The
HOLY
GRAIL

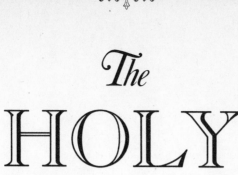

The
HOLY
GRAIL

NORMA LORRE GOODRICH
Kt. T., FSA Scot.

HarperPerennial
A Division of HarperCollins*Publishers*

The Library of Congress has catalogued the hardcover edition as follows:

Goodrich, Norma Lorre.
    The Holy Grail / Norma Lorre Goodrich.—1st ed.
        p.   cm.
    Includes bibliographical references and index.
    ISBN 0-06-016686-X
    1. Grail—History.   I. Title.
BF1999.G629 1992
398´.4—dc20   91-58371

ISBN 0-06-092204-4 (pbk.)
95 96 97 98 99   RRD(H) 10 9 8 7 6

Eleanor J. Greenan,
great lady, true and admirable friend.

For many in the Christian tradition the search for the Holy Grail is to be seen as a metaphor of Abrahamic dimensions, concerned, as he was, with both a process and a goal. The command "Get thee out of thy country . . ." and the promise "I will make of thee a great nation . . ." (Gen. 12:1–2) together become a pattern of much that is to follow, a pattern echoed in that sacred task committed to the Knights of King Arthur. Entering into the quest for the Holy Grail, even though separated by close to fifteen centuries from the historical reality, remains a journey that engages heart and mind, faith and belief. It touches the very bedrock of religious experience.

JOHN HIGGINS, Rector of the Church
of St. Michael & All Angels, Arthuret

Contents

❖

Illustrations

Graphics by Michael R. Cap de Ville, California State University, Long Beach.

Figure 1 © Tony Wiseman/Central Studio, Carlisle, Cambria, UK. Figures 3, 4, 8, 9, and 11 were photographed from Professor François Pierre Guillaume Guizot, *L'Histoire de France depuis les temps les plus reculés jusqu'en 1789. Raconté à mes petits-enfants* (Paris, 1877), vol. 1, illustrated by Alphonse de Neuville.

Acknowledgments

My thanks to my husband, John Hereford Howard, KOC, KTJ, FSA Scot., for having made possible recent trips to Scotland, France, Finland, the USSR, Denmark, and England; and to patrons: Mrs. Marjorie Greenan Marks, Mr. Harold Brooks-Baker, Dr. Roger Rothrock, CLJ, KM, Mr. J. P. Morgan, and members of SAR.

I also thank those persons who have worked on this book: Senior Editor Craig Nelson who suggested it, Editor Jenna Hull, Archivist Jana Seely, and Agent Harold Schmidt.

My indebtedness to the following among many other librarians is greater than can be said: M. Préneron of the Bibliothèque Nationale of France; research librarians at the Butler Library of Columbia University in the City of New York; and for their courteous accommodations over twenty years now: Susan Allen, Joan Edgar, and Ruth Palmer of the Honnold Library, The Claremont Colleges.

Thanks to family and personal friends: Jean J. Lorre, Nita T. Falby, Phyllis Leslie, Marjorie Onsgard, Janice Chambers; and to kind Editors: Barbara Paul Fanshier, Dr. Molly Ann Squire, Terry McKay, Margaret MacKay, and Ethel MacBrair-Koller.

Cordial thanks to many faithful correspondents, who have cheered me with visits and/or frequent, long letters: Knights Templar Dr. A. R. L. Bell, FSA Scot., A. M. Davie, Robert D. R. Brydon, Grand Master Thomas and Matron Jane Bell; Rev. Scott and Mrs. Hall; Col. J. Ross Oborne; Councillor Allan Forsyth; Dr. William Douglas Bookwalter; Author William S. Stimson; Clan President Willis L. Cunning; Attorneys Frank Calvert Tribbe, Michael W. Hinkle, Nancy J. Siegel, and John P. McKay; and my dear, former colleague, Professor of Architecture Eric Pawley.

Introduction

The aim of this book is to track slowly the unrevealed Holy Grail until it emerges finally from its myriad theories.

We shall have to begin at its beginning in time and place if we are to follow it from then to now, there to here. Our greatest task will be to unveil the shrouded Grail itself. What precisely has constituted this revered Holy Grail? What remains of all that today?

We know that the Grail was long worshiped in solemn ceremonies, but we are not sure whether by means of some holy drama, Jewish service, or prehistoric rite resembling Christian baptism, or Eucharist.

The Grail could have been either one object or a group of objects such as are employed today in celebrating the Mass: ciborium, paten, ewer, corporal, missal. Was it originally some hidden and sacred relic such as the Shroud of Turin? Or was it a hallowed body part of some early saint? Even today many such relics may be viewed underground in the treasuries of European cathedrals. One early visionary declared on oath, however, that the Grail truly was a lost Book of the Bible written by Christ. Others said it was his Precious Blood.

We can already say that the Grail was worshiped either before a table or an altar, and at such a temple as the one in Scotland called the "Round Table." We also know that it was or still is preserved in Genoa, in Valencia, and in New York City. But perhaps the Holy Grail is in Scotland, just south of Edinburgh. Some have preferred the view it was that lost, precious Book of Christ; others, that it was a golden chalice so precious it blinded the viewer, or even the silver platter that bore the severed head of a holy man, or it was an inestimably precious bowl, chalice, emerald, stone, or ark. Thus, confusion reigning, rediscovery of the Grail has fallen to us: our present quest and central theme.

What will constitute acceptable evidence? It would seem that, considering the size of this unsolved problem, which stretches from the death of Christ and fall of Jerusalem in A.D. 70 to this present aftermath of World War II, we ought to allow any and all pertinent material to be weighed, be it eyewitness testimony from manuscripts written in the twelfth and thirteenth centuries, biblical scholarship, history, geography, and also mythology, again defined as records of extinct religions.

Our Grail search will have to sprout wings if it is to fly across nations and down centuries, from A.D. 70 to the present day. For worship of the Holy Grail still continues today, as we study it.

Even a first, summary glance will convince us that we really must overfly Europe and the Middle East for nineteen centuries: ancient, medieval, and modern.

A.D. 70–500	Early Apostles and missionaries depart from Jerusalem to spread the Gospel in Italy, Spain, Gaul (France), and Britain. Saint Mary Magdalene soon establishes Christian pilgrimage centers at "Sarras" and elsewhere in France, and into England.
475–542	A Christian King Arthur worships the Grail on the Isle of Man and in Scotland. His breast, said Layamon, was the Round Table. His foremost Grail Questers were: Gawain, Lancelot, and Perceval.

The ancient world ends here.

987–1328

For hundreds of years the Capetian Dynasty rules northern France, and by a series of coups not only conquers its Angevin rivals but annihilates southern France (the Languedoc). The rule of the Capetians overlaps that of the Angevins in England. The Angevin Dynasties, which ruled England and parts of France, plus occasionally Jerusalem, Naples, Hungary, and Poland, are outmaneuvered in both France and England by the Capetians.

1095–1272

Nine Crusades, Christianity versus Islam, involve Europe in wars for the recovery of the Holy Land. The Knights Templar, expendable warriors, go east to fight and die. In the midst of such wars at home and abroad the Grail manuscripts surface, as does King Arthur.

1136

Geoffrey of Monmouth brings King Arthur and Arthurian literature to the attention of the world with his Latin text, *History of the Kings of Britain.*

c. 1170–1185

Chrétien de Troyes, France, brings the Grail, and questers Lancelot and Perceval to the attention of the world.

c. 1170–c. 1220

The major Grail texts surface immediately following. Major Grail manuscripts in the twelfth and thirteenth centuries come from Wales, England, France, Spain, and Germany.

c. 1118–1314

The Sovereign and Military Order of Knights Templar flourishes, serves, guards its relics, fights, and dies in the Holy Land. The survivors in France are accused of heresy, tried, and massacred. Others survive inside Spain, England, Scotland,

Germany, and Hungary. Their massacre
in France shakes that realm.

1002–1271   Followers of a religion called Catharist
(Puritan) or Albigensian heresy are finally
accused, tried, and massacred in southern
France, but also as far north as Oxford,
England. Millions die in the Languedoc,
and their language (Provençal) and
civilization are obliterated. This massacre
of men, women, and children will shake
the world.

The Middle Ages end in 1453 or 1492.

The Renaissance   Religious Wars continue throughout the
Renaissance. Refugees pour into the New
World. In Spain Cervantes and Saint
Theresa of Ávila seem to seek consolation
in Arthurian literature. In other words,
the Grail seems to resurface in terrible
times of massacre or expulsion of Jews, as
from Spain in 1492. Western Europe
could not believe the fall of
Constantinople in 1453. (King Arthur
had claimed descent from a Constantine,
and from a grandmother who founded
the Church of the Holy Sepulcher in
Jerusalem.)

In intervening centuries the Holy Grail, and King Arthur also,
become legendary. The Victorians especially debase even
the legend.

1938–1945   The Holy Grail resurfaces during World
War II, particularly because of the
world's second-worst massacre, or worse:
six million Jews killed by Nazi Germany
before the eyes of the world.

At this time the Grail reappears in the Languedoc,
southern France.

Whenever Arthurian literature has become known, it has been beloved beyond measure. Even today the study of this body of literature, the largest in the world, evokes deep emotions. The tension between viewers of it as legend and viewers of it as fact and history has become more and more aggravated.

Historians like Sir Winston Churchill have deplored the hatred showered upon Dark Age historians, particularly those inside Scotland, who still maintain that King Arthur really lived and died defending his realm. The quarrel has moved from Scotland and England to France, Italy, Germany, and Spain—thence to the Low Countries, Ireland, Iceland, Switzerland, the United States, Canada, and Australia.

All these, then, have become native lands where dwell principal worshipers of the Holy Grail. Century after century, this Grail has never died but been miraculously reborn.

We need now to look most closely therefore at the original master texts from the twelfth and thirteenth centuries in order first to isolate their findings about the Grail itself. Then other principal considerations naturally follow:

Grail Ceremonies
Grail Heroes
Grail Priestesses
Massacres
Grail Temples
Grail Initiates

The chief Grail manuscripts emerged as a direct response to wholesale wars and massacres like the Crusades. Their authors protested the massacres and expulsions of Jews from England as well as from the Continent. These texts about the Holy Grail seem finally to be olden-time lessons, from the very learned, to the less learned, about their freedom. The authors decry warfare, massacre, religious bigotry, persecution of men and women, and slaughter of children. They offer alternative views of better times that could come for all people, and a better world for women and children. They long for the return of King Arthur's vanished realm, where spiritual values overrode avarice, tyranny, greed, and oppression. The Grail texts portray an ideal society of true aristocrats, where virtue is rewarded and noblewomen stand as regal and as priestly as noblemen. For this the Holy Grail has never ever vanished from our minds and souls.

The Holy Grail stands nevertheless in a category all by itself, one of the world's major, unsolved mysteries. For this reason, because the mysterious Grail has tantalized for ages, we need a history based upon eyewitness testimony made by those persons who ages ago saw the Grail, touched it, and recorded their revelations.

Written testimony abounds, and particularly, or first, in ten hand-written accounts largely from the twelfth century.

Since veneration of the Grail also continues in France today, however, this book will follow the Grail from its origin in Jerusalem to its ceremonies, personages, and processionals now as the twentieth century draws near its end.

The Holy Grail is an awesome and terrible mystery. Concerted efforts by thousands of believers over decades at full thrust stamped out the Holy Grail. And not only once. Several times. But here we find it, thriving again today.

Ten major, medieval authors were engaged to write books about the Holy Grail. Two German authors, one of whom was a Knight Templar, which was a medieval, chivalric society, wrote famous texts during the Crusades. Another text was written in Welsh and recopied later, about 1300. The other major accounts were written in Old French. (One short English text of lesser importance was recopied around 1440.)

We can safely conclude even now, then, that what we know, what we can learn about the Holy Grail in the Middle Ages, comes largely from these French-language, *hand-written* and hand-copied books therefore so called: *manu scripts.*

Such texts in Old French do not allow us to presume we are reading books by French men and/or French women, however. During the entire Middle Ages, from 1066 to 1399, Great Britain also was being ruled by French, or by Angevin princes of their dynasty. And one of our most brilliant, seven "French" authors was certainly French, and a converted Jew.

The Holy Grail may therefore be considered primarily a French subject, requiring for its study persons trained to read variations of Old French even as written beautifully by an author whose native language was Hebrew. Not only were these major Grail works commissioned during the Middle Ages, while Europeans fought Arabs in the Middle East for hundreds of years, but also while the

Angevin Dynasty ruling England, southern France, and parts of Spain and Portugal met in combat to the death, again over hundreds of years, the Capetian Dynasty ruling Paris, northern France, and parts of Italy. The Grail manuscripts emerge, then, courageously, under an actual terror of history so stupendous as to leave authors aghast now with loss of breath.

My colleague Madame Régine Pernoud, author and librarian at the National Archives of France, Bibliothèque Nationale, in the center of Paris, wrote of the great shining light and enlightenment of these same Middle Ages. If there shone on the Grail this great white light, then it also revealed black masses of dead Arabs under Richard the Lion Heart's mailed fist. The beams of a helicopter's searchlight over a modern airport disaster would have shown the same Middle Ages other piles of burned corpses and mountainsides stripped and littered with slaughtered children. A study of the Holy Grail demonstrates plainly the terror of history.

Two of the most famous theologians of our times, Paul Tillich and Mircéa Eliade, have insisted equally that in times of great terror such as the Middle Ages, which suffered the Crusades plus continuous dynastic wars to the death in western Europe, both time and history become ultimate concerns of theology. In such dire days great religious symbols such as "the Holy Grail" strove to point beyond suffering toward hope and a better world. Whole groups of people, entire societies, in fact, clung to the Grail's gentle sur-reality that shone beyond the stress of battle, corpses, death, hatred, and cold revenge. Only the Grail dream or vision invited persons to share some new reality that might open out into a cleaner land-scape—like Salvador Dali's uncluttered vistas inhabited only by innocent objects.

Alongside the Holy Grail, history developed its great, comforting, Celtic legend called "the Breton Hope": King Arthur had 'been born, and of a royal race, recorded the Breton scholar Count Villemarqué in 1862. The king will come again, claims the Grail legend, to reign over us. He will stand before us like a wall. He will see the Holy Grail at its castle in the sea, and he will rule our world in peace. He is our once and our future king.

He alone of all men, in his time on earth, saw "all" aspects of the Holy Grail, adds the Grail author/scholar at Glastonbury Abbey confidently. Into this king's very fist the sword was offered by a lady's white hand that rose out of the Irish Sea. And the brave Arthur, strong as a bear, daring as a wild boar, grasped it in defense of his people. That hand, said another Breton historian, Ernest Renan (Paris, 1863), was the hope of the defeated Celtic peoples, who had bravely suffered one major defeat after another all the way from eastern Europe, to the land's end, Finistère in Brittany, and Scotland in Britain. With his iron hammer Arthur would eventually break the sun free from his towered prison even, and make the Grail shine on the Western world again.

While the Holy Grail leads us ultimately to theologians, it commences certainly in history defined as a narrative of events, our Grail manuscripts. Each major text, as written by the best authors of the twelfth and thirteenth centuries, as composed and ordered by the best brains at work in those days, constitutes a record of facts written for the purpose of analysis and conclusion *by the reader.* The events delineated form the very subject matter of history, which is by itself one branch of knowledge. Each written account can be pondered, now that we have learned to read Old French, and now that we have direct access to the manuscripts themselves in the Bibliothèque Nationale of France.

All events connected with the Grail, as they are narrated in Old French, fall correctly into what French scholars themselves now term "history," which is to say, what occurred before the defeat of Napoléon at Waterloo. Their cutoff date between history proper and current events, too close to us to call historical, is, thus, the year 1815. By that year, in fact, our Grail manuscripts were being resurrected by textual scholars and printed in scholarly editions footnoted so that all the variant copies could be consulted page by page. By 1815 also, the old avoidance of sacred material and tabooed names such as Arthur, Guinevere, and Perceval—all three still of unknown etymologies—had relaxed. The lesser personages such as the hero Gawain had avoided the stringencies of silence, of course. His name could be freely spoken.

Since our masterful texts are French for the most part, or French except for the occasional superb Welsh, English, and the German tellings, contemporary historians who have devoted full-length books to the subject of the Grail are mostly French-speaking also. It was French historians who first began speaking of a *mystique* of history, a French word which has since 1889 and 1891 gained popularity and considerable status in English also. The French call a mystique of history a system or a belief which has been formed around an idea, or a feeling, or a person.

We shall now speak in English (*Oxford English Dictionary* 1986) of mystique as being the old atmosphere of mystery and veneration attending to such an activity as quest for the Castle of the Holy Grail. Certain doctrines are truly surrounded by a mystical aura, and so are certain persons, which is the raison d'être of public relations departments and advertisers' propaganda. The word *mystique* also defines or exposes the savagery of matadors and brutal dictators like Adolf Hitler. Rightly so, for Hitler's massacre of the Jews in World War II was, as we shall see, directly related to his veneration and search for the Holy Grail. And more is the pity.

The word *mystique* does imply, to some degree, irrationality, and this in the Romance languages generally because by "la mistica" is understood a branch of mystical theology. Such theology implies prayer, or other direct communication of the soul with God. It constitutes also a visionary method of scriptural interpretation, as well as contemplation, spirituality, and meditation. All are sought via self-surrender in order to obtain union with God. Perhaps the Holy Grail will even have to be considered a mystery religion. It certainly involved several, fascinating mystery women, interesting enough to warrant a considerable effort to understand their performance and decipher the aura surrounding them.

It is truly wonderful personally to follow this Quest of the Holy Grail through marvelously mysterious texts, each author going it alone in his inquiry and so without our advantage today of all the known Grail texts, ten of which stand unquestionably as major works of art. All authors sought only to understand this complex of beliefs that linked King Arthur's Questers. Each accepted as undeniable the sovereignty of the individual conscience if and when it must authorize protest leading to dissent. Deep in thought, French historians of today, like Dr. A. Barthélémy of Toulouse, ponder the terrible lessons of history. Century after century King Arthur's Grail heroes spring to life again as Knights Templar, for instance, ready to die—and die they did either before the walls of Jerusalem or condemned to death in their native land, where they had returned after having been trounced and shamed in Syria.

Because the Grail spirit survived such massacres, it rose again somehow more veiled, more mysterious, even more figurative and concealed in the works and teachings of Saint John of the Cross, Saint Francis of Assisi, Saint Catherine of Siena, and most compelling of them all because of her mystical book, Saint Theresa of Ávila, Spain. In her *Las Moradas* (literally, The Chambers) the Grail mystique resurges sweet enough to tear at the heart strings. Its meaning in Spain's Golden Age became more hidden, more figurative, almost an allegory of Everyman's quest. Hers was a science of mystical adoration, truly the same, prehistoric, Grail belief or mystique encountered under King Arthur. Thus, exaltation becomes a regular resource. The Grail ecstasy is also sought today in an Antioch Chalice, or on its oldest site beside the Isle of Man, in La Seo Cathedral in Valencia, in Spain's national monument at San Juan de la Peña, as at Montserrat (once called Montsalvat—Mountain of Salvation), in Genoa, in Jerusalem, at the Rosslyn Chapel outside Edinburgh, and last by the Rosicrucians at Montségur in the Oriental Pyrenees.

The nature of the Grail will dawn upon each one of us: object? idea? relic? hallow? gold chalice? silver platter? ciborium? paten? bowl? candelabra? ewer? altar? round table? corporal? book? missal? emerald? stone? ark? What was its ceremony? A mystery is the answer.

The Grail was a mystery, and it remains a mystery—or it was a *ministerium*, which means any religious service—or a Mystery such as baptism, Communion, Eucharist, or other divine liturgy. Certainly its service culminated with the initiation of King Arthur's Questers like Gawain, Lancelot, Perceval, Galahad. Otherwise, those prehistoric days remain stubbornly close-mouthed. Was it a play? Was it holy drama? The enigma is cryptic, dark, profound. So far, one can say no more.

How do we set about solving the mystery of the Holy Grail? There seem to be two routes: (1) study of the Grail as it appears not so much alive as thriving today, and (2) study of the Grail as past, as history. The second approach appeals as being more orderly, certainly more consonant with my French education, ergo, my teachers' teachings. And surely the second method via the gates of chronology and geography will lead to Dali's uncluttered vistas, where thought roams freely in a free country like our summer fields of Indiana and Iowa.

Like the Shroud of Turin to which it may be closely related, the Grail today is worshiped in two mountain lands: Scotland and the Languedoc. It is also worshiped where Saints Mary and Mary Magdalene are venerated: in the Alps, in southern France, and along the mountainous Basses-Alpes of the Mediterranean coast.

Our history of the Grail starts out from the hills around Jerusalem because Jerusalem is the oldest site mentioned in our ten major Grail manuscripts. One text clearly identifies the Grail, by eyewitness observation and shattering revelation, as an object made in Jerusalem and brought from that holy city to Scotland. Our next Grail text explains how the Grail Castle itself was derived from Solomon's Temple, and how King Solomon and his queen devised a way for the Sword to be brought safely out of the devastation wreaked on the Holy Land in A.D. 70. Another Grail text moves the Grail from and then back to an intermediary site called "Sarras," which seems possibly to have been the most ancient seaport metropolis of those virtually prehistoric days: Marseilles. So far, our method works logically as laid out in Grail texts.

The evidence leading us to Marseilles raises severe problems in early Christianity, but those are questions that must be returned to learned Church historians of all denominations. Our focus centers narrowly about the Holy Grail. Our really severe problems concern the transmitters of the Grail from Jerusalem into the far Western world. In their thorny cases, they are unfortunately not those holy persons whom we all recognize, but a handful of famous unknowns. These first Grail Bearers do have names: Joseph of Arimathea, Mary Magdalene, and Saints Mary of the Sea, Bartholomew, Philip, Lorenzo (Lawrence), and Lazarus, among others. Our Lady-Mary-on-Guard Church looks out over the Old Port at Marseilles, across the Count of Monte Cristo's prison isle, and sweeps the blue Mediterranean gratefully. Nobody has ever disputed her throne there, much less her right to it.

In Great Britain's Glastonbury we meet the first of the prehistoric and royal women who became Grail Queens: Guinevere, or Guanhumara herself. No Grail manuscript places her reign at landlocked Glastonbury; but she was identified, recognized, described by eyewitnesses during her lifetime as a Grail Queen before an altar at the seaside Castle of the Holy Grail. One text written undoubtedly by a Benedictine monk at Glastonbury Abbey placed Queen Guinevere at Glastonbury, to which holy place she had been kidnapped and held prisoner for a year, he testified. As corroboration he placed her near contemporary Saint Gildas, yet we are pretty sure Gildas never was at Glastonbury. However, millions of people have for centuries believed that Guinevere was buried at Glastonbury, and so we put her there conditionally, as the first Grail Queen.

When we turn next to Spain, even *we* doubt the validity of our system because Saint Lorenzo assuredly brought the Grail into Spain long before Queen Guinevere may have been taken hostage to Glastonbury. The reason for continuing immediately with Spain as the site of a Grail Castle is first of all a serious preoccupation with medieval history. The Holy Grail thus becomes very complicated because of the Grail texts themselves, which, we are forced to admit, derive from the ending of the twelfth century or thereabouts.

Why after centuries of silence do we suddenly have a rash of Grail manuscripts? One satisfactory answer may be found in Spain. Second question: Why do these manuscripts draw the attention of major authors for a limited period and then get dropped into an even deeper silence? What happened during their years of composition? Third question: Who broke the silence again after the last shot was fired with a new weapon, which was gunpowder, and after the peace treaty ending the Hundred Years' War had been ratified at Cadillac in 1453? Who broke that silence? None other than two of the most beloved writers of all time, both Spaniards: Miguel de Cervantes and Saint Theresa of Ávila.

As the Grail texts are largely French, the Grail is therefore a French subject, just as its mystique was originally a French idea first promulgated by French historians, still used by them as late as 1989. We go next to France itself, which is represented in Grail lore by the hero Lancelot. No matter that Lancelot in King Arthur's Court was a Scot. In Arthurian lore, as in Grail texts, Lancelot typifies French heroism, the medieval French epic hero, a Frankish military ethos, and a Languedocian (i.e., from southern France), courtly lover. He is so French, in fact, that he rules their centuries: military man par excellence, Grail Quester who abandons the quest after a second-degree initiation, father of the Grail hero Galahad, and mythological solar hero. Lancelot also personifies what is most French of all: a glorious and perfect Knight Templar. There is no doubt at all about it: ladies' hearts beat faster at the very mention of his name. Lancelot is the most glamorous man who ever lived. Ask any lady.

In chapter 6 we have to plunge into the life stories and Grail Quests of the greatest of Grail heroes: Perceval. Whether once from the kingdoms of ancient Wales, from England, or from France, Perceval is the most renowned when he bears his German names: *Parzival* and *Parsifal.* There from Wolfram von Eschenbach we learn that his Grail story originated in Toledo, Spain, which we might already have surmised, given also the Jewish ancestry of Saint Theresa, the author of the Holy Trinity Grail story from Fécamp,

France, and also the French-Jewish celebrity and brilliant author Chrétien de Troyes.

Parsifal enters the Grail Castle this year again (1991), in a new production at the Metropolitan Opera in Lincoln Center, New York City, as he has done every Easter Sunday in Richard Wagner's own theater at Oberammergau. When great music dwells upon book, it raises it immeasurably above mere pen and paper. Sung words at the Grail Castle bring us all to tears—in flood. This opera is the Grail's apotheosis.

But even Wolfram's lovely Grail Queen's going east into India must take second place before the Languedoc's Grail Queen named Viscountess Esclarmonde de Foix. The Lady probably starved to death around the year 1314. It is sad that this royal Esclarmonde did not live to see her grandson crowned King of France. Even more sad is that none of her sermons has survived. More sad still, no record that we know of remains of her arguments offered in debate against learned Church theologians. No such record has ever, to the best of my knowledge, been even mentioned.

Nature on this earth had created wonderful places. And man has made wonders too, like the Mont-Saint-Michel to which everyone goes when in France, on pilgrimage every May Day. Nature herself made the Yosemite Valley, Oahu, and the Bay of Naples, and Arthur's Seat in Edinburgh; but above all these, for pure splendor, towers the Grail Castle site called Montségur, Mount Security, in the Oriental Pyrenees. This was the Viscountess Esclarmonde's property, which she deeded to refugees toward the end of the Albigensian Crusade. Whether or not Montségur always was, from Day One, a Castle of the Holy Grail, it has been such since World War II. But the religion of nonviolence and the tragic end of the Catharist, or Puritan, or peace church there is another, longer story: chapter 7.

To end the book we shall return again to the King Arthurs, for there were two: the warrior king who won twelve victories in defense of Scotland, and his second self, who was the sixth and only supreme initiate at the Grail Castle in Britain. There before the year 542 he personally saw the Grail lying "open and dis-covered" before him alone. His first Commander in Chief, the royal Knight Gawain, had come very close to this sighting. Call it "revelation" or "apocalypse," as you will. King Arthur's fame and reputation lie equally upon both persons, the head of state and the head ecclesiastical initiate. After his death in 542, claim the *Annals of Wales,* the Grail surely, rightfully, returned to "Sarras."

By counting the years, Perceval's young father concluded, after he had taken his small son to the tomb of Joseph of Arimathea, that there were some five hundred years or thereabouts between themselves and the living presence of Christ in Jerusalem. The celestial city fell to the Romans in 70, after which Mary Magdalene and her missionary associates journeyed to Sarras. Her cave and annual pilgrimages there today perpetuate this tradition. Meanwhile other disciples who became saints traveled into Gaul, Spain, and Britain. By the sixth century when King Arthur died, Clovis had already established his empire in northern France, and the Visigoths, their capital at Toulouse. Charles Martel and Charlemagne drove the Saracens out of France, but in the Grail manuscripts all heathen peoples are called "Saracens," so great was the general fear of their armies. After 542 the Grail returned to "Sarras," as Perceval's son Lohengrin migrated east to Brabant. During the Crusades of the twelfth and thirteenth centuries, while the Grail texts were being written, Angevin royals and Knights Templar spread and upheld a secret Grail tradition. In the fourteenth century it revived again under the peace church of the Catharists in southern France. By all appearances the Holy Grail has constituted a mystique of history.

Note to the Reader

A list of major Grail texts is included in the Selected
Bibliography (see page 345). This first list is supported by a
second summary list of notable scholars, historians, and
theologians whose writings have been of great assistance to me.
Each name precedes a date, which refers to a work found
particularly inspiring (see pages 343–44). Most names and dates
reappear more completely in a following, longer section of the
Selected Bibliography. The purpose in all this has been uniquely
to assist interested readers in pursuing this subject of the Holy
Grail and in checking sources.

**THE EAST WINDOW OF THE
CHURCH OF ST. MICHAEL &
ALL ANGELS, ARTHURET**
*(© TONY WISEMAN/CENTRAL
STUDIO, CARLISLE, CUMBRIA, UK)*

Chapter

I

JESUS
IN JERUSALEM

THE BOOK OF JESUS

Passing from deduction to induction, we shall in this chapter seek manuscript evidence to prove that the Holy Grail derived from the city of Jerusalem, from the lifetime and ministry of Christ, and from the lives and writings of the Apostles. The first text to be summarized is the *Grand-Saint-Graal* because it offers a first identification of the Grail itself. Therefore we can come down to business right away. The author argues that the Grail is a Book, associated with blinding light, which we already recognize as a Grail phenomenon. He goes on to argue the pedigrees and genealogy of Lancelot and Perceval, all of which makes us want to identify him as a prototypical Scot. We then offer support for this author from theologians, from the Book of John, from the legend (or fact) of Joseph of Arimathea, from a Bible geographer and the suggested birthplaces of Saint George, the trial of the theologian Pelagius, and the life of Saint Mary Magdalene. Then we move on to Solomon's Temple as pattern and original of the Grail Castle, and include its Oriental treasures also.

We look briefly at several other texts such as *Parzival* (the Ger-

man Perceval) and the *Perceval Continuations* to learn that Jewish
scholars wrote the Grail lore in the first place. We there find our
second identification: the Grail was a stone fallen from heaven.
Turning to the *Queste del Saint Graal,* we hear Queen Morgan le Fay
lecture on the "tables" of the Grail ceremony. Then we allow the
wonderful Sir Thomas Malory to speak his piece on the subject. The
Grail *Queste* again appears to wind up our derivation of the Holy
Grail from Jerusalem by supporting the *Grand-Saint-Graal:* not only
did Solomon arrange transport for the missionaries to Britain, but
Perceval's sister also there met her death.

Those persons who suddenly saw the Grail in front of them, open
and unconcealed, suffered a severe shock. In some cases this sight,
or sighting, caused the viewer to experience a loss of memory
accompanied by confusion, even by a disorientation that lasted into
the following day.

At the moment of sighting the Grail, some persons were actually
blinded. Others lost their power of speech, and this despite a prior
indoctrination over a long period of time. Relatives and teachers
had coached the persons searching for the Grail, and especially
cautioned them to speak, to remain conscious, to be alert, to rise
to the occasion, and, at least, for God's sake and their own, to ask
a question.

The ones who managed to keep their wits about them were so
few and far between in King Arthur's day and presence that authors
recorded their experiences. Therefore these names are known. As
for the viewers' reactions under extreme stress, we could also puzzle that out, and even eventually describe it clinically, as it were,
if we were clinicians.

To us also, at this point in time, for we are nothing to ourselves
but ordinary people also, trying to live our own lives safely and as
best we can, the Grail is a total mystery. We even wonder if we too
have already seen it, and can't remember either, in some museum,
in some cathedral, at sunrise over a mountain peak, in the treasury
of some castle, among the relics of some sanctuary, or in our own
temple, or synagogue, or church. It could be. It could certainly be.

For we too have been searching for the Holy Grail, but not all
of us full-time, as a career, like Lancelot, or Gawain, or Perceval,
or Galahad, or King Arthur himself. They did not merely search.

They quested. They devoted their lives to the Quest of the Holy Grail. We travel.

One person saw the Grail twice, was able to touch it and recall it later, and was even subsequently empowered to write down his experiences with his own hand and pen. He tells us quite frankly at the commencement that he has decided to remain anonymous. He gives us three reasons: firstly, anyone who heard him say that God had shown himself to him by allowing him to write "The Holy Grail," which is the holiest of all stories in the world, would call him a vile, arrogant scribbler. Secondly, anyone who knew the name of such an author, or anyone personally acquainted with such-and-such as author of "The Holy Grail," would not find the account worthy, or even worth reading. We know familiarity breeds contempt. Thirdly, those readers who found errors in his account, or lies, or mistakes in grammar or, worse yet, in theology, would besmirch his name forevermore. To save himself from loss of reputation, then, this author remained anonymous.

One must respect these reasons for anonymity. One must also respect this anonymous, French-speaking author of the Middle Ages for his honorable intent, which contrasts well with those of his contemporaries.

The text in question, where the anonymous author recounts his firsthand, and very traumatic, viewings of the Grail, goes by several names (listed in the Selected Bibliography), from which we choose to call it simply the *Grand-Saint-Graal.* It is a grand achievement indeed, offering the first identification of the Grail itself. None of the other ten or so Grail texts touches the heart as does this anguished, sincere, personal experience.

Our anonymous author writes prose in the Old French language of northern France, addressing his account particularly to those who believe in the Trinity: Father, Son, and Holy Spirit ("saint esperit").

"It was seven hundred seventeen years after the death of Christ," says our author, meaning it was A.D. 717, when he had this terrifying experience of the Grail. Seven hundred seventeen years after Christ's Passion, he says, he found himself in a wild part of a country he does not wish to identify any more closely, and furthermore, it was a heathen land, not Christian, that is to say, but a very delightful, pleasant country. It was coming up for Good Friday, after vespers service, when the author says he felt so sleepy he began to nod and doze. Very soon thereafter he heard a voice calling his

name. The voice called him by name four times ("iiij. fois"). It said,
"Wake up and learn of three things one and one as three." He saw
before him the most beautiful man that ever there was. And when
he saw this man before him, he was so stricken he couldn't think
or do anything, or even decide what to do. The man had to ask if
he heard him. And he managed to get out haltingly that he still
wasn't sure. And the man said it was an experiencing of the Trinity
he brought. And it was because the author had doubts as to whether
there were three persons or only one God and one Power. Which
has been a troubling question.

Then he asked, as we follow in rapid summary, if our author had
any other problem in faith. And he asked if the author was capable
of hearing and if he was blind or could see who loomed over him.
The author replied he was mortal and, to be truthful, could not
sustain the sight of blinding light. Nor could he put into words what
nobody else had been very able to express. Then the beautiful man
bent down and blew in his face. At which point our author's vision
became a hundred times stronger. And he felt empowered to speak
in tongues, which was a great marvel. And the man said: Can you
understand? Do you know who I am?

Then the author felt stifled by a torch between his teeth. He was
so terrified he could not utter a sound. And the other said: "Have
no fear. . . . I am the Fountain of Wisdom. I am he to whom
Nicodemus said, 'Master, we know who you are . . . I am the
Perfect Master . . . come to resolve your doubts . . . and those of
your readers.'" (Sommer, vol. 1, p. 4.)

"Then he took my hand," resumes the author, "and he presented
me with a Book. It was a small Book no bigger than the palm of
a hand. The Book he had presented to me contained marvels never
before thought or known. The man *wrote this Book*.

"The skies can rain! The air can whirl! The earth can crumble.
The waters can run red. . . . But never shall man die of sudden
death," the Master said.

The author heard the voice through thunder. The sky fell down.
The earth groaned and quaked. The brilliance grew more blinding.
He really went blind. He staggered and fell down.

But when he opened his eyes, he saw no trace of that.

As soon as it was day, he began to read, at the beginning, his own
genealogy, which he desired to see. After he had looked it over,
he marveled to think how such a tiny Book could hold so many lines
and letters on its pages.

After having been plunged into thought for a long time he looked at the Book and saw: "Here Commences the Reading concerning The Holy Grail." Then he read: "Here Commences Terror." As he pondered this title, he saw the flash of lightning that dropped him into unconsciousness.

The next day was Good Friday. Before it dawned, an angel took him to heaven and down again. His doubts were resolved. He locked the Book in the cabinet to the left of the altar.

Next morning he said Mass. Then he opened the cabinet only to discover that the Book was missing. The cabinet was still locked.

He was astonished, but a voice told him not to be. Christ too had vanished from his tomb although He had been enclosed.

A voice told him to go for a walk along the path that led to the Stone, or peron (perron) and the Valley of the Dead.

Then he was to leave the main path and walk toward the Junction of the Seven Roads, probably at Carlisle, because from that point he could proceed toward the Valley of Scotland. He also came to another landmark, the Great Cross that rises above the Fountain. These markers are characteristically Arthurian. Along the way the author encounters another adventure characteristically Arthurian or meets the same Questing Beast which King Arthur and Queen Guinevere followed through the deep forest. As we shall see, this Beast will reappear soon in France. There too will occur the nunnery and chapel we know from Arthurian literature.

On the altar of this chapel, the author found his priceless, disappearing Book. It was Christ Himself who now ordered him to make a copy.

Next morning the author found laid out for his use the Book, plus pen, ink, parchment, and a little knife for sharpening quills.

He copied the Book. The copy he made is known now as the *Grand-Saint-Graal.* This text is perhaps the most tender and touching of all the Grail manuscripts. In fact, none of the other texts touches the heart as does this one.

The reader is astonished to think even that there may once have been a Book by Christ. To think that there may once have been a Book of the Bible actually written by Jesus Christ, in his own handwriting, and that it contained his genealogy, brings shivers to the reader; for the genealogy of Christ takes us afar, to Bethlehem and Jerusalem, and to Kings David and Solomon. As biblical scholars have thought, both Greece and Israel have traced their civilization and culture, and inhabited their lands for at least the past 3,350 years. Greek and Hebrew civilizations appear to be parallel structures erected upon an East Mediterranean foundation of the second millennium B.C. Therefore the New Testament was written in Greek and/or in Aramaic.

Both Lancelot and Perceval (who were more than once candidates for initiation at the Grail Castle), stand above all other Arthurian heroes except Arthur himself, and perhaps Galahad. Both boast pedigrees that are at the same time "royal and sainted." In plain words, Lancelot and Perceval are descendants of the Kings David and Solomon.

What rises equally important from the first Grail text we examine here is the prophecy of Jesus it contains. The two chapter headings, "Here Commences the Reading concerning The Holy Grail" followed by "Here Commences the Great Terror," refer the reader to the history of Britain in the Dark Ages, from the death of Christ to the death of King Arthur some five hundred years later. This period of the Holy Grail represents the early history of Christianity, which follows both the Passion and Crucifixion of Christ. The destruction of Solomon's Temple then follows Christ closely in the year A.D. 70, as the Venerable Bede calculated for us the passage of time. It is the general consensus that it required this same period of five hundred years for the early Apostles, missionaries, and Christians to spread this new religion across western Europe, into what are now Italy, Spain, France, Germany, and Britain.

Controversy dogs our every attempt to speak clearly, of course, where even the names and origins of missionaries and Apostles, plus the names and places of their conversions, are unclear and still hotly disputed. Nor is there close agreement even about the first four Gospels that also launched Christianity. In any event, the *Grand-Saint-Graal,* in its variant copyings made in the Middle Ages, has led us far from Jerusalem—to Scotland and northern France—and back again to the Holy Land and the Celestial City of Jerusalem.

Our first author, whose name will probably never be known, haunts the memory. He is descended from one of those shadowy figures who knew Christ, who left Jerusalem after A.D. 70 to journey into the unfamiliar lands of western Europe. Their names today are hardly recognized even when their depiction in mosaic stares down at us from an ancient church: Saint Joseph of Arimathea (and Britain), Saint Lawrence (of Spain?), Saint Philip (of France?), Saint

Bartholomew of Occitania (southern France), the later Saint Martin of Tours, and Saint Patrick of Ireland (born in Scotland?).

Our author, who writes in Old French prose but who is descended from the family of Christ himself, still speaks to us in all sincerity, in his own voice, from his own personal and so impassioned spirituality. He lived in an unsettled area, he says, which was thinly populated—like Scotland then and now. He had been educated in a French school that, then as now, encouraged creativity and originality above all else. He was doubly a product of French education, for although very learned theologically, he could speak to readers far and near, academically trained or not. One further clue situates him, or at the least links him to Britain and to early British Christianity. Our author mentions by way of authority the personage of Nicodemus the Pharisee, who is also mentioned in the Fourth Gospel, of John (3:2). It was Nicodemus who brought the expensive myrrh and aloes to Joseph of Arimathea, and who therefore helped prepare the body of Jesus for burial. Thus, our author derives from Britain, Glastonbury, and later Scotland, where in the Dark Ages Joseph is believed to have sired not only King Arthur, but also the other most noble and most prominent questers after the Holy Grail: Lancelot and Perceval.

Nor is our author of the *Grand-Saint-Graal* alone in his belief that Christ wrote a Book that survived his death and the subsequent fall of Jerusalem in A.D. 70. The most prominent of known French authors of Arthurian texts in the Middle Ages is the celebrated, much admired, Chrétien de Troyes (from Troyes in Champagne, northern France). Chrétien also wrote a Grail text called *Conte del Graal* (Tale of the Grail), in which he writes:

> . . . *Biaus sire chiers*   (v. 6,254)
> *Don ne creez vos Jesucrist,*
> *Qui la novele loi escrist,*
> *Si la dona as Chrestiiens?*

> . . . *Dear noble Lords,*
> *Do you not then believe Jesus Christ*
> *Who wrote the New Law thusly*
> *And gave it to the Christians?*

Here Chrétien, who was very probably a converted Jew, employed as a writer by his local Duke, distinguished between the "New" and "Old" Law; that is, Christian and Hebrew, New and Old Testaments, Christianity and Judaism. But he too makes Christ an author, and apparently of a book once included in the New Testament. Both Chrétien and the less intrepid author of the *Grand-Saint-Graal* also reassure readers of the Arthurian/Grail texts that in their pages both great religions meet harmoniously, in open dialogue.

In 1965 Rev. Dr. Charles Francis Potter also thought that Christ wrote a book, and that he had found it. He relied for his authority on the closing words of this same Gospel of John, which probably was the book most treasured by the early Christians:

> And there are also many other things which Jesus did, the which, if they should be written every one, I suppose that even the world itself would not contain the books that should be written (21:25).

There is a book discovered in Serbia (1892) but written between 30 B.C. and A.D. 70, which is called the "Slavonic" or "Second Enoch," from Enoch, Son of Jared (Gen. 5:18, 24). This book also, like our *Grand-Saint-Graal,* recounts a revelation, but one given by God to Jesus, or relayed in the words of Christ to John by an angel. This "Slavonic" gospel belongs among the scriptures called non-canonical, and also called pseudepigrapha because printed under olden names such as Enoch. Enoch's book contains Jesus' promise of a future life, which recurs as John writes: "In my father's home are many mansions" (John 14:2). It tells how Jesus prepared places for a Messianic Supper, and these injunctions: . . . clothe the naked, feed the hungry, be kind to animals, follow me afterwards . . . angels await me. Theologians conclude: it is traditional to assume that Jesus wrote no scripture.

Others still go on to correlate this book of Enoch's secrets with the ethics of Jesus, which included also his exalted view of man, his charity and benevolence, his patience under affliction, and his love of others. In particular the Enoch book stresses what Matthew, Mark, and John also stress: the kindness of Jesus toward animals, fowls of the air such as sparrows and doves, and the draught creatures like the ass and the ox.

Both ox and dove became symbols closely associated with the Holy Grail, the former by being not only the symbol of Saint Luke but also the secret symbol of the Grail Castle (patience under suffering). The dove also symbolized the Grail Castle and its sign was branded upon horses owned by the Lady of the Lake there. The doves that hovered over the head of Christ at his baptism by John recur in the synoptic Gospels as the descending dove of the Holy Ghost (Spirit). In Arthurian literature it indicates the blessing of God upon Perceval on the day of his inauguration as last King of the Grail Castle. The descending dove as this symbol figures most prominently in the Old German version of *Parzival,* as in Richard Wagner's modern opera *Parsifal.*

A great Hebrew scholar in France, Ernest Renan, who wrote a controversial *Life of Jesus* in 1863 (translated 1910), considered the four Gospels as little better than "legendary biographies" (p. 67), corrected by the Jewish historian Josephus. In his long-considered opinion, our Grail text was incorrect, and Jesus did no writing at all and left the world "no book" (chap. 28, pp. 408–09). Renan's *Life* was banned (placed on the Index Expurgatorius) by the Catholic church, but defended recently by the English historian Arnold Toynbee in his introduction to *The Crucible of Christianity.* After censure, Ernest Renan was removed from his chair as Professor of Semitic Languages at the Collège de France.

Toynbee defended Renan first of all because he was a great scholar and secondly because he was only a layman in matters theological, merely a member of the general public for whom he wrote the life of Jesus. French writers, or writers such as our author of the *Grand-Saint-Graal* who wrote French as a result of their French education, or because they reside in a country, like Scotland, which was being governed by French persons during the Middle Ages, perform a real function, Toynbee concluded:

> This abiding solidarity between the academic and the non-academic members of the Republic of Letters in France is, no doubt, one of the reasons why French culture has been so continuously full of vitality and so continuously pre-eminent (p. 17).

Thus, because of Renan's attempt to portray Jesus as a human being whose biography could be written, others may respect the medieval author of the *Grand-Saint-Graal* who saw Jesus in his vision and who received into the palm of his hand the little Book. And furthermore, Geoffrey of Monmouth, historian of the kings and queens of Britain in 1136, claimed that his source was a little, small book. To his credit, it must be repeated, the prehistoric or ancient books of Wales are just so: little and small with an incredible amount of writing on each page.

To close this praise of the *Grand-Saint-Graal,* which has brought us all closer to the year 1 and the beginnings of Christianity, we should turn to a modern theologian from Scotland itself, William Barclay, late Professor of Divinity at the University of Glasgow. In one of his many books, *The Mind of Jesus,* Barclay wrote (chapter 13) authoritatively that Jesus was not a writer, and therefore not the author of any book. For this conclusion Barclay turned to what Jesus said about himself. He gave himself, said Barclay, three descriptive titles: Preacher, Prophet (or Herald), and Teacher (Rabbi). As preacher he spoke by divine proclamation. As prophet he foretold the future. As teacher he was the divine physician, the servant of men, the seeker of the lost, the fulfiller of past hopes and dreams, the divine liberator, agent of judgment, and touchstone of God.

Our author of the *Grand-Saint-Graal* expressed his reasons for wishing to remain anonymous in a world of theological controversy. Actually, when he presented Jesus as human and willing to appear in the flesh to our author, the latter was even then perhaps treading, like ourselves, upon dangerous ground subject to earthquake. At the Council of Chalcedon in 451 a major controversy erupted on the human and divine natures of Christ. As a result five Christian churches withdrew from the fold, and turned to isolation: Coptic, Ethiopian, Armenian, Syrian, and Syrian of India (Malabar). But the Grail Castles then as now spread over western Europe, welcoming and celebrating, and opening arms to all who would come humbly.

THE BOOK OF JOHN

In chapter 21 of the Gospel of Luke, Jesus eloquently predicted the days of terror to come in Jerusalem and the terrifying storm and earthquake of its destruction. He foresaw the flight of its people and the dispersal of his Apostles. Some of this applied directly also to the lifetime of King Arthur. Then too the earliest Christians in Britain, as the eyewitness Saint Gildas described it, fled into the more uninhabited mountains and valleys of Wales and Scotland. Centuries after this mad flight of starving people during another Age of Terror—the fifth and sixth centuries—the two great Christian centers of Glastonbury Abbey in England and Fécamp Abbey on the Normandie coast were founded by Rome.

Understandably, then, the name "Rome" hardly occurs (except to describe Arthur's heredity) in the Arthurian corpus, immense though that body of writing is. The Christianity practiced at the Grail Castle is entirely pre-Roman. The claims of authority in Arthur's day were not Rome, but Jerusalem and Constantinople. The earliest missionaries into France, Spain, and Britain were not the major Apostles, not Peter, and not Paul either, but such ones as Joseph of Arimathea, Saint Philip, Saint Lawrence; and they knew of the Empress of Constantinople, Lady Helena, who had been born in Britain. Her son was the Emperor Constantine the Great, also born in Britain. He declared Christianity to be henceforth his State religion. And King Arthur claimed descent from a Constantine. Furthermore, King Arthur donated a piece of the True Cross (Holy Rood) to Melrose Abbey in Scotland. His ancestress, this Empress Helena Augusta, had not only found the True Cross but had also built the Tomb of Christ within her Church of the Holy Sepulcher in Jerusalem. The flood of pilgrims to worship in this holiest of churches played its part in causing the Crusades and the Crusading Order called Knights Templar, charged to protect them and their routes across western Europe, and *outre mer,* across the Mediterranean Sea.

The early Christians who worshiped at the Avalon Grail Castle seem to have known the Gospel of Luke. They follow especially the life of Jesus as lived in a time of salvation, a time of crucifixion, followed by Pentecost. In fact, King Arthur always held the plenary sessions of his Court at Pentecost when petitions for his warriors to undertake adventures and right wrongs were entertained. They follow in Arthurian texts this yearly progression when the Holy Spirit descended on the Church fifty days after the Passion like a roaring wind settling upon the followers until all spoke, as the author of the *Grand-Saint-Graal* remembered, in tongues otherwise unknown to them.

They do not seem to have had copies of the Book of Acts, however, which transferred authority from Jerusalem to Rome. And yet Christianity had rapidly taken hold in Rome when some thirty years after the death of Christ the Roman Emperor Nero blamed Christians for burning his city. By A.D. 70 the Christians began to disperse, and the Jews lost their ancestral homeland.

The early Christians in Britain, and this is even more certain for those in the Pyrenees Mountains of what are now southern France and northern Spain, knew the Gospel of John. John spoke of both Nicodemus and Joseph of Arimathea. Delightedly they made great use of the actual words of Jesus in the long passages quoted by John and reconstructed in the *Grand-Saint-Graal*. They thought of his ministry, which overlapped that of John the Baptist. Their great clergyman, prophet, and warrior Merlin had adopted John the Baptist's life-style. They found in John not only the coming of Nicodemus, but also the words of Thomas, the personality of Philip, the raising of Lazarus, the reality of Andrew, and all of John's vivid recollections. From this Gospel they came to know Jerusalem and the Holy Land. The Gospel of John traveled immediately to the Pyrenees Mountains by way of John's pupil Polycarp, said the theologian Barclay in his two-volume edition of John, and then via Polycarp's pupil, Bishop Irenaeus of Lyons. Barclay believed that the Gospel of John was written circa A.D. 100 at Ephesus, the very city where the Virgin Mary's last home is shown to visitors today. The Bishop Irenaeus expressly named John, "the beloved disciple," as author of this Gospel.

Among theologians today there is no agreement whatsoever concerning this Gospel so preferred by early Christians in western Europe. As many find the Gospel of John heretical and Gnostic as find it orthodox and Roman. Where the worship of the Holy Grail attracted many persons, that question is immaterial now. Perhaps fifteen thousand Knights Templar died for their faith. The entire population, in the millions, some say, of southern France, or Occitania, was burned to death, including women and children, because of their understanding of the Gospel of John. Those who sought spirituality above all, who loved Christ as a god of light just as did our author of the *Grand-Saint-Graal*, felt alienated otherwise in their own land. They abhorred a world of crass materialism, industrialization, filthy urban centers, pollution, and overpopulation. In worshiping the Holy Grail they sought a God beyond matter, a life of simple abnegation, the joys of spirit rather than those of gold, or flesh, or appetites always unsatisfied, always consuming gluttonously. They sought a Christ who was both divine and human, but altogether *perfect* in all respects. Our author of the *Grand-Saint-Graal* uses such words: *pure* and *perfect*. They are, theologically speaking, dangerous words. Those who died first were the "Perfects," or fifth-degree initiates at the Grail Castle in southern France. The Templars followed them into death.

The very introductory verses of the Gospel of John launched a religion that preferred a spiritual interpretation of Christ himself, as being the Word that existed before the creation of our world. It is a preexistent universe where miracles occur, and where the falling dove of the Holy Spirit allows the worshiper's mind to wander freely in his own garden of images, and read his own consolation into the symbols he creates. There the dazzling light shed about the real presence of Jesus blinded the viewer perhaps but also drew him up out of the evil and darkness of his everyday, painful, working existence. Because of Christ a light came into a world that had almost lost all hope as it struggled against evil and the natural darkness of the cruel universe.

The Gospel of John, whether it accepted a philosophy of opposites or condemned dualism, offered a theory of life that thousands understood, applied to their own lives, and consequently comforted them. The knowledge of the Grail was a quest everyone could, in imitation of his royal lords, kings, and great queens, undertake quietly, silently, and humbly.

Opposite the darkness in a man's soul shone the blinding light of Jesus, as presented by the sight of the Holy Grail. Opposite falsehood is the truth that sets us free, such worshipers said. Opposite the fear of old age and death is Jesus' promise of resurrection and victory. Against the fires of hell and the pull of the underworld is the bliss of paradise and the glory of heaven. Not all exists in this world, for there are other worlds, Jesus said. The sorry, warring world of human persons is only one of the worlds. Others are divine. Man too is capable of striving for perfection. The quest of the Holy Grail is a search for purification on the road to whatever degree of perfection may be possible. Gawain took one giant step along that road, at the end of which rose Lancelot's son Galahad, perfection in man.

Because of John's Gospel, the worship of early Christians peaked in southern France, where it is referred to now as "Catharism." Actually, the Greek word for "Catharism" covers up the Latin and English name, which is simply "Puritanism." The major difference is that the Catharists were massacred whereas their spiritual descendants, the Puritans, fled to America and legislated religious tolerance.

In medieval Occitania in the Pyrenees Mountains the Catharists read the Gospel of John aloud at religious services viewed as consolatory:

> In principio erat Verbum . . .
> In the beginning was the Word . . .   (v. 1)

> . . . Gratia et Veritas per Jesum Christum facta est.
> . . . grace and truth came by Jesus Christ.   (v. 17)

René Nelli, who is the world's authority on Catharism in France, points out that the Gospel of John was very early translated into Provençal. That language too was stamped out as a result of the massacre of all of southern France west of the Rhône River. Christ says in Provençal:

> Celui qui me suit ne va pas dans les ténèbres . . .
> He who follows me does not go down into darkness . . .

> Crezetz en la lutz, que siatz filh de lutz . . .
> Believe in the light that you may be a son of light . . .

The teachings and beliefs of the Catharists stemmed directly from the first or introductory verses of John's Gospel. Nelli explains that they taught a double creation: heaven versus hell, light versus darkness, earth versus eternity, spirit and/or soul versus the body, and the devil or prince of the world versus Christ. Souls to them were lost lambs, indeed. Christ promised each man necessary grace. They also believed that the end of time had already arrived at the death of Christ. Nelli agreed with George Adam Smith, who wrote a historical geography of the Holy Land, that "the Semites are the

religious leaders of humanity," because their "prophets saw Jeho-
vah exalted in righteousness."

It would therefore be not only right and rightful but also understandable that at the collapse of King Arthur's kingdom the Holy
Grail was sent out of Britain—perhaps to the faithful in southern
France, perhaps returned to Jerusalem. At the time of the massacre
of the Catharist population of Occitania, the Holy Grail again vanished. Shortly before the last Catharist heretics volunteered to be
burned at the stake in a mass execution, the "sacred treasure" of
the Catharists is said to have disappeared. It has never been proven
found, and that through no lack of unceasing searching during the
last centuries.

The Reverend Smith, who was Professor of Hebrew at Glasgow
University (c. 1896), supported in his historical geography the
beliefs of the Arthurian writers of Grail texts. What they claimed
was historically accurate. Bethlehem was a town west of Nazareth
and Galilee. It had neither harbor, nor river, nor main road, nor
marketplace, but stood "aloof, waterless, on the road to nowhere
. . ." (pp. 318–19). But it was far greater than Athens or Rome
because it was an "ideal city."

Jerusalem too was correctly immortalized by the Grail texts
speaking of it in King Arthur's day, with its "great long lines of the
land . . . spread out . . . as now . . . the range that rolls from our
feet north and south . . . falling to . . . the Jordan Valley . . ." (p.
123). Lydda in Sharon supplied a refuge after the fall of Jerusalem.
The great Irish theologian Pelagius was tried there in the same fifth
century in which King Arthur was born and Saint Patrick preached.
It is also the site of the Syrian Saint George, who became the patron
saint of England under King Edward III. There on the Lydda
Church is still to be seen an ancient bas-relief of Saint George and
the Dragon, and his tomb. Magdala is there also, the home of Saint
Mary Magdalene of France. It was one of the nine cities, around the
Lake of Galilee, formed long ages past around now-barren sites.
Inscriptions from the Holy Land westward mark the Phoenician
voyages: Cyprus, Rhodes, Sicily, Malta, Carthage, Sardinia, Marseilles, Spain, Gaul, Britain.

Christ himself chiefly labored near the Lake of Galilee, concluded Smith. There was the focus, in this deep valley of tropical
heat, in a trench 680 feet below sea level. One descends from the
hills of Galilee past basalt dikes where Crusaders and Knights Templar were finally defeated. Christ came down from the higher val-

leys of Nazareth to find a home there by the blue lake, and his disciples. The ancient historian of the Jews, Josephus, described it all, including the fall of Jerusalem. "And so," whispered Smith, "the speech of the fishermen of her lake . . . have become the language and symbolism of the world's religion" (p. 463).

King Solomon's
Temple

The Old Testament, which covers a thousand years concerning the Jews (who are considered "the most profoundly religious people of antiquity," said Henry Wheeler Robinson in Edinburgh in 1911 [p. 68]), bequeathed to the Western world a concept of man and a design for a temple. Stressing the dignity of man, the idea of the individual person, and the relationships of man in society, and man to God, its writers elaborated. Basing his thoughts upon Hebrew prophecy, in his Gospel John spoke of man's possible, new birth and of his eternal life. The Hebrew concept of a temple was that of King Solomon.

In his *Wars of the Jews* (vols. 5 and 6) the Hebrew historian Flavius Josephus described Solomon's Temple (§3) as having been constructed on the Mountain of Jerusalem called Moriah. The temple had altogether nine gates covered with gold and silver, as were their jambs and lintels. Corinthian brass had also been used lavishly. The front of this holy house (§4) was all-over gold—that gate was golden—with golden vines above it—and clusters of grapes as tall as a man. There hung a Babylonian curtain embroidered with the five colors mystically interpreted—like hues of blue, scarlet, and purple. There flax represented the earth, blue stood for air, purple was the Mediterranean, and scarlet was fire. Worshipers entering were thus reminded symbolically of the four ancient elements: earth, air, fire, and water. The subject embroidered was the Twelve Figures of the Zodiac.

Beyond a veil were the three most famous objects venerated by mankind over the earth, it was believed. They were God's possessions (§5): (1) a candlestick representing the Seven Planets, (2) a table with twelve loaves representing the Zodiac, and (3) an altar and incense made from thirteen sweet spices brought from or over the sea. These were the Holy of Holies.

Even reading Josephus thus far, it seems clear that this same candlestick, which is to say a replica thereof, is the one borne by a royal maiden before the Holy Grail. The table with the twelve loaves is King Uther's Round Table made by Merlin, with its sometimes, or original, twelve members and later, empty thirteenth Seat of Dread for Christ's Judas. Queen Morgan le Fay delivered a learned oration thereupon, and it is one of the finest set pieces in Arthurian literature.

At King Arthur's Court, prior to the year 542, only priests and priestesses were educated in reading, writing, astronomy, oratory, and philosophy. The princes were educated principally in warfare, etiquette, physical prowess, and oratory. Lancelot was able to read the names on tombstones. Arthur was not able to do that, but Perceval could read. Arthur's half sister Morgan was known from early childhood to be the most intelligent, and the best educated of the priestesses, and she outlived Arthur, with whom she was never on good terms.

Josephus writes (§6) that the east side of Solomon's Temple was faced with "plates of gold of great weight" so that persons approaching it from the west were forced to avert their eyes. From a distance the temple looked "like a mountain covered with snow" because what was not gold was white.

Its chief altar was square with four raised corners, which resembled horns. Illustrations of just such an altar have survived. Now, the Avalon Grail Castle was also called "Horned," because it stood in a hooked or horned, semicircular bay—or because its altar too was horned, or, lastly, because horns were sounded at its four corners—and such illustrations too have survived.

Today, as for the past 5,750+ years, the Jewish calendar starts with the New Year, Rosh Hashanah, and culminates the New Year festivities ten days later by celebrating sunset on Yom Kippur, October 9. The Rabbi blows a curved horn to usher in each New Year and herald the start of the Jewish High Holy Days. They have done so, say some, since 3760 B.C.

Josephus says that Jerusalem was taken six times before A.D. 70, when it fell to Romans. He calculated 1,179 years from King David to its destruction under the Roman Emperor Titus, and 2,170 years from the Temple's first building. Thus, for its beauty and wealth, and for its longevity, Solomon's Temple must have been the architecture copied by builders of the Grail Castle, which also stood on a mountain. And yet, marveled Josephus, nothing could save Solomon's Temple from the hatred, envy, and ignorance of its conquerors:

> . . . yet hath not its great antiquity, nor its vast riches, nor the
> diffusion of its nation over all the habitable earth, nor the

greatness of the veneration paid to it on a religious account,
been sufficient to preserve it from being destroyed (p. 342).

And so Solomon's gorgeous Temple was plundered, restored,
cleansed, polluted again, repaired again, despoiled. Ezra tells in
chapter 6 how the Persian Emperors Cyrus and Darius decreed its
restoration. Christ in Matthew, Mark, and Luke foretold its destruction in A.D. 70. John wrote that it symbolized the body of Christ
(chapter 2).

In his recent book on the mysteries of the Knights Templar of
Jerusalem, Louis Charpentier explains how treasures disappeared
over the ages, including the four parts gold and one part silver of
Solomon's Temple in Jerusalem. Was not the Holy Grail one of the
treasures saved from it? What other treasures might there have
been in the world: the Cauldron? the Golden Fleece? the Golden
Apples of the Hesperides? the Tables of the Law? Lucifer's Emerald? the Stone of Scone? the Eye of Horus? the Cup of the Last
Supper? the Holy Grail?

A French legend, says Charpentier, insists that an Asian Prince
Pérille carried the or a Holy Grail from Jerusalem to Gaul. There
he built a temple resembling Solomon's to house it. He then established a military Order to defend it, for all the world's ancient
treasures have had famous defenders: Antaeus, Isis, Moses, Prome-
theus, Medea. The members of this military Order were called
"Templists."

The Templists of ancient Gaul, continues Charpentier, swore to
reply to no question, neither concerning rank nor condition, and,
if questioned, to return posthaste to the nearest Commandery. The
Supreme Commander of this secret Order was also a secret, and he
lived in a secret place. But it is believed that he was called the Grail
King.

In mysterious terms the Grail Castle of King Arthur was once
referred to as the "Orient." What did "Orient" designate to these
fifth- and sixth-century guardians? Charpentier replies to his own
question: Beauty, Christ, Place of Light, Temple, Church, Sanctuary, Dawn. Then "Orient" is where the Grail once was if it came
originally from the eastern, or "Oriental," city of Jerusalem.

Not much more than a hundred years after the fall of Jerusalem,
which caused a massive displacement of population, the Bishop
Irenaeus (Irénée) of Lyons in Gaul, who lived during the years
130–202, proclaimed that the Western world stood four-squared,

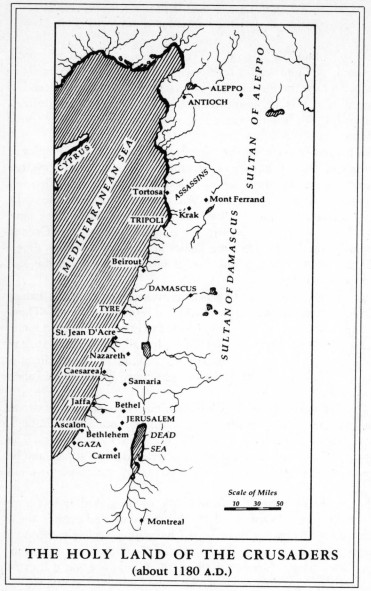

THE HOLY LAND OF THE CRUSADERS
(about 1180 A.D.)

having reasonably four quarters since it rested upon Four Pillars, which were Matthew, Mark, Luke, and John. Jesus' "Book of Revelation," declared the Bishop of Gaul, which he "gave" to Saint John the Divine, declared Saint Matthew to be a youth holding a Book, Saint Mark to be a lion like the Lion of Saint Mark's Cathedral in Venice today, Saint Luke to be an ox, and Saint John to be an eagle. Actually the four creatures appear earlier together, in the Vision of God by Ezekiel (1:10):

> As for the likeness [of four living creatures] of their faces, they four had the face of a man, and the face of a lion, on the right side; and they four had the face of an ox on the left side; they four also had the face of an eagle.

Both lion and wild bull (ox), which roamed the Holy Land in the days of Christ, symbolized strength and the tribe of Judah, and Christ himself, says Revelation. The eagle too is expressed metaphorically as a great teacher, like Christ, who found his pupils in a desert or howling wilderness and kept them like the apples of his eye. That teacher resembled an eagle that cares for its nest, and looks after its young over whom its wings spread protectively. Like an eagle, the Apostle also led his readers, "and there was no strange god with him."

Saint Jerome drew up his list, which Saint Ambrose also accepted, as follows: Matthew = man, Mark = lion, Luke = ox, and John = eagle. Saint Augustine termed Matthew a lion; Mark, a man; Luke, an ox; and John, a lion. Saint Irenaeus thought Matthew was the man; Mark, the eagle; Luke, the ox; and John, the lion.

A modern view is inspired by Barbara Walker's recent *Woman's Dictionary of Symbols and Sacred Objects* (1988), a 564-page book that is wonderfully arranged and very clearly illustrated by the author. In Walker's text, Platter, Diamond, Emerald, Cup, Chalice, Blood, Lion, Gold, and Copper are all either identified as the Holy Grail or as being seen at the Grail Castle. Moon, Sea, Water, and Ox are mentioned frequently as necessary to worship there. King Arthur is called Roman (Eagle) and Emperor. Queen Guinevere is represented on her funeral stone as an Angel.

A modern Knight Templar, Chevalier Robert Brydon of Edinburgh, City of the Lion, agrees that the Holy Grail refers directly to Solomon's Temple. It alludes to it, however, not necessarily only in a physical and materialistic sense, but as a spiritual kingdom. For

THE FOUR PILLARS

1	2	3	4
Matthew	Mark	Luke	John
Man	Lion	Ox	Eagle
Air	Fire	Earth	Water
Breath	Heat	Flesh	Blood
Angel	Gold	Diamond	Cup
Platter	Copper	Emerald	Chalice
SEPTEMBER 21	**APRIL 25**	**OCTOBER 18**	**DECEMBER 27**
Sky	Sun	Moon	Sea
Queen Guinevere	Lancelot	Perceval	King Arthur
Temple	Jerusalem	The Grail Castle	Empire

this reason the Grail Castle stood—as the medieval Knight Templar from Germany, the Chevalier Wolfram von Eschenbach, said—atop the Mountain of Salvation. The trials also, Chevalier Brydon adds, are allegorical. Gawain did not literally journey in winter through snowy forests filled with ravening bears and boars. Nor did Lancelot literally crawl on bloody knees across a Sword Bridge in order to reach the Grail Castle.

The worship of the Holy Grail, Brydon adds, was a secret gospel. Its chalice of Christ's blood, or Holy Grail as is sometimes said, was no less than a universal symbol, like the Celtic vessel of resurrection, or Cauldron of artistic inspiration. Because this worship posited a tradition of a spiritualized knighthood that was incorruptible, highly moral, spiritual, and in every sense noble, the Templars (or Templists of Charpentier) were both real and mystical guardians of the Grail as of the routes to Jerusalem.

Worship of the Grail stressed these concepts, added Chevalier Brydon in Edinburgh in 1990: sacrifice, courtesy, duty, care of the poor, and the idealization of woman. Those are the strict obligations of knighthood today as during the Middle Ages when the German Wolfram von Eschenbach, a Knight Templar, traced the origin of the Holy Grail back in time to King Solomon in Jerusalem.

KING SOLOMON AND THE GRAIL

The German Knight Templar Wolfram von Eschenbach wrote what is probably the most beautiful Grail text based upon the adventures of Parzival (known in French as Perceval). Halfway through his quest, the young hero Parzival stops at a sacred fountain (English edition, bk. 9) to receive instruction from a holy hermit.

There are mysteries concerning the Grail, the hermit Trevrizent told Parzival. It would be fortunate if the youth were ready to learn them before he wore himself out in aimless journeys.

The Grail texts were first discovered by accident in the ancient Visigothic capital of Toledo, Spain, which was renowned later as a center of Jewish and Moorish culture, says the hermit. They were written in a Semitic(?) language, which had to be learned so they could be read (German text, Munich, 1980, p. 233).

The original author of these Grail papers was a Jew named Flegetanis, a scholar of great learning and reputation. He was also descended from Solomon's royal line in Jerusalem. Thus, he was an Easterner who had been baptized. Now, this scholar Flegetanis was also an astronomer able to calculate both the rising and setting of the stars and the intervals between them as they pass along the ecliptic. He was also able to determine their influence upon the achievements and fortunes of man. It was in the dark heavens at night that he first had read the word "Grail."

The Grail was brought down by angels from the stars to the earth and left there, says Wolfram. Since it has been on earth, it has had to be guarded. That band of dedicated knights who swore to guard themselves from defilement have since that time undertaken custody of the Grail. Researchers later found similar records in the chronicles of Anjou, France, and the lineage of the medieval Angevin Dynasty (which then governed Britain, large parts of France, Provence, Occitania, and had formed alliances in Spain and the Holy Land). The name of Parzival is found in this royal line. . . .

For fifteen days the hero remained in the hermit's bare cave to absorb his teachings, which began with the story of Adam and Eve: "Die Erde war Adam's Mutter" ("Earth was Adam's Mother") (p. 239). Wisdom is contained, the hermit explained, in these ancient tales that teach young adventurers how to discern the truth. A young person is allowed by God freely to choose between ignorance and learning, as between good and evil, between purity and corruption. Only God can anticipate the thoughts of people and judge them beforehand for their purity.

Parzival complained, however, that no matter how hard he had quested, he had received only pains, sorrow, and failure. He yearned and sorrowed for the Grail, which he had not found, and for his wife and child, whom he sadly missed.

Then Trevrizent scolded him for believing foolishly that anyone searching for the Grail was in any way guaranteed success:

> niemand Kann den Grail erjagen, der
> nicht im Himmel so bekannt ist, dass
> er mit Namen berufen werde zum Grale.   (p. 251)

No man can ever conquer the Grail,
unless it is known in Heaven, that
he is summoned by name to the Grail.

Many brave knights ("Ritter") live at the German *Munsalwäsche* (Mountain of Salvation) in order to guard their Grail, the hermit explained to Parzival. They also are Templars. They live from the power of a stone that fell from Heaven ("Er heisst Lapsit exillis"). This stone has such power that when it burns the phoenix, or fire bird, to ashes, the (immortal, sun) bird comes back to life at sunrise again. The same is true for mankind. Whoever sees this powerful stone will never grow old even in two hundred years, except that his hair may perhaps turn white. Every year his bones and his flesh grow like the fire bird young again. This stone is called "the Grail": "Der Stein wird auch genannt der Gral" (p. 242).

Because it is Good Friday today, Parzival learns, the company of guardians at the Grail Mountain of Salvation await the descending white dove, which dives down from Heaven bearing a white wafer in its beak. It drops the wafer on the White Grail Stone (such as the later *Edelstein* in the Kaiser's Crown) whence all good nourishment is provided, and drink, and dinner like those future perfect foods in Heaven.

The names of the noblemen and noble maidens who serve the Grail are inscribed around the rim of the White Stone. Having been called, each one by name, they will all have achieved Perfec tion. . . . The Stone is always (white and) pure: "der Stein ist immer rein" (p. 243).

❀

(Summary of the *Continuation-Perceval,* Mons MS, v. 33, 755ff.)

Perceval set out again. He continued on his road until he came to the portal of a castle. As soon as he rode onto the drawbridge, he saw sergeants stepping forward to greet him with all signs of great joy. They helped him dismount, led away his horse, and assisted him to disarm. Then they wrapped a soft mantle about his shoulders and escorted him into the Great Hall. No such splendor in an interior was ever seen since the days of Judas Maccabeus. . . .

Here this author, like others whose words betray their Hebrew education, refers the reader to *Maccabees,* which are two books in Hebrew relegated to the *Pseudepigrapha.* They tell the story of warfare in the years circa 167–135 B.C. and the career of Judas Maccabeus against Antiochus IV, King of Syria, who attempted to Hellenize Judaea and wipe out Judaism.

❀

Since the days of Judas Maccabeus, Perceval thought, no Hall was ever decorated in such a distinctive and recognizable style. If one looked up at the ceiling, one saw it was illuminated with pure gold and a host of little, tiny stars made all of silver. The walls were by no means painted with paint, neither vermilion, nor azure, nor heraldic green, nor plain green any more than with any other color there is. The walls (like those of Solomon's Temple) were entirely plated with sheets of gold and silver that had been worked to represent thousands of images, and set with so many priceless gems that they lighted up the whole Hall. Nobody could enter without being struck dumb with amazement.

The Fisher King was present there, seated on a scarlet cushion. Perceval greeted him in God's name, and the Good King replied to him gently. The youthful knight wanted right away to know the full meaning of all he glimpsed, but it was not yet time . . .

❊

Toward morning Perceval lay wakeful for some time until he heard a voice calling him, "Perceval, my brother!" And the voice continued saying that a daughter would be born to him and his wife Blanchefleur, and that she would be both promising and beautiful, and that she would wed a glorious king. However, through sedition and sin, this king would be threatened with seeing his realm destroyed except that one of his sons would avenge this treason and reseat his father on the throne. The latter would have another heir who would conquer vast territories, and a third heir who, although handsome and gracious, would be changed into a bird (Lohengrin the Swan Knight?) to the great despair of his parents. The oldest brother would take to wife a maiden who, because of her great worth, would help him restore his fortunes. To them would be born a daughter whose son would become the Glory of all the world, for his three descendants would free Jerusalem and the True Cross (Godfrey de Bouillon, First Crusade, 1099).

❊

(*La Queste del Saint Graal,* Incident 13, Nutt, *Studies,* pp. 42–44)

During his travels far from home and weary, Perceval came late one night to a hermitage where dwelled in absolute abstinence a hermit Lady. When he knocked at her door insistently because he was wet, cold, and hungry, he finally heard her allow her servants to admit him. She recognized Perceval at once, told him she was his aunt and formerly the Queen of the Waste Land. It was King Arthur's half sister, Queen Morgan le Fay. After they had spoken and Perceval had learned that his mother had died of sorrow soon after his enrollment in the Grail Quest under King Arthur's direction, Queen Morgan undertook the youth's education. Here follows the Lady's lecture:

Three Fellowships followed the life of Christ, as you doubtless know. The first of these communions was the Table of the Last Supper where his Apostles joined Christ as they had customarily done at other suppers in common. At this last table it was not earthly bread but heavenly bread that sustained the Fellowship. You will recall the words of King David:

KING DAVID'S SONG OF ASCENTS

Behold, how good and how pleasant it is
For brethren to dwell together in unity!
It is like the precious oil upon the head,
That ran down upon the beard,
Even Aaron's beard;
That came down upon the skirt of his garments;
Like the dew of Hermon,
That cometh down upon the mountains of Zion:
For there the Lord commanded the blessing,
Even life for evermore.

This Fellowship at table was founded by the Lamb of God, who was sacrificed for us all. Such peace and harmony reigned at that table that all their good works could be seen and believed.

Centuries later a second table was founded in memory of the first and according to its rule. This one was known as the Holy Grail, or used in its worship. That announced to the world the coming of Christianity. Joseph of Arimathea brought this service from Jerusalem, landing in a new land with his family and friends, some four thousand poor souls. They lacked the necessities of life, and especially food enough for such a great number of people. All the first day they trudged through forests that seemed totally uninhabited. On the second day they met at last one old woman carrying twelve loaves of bread from an oven. The men bought her loaves from her but fell to quarreling about how to share so little among so many. Report of the quarrel caused Joseph of Arimathea to summon a general meeting at the table. There he cut the bread in so many pieces as all stood in crowds around and watched him. After he had laid out the pieces of bread, he placed the Holy Grail on the Grail table, in plain sight. Before their eyes the pieces of bread multiplied until all the four thousand had eaten their fill. Thereafter those present offered prayers of thanksgiving to the Lord who had come to them in their day of need. (Joseph of Arimathea was the uncle of Perceval's mother.)

The third table was devised by Merlin himself to teach a very clever lesson at King Arthur's Court also. The table was round like the earth, circular like the spheres where roam the stars, whence Round Table means our universe. The best of youths therefore leave home, mother, and family to apply for this Fellowship at the rank of Companion, and in the hope of becoming knights.

> Merlin made the Round Table in token of the roundness of the world, . . . for all, Christian and heathen, worship at the Round Table; they have been chosen to the fellowship of the Round Table. They think they are more blessed than as if they had got half the world. You have seen that they lost their fathers, their mothers, and all their kin, their wives, their children, in order to be of this fellowship . . . When Merlin had ordained the Round Table he said that they who should be fellows of the Round Table would learn the truth of the Holy Grail. (Sir Thomas Malory, *Le Morte d'Arthur,* bk. 14, chap. 2)

KING SOLOMON'S SHIP

This chapter on the origin of the Holy Grail in Jerusalem would not be complete without turning once more to two manuscripts, the *Grand-Saint-Graal* and the Grail *Queste,* which explain how early missionaries undertook the long and dangerous voyage overseas to western Europe. We now learn that King Solomon had a ship constructed to bear them thence, and that this sacred ship was later called Holy Church. Then the Grail *Queste* comes in to tie this ship, with its sacred sword and altar, to the Perceval (Parzival) personage who achieved sight of the Holy Grail. To make his story quite unforgettable, the author of the *Queste* relates it to the young sister of Perceval.

❋

Summary: (*Grand-Saint-Graal,* pp. 131ff.)

When Solomon realized that even he, wise as he was, could not protect himself against the wiles of his wife, he devised a parable for his book. He had walked around the world and never was able to find one good woman. He really marveled that women were so clever and malicious. For even our first mother didn't end up without being hurled out of Paradise.

While he was saying these words, a voice answered him: Solomon, don't despise women even though through the woman Eve man first came to grief. In the place of that woman will come another.

When Solomon heard this word, he realized he had been foolish to have blamed Woman.

Therefore Soloman decreed that the one woman should be called "mother" and the other, "stepmother."

"Alas," thought Solomon, "I would have been so pleased to have seen this blessed person."

Solomon was wrapped so long in thought that his wife, whom he loved, perceived he couldn't pull his heart up. She was afraid he would make himself sick over it.

One night he was more troubled than usual. She begged him to tell her what he was so deep in thought about. Solomon, who realized her so much more subtle and wily than any man could ever be, thought that if a mortal could counsel him in his cogitations, she could probably do so best. Then she spoke.

"Sire, I have thought how a knight will be descended from our lineage."

"So tell me," he told her.

"Tomorrow morning, call together the carpenters in your kingdom. When they are assembled, command them to make a ship so that it can never rot, neither from sea water nor any other cause, for a period of four thousand years. . . ."

On the following day Solomon handed down messages to seek carpenters. When they were in his presence, he commanded them to construct a ship which would be seaworthy and guard against rot for four thousand years. They pained and labored until the ship was made and was ready to launch in a half year.

When the ship was ready to go, the wife said to Solomon, "Sire, since he you spoke of will surpass in high birth and chivalry all who will be born ahead of and after him, it seems to me that it would be proper for you to prepare the most priceless weaponry which he will bear. These arms must be precious as he shall be best above other knights."

"Tell me," he says, "what arms these could be."

She tells him what will be suitable. In the temple made in honor of Christ is the sword of King David, she says, and sharpest bladed which was ever handed to a warrior. Take off the handle and scabbard. Those who know herbs and gems will make a new handle of precious stones. Any one person seeing it will see one single stone . . . We shall have smithied a scabbard so marvelous that it will be unique. When these things are completed, then put on hangings to please.

A learned man removed the sword from the temple. Then he also did everything she had commanded. After that he made the hilt as rich and as beautiful as the story says. When he had ornamented the hilt and the sheath and had begun to examine them and saw a superb sword, he formed the opinion that no knight was ever to be appareled so nor ever to be so virtuously provided as Perceval would be.

Solomon wanted to tie on hangings suitable to such a sword; but his wife said no. So what she did was to bring some as ugly as old hemp. They made a belt so weak it couldn't even hold a sword.

"What is this stuff," asked Solomon, "you want to put on here?"

"Yes," she said, "in your time there won't be any other."

"Oil fait ele ia a uostre tans ni aura autres," she said, but there will come an hour when a damsel will change it and will put others so lovely and so expensive that the sword will become a wonder worth seeing. So in this sword you will be able to recognize the faces of two women. For just as the Virgin who is to come will mend our first mother Eve's misdeeds, just so will this maiden repair this sword. For she shall put cords she shall love. These words made Solomon easy on that score. He did marvel that her words would one day come to pass.

When the ship was completed, roofed as richly as the story claims it was, Solomon had made in it a bed [an altar], beautiful and marvelous for placing a sword at the foot. At the head the king put the crown which King David his father had worn, so saying he left it for the knight because it could not be better employed elsewhere. When all was done, the Lady said something was still missing. Then [she] took carpenters and guided them to the tree of life under which Abel was slain. Then she told the lords that it was fitting that this crimson tree and the others, one white and the other green, should give three branches, one crimson, one white, and one green, with leaves around. They said they hesitated greatly to cut into the tree of life. She told them that she would shame them if they did not execute her order. They struck their axes inside it and immediately saw the tree bleeding like a man with his arm cut off. They were aghast at what they had done. They stopped hacking, and repented sorely their acts. Then three branches were carried on board the ship and placed where she had directed, one behind the bed [the altar], one before it, and one laid upon it. Nor was this done without its having deep significance. While she and Solomon were speaking of the three branches, the news was brought that those who had broken into the tree had become blind, which made Solomon sorry.

The ship was launched then.

An old man sent by God later revealed that the ship signified Holy Church, beautiful edifice and most delightful in the world. For from faith and truth was Church constructed. By ship we must understand Holy Church by the sea. . . . Just as the ship carries a man across the sea without peril, upholding him over water, so

Christ carries ministers ["menistre"] through the world and through sins which do not contaminate them. The ship also signifies the holy table, the bed [altar], the holy cross. The white branch signifies God's virginity; the red one, Christ's love of man; the green branch signifies patience. Thus, virginity, charity, and patience are the altar cloth.

※

(Summary of *La Queste del Saint Graal,* Incident 35, as in Nutt, *Studies,* p. 47)

When Perceval, Bors, and Galahad (centuries later in Britain) found Solomon's ship, they discovered King David's golden crown still there, overlying a purse of lustrous fabric and a book explaining the ship and its significance. Perceval read this to his two companions. The maiden who supplied the marvelous hangings and the belt for the sword was Perceval's own young sister. She had prepared the belt from braids of her own golden hair, which was her richest possession. She removed the tattered hemp belt and tied her own in its place, which pleased Galahad because he had told her once how precious and lovely her golden hair was. Galahad was first to grasp the sword by its pommel, which it allowed him to wield. The maiden then girded the sword about him, saying that by this privilege she engaged herself to die the most blessed of all royal maids for the noblest of all noble knights. Next day the ship landed the four of them at a fort on the Marches into Scotland, or north shore of the Solway Firth.

※

(*La Queste del Saint Graal,* Incident 41, Nutt, *Studies,* p. 49)

The three companions, Perceval, Bors, and Galahad, accompanied by Perceval's little sister, came to a castle nearby where they were nobly served. When they inquired after the castle's custom, they were informed of a sad circumstance: the chatelaine had been ill with leprosy for the past two years. No physician sent for from far or near had been able to arrest the progress of her disease. One prophet only had given a prescription, but unfortunately it involved an unknown maiden, sister to the questing knight Perceval. The sick Lady required a basin full of blood from a girl who was a virgin in fact and by intent. If that virgin were by some chance Perceval's sister, who was a king's daughter, a queen's daughter, and a perfectly pure maid, then the chatelaine would be cured at once. The castle guards had been alerted to halt all maidens and demand their blood in any case.

Perceval's sister Dandrane asked the three companions to advise her as to what she ought to do. Galahad warned her not to comply with such a demand, which would surely prove fatal, given her extreme youth and small body. The maiden begged them all three for their consent, however. They reluctantly yielded.

Before Perceval's sister requested the castle personnel to commence the phlebotomy, during which she would bleed to death, she asked them to lay her after death on Solomon's ship so that she could be carried to Sarras. They were to bury her there beside her brother Perceval and her beloved Galahad at the end of their lives.

The chatelaine was bathed in the maiden's blood. Her blackened flesh turned rosy again. By night she had fully recovered.

Chapter
II

MARY MAGDALENE
IN MARSEILLES

THE MYSTERIOUS SARRAS

The death of Perceval's sister leaves us with the problem of where the Grail went after the collapse of King Arthur's realm around the year 542. It would seem at first glance that an intermediate harbor existed between Jerusalem and Great Britain. And, secondly, that the journey was frequently made in either direction: Jerusalem to Britain, Britain to Jerusalem. That harbor appears to have been Marseilles, adjacent to the most sacred necropolis of ancient Gaul, upriver from Marseilles, at Aliscans. Nearby Lyons was the "head of Gaul," near which, at the confluence of its rivers, all Celts desired to be interred.

Our second problem now is the search for a prototype priestess after whom the many priestesses, and especially Queen Guinevere, were modeled. Dandrane must have had a precedent. There must have been a preeminent woman saint whom they followed. In this same area of Marseilles we come upon the life and churches of Saint Mary Magdalene. She was a perfect example not only for Dandrane and Guinevere, but for all women in Christendom. We shall have to protest her having been called a "prostitute," when all the time she is referred to as the "supreme initiate" of Jesus.

The story of Saint Mary Magdalene adjoins that of the other Marys who are honored still today in huge processions every May 24. Here, then, is the original procession of holy women, priests, and laymen that the Grail ceremonies could well have copied. We conclude by sweeping through the Arthurian manuscripts to search for accurate, detailed descriptions of Grail Processions. We shall see who figure principally: maidens, ladies, matrons, princesses, and finally the august Grail Queen herself.

Where were Perceval and Bors to go after King Arthur's kingdom collapsed? Where was the "Sarras" where they had sworn to convey aboard Solomon's Ship the dead sister of Perceval? As last King of the Grail Castle, and last, adult nephew of King Arthur, what dispositions had Perceval made for the repose of his sister and the safety of ship and altar of the Holy Grail? Where and what was this Sarras?

It might be well to stand in her place first, walk in her shoes, and imagine what Dandrane wanted by way of a final resting place. She said she wanted to be buried in Sarras because it was a holy site. She knew furthermore that Perceval and Bors, and perhaps Gala-had too, would eventually lie there. Lancelot had already removed the sarcophagi of Kings Lancelot I and II to greater safety in the Highlands—north of Edinburgh where he had been crowned. Dan-drane was alone in the world, an orphan like her brother Perceval, whom she had assisted, counseled, and advised as he pursued his Quest for the Grail and his inauguration as last King of the Grail Castle. Both knew that when King Arthur called up Perceval, the last of his nephews, he had only six more years to reign before he too would suffer defeat and death. Time for Perceval's sister Dan-drane had already run out.

To begin with, Sarras must have been (perhaps must still be) a place of holy burial for Celts, and especially for Celtic royalty. Being of royal birth on both sides of her family (Dandrane's mother had been the Widow Lady of Camelot), and also of holy birth because she was a descendant of Saint Joseph of Arimathea, Dan-drane in her last will and testament specified "Sarras." It was there-fore more prestigious than Calton (Caledonian) Hill in Edinburgh, where Merlin in Arthur's father's days had constructed the royal necropolis for the Celtic royal dead. Even today Calton Hill is reserved for white, marble monuments to the illustrious dead of Scotland. Dandrane did not choose the nearer necropolis, and, in truth, Edinburgh was once to fall to the enemy. Even so, she would have chosen another, greater City of the Lion. "Sarras" must have meant to her such a burial ground as Lyons in France, called Head of Gaul *(Caput Galliae).*

We look therefore to a site older than Edinburgh, but also to a port city where Solomon's Ship could have dropped anchor and arranged for the funeral services of the royal Dandrane. The oldest western city that was and is a principal trading center, located in a small, deep-water harbor encircled by high mountains, but also near the mouths of an enormous, navigable river, five hundred miles long, in fact, is that most ancient of all French metropolises, Marseilles.

Marseilles is a huge commercial city advantageously placed by nature behind an almost-landlocked and therefore very secure harbor, a city very reminiscent of the bustling, modern Glasgow, or Chicago, or New York: fast, exciting, beautifully reflected in water. But blue and white Marseilles is the oldest city in France, unbelievably ancient under its modern red and green colors the native lads love to wear. It is also the oldest Christian site in the west of Europe—one giant step to the west of Jerusalem, another giant step along the Phoenician's tin route to Cornwall and southern England.

No less an authority than the lecturer and specialist on the Shroud of Turin, Frank C. Tribbe, author of *Portrait of Jesus* and many articles on the life of Jesus, and editor of *Spiritual Frontiers,* believes that Joseph of Arimathea and other refugees from Jerusalem after A.D. 70 stopped in Marseilles for a long period of time or visited it regularly in their trading and shipping ventures. From Dandrane's point of view, then, Marseilles was widely recognized as a spiritual, ancestral home of the Celts.

More importantly perhaps, Dandrane would have heard of this chief city of the ancient Roman province, i.e., Provence, as down the Rhône River from some of the lesser Roman cities such as Arles, Aix, Orange, and Avignon, but not Toulouse. Their great common necropolis at Arles was Aliscans, more properly *Alise Champs (Champs Elysées* in Paris also today), which means the Alder Tree Fields. Ancient Celtic kings like Arthur were named for the alder, which is a chieftain tree: "Bran art thou called by the branch in thy hand." In battle the king could be distinguished by the alder branch in his raised hand, although some kings wore it on their hats.

The Plantagenet kings wore the yellow flowers of the moorland broom *(genêt)*. Alder trees were planted around this most ancient necropolis in or on the banks of the lordly Rhône because it was a sanctuary for the noble and royal dead of the Gauls. It was tended by virginal priestesses, which was Dandrane's condition also, the object of her education, and her raison d'être.

The modern painting of Aliscans by Vincent van Gogh gives us today his wonderful notion of what was the grandeur of this now ruined necropolis. Van Gogh painted it in his century, of course, by which time the prehistoric sanctuary had long been plundered and overgrown. Even so, his lovely painting has captured centuries long dead and gone but haunting still in their listening silence.

Aliscans is also one of the world's oldest epic cycles whose heroes like Aymeri de Narbonne never die but stand as tall and as herculean as Arthur—who has as yet no epic cycle to commemorate his name. Marseilles includes within its scope Narbonne also, plus the rest of the wide estuary of the Rhône as it splits into two rivers before reaching the sea.

Frank Tribbe suggested* that "Sarras," as it is spelled in Arthurian manuscripts, was Marseilles, and not a short form of "Nazareth" as I suggested in *King Arthur* of 1986. He is certainly correct, it would appear today. The word is probably derived from "Saracen" as a generic term meaning a place where persons spoke a Semitic language. The medieval authors name Marseilles and its environs "Sarras," because three hundred or so years before their time southern France was conquered by invading Saracens, who in those days were Arabs. Charles Martel halted their advance at the Loire River, central France, in the Battle of Tours in A.D. 732. The same or allied Saracens remained in Spain until their expulsion in 1499, but in Spain they were called "Moors."

It staggers the imagination to realize that Marseilles and rose-colored Toulouse, Aix and Arles, Orange and Avignon, are Christian centers that go back in time almost to the death of Christ. More stunning is the corollary: that worship of the Grail, or possession of the Grail as a holy object, may antedate King Arthur by five hundred years. Thirdly, one gasps to realize that when Dandrane wished to be buried there or at Aliscans she already knew it as a focus of worship of Mary, ergo as a woman's center, first and

*Per telephone conversation, January 20, 1990.

foremost a necropolis where a priestess's body could still be accepted gratefully.

But still that is not all. The most staggering realization comes at the end: the worship of the Holy Grail continues today, now in our day, in the mountain valleys of the Pyrenees close to prehistoric Toulouse, ancient capital of the Visigothic Empire. And holy processions of masses of people continue annually today in the Rhône delta as they continue privately in the mountains south of Toulouse. The Grail texts recount the appearance suddenly, without preamble, and the stunning beauty of similar processions at the ceremonial Grail Castle in King Arthur's time. Royal maidens, of whom Dandrane was probably one, entered bearing a Grail. They were wreathed in flowers. They were incredibly graceful, lovely, as young girls of any rank in society are always graceful and adorable.

The memory of the Grail, and of Grails, comes mysteriously down the centuries, very much like that of the mysterious "Sarras," which probably after all is no needle in a haystack, but the hidden harbor of Marseilles with its white island in front of it (with the Château d'If of the Count of Monte Cristo) masking it from view by sea.

The splendid city of Marseilles, which is a feast for the eyes, was founded at least six hundred years before the birth of Christ, at the mouths of the Rhône River (Bouches-du-Rhône), and called Massilia and Magsalia. It stands, or rather rises, in the center of the Gulf of (the) Lion, which is forty-two kilometers wide. It has always been the chief center of east–west (Asia–Europe) trade and also of trade north and west along the coasts of Africa. This thriving trading center was not annexed by Rome until 49 B.C. Marseilles was founded by Greek colonists, and the visitor believes it, for the young men who throng its wide boulevards much resemble in body and pose the Cretan bull-vaulters of the famous frescoes in Cnossus, or Knossos: broad, lean shoulders, flat bodies, narrow hips, olive skins, black eyes and brows, proud stances. Marseilles has always proudly declared itself a "meeting place of all races." Like New York, it is therefore an open city.

The shoreline of Marseilles, with its old port and old quays still intact, is a marvelous sight, to be sure, but all that aged beauty is nothing compared with the view of Marseilles from the deck of an ocean liner as it cuts its swath from Naples en route to Gibraltar. The sight of Marseilles as Dandrane's brother Perceval would first have viewed it, from the sea, is world famous: a semicircular bay with bare hills rising to great mountain ranges of the Basses-Alpes behind it, marble-veined balustrades under the brilliant, hot sun of the Azure Coast. Of course, Marseilles is relatively poor in ancient buildings now—having suffered razing during the German occupation in World War II, and having subsequently been gutted by Allied naval bombardment in August of 1944. Its Canebière, though, ranks among the great avenues of great cities. And its cold wind, the *mistral* (a Provençal word from this almost dead, ancient tongue) sweeps violently down from the Alps like the northerners through windy Chicago.

Some 150 meters above the city towers the church and hill of the Virgin Mary, Notre-Dame-de-la-Garde, mounting guard over her city of the ten saints or maids named Mary from Jerusalem, adored there after the death of Christ. After his death the other Marys also migrated to Marseilles. And it is a Mary-city today. With a coat on and a heavy arm to steady a person, one can climb out on the outer balustrade of her church and look breathlessly down on Marseilles laid out in her curved, blue bay. But watch out for a gust of the *mistral,* which blows until it gives up trying to plunge the huge, blindingly white church down the marbled mountainside.

The ancient Greek historian Strabo marveled at Marseilles with its busy port and hinterland rich in olive trees, vineyards, mulberries, silk worms, and fruits, and its island, the Camargue, insulated by the two branches of the Rhône, always prime breeding pastures for the famous white horses called "White Manes." He noted how goods from the Marseilles *emporion* filled inland markets upriver as far distant as eastern France, southwestern Germany, and even northwestern Switzerland, for the Rhône also flows downstream through Lake Geneva.

In later Roman days the fifty-oared war galleys of Marseilles defeated the Carthaginians. Strabo and another historian, Pausanias, both told how the *Marsellais* brought in educated women as priestesses after each military conquest so their altar fires could be rekindled and their peoples consoled and encouraged by lovely, foreign women. Marseilles in those days had trading posts and counters not only from Senegal to Spain, but from Narbonne to Thulé, which ancients said was the Shetland Islands and Jutland, Scotland, and Denmark, by 320 B.C. Therefore Dandrane also longed to lie in Marseilles after death because it boasted temples to Artemis and to the Marys.

Many Romans preferred to be educated in the Oriental schools in Marseilles by great Hebrew scholars rather than journey east to Athens. In Marseilles they could choose other subjects also perfected in Asia: medicine, astronomy, rhetoric, law, politics, religion, and philosophy. Other faculties made Marseilles equally famous as the Greek university of the West.

After having fought long against Julius Caesar, the city, sadly, fell to that monster in 49 B.C. Christianity was well established, however, by 846 when the Saracens sacked the city. It became an independent county after the Carolingians died out in northern France; enjoyed a new prosperity during the Crusades when the erstwhile King Richard I, the Lion Heart, was its king; and became a royal city in 1481 after its centuries of opposition to Catharism and Protestantism. Throughout religious wars and massacres Marseilles clung carefully to its Christian women saints and to Roman Catholicism.

Madame Myriame Morel-Deledalle, Conservator of the Museum of History in Marseilles, writes (July 18, 1990)* that archaeology in the port area has uncovered the ancient ramparts from the day of Christ, the hook at the harbor entrance, the city's fountain of ancient, sweet water, the main city reservoir, and the harbor itself, all of which point to its importance in the ancient world. A Roman ship was also found under layers of the ancient port. The city has therefore finished building a museum around a *Jardin des Vestiges* (Garden of Ruins). The antique fountain has been restored and filled with sweet water again.

*Personal correspondence.

SAINT MARY MAGDALENE

Mary was named Magdalene from the place-name Magdala, the "castle" where she was born.* Mary Magdalene, her brother Lazarus, and her sister Martha jointly owned Magdala, which is two miles from Nazareth and Bethany, plus another castle near Jerusalem, plus a great section of Jerusalem City itself. In the division of their inheritance, Jacobus asserts, Mary took Magdala, Lazarus chose the property in Jerusalem, and Martha received Bethany. Mary devoted herself to pleasure. Lazarus trained for war. And so Martha administered all three estates, including men-at-arms, servants, and the poor. Even so, after our Lord's death and ascension, all three sold everything and laid the money at the feet of his Apostles. But by then Mary had already deserved her reputation as a rich sinner.

Mary had often heard Jesus preach. Every time she heard him, she became more and more inspired. She therefore followed him to the house of Simon the Leper, where he was dining. Because she felt herself such a sinner, she hung behind at his feet, washed them with her tears, and anointed them with precious ointments. (Baths and ointments were customarily used there because it was such a hot, dry climate with a blazing sun that burned the skin.)

Simon expressed surprise that Jesus as a prophet should have allowed a sinner like Mary to touch him. But Jesus reproved him and forgave Mary her sins.

This is the same Mary Magdalene whom Christ customarily favored with many indulgences. He once took seven devils out of her, for instance. He folded her about with his love. He wanted her to be his hostess and for her to plan his journeys, and he often asked pardon gently for her. He had reproved the Pharisee Simon when he called Mary Magdalene sinful. He corrected Judas, who claimed she squandered money. When she wept, he consoled her, but also wept with her. Because he cherished her, he raised her brother Lazarus from the dead after four days. Because he loved her, he healed her sister, who had been hemorrhaging for seven years.

This gives you evidence of Mary Magdalene, who was the first

*This is her story summarized, but as told by Jacobus de Voragine (1230–98) in his book *The Golden Legend (Legenda Aurea),* or Saints' Lives, Englished by William Caxton, circa 1483, and now re-Englished.

to wash our Lord's feet, which were his holiest parts (for holy persons were anointed on the feet), and who did penance for her sins. It was also she who anointed his head when his passion on the Cross drew near. It was also she who prepared the ointments that would dress his body, and she was the one who refused to depart from the tomb when his disciples departed.

It was to Mary Magdalene that Jesus appeared first after his resurrection. She had come among the Apostles and was Christ's witness. She too was an Apostle, female among the men Apostles. And so, fourteen years later, after the martyrdom of Saint Stephen and the ostracism of the others, she too went into a distant country to preach the word of Christ. There were seventy-two disciples, and Saint Peter himself permitted Mary Magdalene among them.

Many disciples and saints, among whom were Mary Magdalene, Lazarus, and Martha, were sentenced to death by being thrown in a derelict hull, which had neither rudder nor gear, and let drift out to sea to be drowned. However, by God's help, they all came safely across the sea to the port of Marseilles.

Nobody there would invite them in, and so the poor Christians had to live under the porch of a pagan temple. But the first time the people of Marseilles came to worship, they were amazed to see the beautiful Mary Magdalene rise up before them. She stood very calmly before them all. She showed them her lovely, happy face. She spoke to them quietly like an educated lady. She then began to preach to them of the teachings of Jesus Christ. The people who heard her agreed with her reasons, enjoyed her pleasant words, and already in their hearts ceased worshiping their pagan idols.

Hers were the lips that had kissed our Lord's feet so elegantly. Of course, she was more inspired with the word of God than anybody else.

One day the ruler of Provence and his wife came to the temple to worship and ask for a child. Mary Magdalene was there. She forbade them to sacrifice to their pagan gods. After this meeting, the princess dreamed that Mary Magdalene instructed her to intercede with the prince on behalf of the needy, and then in a second dream, threatened her. The third night both prince and princess were terrified to see Mary Magdalene before them with a burning face as if the palace were afire. And in her dream she cried out: You dictator! You son of a devil! With that snake of a wife who will not say what I told her to tell you. You enemies of the Cross! You pigs who stuff yourselves but deny all food to the Saints of the Lord. Do you not roll around in silk? And then do you not walk out and see the Christians without a roof over their heads? And you look the other way? You shall therefore not escape the punishment you deserve. You are tyrants and criminals!

When the prince and princess awoke, they saw that Mary Magdalene was no longer there. But the prince still trembled. "We had better obey her," the princess told him. So they took in the Christians.

Another time the prince confronted Mary Magdalene: "Can you defend this law of Jesus you preach?"

"I can," she said, "because it is confirmed every day by miracles, and by the word of Saint Peter in Rome."

"We are ready to accept your teachings," he said, "if we can conceive a child." So Mary Magdalene prayed, and as a result, the princess conceived.

To make a long story short, the prince and the princess had a ship loaded with cargo before they embarked for Rome to hear Saint Peter and judge him for themselves. But unfortunately they ran into a terrible storm, which sent the princess into labor prematurely. She delivered a son, however, and then died. The sailors refused to keep a corpse aboard, and knew the baby would soon die of starvation; but the prince persuaded them to lay the corpse on a mountain they saw nearby, with the baby on the mother's breast. The prince then prayed to Mary Magdalene's god, covered his wife with her mantle, and left the dead mother with her living baby. He then proceeded, aboard the same ship again, to Rome.

In Rome the prince found Saint Peter, who advised him to trust in God, not to grieve, for all would end joyfully. With Saint Peter the prince journeyed on to Jerusalem where he visited all the holy places made famous by Christ. Two years later the prince reembarked for home.

During the return cruise they again passed within sight of the same rock (mountain?) upon which they had laid the dead mother with her babe. The prince pleaded with the captain, and gave him expensive gifts, until he consented to drop anchor there again.

They all saw a little child standing by the seashore throwing stones in the sea, as children will. When he saw the ship, he ran away. They found him huddled against his mother, under her mantle. The prince knelt down and prayed that Mary Magdalene would help them again. . . . His dead wife awoke.

She too had been all this time on a pilgrimage to Jerusalem with

Mary Magdalene, she said. And it was Mary Magdalene who had delivered her child and cared for him. The little family reembarked for Marseilles. When they arrived home, they knelt before Mary Magdalene, who was preaching, and asked her if they could become Christians. They were baptized by Saint Maximin.

Thereafter the Prince of Provence had all the pagan temples torn down. He chose Saint Lazarus to become the first Bishop of Marseilles. Then he made a procession to the city of Aix where he had Saint Maximin also raised to the bishopric.

Afterward, Mary Magdalene left Marseilles. She needed a life of solitude and meditation, she explained. She longed to leave the world and reside henceforth alone in a solitary, uninhabited place.

She retired to the cave and cliff now called Sainte Baume, or the Holy Balm, north of Marseilles. On this bare precipice there was neither running water, nor grass, nor any trees. From that time on Mary was no longer nourished by earthly food, only henceforth by celestial provender.

At every hour of prayer her whole body levitated. Angels raised her up through the air. Heavenly hosts made music then. Glorious choirs sang for her delight.

Then a hermit priest came to reside in a cell at no great distance from her cave. He himself bore witness to all comers that she was raised up into the air several times a day, that she remained suspended for the space of an hour—and this by no human intervention—and then lowered into her customary place.

The priest then desired to go closer and really know the truth about what could have been visions on his part. He prayed first, and approached devoutly. But as soon as he reached a point a stone's throw away he felt his legs begin to bloat and his innards shrink. He panted from fear. The minute he turned away, he felt easy again. A second time he tried to approach her, but he suddenly couldn't move at all. The priest finally understood that hers was a mysterious and heavenly sanctuary impenetrable by mortals. He called upon her then to speak, and she spoke, saying, "Come and know."

Then she said, "Do you recall the holy book about Mary Magdalene, that famous sinner who bathed the feet of Christ with her tears and dried them with her hair, and begged forgiveness for her sins?"

"Yes," he replied, "and Holy Church has told it for the past thirty years now."

"I am she who did that and have been here alone for thirty years."

The Sunday after Easter Saint Maximin also saw Mary Magdalene surrounded by her attendant angels standing in the choir of his church, thirty or forty inches above the pavement. "Come nearer, Father," she told him.

And it was, of course, Saint Maximin who first wrote this eyewitness story of Mary in his book. And he further wrote that every time Mary Magdalene appeared, she always wore her same beautifully composed face, which shone like skin in sunlight. Then she came to the altar and received communion, after which her soul departed her body.

Afterward there came all around where she had been the sweetest perfume imaginable, and this lovely fragrance persisted for seven days at that spot. Saint Maximin requested that her body be anointed with precious balms and that it be suitably interred, and that he be buried in the same tomb thereafter. Other well-known authors such as Hegesippus and Josephus agree with this story or relate it identically. The latter claims also that Mary Magdalene endured such piercing grief after the death of Christ that she would never more look upon any man for the rest of her days.

Some authors have said that Saint Mary Magdalene was the wife of Saint John the Evangelist. When Christ called him from the wedding, he angered Mary Magdalene so much that she gave herself over to all pleasures of the flesh. However that may be, it was not suitable for John to be the cause of her damnation, for which reason she was given penance and converted to a holy life. Instead of enjoying the delights of the flesh, then, she was rewarded by having bestowed upon her the supreme delights of the spirit. For giving her up, Saint John was similarly recompensed.

Those poor sinners and those afflicted with disease or blindness who were saved by Saint Mary Magdalene experienced at the hour of her death the vision of her sweet presence. They saw her then in the full bloom of her great beauty, and flanked by angels. At their deaths she sent angels who bore their souls up to heaven in the semblance of white doves.

Because Marseilles was the home of Saint Mary Magdalene, it was also the sort of very holy sanctuary that Dandrane, Perceval, Bors, and Galahad would long to visit. The Sainte Baume sanctuary is today also one of the most sought after places of pilgrimage in the world. It falls into the area stretching from the Rhône delta north into the Alps on the east with Lyons, City of the Lion, at the junction of Alpine rivers. This entire ancient area of Provence is saturated with biblical history. It also shelters the most awesome necropolis in western Europe.

During the Middle Ages, Mary Magdalene was interpreted as, according to literal readings of Luke and of *The Golden Legend,* "sinful," therefore a prostitute or a harlot. This influential reading caused houses of prostitution in England to be routinely called "Magdalenes." Some biblical scholars have blamed this accusation upon Luke alone, finding his view of women too Greek, too puritanical, too easily derived from the old dictum that flesh is evil and woman's flesh disgustingly so. Marina Warner argued (1976) that the New Testament treated Mary Magdalene no more shockingly than the Old Testament treated Eve—misogynistically. Emile Mâle reported (Paris, 1949; New York, 1958, p. 21) that the legend of Marie Magdalene in France was invented out of whole cloth in the eleventh century and had no basis whatsoever in fact. In the French language a Magdalene *(Madeleine)* is an endlessly weeping woman.

Saint Mary Magdalene is by no means the only Saint Mary venerated in Provençal religious services and by the processions that include thousands of worshipers every year. But Mary Magdalene stands taller because she preached the gospel, because she was called apostle, because she donated a great fortune to Christ, and because she was beloved especially by him. Even so, the age-old insult hurled at her from every pulpit, that she was a prostitute, rankles.

Rich women do not become prostitutes, and Mary Magdalene was an immensely wealthy woman by any standards. Elizabeth Cady Stanton observes:

> Thecla, Paula, Eustochium, Marcella, Melanie, Susanna, are but a few of the women of wealth who gave both themselves and their large fortunes to the establishment of the ethics of Jesus (*The Woman's Bible,* New Testament, p. 137).

Yet, she continues, their great works are rarely even mentioned in histories of Christianity, or elsewhere. In fact, the degradation of women "in Christendom" has been so great that, in the case of

Mary Magdalene, few will even respect her memory by dropping the old insults.

The men who visited the tomb of Jesus saw no visions, Stanton continues, "but all the women saw Jesus and the angels. . . ." Jesus even then called Mary Magdalene by name. Overcome with joy, she answered, "Rabbi" (Comments on John, p. 143). The theologian William E. Phipps considered her "the supreme initiate" of Jesus, and the teacher of the other Apostles. Phipps argues that Jesus did not believe in abstinence, and even that he may have been Mary Magdalene's husband, if anyone was.

THE SAINTS MARY OF THE SEA

Thousands of persons in France annually celebrate the Saints Mary, of whom there are by the latest count ten, which is also Marina Warner's finding (1983, pp. 344–45 and app. B). The theologian William Barclay in *The Mind of Jesus* (1960) explains:

> The contradictions within the story [of the Resurrection] have been advanced. In Mark it is Mary Magdalene, Mary the mother of James, and Salome (Mark 16:1); in Luke it is the two Marys and Joanna (24:10); in Matthew it is simply the two Marys (p. 291).

Ernest Renan had argued in chapter 1 of his *Life of Jesus* (1895) that such details make little difference in the overall march of the centuries, for what Jesus did anyway was to cast a black shadow on the civil power of the Roman State. That Empire, he said, was far "from suspecting that its future destroyer had been born" (p. 406), that Jesus would create a new power, which was spiritual only. "In presiding at the scene of the Calvary, the ancient Roman State gave itself the most deadly blow" (p. 407); the Roman eagles had sanctioned "the most unjust of executions." Ever since that day, "the armed police" have been regarded "with a certain pious repugnance." In his book *The Quest of the Historical Jesus* (1926) Albert Schweitzer had concluded similarly—that accurate, historical precision, as concerning the number of Marys, was subordinate to their and our spirituality:

> The abiding and eternal in Jesus is absolutely independent of historical knowledge and can only be understood by contact with His spirit which is still at work in the world (p. 399).

What is paramount is, thus, the belief thousands have in the Saints Mary of the Sea. Their worship also, like that of Mary Magdalene, may simply have entered the Church by popular demand, via some west transept.

There is in Provence another most ancient place—not a city like Marseilles, not even a town, never or no longer a harbor—merely a little hamlet: *une petite bourgade* called Les Saintes-Maries, the Saints Mary. During the Middle Ages it was called Town House of the Sea *(Villa de la Mer)*. This little place of scattered dwellings was strangely not only patronized by the august Counts of Provence but magnificently dowered by HRH Queen Jeanne de Provence according to the following rules:

1. It is hereby forbidden to collect any taxes whatsoever in Les Saintes-Maries.
2. It is also forbidden henceforth to make any seizure there (such as of clothing, weapons, furnishings, or livestock).
3. A judge from the city of Tarascon will travel there to preside *in situ*. No resident will be required to travel to any superior court.
4. The Counts of Provence undertake to patrol forever the coastal waters off Les Saintes-Maries and to defend them henceforth at their cost.
5. The last, celebrated church dedicated (twelfth century) there to Saint Mary the mother of Saint James and to Saint Mary Salome will be maintained and fortified by the Counts of Provence, at their cost, forever more.

The church portal is therefore sculpted with two lions, which is not only the sign of the Avalon Grail Castle, but also the ensign of Provence.

This lone, fortified church looms over the hamlet, at a distance of forty kilometers from any other habitation. In this respect it resembles the parish church at Arthuret, dedicated to Saint Michael and All Angels, which stands near Longtown (near Carlisle) just north of Hadrian's Wall, on the border between England and Scotland. It too is only a large church that overlooks the sea and stands surrounded on two or three sides by an ancient cemetery, the place named for King Arthur, one presumes. Its history and that of its adjacent baptistery remain shrouded in mystery, but it also was dowered and maintained by the ancient Scottish noble families of Graham and Douglas. Its name seems to go back into ancient time, past the battle fought there by Merlin's son in 573, to the burial of King Arthur circa 542. The name Arthuret might derive from the Pictish Arthur + *pet* (tribal territory) > Arthuret.

Given also the links between Arthurian literature and Provence itself, the two lions of Provence bring to mind the pair of lions that Lancelot saw as he prepared to cross the "Sword Bridge" into the

Avalon Grail Castle. Thus, the Church of Les Saintes-Maries may be another, ancient Grail Castle where mass pilgrimages still occur, as they have for the last millennium, every summer.

The processions every year to Les Saintes-Maries will lead us to those once held at King Arthur's Grail Castle, and to those once held at Saint Ninian's Cave in Scotland where Merlin and Niniane, the Lady of the Lake, were buried. These processionals occur still today at Les Saintes-Maries, France; at Saint Ninian's Cave, Scotland, on certain Sundays in summer; and for King Arthur at Arthuret and Glastonbury, England. It is no wonder that the cult of the Saints Mary entered the churches, as some scholars say, either from Coptic or Gnostic traditions, but in either case also by popular demand.

The fortified Church of Les Saintes-Maries has its own well inside its massive, thick walls, which make it look like a huge tomb. It has a walkway on its summit for patrols, machicolations, crenellations, a bell tower in the center, flanking towers at its angles, and one central, very high ogival nave. The interior is so vast and so dark as to be invisible, but there are said to be eight columns sculpted marvelously with satyrs' heads, rams, old men (Grail Kings?), and other protective symbols. There is a deeper, interior level below the choir, and a celebrated crypt containing those tombs that have attracted pilgrims for centuries to this stark, holy place under the empty sky, deadly sun, and flat marshland of the estuary. The *bourgade* itself is set on the extreme southwest point of the Rhône delta, slightly east of the mouth called Petit-Rhône. Today a small railway links the place to Arles, crossing the Camargue, which is a distance of thirty-eight kilometers. It was needed to handle the thousands of pilgrims for that one summer day each year.

Thus, we return for a moment to recall that Arles on the Rhône River, which was once, like Marseilles, an important Roman capital, contains the ancient necropolis of Aliscans (Alyscamps) and its own eleventh-century cathedral of Saint Trophime. In the year A.D. 314 a Roman Church Council forbade the local or resident ecclesiastics to side with Bishop Donat of nearby North Africa, who claimed they were the only, true heirs of Jesus' Apostles. Their modern descendants are also heirs and seers, world famous for their Provençal masterpieces: Alphonse Daudet, Robert Louis Stevenson, Georges Bizet, Vincent van Gogh, Frédéric Mistral, and Jean Giono and his friend Pablo Picasso. Not to forget the revered Paul Valéry, the foremost French lyric poet of our day, if not of any day.

It is told by friends in Provence, and especially by Jean Giono in our long hours of conversation while he awaited death, and it was also told by authors and antiquarians such as Jules Charles-Roux, how after the death of Christ Saint Mary-Jacobée (mother of James), Saint Mary Salome, and Saint Mary Magdalene, along with Saints Ruf, Maximin, Trophime, and Lazarus but without their poor Egyptian servant Sarah, were cast adrift from the shores of the Holy Land. When the poor Sarah discovered they were gone, she leaped into a light skiff, put out to sea, spread her sail (veil?), and caught them up. Then an angel took the prow of the first "embarkation," and guided them all straight to the wonderful, warm coast of the Camargue. They loved the low, lovely island of grasslands and flowers.

The two Marys for whom the *bourgade* is named remained close to the shore, always collecting people to them from the pine stands, marshes, lagoons, and ponds of the shore. They watched the *vaqueros* herd the stout, black bulls that have made them famous as breeders, and their wild, white-maned horses. Others do so today.

Saint Trophime, who became the first Bishop of Arles, performed the funeral rites of the Saints Mary. Their tomb was finally incorporated into a church about A.D. 1000, and they built it powerful enough to withstand more raids by the Saracens, who had several times destroyed the older chapels.

Every May 23, reported Jules Charles-Roux (1910), the roads were filled to overflowing with pilgrims, as they are today, by ladies in Provençal costumes, herders, cowboys, and gypsies (from the word *Egyptian*), from France and Spain especially. They come today on foot, in caravans, on horseback, ladies riding *en croupe* and in carriages, all tramping over the prime, salt-layered grazing land of the Camargue. As they come, they sing the ancient hymns and carols of Spain and Provence. The fields at the end of May are ablaze with flowers, especially with so much lavender, that it is a lilac-colored world as far as the eye can see, but also with rosy tamarisk blossoms, yellow Spanish broom, pink heather, and wild, yellow irises. Red flamingos occasionally take fright and beat upwind into the bright, blue sky. It looks less like a religious procession than a Star March to the Mediterranean, say the native poets, away off in that flat distance.

Then comes still every year a procession of sick children being wheeled or carried in chairs or litters. Following are the old people, also carried by their sons and daughters to special seats reserved for those two groups, beside the High Altar.

Then process the deputations from the great, ancient cities upriver or in the delta: Nîmes, Montpellier with its university faculty from the ancient, celebrated School of Medicine, Avignon of the Popes, Perpignan in the Oriental Pyrenees. All have to cross the Rhône Canal at Beaucaire—city of the famous medieval lovers Aucassin and Nicolette—and must cross the arms of the Rhône. Thousands of male gypsies wearing espadrilles walk proudly beside their caravans. They resemble the gypsy Carmen—hooked noses, elegant, and upright torsos, dark-skinned, tall and superb, haughty and supremely elegant, observe the natives, looking, they say, very majestic, like noble American Indians.

As all in this throng approach the sanctuary, they observe on either side, even after these hundreds of years, the old scars left by the Saracens the last time they raided and burned the Camargue. Their Saint Sarah's Church is three stories high over her crypt. The choir too is very elevated above the main floor. It is dark, dark inside, and cool. The relics of the two Marys rest in a double coffer on the nave, behind a wrought-iron curtain.

At vespers on May 24 the formal ceremonies commence. It is a great solemnity. Thousands of candles suddenly light the church. The suppliants commence a low chant. The crowd rises. All arms are outstretched to the two Marys. The relics descend . . . along with a golden candelabrum of seven branches. Above the head garlands sway, with their satin ribbons. Above them are the crowns of every first communicant of that region.

In the choir itself are the masses of suffering humanity—the ill, the blind, the paralyzed, those held up on the shoulders of their sons. All try to touch the garlands. They cry, "Long live the Saints Mary. Long live Saint Sarah the Egyptian."

Then from outside the church come five hundred men in procession, carrying a boat filled with flowers. They turn and maneuver down the narrow path, between the few cottages newly white-washed, on their way to the sea. They halt briefly to permit a priest to climb aboard. He will bless the blue Mediterranean for having borne the Marys safely across its waters. The men continue to carry the boat past the gpysy encampments along the beach. From each house-trailer women lean out and solemnly dip from each hand branches of laurel, olive, and tamarisk over the heads of the participants. In the boat, all know, there is a sacred relic, their Holy Grail:

in this case, a reliquary holding the two forearms of the two Saints Mary.

The first chords of the *Magnificat* are heard from within the church. It has followed a long panegyric praising the two Marys. From time to time the crowd interrupts, but the gypsies themselves always remain absolutely silent and immobile. They adore in their own way, which is their Fire and Water rite, say some.

All festivities end before sunset. . . . The hamlet closes doors, bars windows again, falls empty then. . . .

Christianity began there in Gaul, people there believe, whence it spread into France. . . .

The Marquis de Baroncelli-Javon in Provence added that the gypsies who come every year to the Church of Les Saintes-Maries near the sea are sometimes called "Bohemians," but there in Provence they are "Gitanos" or "Caraco" (Carai), as elsewhere in the Languedoc.

In their lost language they say they came from Atlantis in the Far West and are brothers of the American Indians, Egyptians, and Mexicans. For these reasons they adopted Saint Sarah the Egyptian.

When they travel into the Camargue each year, they are returning to what was once their European homeland. Frédéric Mistral agreed: because the gypsies were displaced by the Ligurians and Iberians, they became homeless wanderers.

Like neighboring Aigues-Mortes (Dead Waters), the port that Saint Louis built for the Fifth and Sixth Crusades, Les Saintes-Maries now lives only from its past, occasionally. Marseilles has over the centuries more than made up for the two ports' decay and sanded-in harbors. Throughout the Middle Ages the city basked in glory, as it does today, a great center of Western civilization.

One of the finest French texts of the Middle Ages puts Sarras there in glory as a first center of the "New" culture from Jerusalem, which was center of the "Old" or Hebrew culture. The French hero Perceval asked his grandfather, who was King of the Grail Castle, to tell him about Sarras where once reposed the Grail hallows: Lance, Grail, and Platter ("Tailloir"). His answer lies in the *Perceval Continuation* (Mons, MS, v. 33, 755ff.) as edited by Armand Hoog (1949, 1974): "How does it happen," asked Perceval, "that we now have them here?" (p. 266).

Very well, young friend, I will explain it to you, said his aged grandparent, since I promised to do so. Joseph of Arimathea took the Grail to Sarras, you see, after Vespasian let him out of the prison where the Jews had put him. Joseph and his friends had preached in Jerusalem and baptized many people there. Forty-five of their converts accompanied them to the Western world. There they carried the Grail.

They arrived one day at the great city of Sarras where the local king was praying in the Temple of the Sun. He was hard put to win a war he was waging. Joseph promised him victory if he would paint a red cross upon his white shield. The king obliged and proved victorious. Joseph converted the people of Sarras to the New Law.

Thereafter he journeyed into Great Britain where he built, continued the Grail King, this very manor where I dwell. I am myself descended from Joseph of Arimathea, and so are you, Perceval. It was God's will that the Grail come here.

GRAIL PROCESSIONALS

The processional character of early worship in Provence brings to mind the famous ceremonies in other Grail Castles where with equal reverence a few royal personages conducted services. One of the oldest and most interesting accounts comes from a Perceval Manuscript in Old French prose, as here summarized briefly:

Perceval once rode on, sadly, always looking for the elusive Grail Castle, to which there were no directions, until he came once by accident upon the man whom he failed to recognize as the Fisher King. This lord was riding in his boat on a river. He gave Perceval directions, for there was otherwise no castle in sight: Try to go back up the hill and down the other valley, was the cryptic instruction. Thus, Perceval retraced his route and finally saw the castle. The drawbridge over the river, or over the sea, was let down for him. Some boys rushed out to take his horse. Others escorted him into the great hall. Then the Fisher King was carried in by his body servants. The customary courtesies were exchanged, for each now suddenly recognized the other. The Fisher King, it now turns out, was Perceval's grandfather who would never be healed of his suppurating wound until this last grandson asked the correct question. Perceval was very hungry. He was therefore offered dinner. He and the Fisher King sat at table.

❦

(The *Didot Perceval* [Modena MS, p. 59], English translation by Dell Skeels, p. 46.) The bare facts follow here:

They were no sooner seated than dinner was served. Then they saw a lone maiden enter the hall from an adjoining chamber. Nobody introduced her. She was very expensively dressed, and she was noble. Around her neck she wore a white cloth. Again, nobody explained. In her hands she held two, small silver platters. Behind her walked a young man carrying a lance. Both crossed the hall without a word being spoken. Perceval saw the platters and the lance from which point dripped three drops of blood. Then entered another young man carrying the vessel which Our Lord gave Joseph of Arimathea while he was still imprisoned. The youth held the vessel high over his head. We must conclude as we can.

When all this passed before the Fisher King, he bowed his head and prayed. Everybody else did the same.

Perceval thought all this was something wonderful. He occasionally thought he might possibly venture to ask a question, but he did not ask anything for fear of making a blunder that would irritate his grandfather. He said nothing.

The Fisher King for his part kept hinting about "asking" and kept using the words "question" and "keeping your wits about you"; but Perceval gobbled his dinner and was otherwise as closed as a clam. His head got pretty heavy anyway, and grew heavier; and the hot food he was unused to eating made him more and more drowsy. He had wandered so long over hill, over dale, as we know, and through forests and bogs, without any sleep for perhaps forty-eight hours, that he could hardly keep his face out of the plate.

The boring, young man returned again, once more carrying what the reader must suppose is the Holy Grail, and this time he passed right in front of Perceval . . . from right to left this second time. Then processed a second boy bearing a bleeding lance. Perceval nodded. Finally came the maiden following them . . . Perceval never said a word. The Fisher King finally had a bed made up for him . . . none too soon.

When Perceval awoke next day he was still marveling at what he had seen. But all that morning in the castle and after he rode out, he couldn't ask a question because nobody was there.

✳

The most famous of all Perceval texts by the French author Chrétien de Troyes contains a similar procession here summarized:

✷

(*Conte del Graal,* v. 4,398ff., English translation by Jessie
Weston, 1913, p. 144.)

A maiden who was noble, 'therefore well bred, and beautifully
gowned entered the hall in front of two young squires. In her two
hands she held what the reader must suppose is the Grail. So great
a brilliance shone about it that candles dimmed just as the rising sun
dims stars or moon. After these persons came one who bore a silver
platter. When Chrétien tells us the Grail was of pure gold, adds the
author, who is Chrétien, and set with precious gems, he speaks the
truth. This Grail was of all precious treasures in the whole world
the most priceless. Its Grail gems outshone all other precious jewels
on earth, no doubt about that.

✷

Sometimes it is Gawain who finds the Grail Castle and is asked if
he can mend the broken sword he sees in the hall, but he fails to
solder the pieces together, as it were. Thus, despite the fact that he
learns why the lance bleeds, he also flunks the test altogether. The
lance bleeds (v. 13, 47), the reader learns for himself, and it will
continue to bleed until the Day of Judgment because it is the very
lance of the Roman soldier Longinus, which pierced the side of
Christ.

✷

(*Perceval Continuation* I, Section 4, Episode 4 from v. 13, 141,
ed. by William Roach [1949], trans. by Weston, p. 152.)

From the doorway of an adjacent chamber a lovely, noble maiden
stepped forth. Gawain, who is a lady's man, concentrated upon
studying her, and decided she pleased him immensely. The maiden
bore a small silver platter *(tailleor)* before all the persons present,
and walked beyond them after the *Lance.* After this, Lord Gawain
was less interested in two squires bearing candelabra full of lighted

candles. Lord Gawain said he burned with desire to ask what people these were, and from what domain; but he kept quiet. While he was mulling over these thoughts he also saw a lovely, noble maiden come in weeping and sobbing. Between her hands she apparently held the Grail high in the air. But Gawain still kept quiet. The object was completely uncovered. Gawain saw the whole thing clearly. And so all he did was marvel greatly that she should be crying so hard, wonder where she was going, and what she thought she was carrying, why she kept on weeping, why she was not being consoled by somebody, or why she did not become weary from all those tears. So she passed right in front of him but entered a chamber as fast as she could go. Then after she was gone, there filed past four squires carrying a bier after what could have been the Grail. It was covered by a royal pall. In the bier was a corpse over which, on the silken pall, lay a sword broken in half at the middle . . .

The Glastonbury manuscript—which is generally called *Perlesvaus* from its Old French name for the hero Perceval, and *The High History of the Holy Grail* in its English translation by Sebastian Evans—more or less skirts the Grail also and its processions. The standard theory explains this reticence or mystery by deciding that the Grail itself never was at Glastonbury, England. When Lancelot arrives at the Grail Castle in this text, for example, he is welcomed by his uncle, the same Fisher King. But Lancelot does not receive a viewing at the dinner table. The author explains only that although Lancelot is one of the three best knights in the world, he is not among those fortunate royal personages destined to view the Grail. Chrétien also knew this when he portrayed Lancelot in prayer hearing a voice from the dead that denied him forever access to the Grail.

Lancelot (branch 7, *Perlesvaus,* vol. 1, ed. Nitze, 1972) had arrived at the Grail Castle after a long, arduous journey through forests and flowered meadows. He eventually arrived at a seashore. There he saw a (Solomon's?) ship ("une grant nef") with three knights aboard, a damsel holding a knight's head, he lying on a straw mattress upholstered in ermine fur, another damsel seated at his feet. Another knight was hauling in huge fishes and off-loading them on a little boat. When Lancelot, who is braver, asked what all this was, he was told that the ship belonged to the Fisher King, who was lord of the castle. That night Lancelot came to a hermitage at the mountain's baseline, near a spring of pure water. There Lancelot confessed. He was told to abjure Queen Guinevere. Lancelot refused to abandon his queen. "Mortal sin," replied the hermit.

Lancelot entered the Avalon Grail Castle safely, although he had to go past lions on guard. He was seated first on a couch in the great hall (l. 3,708) and dressed in rich, warm robes. The entire hall was draped in silk hangings. There were holy writings thereabouts. . . . Then he saw the Fisher King in his chamber, lying on a bed, damsels in attendance at his head and feet. His chamber was so bright Lancelot thought the sun must be shining inside the room.

Two knights had already seen the Grail, Lancelot heard. The first was Perlesvax (Perlesvaus, Perceval), and the second was Gawain (l. 3,733). Lancelot was asked to be seated at an ivory table for dinner (l. 3,746), and the table was laid with gold and silver dishes. He was served roasts of boar and venison. Even though he was one of the three best and noblest warriors in the world, he did not receive a view of the Grail. But he persevered in the Quest. He was inspired by Queen Guinevere with "sens et cortoisie et valor" (l. 3,866)—direction, chivalrous behavior, and valor.

Gawain's earlier visit to a Grail Castle in the *Perlesvaus* telling was, however, a more complete fiasco (branch 6: 19–20). He saw two maidens come from a chapel into the great hall, one holding what could have been the Grail and one, the bleeding Lance. They were accompanied by (Saint Mary Magdalene's) holy balm. But then Gawain's vision blurred and he saw not two live maidens but two angels bearing golden candelabra filled with lighted candles. They filed past in solemn procession and disappeared into another chamber—or was it another chapel? Gawain said he was deliriously happy to have been so favored. All he could think of, he said, was God. The knights who sat beside him realized his ecstasy amounted to loss of his wits, boredom, and confusion. . . .

Very soon the whole company repeated their procession past Gawain all over again. That time he no longer saw two damsels, however, but a child. He was so embarrassed to see the three drops of blood that he uttered not even one single word. He leaned forward as if he thought to kiss the three drops of blood. A third time the three maidens filed past him, but this time all Gawain managed to see was a vision, which he later testified must have been the Grail. He saw a crowned king nailed to the Cross, he said, with the spear (of Longinus) in his side.

Finally, all the diners withdrew. Dinner had been served. The tables were cleared. The lights were put out. The hall fell silent. And still Gawain sat there, sleepy, blind, and dumb, all by himself.

Wherever processions and the Grail are sought, the two best imagined and longest versions lie in two German texts, the one by Heinrich von dem Türlin and the *Parzival* of Wolfram von Eschenbach. In the version written by Heinrich and called *Diu Crône,* or *The Crown,* translated by J. W. Thomas (1989), the author ends his story with the final adventure of Gawain, which is his completed visit to the Grail Castle.

It was as usual evening in the Grail Castle this last time (ll. 29, 316, 326ff.), and dinner was again being served. Having just passed through Purgatory, however, Gawain remembered the fairy injunction not to eat or drink if he wished to return to the land of the living. After dinner, two noble maidens, each bearing two candelabra set with jewels, commenced the procession. Two squires followed them, bearing a beautifully worked spear. Then processed two more high-born damsels bearing a golden bowl set with precious gems.

Then entered God's perfection in a lady: the most beautiful lady in the world. She held in her hands an embroidered pillow (?) of red gold upon which lay a jeweled reliquary of gold and gems so splendid it cannot be described. The lady was the same, golden-crowned queen who had instructed Gawain about the Grail (l. 28,440): that he should remember her, her costume, and her attendants. If ever he saw them again, he must pay heed. He would be inside the Grail Castle where he was immediately to ask a question. Gawain knew the golden-crowned queen was a "goddess."

(His knowledge of her identity sends us back, to the most celebrated of English texts, *Gawain and the Green Knight,* where the Fairy Queen, who is Queen Morgan le Fay, King Arthur's half sister, is also recognized as "goddess.")

Gawain watched as the "goddess" placed the reliquary on the table (altar?). Inside the reliquary was a small piece of bread for the Fisher King to eat.

Gawain then asked: "What is this ceremony? What is this miracle?"

The Fisher King answered: "It is the Grail, which must be kept secret. . . . You shall win the world's esteem for your courage and for the success of your quest."

Another famous Grail procession by the talented author, Wolfram von Eschenbach, occurs in what English translations customarily call book 5 (trans. A. T. Hatto, 1980, p. 124): At the end of the hall a steel door was thrown open ("Am Ende des Saales wurde eine stählern Tür aufgeschlossen" [*Parzival,* ed. Wilhelm Stapel, 1980, p. 120]).

Two lovely, gracious young maidens led the procession. Chaplets of flowers over the silken fillets (of priestesses) bound their curls, which had never been cut and so reached the ground. Each damsel carried a golden candelabrum with lighted tapers in each holder. Both wore reddish gowns belted with precious sashes at their slender waists. Behind the maidens walked two duchesses with lips as red as fire. Each carried a pure white, ivory stool. The four ladies bowed to the assembly. The stools were set beside the Fisher King. The ladies took their places, side by side.

Then entered four pairs of ladies bearing tall tapers and one enormous Precious Stone that was pure red flame like the dark orange jacinth, or dark red hyacinth "Granathyazinth." It was the color the sun made as its light passed through the "Stone." These eight matrons were clad in dresses as green as grass, made of North African samite (from "Azagouk"). They set the ivory tables for dinner and then took their places. They were lovely with fresh wreaths upon their heads.

Then came two princesses who had been invited from a great distance. They bore two finely honed knives on trenchers ("zwei Tüchern"), white and shiny like silver, but sharp enough probably to cut steel. Four maidens preceded them, bearing tapers before silver. The two princesses laid their silver on the "garnet hyacinth" (Hatto's translation). Now there were eighteen maidens in the hall, but after them came six more dressed in silk interwoven with threads of gold from bright Nineveh in the East. Their gowns were multicolored (like those of high-grade Druid priestesses).

The Grail Queen entered last. Her face glowed like sunrise. She wore a brocaded gown from the silk of Arabia. She was perfection in person. Her name was Repanse de Schoye, and she was the daughter of the first Grail King Frimutel.

In goblets of purest glass young ladies then bore in balsam that burned with red light and sweet perfume.

Queen Repanse set down the Grail before the noble Fisher King, as the queen's attendants moved into places so that they flanked her, twelve on either side.

Chamberlains brought in golden bowls. Servants carried in one hundred tables. What splendor!

And yet Queen Guinevere was certainly the greatest of the Grail Queens. A study of Sarras, Saint Mary Magdalene, and the Saints Mary of the Sea has led us back to her inside Britain.

Modern critics inside Britain usually say that the Grail could not have been Christian because of all these women and maidens present in its ceremonies. As everyone knows, they say, women are not allowed to perform functions in Christian Churches.

Chapter
III

QUEEN GUINEVERE
NOT IN
GLASTONBURY

GUINEVERE DEAD?

That Queen Guinevere was alive in Glastonbury is a solid claim only because it exists today in writing done in the Middle Ages. That she lies dead and buried in Glastonbury is also a solid claim doubled: first, because the claim was made in writing done in Glastonbury Abbey by one of the foremost Benedictine monks of the Middle Ages; and second, because the slab over her sarcophagus is shown in Glastonbury, in the ruins of that ancient Benedictine monastery destroyed by King Henry VIII some four hundred years after the second text was written. There exist still other proofs made during the reigns of King Henry II and Queen Elizabeth I when both monarchs are said to have tried—unsuccessfully, however—to authenticate her burial there. King Henry II is said to have ordered her exhumed, and it was done. The problem here is that he had been dead for two years before the exhumation.

What must be done all over again, as it has already been done by many generations of inquirers over nine centuries now, is to reevaluate the evidence, which consists, then, of the following:

1. The Caradoc of Llancarvan text called *Vita Gildae* (Life of Saint Gildas), which made the original claim that Queen Guinevere was for one year alive in Glastonbury.

2. The second text called *Perlesvaus,* which followed closely upon the first but claimed *Queen Guinevere* only lay dead in Glastonbury, and this is the prose account written at Glastonbury's Benedictine Abbey.

3. The story of her exhumation, which King Henry II ordered his cousin Henry de Sully, Abbot of Glastonbury, to effect, and the report made to the dead King Henry II by his witnesses.

4. Some mention of the aftermath that drew Queen Elizabeth I, her historians, and King Henry VIII into this acrimonious cause célèbre.

All these further details, about both King Henry II and Henry de Sully, are also apparently false.

Another investigation might commence by looking at Queen Guinevere as queens are portrayed generally by the Benedictine monk who wrote *Perlesvaus,* and who claimed, perhaps in all honesty, that she lay buried there in the Abbey where he sat writing and looking about him as he wrote. One wants to credit him first because he is one of the truly most talented writers of the Middle Ages. The talent and industry of this anonymous religious are gigantic. His authorial voice is almost immediately familiar, unique, eminently recognizable. Furthermore he should at one time have had access to one of the greatest libraries in the Middle Ages, in the largest monastery, a Cluniac house in the Western world of his day—ergo, access to very ancient, *archaic* material unknown elsewhere. What paradise for an author: to be peaceful and quiet in a beautiful locale like Glastonbury, to be free to study and write as many hours as he could possibly stay awake every single day of his maturity, and to have free and unlimited access to sources it would take a lifetime to read, sources unavailable elsewhere.

First, then, we will look at what our *Perlesvaus* author had to say about Queen Guinevere and then we shall see what he had to say about those queens who were her contemporaries. Then we will move to the rival author from Germany to see the same on his part: what he said about Queen Guinevere, what he said about the queens who were her contemporaries and acquaintances; and then we can move to dates and chronologies of this whole Guinevere controversy. Our second author who will be compared to the *Perlesvaus* author is the German Knight Templar Wolfram von Eschenbach. Both authors were more or less contemporary, and both were monks who had renounced the world and taken vows of poverty and celibacy. (Readers will be referred to the available English translations of *Perlesvaus, The High History of the Holy Grail,* rather than to the diplomatic or scholarly two-volume text edited by Nitze and Jenkins, *Perlesvaus* [New York, 1972], 10,192 lines from the Hatton 82 manuscript of Oxford University, *Le Haut Livre du Graal.* Chapters in *Perlesvaus* are called branches 1–35.)

The Grail Castle had three names: (1) Eden, (2) Joy, and (3) Souls. In other words, it was once called Paradise. Then it was called "Joy" when Lancelot and Elaine resided there and she bore Galahad. But when it was Christianized or re-Christianized by Perceval, it was renamed Castle of Souls.

Only the *Perlesvaus,* which textual scholars like W. A. Nitze have considered the most archaic of all Arthurian accounts, makes it clear that King Arthur transferred the worship of the Holy Grail from Scotland to the Isle of Man. After the preaching on that Isle by Saint Patrick himself around the year 440, King Arthur in around the year 540 transferred (as claimed in branch 21), his treasure, his royal dead, and his worship of the New Law to that place. From that day on, whether she really was already dead which is very doubtful, at least Queen Guinevere ceased participating in a worship that henceforth excluded priestesses. Christianity has by and large upheld that taboo for fifteen hundred years now, which is quite a record of opposition to its women converts, or to half its members.

In branch 24 the *Perlesvaus* author trips himself up marvelously in his version of Queen Guinevere's death and burial. He says there that Lancelot journeyed to Avalon, and that Avalon is (was) Glastonbury. His description does not fit, first of all. He says Lancelot arrived into a wide valley between two forests. Now, Glastonbury is marshland almost all the way, say, up to fifty miles, as the crow flies, to the Bristol Channel. And the road is overland, with no main highway, in and around small farms even to the east and Stonehenge. Beside the valley, he says, is a mountain—if a bare conical hill can be called a mountain: the Glastonbury Tor. On the summit was a brand-new chapel, i.e., Saint Michael's Chapel, not ancient, but recently constructed in the twelfth century. That is slip number one.

Then he adds that the new chapel (Norman French Chapel, built c. 1185) had a new lead roof (paid for grudgingly by the very angry King Henry II at the demand of his "cousin," Henry de Sully, Abbot of Glastonbury's Benèdictine Abbey). A spring was there, Glastonbury's celebrated Chalice Well. But—a second slip—Henry did not become Abbot until 1189, the year of King Henry's death.

Next morning Lancelot rode a far piece, almost to Carlisle, which might be something less than a thousand miles away from Glastonbury. Slip number three, at least, by now.

Of course, King Henry II (although he was already dead and buried in France) wanted Queen Guinevere's body exhumed and King Arthur's also, which has by now amounted to a sorry tale of lies and incompetence. Unfortunately the king himself had died in 1189, leaving his realm to his adventurous son Richard the Lion Heart, the darling of his French subjects but no administrator like his father. As another sad result, the Abbot Henry de Sully of Glastonbury succeeded in impressing nobody with his spurious claims to King Arthur's and Queen Guinevere's bodies. Perhaps even then skeptics thought the bodies inside the log coffins were those of some Anglo-Saxon king and queen who could not have died much before the year 800. And so, regrettably for the French who truly regretted it, a Henry de Sully became the next Abbot of Fécamp Abbey in Normandie—and lost his bid for the Archbishopric of Canterbury.

The prime, personal characteristic of the *Perlesvaus* author, and it sets him totally apart from authors of other Arthurian texts, remains a strong inclination to depict cruelty in its more ghastly forms. This twist of his personality actually suffices, the literary critic would say at once, to remove him from the ranks of major authors. He is, in other words, a psychopath like the filthy Marquis de Sade who deserved his prison sentence. *Perlesvaus* commences ten years into the reign of King Arthur. Or, the author presents a dead queen in southern England, where dead or alive she most certainly never was.

Perlesvaus ends its gory tales of murdered queens and cruel, murderous ladies with scattered references to the noble Queen Jandree, which is the same name as Cundrie, a person sometimes said to be Gawain's sister, or elsewhere to be simply a Grail messenger from that castle belonging later to the Fisher King. "Jandree" is the Manx spelling, which is to be expected if King Arthur's lost Grail Castle was on the Isle of Man in the Irish Sea. But this Queen

Jandree of *Perlesvaus* belongs not at the end of his text but at the commencement, before the Isle of Man was Christianized or re-Christianized by Perceval. At the end of *Perlesvaus,* just before Perceval enters Solomon's Ship and puts off to sea (branch 33), Queen Jandree is at last converted to Christianity, christened, and baptized. Gawain bears witness to these last events, knowing in his heart that there never more will be written an account of them all. Nor shall any later warrior possess the power of Perceval.

Even there the *Perlesvaus* errs, for Perceval's son by his dear wife Blanchefleur (White Flower) will be the Swan Knight Lohengrin. The Swan Knight sailed from the Isle of Man to Belgium where he founded the Royal House. One of his descendants was that Godfrey [Godefroi] de Bouillon who in 1099, at the completion of the First Crusade, freed Jerusalem. Then the Knights Templar, the Poor Soldiers of Christ, were founded to defend the holy city. Their Order lasted for some two hundred years under the Kings Baldwin of Jerusalem. When they lost the city, they were killed and outlawed in their original home, France.

Not only are distinguished women described in the Knight Templar's poem *Parzival,* they are also permitted to speak, to address King Arthur's Court, and to deliver orations. Thus, we here know both the sorceress Cundrie from the Grail Castle and Queen Guinevere herself (spelled Ginover in German) as orators. In book 7 Cundrie chastised Perceval publicly for not having asked a question during his first visit at the Grail Castle. Had he remained in possession of what few wits he has, she cries, he could have ended the Waste Land, Perilous Times, and the Fisher King's sufferings. He is descended from the royal Angevin Dynasty—for here Wolfram also steps out of King Arthur's day in order to compliment his contemporary monarchs of England, France, and Spain, many of whom are Angevins or married to Angevin noblewomen far and wide. Perceval thus sought the Holy Grail (Saint Graal), which by a horrible pun makes him of Royal Blood *(Sang Réal* [Réel], or *Royal).* By extension he was to seek sight of the Grail on its Mountain of Salvation (Munsalvaesche), which follows the pun into Mount Royal, or Montréal in Aquitania, or the Languedoc. These puns truly flatter the Queen of England, wife of King Henry II. She is the beautiful and notorious heiress Aliénor de Guyenne, Eleanor of Aquitaine, mother of King Richard the Lion Heart, her next-to-last child.

Before bursting into tears, Cundrie calls Parzival every bad name she knows: snake, snake's fang, accursed, monster, faithless, hell-bent, shepherd of hell, and a bane of her existence. On such occasions, Wolfram adds carefully, Cundrie did not speak her native tongue (Gaelic), but Old French, which he, the author, hated having to translate into German.

When she delivered a proper oration in the manner of the Roman orator Cicero, and according to the rules of discourse first spelled out by Quintilian in Rome before A.D. 99, Cundrie spoke Arabic. It is totally amazing to consider the possibility that she had studied in Toledo, whence, as Wolfram believed, the Grail material and worship originated. Or that her teacher was the same person who taught Niniane: Merlin, the learned astronomer.

Cundrie delivered the set oration after Parzival was inaugurated King of the Grail Castle (book 15):

> *Nun merke, Parzival!*
> *Zwal, der höchste der Planeten, . . .*

> *Now pay attention, Parzival!*
> *Saturn is highest of the Planets,*
> *Fast flyer Jupiter comes second,*
> *Red Mars next, then golden Sun,*
> *All have made you the Grail King.*
> *Friday's planet is Venus.*
> *Mercury rolls round as six.*
> *Moon is nearest to us of all.*   (p. 395)

When as a lad Parzival had foolishly slain the Red Knight and ripped off his armor savagely because he knew no better, Queen Guinevere was permitted to speak, by Wolfram in his account of what she saw as this sad death (book 3): Alas, that we should lose so gallant a knight to this foolish boy Parzival. Our Red Knight should have sat at the Round Table. What did he win for himself? Death! He was a warrior without deceit, open and honorable. Now I give his funeral oration and must consign him to the grave. See how his mortal wounds seep red sorrow. See how much more beautiful than these red flowers are the red curls on his dear head. Now we shall hear no more laughter among the ladies of our Court.

With his adoration of queens the Templar Wolfram makes a genealogy for Arthur's world, and a geography of the Angevin Empire, that remains to puzzle and amaze the centuries:

The Grail King Titurel has a son Frimutel, whose son is the Fisher King Anfortas, whose brother is Parzival's tutor Trevrizent and whose sister is the Grail Priestess Repanse de Schoye. Queen Herzeloyde weds the hero Gahmuret and their son is Parzival who weds Condwiramurs, whose son is "Loherangrin," the Swan Knight. In Britain Uther Pendragon weds Ygerne (Wolfram's Arnive is an anagram) whose child is Arthur, whose son is Lohot (Ilinot) and whose queen is Guinevere (Ginover in Wolfram). Both Arthurians and Angevins are to claim Mazadan as a common ancestor.

Wolfram kept this genealogy, and much more, fully under his control. In so doing, he successfully united the two worlds, Dark Age Arthur's Court circle and the medieval Grail Castle royals and their questers. His poem moves from one circle to another in a physical world where personages travel back and forth as they are dispatched and released like puppets on the strings of their desires.

None of the authors viewed so far, and all were authorities on British queens, has had anything to say about Queen Guinevere having been in Glastonbury, England. In fact, only one author of one text so stated. He was Caradoc of Llancarfan (Llancarvan), and he wrote, or supposedly wrote, a text astonishing for its falsity and brevity, called *Vita Gildae* (Life of Saint Gildas). Now, Saint Gildas was not in Glastonbury either, as his real biography has shown. We shall, however, be obliged in our next pages to refute Caradoc. In so doing, we have an opportunity to broach another subject closely linked to our quest of the Holy Grail. That subject is cemeteries. Grail Castles always stood in close proximity to a necropolis.

THE EXHUMATION OF
QUEEN GUINEVERE AT GLASTONBURY

King Arthur did not—despite his organizational skills, or because of them—bring Glastonbury to world fame. Nor was it love, alas, although Guinevere was a great beauty, which induced Arthur to seek a bride in Pictish country, northeastern Scotland. His aim was to wed Sovereignty herself, and she was It. Therefore Arthur was not at Glastonbury; but Queen Guinevere, said Caradoc of Llancarfan, was.

There crops up one kernel of truth in Caradoc's misshapen, fraudulent text: the cemetery. Wherever there was a Grail shrine, there had to be a cemetery in close conjunction, and, hopefully, many royal graves. Those bodies inside logs that were exhumed in 1191 at Glastonbury were doubtless Saxon royalty, but they still bear Arthur's name and that of his very royal Sovereignty. William of Malmesbury also struggled mightily to create in this Glastonbury a Perilous Arthurian Bridge from which to toss Excalibur, and he labored a lifetime lauding the sanctity of this Saxon necropolis. John of Glastonbury (1290–1400) grew old connecting the cemetery (*âtre*) to the *Blaunche Launde*, or Moors on either side of Guinevere's Firth of Forth (eastern Scotland), a hopeless task. Perceval fell under the Glastonbury graveyard's marvelous spell too, and ate supper at their "Grail Castle," the ruins of which never were there, and are nowhere there now. Gawain too entered the Perilous Cemetery (*Atre Perilleus*), and even he saw the stone coffin open, and even he shrank before her raised, skeletal arm! But not at Glastonbury really.

Such is the aura of majesty that Guinevere bathed in. The whole world once had looked at her naked loveliness . . . until Lancelot threw his cloak about her. But King Arthur too, says the author of *Perlesvaus* at Glastonbury itself, went with her golden crown to the Grail Castle, *which was at Glastonbury,* he said. A French poet named Renaud de Beaujeu, in his *Le Bel inconnu* (or Handsome Stranger Knight poem), puts his hero at Glastonbury, after which, unsure of the geography of Great Britain, he has him awaken at Snowdon (Stirling in Scotland) and Carlisle (England, but formerly in Scotland).

Queen Guinevere went to the Grail Castle, to be sure; however, it was not to that sanctuary of Glastonbury, but to another such on the Isle of Avalon, and that one was an Eden, or an Island of Joy, and not an "apple orchard." The myth of the Grail Castle has exerted such a powerful pull upon the world's tender hearts that generations of kindly scholars, like the Welsh Professor Sir John Rhŷs, have twisted around the problem of *Avalon* until it is derived from *apple* in Welsh, et cetera. And, to be sure, Glastonbury, which is a pretty, little place, has meadows, cows, and apples.

But Guinevere, Virgo, was not at that Grail Castle to eat apples, but elsewhere to initiate Lancelot during a sacrament in which she functioned as High Priestess: another diamond in Sovereignty's golden crown. All such candidates were warned not to eat an apple (or was it a quince?). Robert Graves's *The White Goddess* warned Lancelot too, for otherwise he could not, said Sovereignty, the Fairy Queen, return ever again to the upper world of mortals.

King Arthur was a warrior made of stronger stuff. He once survived an initiation requiring him to lie for "three days under the slab," say Welsh mnemonics. When Sovereignty went to the Grail Castle, she also liberated King Arthur's prisoners, including his foster brother Kay the Seneschal. Any great lady liberating prisoners follows the eastern biblical tradition of Harrowing Hell as done by the Virgin Mary. Thus, Queen Guinevere was, or became, a Christian priestess of sorts.

Therefore was it not more likely, asked R. F. Treharne, Professor of History at the University College of Wales in 1975, that royal bodies exhumed at Glastonbury in 1191 were those of Saxon royalty, perhaps King Edmund of Wessex, who died in 946, or Edmund Ironside, who died in 1016, buried beside his Danish wife? Either should have been glory enough for Glastonbury.

The roster of scholars who have debated this question of the supposed exhumation at Glastonbury in 1191 of King Arthur and a golden-haired Queen Guinevere would fill this book. Suffice it to say, first of all, that two royal bodies were exhumed and reburied. The bodies were found interred inside a log, or logs, which was certainly not the Arthurian custom. Arthurian sarcophagi were stone, sculpted in advance of death, and they lay waiting. Queen Guinevere was having hers made and Arthur's too, finely sculptured. Merlin had his and the Lady Niniane's made and their niches carved in Saint Ninian's (?) (or Merlin's) Cave on the Rhinns of Galloway. The reader has only to go see for himself or herself: The niches on the left-hand wall of the cave are very plainly visible. Any one of the empty, narrow coffins that lie today under the weather on the unroofed flooring of Holyrood (Holy Cross) Abbey in Edinburgh, Scotland, would fit those niches. Merlin's Cave, now called Saint Ninian's Cave, is such a sight as one could find nowhere else. Below it is the Irish Sea, rolling stones and rushing up the shingle. And far off across the hazy water looms the blue Isle of Man.

The exhumation of the royal corpses, or skeletons, at Glastonbury took place at night. The Abbot had ordered a curtain wrapped round the open grave. None of the witnesses could see a thing in the darkness. One of them recalled later, though, that he saw a queen's head with locks of golden curls. All vanished or disintegrated when the night air hit them. Somebody handed around a lead cross with the uncials "here lies King Arthur" and "the once and future king" carved on it—not in letters of King Arthur's day, however, but in letters of the Glastonbury Abbot Henry de Sully's day. No matter. The so-called cross and so-called lettering has long since conveniently disappeared. Nobody has yet found Guinevere's golden crown. Nor her jewels. Nor the severed head of Arthur's son Lohot, which the Glastonbury author of *Perlesvaus* said Guinevere had ordered buried beside her, inside her stone sarcophagus.

The entire Glastonbury cause célèbre revolves about royal personages and not only about the king and queen who were interred there, exhumed, and reinterred. This exhumation of 1191—with its unreliable witnesses, unreliable testimony, manufactured evidence patently false, and missing evidence—stems from the terrible times just past and the ongoing Third Crusade. In such awfully dreadful days we would doubtless all have been searching for royal personages, dead if not still living, upon whom we could hang our breath—and for a Holy Grail to sustain us upon that sea of nothingness.

In April of 1185 a terrible earthquake struck all of England. In 1187 the holiest of cities, golden Jerusalem, fell to Saladin; and the future King of England and Anjou, Richard I, took the Cross—without asking permission of his mother and also without even telling his father beforehand of his intention. They should have named this careless youth Richard Spur of the Moment and not Richard the Lion Heart.

The so-called Caradoc of Llancarvan had by 1160 sown the seed of exhumation by his or somebody else's *Vita Gildae*. In 1189 an unscrupulous Abbot named Henry de Sully, rumored to be closely connected to royalty, or even royal himself, came to rule Glastonbury Abbey. The place was a desert. The Abbey had burned to the ground in 1184. It had been a terrible century for England. Winchester had burned to the ground in 1180, and Chichester in 1187. Then, King Henry II died, around July 3, 1189.

Therefore all those friends of Glastonbury who have claimed for so long that King Henry II personally ordered the exhumation of King Arthur and Queen Guinevere at Glastonbury—either because, their being vampires, he wanted to drive a stake through their hearts or because he shivered on his throne and dreaded the return of the once and future King Arthur—are most likely very mistaken. As far as Henry de Sully is concerned, confusion also reigns. We shall come back to him again when we come to search the riches at Fécamp Abbey on the Normandie coast for evidence of the Holy Grail. In any event, no Henry de Sully won the Archbishopric of Canterbury. But a person of this name presided at the exhumation in 1191.

King Henry II of England, whom one can only pity for the sad tale of his wounding and sudden death in his native Normandie, never went to Glastonbury in his entire life. The Eyton Chronology of Henry II gives his itinerary, showing him ceaselessly en route over England and France, his Angevin Empire, from 1154 to 1189. His biographer says he spent Christmas in England several times, each time getting his gorgeous Queen Eleanor of Aquitaine pregnant. In any case his three sons Geoffrey, Richard, and John were terrible. After Geoffrey became Bishop of York, he allowed terrible persecutions of wealthy Jews. Richard was in Normandie warring against his father also in 1189. He did go to his father's deathbed, but Henry II turned his face away in sorrow and disgust. Before he became King of England, and long before he was forced to sign the Magna Carta (June 15, 1215) at Runnymede Meadow, the younger brother John had terribly disgraced himself in Ireland. Sent to receive the homage of conquered Celts, John had hooted and screamed with laughter at their appearance and ripped at their chieftain insignias and garments in derision.

Among those authorities who have written books and essays siding with and against Glastonbury's account of the exhumation performed there in 1191 are most notably: Rev. Lionel Smithett Lewis of Glastonbury (1922), Dean Joseph Robinson of nearby

Wells Cathedral (1926), Edmond Faral (1929), Geoffrey Ashe (1968), Helen Hill Miller (1969), Professor Nitze (who edited *Perlesvaus* at the University of Chicago from 1931 and who returned to the question in his article published in 1972 in *Speculum*), and Professor Treharne in Wales (1975).

Rev. Lionel Smithett Lewis established a chronology of events at Glastonbury, as follows: all dates are A.D.

37–63	First church built there
58	The Blessed Bran kinged and converted there
July 27, 82	Joseph of Arimathea died there
167	Saint Michael's Church built there, on the Glastonbury Tor
c. 450, or 472	A Saint Patrick was Abbot there and buried there
488	A Saint Brigit, or Bride, was there
540	King Arthur was buried there
c. 540	Maelgwyn of Llandaf, who lived before Merlin, wrote a first history there
546	Saint David of Wales built a chancel there
612–620	A great plague devastated the area
c. 652–658	The Saxons conquered Glastonbury
c. 1066	King William the Conqueror granted no taxes to be paid at Glastonbury
1129–1342	Glastonbury historians are William of Malmesbury, Adam de Domerham, John of Glastonbury

1184	Glastonbury burned to the ground
c. 1542	John Leland wrote that Glastonbury was greedy for burials of the great and famous
c. 1577	Raphael Holinshed reported in his *Chronicle* that Joseph of Arimathea's tomb was still to be seen there

The Reverend Lionel Lewis concluded as he had begun, that Glastonbury, and not Canterbury or York, *is* the Mother church of Great Britain because it was "a British Catholic Foundation older than Rome itself" (p. 41), which is, as the French say, "beaucoup dire." Whatever one may say to the contrary, he continued, Britain was outside the Roman church and also outside the Roman Empire. Rome to the contrary in both cases, of course.

Almost everything said so earnestly by Rev. Lewis (whose book is easily available in Glastonbury today) was earnestly contradicted by Dean Joseph Armitage Robinson in his magisterial *Glastonbury Legends* (1926). The Glastonbury legend, as much expanded over their writing careers by both William of Malmesbury and John of Glastonbury, grew into a complete scenario in five parts: (1) Gospel of Nicodemus: Story of Joseph, (2) The Sea Crossing from Israel, (3) The Conversions by Saint Philip of Gaul, (4) The Second Sea Crossing from Sarras on Josephe's Shirt, and (5) The Arrival of the Missionaries at Glastonbury.

Dean Robinson takes such trouble with the passage from the *Estoire* about the second sea crossing on Josephe's shirt that we shall have to offer our assistance in the next few pages. The Dean translates it as meaning either that the missionaries were buried in their shirts, or that they (surely not "they"), or one of them perhaps, crossed the sea on his shirt, or failing that they were interred in a bifurcated line and not in a shirt at all. So they could have been interred, he concludes, *in linea bifurcata,* on a line diagonal to or from King Arthur's bones.

The Grail legend, he concludes, remains obscure because it could be either the Celtic food vessel or talisman on the one hand, or the Christian "cup" for blood, "dish" of the Last Supper, Sacramental Cup, or simply a Quest thereof: "All this is in harmony with the fact that the Holy Grail was purely an invention of the ro-

RICHARD COEUR DE LION
LEAVING THE HOLY LAND

mances, and never at any time received ecclesiastical sanction" (p. 39).

R. F. Treharne added (1967) that the pilgrimage to Glastonbury is now organized every June by the Anglican church. It is a solemn procession in our days despite all the persons to the contrary who have over the ages laid "sacrilegious hands on devoutly held beliefs" (p. 10). As Treharne discovered, William of Malmesbury early in the twelfth century conceded that King Arthur's grave at Glastonbury, and Queen Guinevere's also, *were not known.*

The purpose of the Glastonbury propaganda was, of course, to raise money so that the burned Abbey could be rebuilt. Therefore William altered his subsequent copies.

King Henry II was not involved personally. All his time was spent in such local wars as finally ended his life. King Richard I was probably never at Glastonbury either, especially since he spent so little time in England anyway, and that only for his coronation and for extorting the vast sums he needed for the Third Crusade. His mother, Queen Eleanor of Aquitaine, may have visited Glastonbury after the exhumation. She had to raise thirty-five tons of pure silver to ransom Richard after he left the Holy Land. And this despite the fact that he would not consummate his marriage to Princess Berengaria of Navarre, whom Queen Eleanor had fetched from Spain to France, from France over the Alps in winter, and down to Sicily. Naked except for his britches, Richard I had already appeared in church there, declaring homosexuality.

Treharne summarizes the state of modern knowledge: "Grievous . . . loss, we must . . . dismiss Arthur . . . from any proven historical connection with Glastonbury" (pp. 106–7).

To Britain by Shirt

Two Grail manuscripts (*Grand-Saint-Graal* and *Queste del Saint Graal*) take the trouble to relate how the early missionaries of Christianity left Sarras, which we have located as in and around the area of Marseilles. By reading now their accounts we shall be able to decide if they really crossed the English Channel and then traversed England to Glastonbury. In their pages the Grail is connected to Joseph of Arimathea, who many church historians say never went there.

We shall have an opportunity to judge for ourselves when our authors give us patently false etymologies:

1. *Saint Graal* = *Sang réel* (Blood Royal)
2. *Saint Graal* = what agrees (with you?)

They betray themselves when they claim that the British Grail Castle was in a foreign land. Glastonbury was not originally a foreign land to the Celts.

Finally confronting the history of Geoffrey of Monmouth our texts fall mute, for Geoffrey knew both Glastonbury and Caradoc of Llancarfan. He expressly omitted Glastonbury from his identification of the sites of King Arthur's kingdom and his victories. What follows is the Glastonbury legend, and the reader must decide for himself what can be believed.

❋

(*Grand-Saint-Graal,* Incident 31ff., Nutt, p. 60; *Queste del Saint Graal* [*History of the Holy Grail,* vol. 2, chap. 41])

Joseph of Arimathea and his companions wandered away from Sarras until they came, after much journeying, to the seashore. That night the brave Galaaz was by the grace of God conceived.

The next day Joseph and his company prayed before their sacred Hebrew Ark of the Covenant, kneeling before their Hebrew or Holy Grail, weeping and requesting that they be made strong to cross the sea into that promised land where they would multiply and become the best people.

They plodded along the path to the very sand and edge of the sea. There they saw neither galley nor ship wherein to embark. They crowded moaning and weeping, praying to the Lord to assist them in their distress, to bring them over the sea. "What are we to do?" they asked Joseph's son Josephe, their Bishop. They knew this was to be the last leg of long travels.

Josephe replied that only some should go. Those who had kept the commandments would be paid according to their virtues. Those who were filled with holiness would pass over the sea.

As it turned out, 250 were declared pure. As it happened also, they were the closest in blood to Joseph of Arimathea. The remaining 460 were sinners.

> *The night was both fair and still*
> *And the sea peaceable at her own will*
> *Without any storm or other distress*
> *And the moon shone in all her brightness* (v. 206)
>
> . . . .
>
> *And it was Saturday certainly*
> *Before Easter day most truly*

. . . when Josephe went to his father, kissed him and all the company good-bye, and prepared to depart. However, a voice warned him to halt.

The first to go were the Grail Bearers. They departed on foot, bearing the Holy Vessel, without dread of the sea, and walked across water dry shod.

When Josephe saw the Grail Bearers safely embarked, he offed his shirt before the others there and changed his clothes. Then he spread "that Schirte" upon the sea as if it were dry land and bade his father set his feet aboard. After that, Joseph embarked the others by order of rank until there were 150 standing thereupon. Then Josephe blessed the "Schirte" and the water they stood up-on. . . . two wicked men fell off and drowned.

They made a safe crossing. Next morning they were in Britain. Josephe had held up the shirt all night by its sleeve. Thus, it moved easily in the water, fortunately, for the rest of their work was cut out for them. Britain was full of wicked folk, all Saracens.

Josephe predicted the reign of King Arthur, whose adventures would last for twelve years.

An angel had already told Josephe that the Grail meant something that did not displease *(li degraast)* but that pleased *(li grée).* One looking inside the Vessel, after first lifting off the lid, would be blinded. The Holy Lance would draw healing blood from a wound into the Grail. That blood could cure blindness. Therefore the Lance meant the commencement of the adventures at King Arthur's Court during which the true descendants of Joseph would be shown.

Then great, terrifying wonders caused by the Grail would occur in Britain. There the Fisher King would be struck through the two thighs by the Lance and suffer ages of pain only to be cured by the one pure descendant who would persevere until all the wonders of the Holy Grail were revealed: that the Grail provides food endlessly, that the Sword could never be mended until Galahad by his touch alone mended it, that the Grail King Aleyn (Noble) was one of the Fisher Kings casting his net about for damned souls, that Joseph of Arimathea brought the Hebrew wonder, which was his Holy Grail, to Glastonbury where he was interred, that the Abbey where he was buried stood under the "Cross of England," that "Corbenie" was the name of the castle built to house the Holy Grail, that "Corbenie" was located in a foreign land *(Terre Foraine)* where during services at this Grail Castle the Grail was placed on a silver table. The priest there stood under the sound of a thousand voices (choristers?) and the beating of hundreds of birds' wings overhead.

The English ends (chap. 56):

> Now I end my Graal and begin the *Prophecy of Merlin* which Robert de Boron (Borron) translated from Latin to French, and added to his *Sank Royal.* Please say a prayer for me and a "Hail, Mary" that I may be able to bring my book to a satisfactory conclusion.
>
> Signed: Henry Lonelich

Looking back somewhat critically at this Glastonbury legend concerning principally the arrival into England of missionaries from France, one can discern certain elements that hold water. Missionaries do travel abroad for the purpose of converting other peoples. These particular missionaries had traveled from Sarras for a consid-

erable time and long enough to bring with them an old tradition
of a Saint Philip of Gaul, of whom the Franks were apparently
blissfully ignorant. Their own saints would be those such as Saint
Denis (Sidney) of Montmartre and Saint Geneviève also of Paris,
whose statue in the Luxembourg Gardens precedes those of all the
queens of France.

These future Glastonbury missionaries must, if we take their
account realistically, have followed the ancient trade route up the
Rhône River to Lyons, then overland to Paris, then down the Seine
River to some point where they could go north to Calais, whence
it would have been merely overnight to Dover, the narrowest
crossing of the Straits.

The problem of the method is more troublesome. Dean Robinson was much perplexed by the word *linea,* which even in classical
Latin would have meant "linen" used for a "shirt" *(camisa).* But the
word *linea* there more likely indicated the fabric (linen, canvas,
muslin) used in the making of a sail and/or a "shirt," says our
colleague Professor A. R. L. Bell of CSULB. Thus, we should have
expected the proud use by the author of a figure of speech, a
rhetorical device usually called *synecdoche.* In such a conceit a part
of something designates the whole: I see a sail (sailing ship), I see
a sheet, cloth, or rag (a sail). Henry Lonelich's strange spelling of
shirt (Schirte) clearly indicates an error on his part. He may have
misread "Schiff" ("Schipe") for "Schirte." Or else he suddenly
underwent a brainstorm when he saw the word "Schipe" coming
up again in his text and decided to write a miracle of his own.

It is uncanny how these Grail texts imitate the Old Testament:
Joseph for Moses, England for Israel, the English Channel for the
Red Sea, English royalty for David and Solomon's line of descent,
Ark of the Covenant replaced by Ark of the Grail, the parting of
the Red Sea replaced by the calm on the usually turbulent Straits
of Dover, the lance of Longinus and the Lance at the Grail, the
Cross of England standing over Glastonbury several hundred years
older than the Saxons and Angles, Galaaz prefiguring Galahad.

At Glastonbury, one can affirm at the least, all currents meet and
not always peaceably: Hebrew, Druid, and Christian; Jew, Briton,
and Saxon; Latin, French, Brythonic, and English. According to
these two Grail texts history carried the Grail from Jerusalem >
Sarras > Glastonbury. One is free either to discard the whole, or
make the best of it. This is about what has happened in Britain at
least for the past two thousand years or thereabouts.

* * *

This vast body of Arthurian literature, which is the largest such in the world, may be considered and classified by its impact into several categories, the first of which is political. Politically speaking, one author remains paramount since his *History of the Kings of Britain* of 1136: Geoffrey of Monmouth. Just by reading the evaluations of Geoffrey in Britain one can date the author by century according to the status in that century of the Crown and the power in that century of Parliament. One such attempt was made, in fact, by Roberta Brinkley at Johns Hopkins University (1932): *The Arthurian Legend in the Seventeenth Century.* When it is a question of a dominant reign, Arthur and Merlin are chiefly in the forefront, pro and con, with Geoffrey, who first wrote their histories, pro and con. When a great king or queen reigns, Arthur and Merlin are respected. When Parliament overshadows the reigns, they are denied and vilified.

Thus, the scholar Alanus de Insulis revived Merlin in 1603–08 by publishing his *Prophecies,* and the Scottish prophet Thomas the Rhymer was lauded at Queen Elizabeth I's funeral. King James of Scotland and England was hailed as King Arthur returned:

> *Charles James Stewart*
> *Claims Arthur's seat.*

Politically speaking, King Arthur supported the Tudor-British claim to the throne. Both Tudors and Stewarts (Stuarts) traced their descent from King Arthur, to which double pedigree Rafael Holinshed brought weight as did William Shakespeare's *Macbeth* by reminding everyone how Banquo's son fled safely into Wales and married Princess Nesta, mother of the Stuarts. Thus, King James was thrice hailed, as Macbeth was hailed outside Inverness. Which returns us once again to the beloved or hated Geoffrey of Monmouth: the British trace their descent to the Brute who first settled Britain. And to our Grail texts: before the Angles and Saxons arrived, centuries before, in fact, the British traced their descent also from Israel. The British kingdoms were Logria (now England), Cambria (now Wales and Cumbria), and Albania or Albanach (now Scotland). And Brut gave Britain its (his) name.

Whenever anyone objected to British genealogies, that person was reminded that they, the Britons alone, and King Arthur especially, were also "noble Roman." Queen Guinevere too was "noble Roman" and educated in reading, writing, and oratory, not to mention the commissioning of sculptured funeral monuments, and the keeping of King Arthur's and Lancelot's records.

The publisher exclaimed in his 1634 edition of Malory, which he entitled not *Le Morte d'Arthur* but *The History of King Arthur:*

> And shall the Jewes and the Heathen be honoured in the memory and magnificent prowesse of their worthies? shall the French and German nations glorifie their triumphs with their Godfrey [de Bouillon] and Charles [Charlemagne], and shall we of this island be so possest with incredulitie, diffidence, stupiditie, and ingratitude, to deny, make doubt, or expresse in speech and history, the immortall name and fame of our victorious Arthur . . . ?

Sir Kenelm Digby replied yes and no, that England was happy to produce such royal persons whom subsequent ages took for characters in French romances! Nathaniel Crouch went him one better in 1687. Anyone who said that Joshua never lived would be called an infidel. If he denied David or Judas Maccabeus, he would be branded an atheist. If he repudiated Alexander the Great, Julius Caesar, Godefroi de Bouillon, or Charlemagne, he would clearly be insane. By the same token, he who refused to honor King Arthur's honored victories ought to be called not only incredulous but plain ungrateful. The reputations of Arthur and Merlin seem truly to ebb and flow with the tides of politics inside Britain.

The second category in which Arthurian Literature can be classified might be termed mystical; for it comprises the Holy Grail itself, its questers such as Lancelot, Gawain, and Perceval especially, plus Galahad and the others. This area is perhaps not necessarily purely British exclusively, but it strikes chords deeper in Scotland and Wales where Merlin built the memorials, paved the streets of Edinburgh, and lies buried in Llandaf Cathedral. Gawain had been almost forgotten. Lancelot has still not been wrested away from the French who translated his name from Geoffrey of Monmouth's Anguselus and the Angus, or Clan Chief, to the French Lancelot.

The third category might be called Pagan/Roman, and it includes the women: Queen Guinevere, Queen Morgan le Fay, the Lady of the Lake Niniane, Cundrie, Dandrane, Orgeluse, the Elaine who was the Grail King's daughter and Lancelot's wife.

A BARBARIAN INVASION BY SEA

These were probably all Druid priestesses originally, who were converted late—or not at all.

As far as the sacred site of Glastonbury is concerned and until new evidence is brought to light, we must conclude that neither King Arthur nor his beautiful queen was ever there. Glastonbury, as English historians have often observed, lies too far from the center of Arthurian battles, which took place in southern Scotland, in the Borders and near both Glasgow and Edinburgh. The Saxon invaders poured savagely into the firths of both Clyde and Forth in the fifth and sixth centuries and were stopped there by King Arthur. Furthermore, and the *Anglo-Saxon Chronicle* so stipulates, the Saxon victories were all in southern England and in the area of York, ancient Bernicia. Saxons failed to conquer all of western England until the 800s, by which time King Arthur and Guinevere were long dead.

Chapter
IV

Saint Theresa
in Spain

The Angevin Dynasty,
France, and Spain

The story of the Holy Grail from the time of King Arthur's Grail Castle and Perceval's departure via Solomon's Ship either to parts unknown, or to the area of Sarras, or to Jerusalem, was captured and set down by those few writers who remain today among the masters of the Middle Ages. Their manuscripts date from 1170 at the earliest to 1230 or 1250 at the latest. These authors lived through this terrible period of civil war, foreign wars called "Crusades," and the years of rising nationalism.

"Nationalism" in both France and Great Britain meant a series of murderous wars during which vast numbers of people were transferred from home rule to the central authority of a king, and from their local or territorial religion to the organized and properly theological and written religion governing henceforth their behavior, ritual, and belief. The accounts of the Holy Grail, which began to appear around 1170, finally dwindled out by the years 1200–1230 or even perhaps as late as 1250 in distant Cyprus. During those last decades the last copyists were still rewriting, recopying, and retranslating. From bits and pieces picked up here and there Sir Thomas Malory wrote his compendious *Le Morte d'Arthur* in the fifteenth century, just before Columbus discovered his America.

No reevaluation of the Holy Grail today can be clearly set out without considering the terrible events of the years 1170–1250. Why is that? Because some awful catastrophe that sets terror deep in the human heart will always turn creative people inward. Some events really do arouse an abiding terror generally in the human heart. One example in the twentieth century suffices: the massacre of six million Jews in Nazi Germany. The utter horror of that crime will never pale. It will never go away. The terror of history is irreversible.

When a person lives through one of these terrible massacres, for example, he will always suffer traumas. In our own days certain persons still try to act out the SS military police of Germany, the concentration camps, the death squads, the black shirts or brown shirts, the firing squads, the freight cars full of human families doomed to gas chambers.

Similarly, writers turned between 1170 and 1250 to study, to solitude, and to the writing of Grail texts. Their work has to be read now that we are ready to deal with the masters of their age, as reactions to terrorizing actions. Against massacre what can be put? What can one view with the eye that looks inward? What can console grief-stricken generations?

When hope in mankind is lost, what hope remains?

It will be time and high time to look again, in slightly more detail, at the rising national state now called France. It became France slowly, at a staggering cost in human lives. Our Grail texts were written for the rulers of France and Britain, themselves locked in mortal combat the length of the Middle Ages. They owned the Grail texts. Before listing them, let us go back and bring up the history of western Europe to them from the ancient world of Joseph of Arimathea.

The hypothetical arrival of Joseph of Arimathea into Glastonbury, or to the holy site that seven hundred or so years later became Glastonbury, would have occurred, of course, during the Roman conquest and rule of Great Britain. Julius Caesar had with great difficulty routed the Celts from Belgium circa 55 B.C., and they had fled overseas, mostly to southern areas such as Devon and Cornwall where today, as at Tintagel, there is a sizable concentration of such royal Belgian names as "Baldwin." The Roman Emperor Hadrian followed the Roman commander Agricola, his conquests of A.D. 37–93, the general having been brought to his knees by the Picts in northeastern Scotland, and returned in some polite disgrace to Rome. Hadrian therefore built his famous Wall across Britain circa 121–27, which even now more than less separates Scotland from England.

After the Roman withdrawal some three hundred years later, or during their evacuation of the outer provinces of their Empire, Arthur and Guinevere were crowned, probably at Carlisle, circa 522. They were not the first royal Celtic personages inside Britain, having been preceded notably by Empress and Saint Helena (c. 248–c. 328), born in Britain as was her son the Emperor Constantine, who found the Holy Cross and helped his mother build the Holy Sepulcher in Jerusalem. He declared for Christianity, thereafter the official religion. But it took several years, several centuries in some cases, for his Edict to reach the Atlantic shores at all its westernmost coastlines. Thus, even during Merlin's lifetime (c. 450–536), and even during Arthur's lifetime (475–542), priestesses still presided at the Grail Castles and probably even thought themselves Christian: Guinevere, Dandrane, Cundrie, Niniane, the dread Morgan le Fay, and Repanse de Schoye. They would eventually die out, and died the last one did, defying those who still branded her a heretic.

By these calculations, Perceval would have arrived at Arthur's Court around the years 535 or 536, when the beloved king had a mere six years more to live. Merlin had foreseen all that, knew in advance the date of his own ending day, and apparently knew Arthur's also. He was one of the greatest scholars of his century, and a renowned astronomer, it is always said. And he was the High Priest, said Geoffrey of Monmouth: "Archbishop."

Immediately after Arthur's death, Saint Columba of Ireland arrived at the holy isle of Iona (A.D. 563) and also founded the Abbey of Deare (Tears) not far from the present city of Aberdeen. Saint Gildas, who never was at Glastonbury, at least not as far as anyone has as yet been able to determine, died in Brittany (now France) circa 570.

It is such a far piece from the year 570 to 1133, when the future Angevin King Henry II was born, and even farther to 1136, when Geoffrey of Monmouth offered King Stephen of England the presentation copy of his *History of the Kings of Britain,* that many English scholars still say there was no King Arthur circa 500. It is true that the *Anglo-Saxon Chronicle,* picking up the story from the Roman withdrawal in the fifth century, never mentions King Arthur. It only chronicles their own victories and, thus, the conquest of their new kingdoms, which are now England, year by year, and winner by winner. And, as usual, the winner writes the history proudly, saying the British Celts ran from the conquering Anglo-Saxons like wildfire. None of them was a hero, ergo, no King Arthur, and none were his victories.

As a result, if King Arthur won his twelve battles, which ended with his resounding victory "the year I was born," wrote Saint Gildas, "at Dumbarton" on the Clyde River just downstream from Glasgow, then in truth he had to have won them in Scotland. For along in 1136 falls Geoffrey of Monmouth out of the blue of Oxford to corroborate Saint Gildas: King Arthur fought at "Alclut," which means "on the Clyde River," and at Loch Lomond, four miles away up the Leven River. One of his battles occurred at "Alclut," and the French medieval manuscripts concur: it was called his "War in Scotland." And so also, claimed Geoffrey, King Arthur was apparently not totally ignorant of history; for he claimed royal descent from the Emperor Constantine the Great, also born in Britain. Arthurian texts occasionally also proudly drop the name of his royal city, built by the Emperor: Constantinople.

While the Northern Annals of Scotland have been lost for some decades now, we do have some corroboration for the reign of King Arthur from the *Annals of Wales,* from the documentation kept by the well-established Church in France, from early and modern historians of Scotland, and from folklore. The hundreds of French manuscript pages begin to fill all the gaps, and they are contemporary with others from Germany, and then from the rest of western Europe and the Isles 1100–1453 until the spread of printing in the fifteenth century. More evidence then occurs in the watermarks of the first manufacturers of the first paper in Europe.

The principal disseminators of Arthurian lore were apparently not its first authors in Latin or Old French, however. Presentation copies mold in libraries. Even today, most authors have neither influence nor control of their text after it leaves their hands. It was, in King Arthur's case, the loud-mouthed broadcasters who spread his history abroad.

Leaving Glastonbury for good therefore, we now must halt a

while to look hard at the broadcasters. Who broadcasted the Arthurian manuscripts? Which points us back to who owned them in the first place. Realizing the huge cost—then as now—of large sheets of *glacé* kid leather upon which copyists traced the authors' texts, and which they then illuminated with solid gold, and which they also illustrated with gorgeous, intricate designs and beautiful pictures of people, castles, and plants, we must understand that only millionaire royalty could afford to commission and/or to own even one or two manuscripts. They were worth their weight in gold during the Crusades when King Richard Coeur de Lion traded them in Cyprus and probably also along his routes to and from Jerusalem. He once owned, it seems, not only the original of the *Lanzelet,* but also the huge *Sone de Nansai* text, which we now have only in a sort of Old French translation, and a poor job it was, really. A single such manuscript was probably the only treasured possession a nobleman could carry easily on his long journey across Europe and the Mediterranean Sea, and barter easily for food, lodging, and transport over a number of years.

The ransom of King Richard I may also have involved the turning over of manuscripts, but that ransom was more obviously required and paid in cold metal. The widowed Queen Eleanor of Aquitaine had heard that bad news in 1193: that she would have to collect, transport, and deliver into central Europe thirty-five tons of pure silver as her son's ransom. *And,* in addition, Richard would have to abdicate the throne of England before he was released. Even then, even after the delivery of the stipulated weight in silver from England and Scotland, the Capetian King of France still tried to have Richard kept longer than the one year in prison. The manuscripts, then, were coin of realms, since they were for the most part written in Old French, that was then the literary, universal language of these realms.

During the six months overall that he went into England to be crowned, first of all, and then to raise the money for the Third Crusade by obliging all officials in Britain to purchase, by the payment of stipulated sums, their jobs, positions, appointments, lands, and churches, it was noted that King Richard I could not utter a single sentence in English. English was a language a would-be poet like him never had occasion to learn. And yet, wrote the English historian William Stubbs at Oxford University in 1902, King Richard I lived in the very age that witnessed the rise of European nations, notably including France and England. King John certainly saw in person the growth of constitutional government when he signed the Magna Carta. It was also, said Stubbs again, the age of "great men." Just consider the careers of these children of King Henry II: Henry (born 1155), Matilda (1156), Richard (1157), Geoffrey (1158), Eleanor (1162), Johanna (1165), and John (1167). Her biographer says Queen Eleanor of Aquitaine became pregnant every Christmas.

The most notable "great men" of that crusading era were the rulers of England and France, who fall into three royal houses. The Plantagenet kings of England also then ruled what looks on the map like 90 percent of France, their realms called the Angevin Empire. The crafty diplomats who were the Capetian kings of the small area around Paris, or the Île-de-France, fall into two branches: the Royal House of France, and the Cadet Branch. The Angevins, and especially King Henry II, were recognized by Spanish and by Portuguese royalty, as the chief owners of these priceless Arthurian texts, and furthermore as their chief disseminators abroad. Queen Maud and Queen Eleanor of Aquitaine, with the latter's two French daughters, Marie and Alix, rank also as chief propagandists and broadcasters here. King Richard I, who was considered the most darling and the bravest fighter in the Crusades, for which he was the best beloved in both England and France, came second to none, or only to his father, as an "Arthurian" enthusiast.

One more distinction needs now to be made before the reader looks at some genealogical charts: "France" of the early Middle Ages means the Île-de-France, or the city of Paris and its environs held by the Elder or Royal Capetian Dynasty. It does not include the Angevin holdings as these territories seesawed back and forth between Capetians and Plantagenets, those two Houses always deadly foes. At least, the wily Capetians knew they were, under their masks of alliance, deadly foes of the English.

All the more civilized, less warlike peoples, who led easier lives in the more peaceful, more clement, lovelier, more Romanized territories south of the Loire River, which also cuts modern France in half, were ruled by neither Capetians nor Angevin Plantagenets. Southern France was nations apart, called variously: Aquitaine, the Languedoc (language of "oc" for "yes," and not "oil" or "oui"), Gascony, Provence, Auvergne on the central uplands, County of Toulouse, city states of Narbonne, Marseilles, Arles, Avignon, Orange, Béziers, and Albi, for example.

A brief glance now at the two Capetian Dynasties should show

how they interbred with the Angevin line proper after the successful victories in the field of Geoffrey Plantagenet and his masterful
wife Maud. Under their son Henry this line moves to the kingship
in England while warring constantly to hold their more valuable
real estate on the Continent. One ought to note also how these
blood lines follow through the whole Middle Ages from the conquest of England by the Bastard Duke William of Normandie and
allied barons in 1066 to the deaths of the last Plantagenet King of
England in 1399 or 1400 at Fflint Castle, Wales, and the death of
Duke Charles in 1486.

The Renaissance is often said to have commenced in 1492 at the
discovery of America by Christopher Columbus for Portugal, and
the expulsion of the Moors and Jews from Spain. Both events
changed Spain forever, and Portugal, and the world: one loss, and
one gain.

Also to consider in such a list of royal personages is the apparent
importance of genetics, which is to say of heredity over environment, the latter, or rearing, being more or less constant in the cases
of royal children. A medieval scholar in France wrote a book on the
education of princes, but the Arthurian *Prose Lancelot* wrote the last
word on the subject of the young Grail Questers' education. Royal
princelings demonstrate a preponderance of recurrent characteris-
tics, it seems to this author, as doubled or accumulated after the
marriage of Eleanor of Aquitaine to Henry II. While neither spouse
demonstrated any signs of either physical or mental weakness, their
children, but not her two daughters by the Capetian King of France,
were or became predominantly sociopathic: unstable, vacillating,
weak, excessively cruel, and debased. Note King Richard's summary execution of Arab warriors *who had surrendered* so that they
were, according to the laws of medieval warfare, supposedly to be
spared.

In 1792, when the French monarchy fell, King Louis XVI and
his Austrian Queen Marie Antoinette were executed as "Capetians." Thus, the memory of atrocities does not fade but returns
centuries later to haunt survivors and descendants. Similarly, no
king of France after those massacres of civilians, and after that
execution, it has been said, ever reigned again with honor in the
eyes of his people. These are among the hard lessons of history, as
are, for Americans, the graves in our cemeteries from our equally
atrocious Civil War.

When we return now to England in the century that follows the

The Median Capetian (Angevin) Dynasties of France/England/Italy
("Angevin" from Anjou, a Ninth-Century County in "France")

ANGEVIN DYNASTY (c. 400 years)

1. Fulk I

2. Fulk, Count of Anjou (1092–1143)
3. Fulk V, King of Jerusalem
4. Baldwin III,* King of Jerusalem (1130–63)
5. Amalric I (brother of Baldwin III)
6. Baldwin IV, the Leper (c. 1161–85)
7. Baldwin V (crowned at age five, d. 1186)
8. Geoffrey Plantagenet, the Fair
   • conquered Normandie
   • m. Maud/Matilda, daughter of King Henry I of England; she attempted the reconquest of England
9. Henry II, first Angevin King of England
10. Richard I, Coeur de Lion

11. King John
12. King Henry III
13. King Edward I
14. King Edward II

ANGEVIN DYNASTY (Cadet Branch) (c. 300 years)

1. Charles (brother of King Louis IX), Count of Anjou and Provence, King of Naples (1266)
2. Charles II
3. Robert
4. Joanna I (d. 1382)

5. Charles III

6. Lancelot

7. Joanna II (d. 1435)

8. Margaret
   • m. Charles de Valois

9. Charles de Valois

10. King Philippe VI (of France)
11. King John II (of France)
12. King Louis I of Naples
13. King Louis II
14. King Louis III

The Median Capetian (Angevin) Dynasties   (cont'd)

ANGEVIN DYNASTY (c. 400 years)	ANGEVIN DYNASTY (Cadet Branch) (c. 300 years)
15. King Edward III	15. René d'Anjou, Duke of Lorraine, King of Naples (1435–80) • King Louis XI of France forced René to will his titles of Provence and Naples to France
16. King Richard II, last Plantagenet King of England (d. 1400)	16. Duke Charles of Maine (René's nephew) (d. 1486) • ended this Cadet Branch

*Baldwin is the same name as Beaudouin, or Baudoin, and Bademagus (Governor of the Grail Castle in Arthurian texts).

The Capetian, or Royal, House of France
(987–1328 English historians)

1. Robert the Strong, Count of Anjou and Blois
2. Eudes, Count of Paris (A.D. 888)
3. Hugues Capet to the kingship (987)
   • m. Adélaïde de Poitiers
4. Robert II (c. 970–1031)
   • m. Rosala d'Italie (?)
   • m. Berthe de Boulogne
   • m. Constance de Provence
5. Henri I (c. 1006–60)
   • m. Anne de Kiev
   • daughter = Maud (1102–67) became the Empress Matilda*

The Capetian, or Royal, House of France (cont'd)

- m. Emperor Henry V of Germany (d. 1125)
- m. Geoffrey IV (Plantagenet) (c. 1128)
- son = the future King Henry II of England

6. Philippe I (1052–1108)
   - m. Berthe de Hollande
7. Louis VI the Fat (1081–1137)
   - m. Adélaïde de Savoie
   - married his son to the heiress Eleanor of Aquitaine, the coup of the centuries
8. Louis VII the Young (c. 1120–80)
   - m. Eleanor of Aquitaine; divorced her, 1152
   - defeated before Damascus (1148), Second Crusade; he supported Thomas à Becket against King Henry II of England
   - m. Constance de Castile
   - m. Adèle de Champagne (mother of Philippe II)
9. Philippe II, Augustus, the Conqueror
   - m. Isabelle, daughter of future King Baudouin VIII de Flanders
   - m. Isambour, daughter of King Waldemar the Great of Denmark
   - m. Agnès, daughter of Count Berthold V de Méran, Tyrol
   - defeated King Henry II of England, 1189
   - defeated King Richard I of England, 1199
   - defeated King John Lackland of England, 1205
   } and confiscated from them Normandie, Maine, Anjou, Touraine, and Poitou
   - defeated the Emperor Otto IV de Brunswick, Battle of Bouvines (1214), and confiscated Flanders
   - took part in the disastrous Third Crusade, after the death of Frederick Barbarossa and the foolish conquest of Cyprus by Richard the Lion Heart, King Philippe prudently withdrew and returned to France whence he furthered the capture and imprisonment for a year, and the bankrupting ransom paid by England for the release of Richard.

The Capetian, or Royal, House of France   (cont'd)

10. Louis VIII, the Lion (1187-1226)
    - m. Blanche de Castile (1185 or 88-1252), twice Regent of France
    - failed in his invasion of England (Lincoln, 1217)
    - fought southern France, the "Albigensian Crusade" (1215, 1219, 1226) behind Count Simon of Montfort, Earl of Leicester (c. 1160-1218), who was the Commander of the French king's forces, a religious bigot, and one of the most hated men in the history of southern France:
        - Montfort captured Carcassonne (1209) and murdered its helpless civilians
        - the Papal Legate then made him Viscount (ruler) of two cities, Béziers and Carcassonne; he then attacked Count Raymond VI of Toulouse
        - he overran Montauban and the County of Toulouse in 1211, murdering all the surviving inhabitants, men, women, and children alike
        - he defeated King Pedro II of Aragon and Count Raymond of Toulouse, was declared Lord of Aragon and Toulouse in 1215, had it confirmed by the Pope
        - he was killed while again attacking Count Raymond of Toulouse (1218)
    - conquered Poitou and, via Simon de Montfort, the Languedoc
    - failed to subdue Gascony or the County of Toulouse
    - (the Regent Blanche of Castile blocked King Henry III of England and by her diplomacy kept him out of France)
11. Louis IX, Saint Louis (1214-70) under regency of Blanche of Castile (1226-36)
    - ended the Albigensian War (Crusade), against Provence, in 1229
    - m. Marguerite de Provence (1234)
    - reconquered, from England, Normandie, Anjou, Maine, and Poitou
    - captured during the Seventh Crusade by Sultan of Egypt (1250-54), during the second regency of Blanche of Castile

The Capetian, or Royal, House of France (cont'd)

- died at Tunis while embarked on the Eighth Crusade
- built the city of Aigues-Mortes, the Sainte-Chapelle in Paris, the Sorbonne, and the Cathedrals of Chartres, Amiens, and Bourges

12. Philippe III le Hardi (the Bold) (1245-85)
    - m. Isabelle d'Aragon
    - purchased Poitou, Auvergne, and the County of Toulouse from England
    - united Navarre to France by his son's marriage
    - fought Sancho IV of Castile
    - invaded Aragon (1285) but died during the campaign

13. Philippe IV le Bel (the Fair) (1268-1314)
    - m. Jeanne, Countess of Champagne and Queen of Navarre (1273-1305)
    - became King of France, Count of Champagne, and King of Navarre (Spain)
    - started a war against Edward I of England allied with Flanders (Philippe allied with Scotland); Pope Boniface VIII successfully halted him (1296-97), but died (1303) opposing him
    - had Pope Clement V elected and moved from Rome to Avignon, France
    - balanced his budget by killing and/or persecuting Jews, Lombard bankers, and Knights Templar (1312), by debasing the currency, and by enacting ruinous taxation on the people of France
    - put to death two Masters of the Knights Templar
    - the Grand Master of the Templars, Jacques de Molay, at his execution predicted his death that year (1314)

14. Louis X (1289-1316)
    - executed his wife, Marguerite de Bourgogne (Burgundy)

15. John I (born and died 1316)

16. Philippe V (1294-1322)

17. Charles IV (1294-1328)
    - last Capetian king in the direct line (according to French historians)

*The Empress Matilda removed to England in 1125 and swore to take succession to that Crown away from the heirs of William the Conqueror, Duke of Normandie. She succeeded.

writing of our major Grail texts, we find the Angevin royals of Great Britain busy marrying in Spain, busy trying to form new alliances that might help them secure their bordering territories in southern France. What have they besides their good looks to recommend them in the eyes of Spanish aristocrats? Henry II dressed like a commoner, but he had received the dedication, say Spanish scholars, of a third edition of Geoffrey of Monmouth's rave success, *The History of the Kings of Britain.* It must be translated at once. One measure of a masterpiece is the stature or quality of its translator: Geoffrey Chaucer translated *The Romance of the Rose;* Charles Baudelaire translated our Edgar Allan Poe.

No less a personage than King Alfonso X of Spain translated Geoffrey of Monmouth into Spanish. Reading the king's Spanish was a real privilege, reports the scholar of Spanish literature William J. Entwhistle. During the thirteenth and fourteenth centuries, and well into the fifteenth also, Spain stood aside but witnessed the end of English dominion on the Continent. Spain watched then the Hundred Years' War, which drove the English out of every yard of French soil except for the port of Calais, opposite Dover.

In 1367 Edward the Black Prince journeyed to Spain, as did the Duke of York to Portugal in 1381, John of Gaunt in 1367, and the Earls of Derby and Salisbury in 1343. A Douglas went down to fight before Valencia, which still says it has a chalice, the Holy Grail, in its cathedral. King Edward I, called Longshanks, went to Burgos in 1254 to the wedding of the Princess Leonor (Eleanor) in Castile. A Spanish poem praised the Angevin ancestry of this daughter of King Henry II of England and his Queen Eleanor of Aquitaine. The lady lived to fight her brother, King John, called Lackland, of England. The troubadour poet Bernard de Ventadorn received the personal patronage of King Richard the Lion Heart.

That lion heart of King Richard, who was always reported as large-hearted as a lion, continued the Spanish tradition, or arose from the ancient Spanish tradition, of heroism. El Cid, who is Spain's national epic hero, daunted a live lion once. And what of our explorer of Florida, in the United States: A Spanish nobleman was watching a Lady once at public games where a live lion was loose in the arena. The Lady, leaning over her balcony, dropped a handkerchief onto the sand below. Without an instant's delay the young nobleman leaped down into the perilous pit below them, face to the ravening lion, recovered the Lady's lost article, and leaped back gracefully to the balcony. For this exploit superbly performed in the eyes of the world, the young nobleman received his sobriquet: Ponce de Leon.

In such an elegant climate is it any wonder Arthurian literature in exquisite Spanish translations swept over Portugal and Spain like a storm? Of course, Edward of Wales, and Edmund, and John of Gaunt too went down to Spain and stayed there as long as they could, from 1386 to 1388. There are glorious castles in Castile from one end of sunny, warm Spain to another, and beautiful heiresses to wed and bring back to the sunless north and the cold of winters. What need had Richard the Lion Heart to learn English? And the only Lady he admired, he told his mother, was Berengaria of Navarre, or she was a princess of the Basque country, say some. Thus, Berengaria followed her future mother-in-law as they pursued King Richard over the Alps and from Sicily, Berengaria following upon the track of her future husband all the way to the Holy Land.

What swept Catalonia, and Navarre, and Castile, and perhaps Portugal first of all, were the Arthurian tales of love, honor, and chivalry. And even more were the tales of chastity, purity, and religion, which is the Holy Grail. Lancelot and Tristan were the heroes who created Amadis de Gaula in Spain and Portugal. The medieval ideals of manhood led out of the terrors of medieval massacre into a newer century of hope and chivalry exemplified in the travels of Don Quixote. A medieval ideal of worship, which was that of the Holy Grail, passed into a book written by Saint Theresa in Spain.

DON QUIXOTE
IN THE CAVE OF MONTESINOS

Rather than list the admirable translations into Spanish and Portuguese of Arthurian texts so as to consider their popularity in Portugal and Spain, it will be hopefully more intriguing to weigh two diverse works from their Golden Age: Cervantes's *Don Quixote* and Saint Theresa of Ávila's *Las Moradas* (literally, The Mansions). Neither author declares for Arthurian literature nor mentions a source from Arthurian literature, but familiar characters people two chapters in Cervantes, and the Saint's work explains and describes the Grail Castle better than anyone else has ever done. It hardly seems possible either one could not have known it.

In *Don Quixote,* which is *Don Quijote* in Spanish, we deal with the most popular book ever written, excepting the Bible. The popularity of *Don Quixote* was immediate the very year of its first publication in 1575. Everybody has loved the thin man from La Mancha, watched his crazy antics as he lived the life of a ladies' man and gallant courtly knight, and wept to see him descend into disillusionment and death. Meanwhile Sancho Panza continually rose from the ignorance of a vulgar boor in contradistinction to the Don's waning idealism. The lesson is too hard almost to bear. Did Lancelot falter also, either before or after he was branded a traitor? Did he fall out of love and die uncomforted?

Don Quixote has been identified as a picaresque novel, a long itinerary of travels taken by a poor nobleman, Don Quixote, and his loutish servant Sancho Panza; but it is also an Arthurian-style "romance," because it is written in Spanish, a Romance language derived like Portuguese and French from Roman (we say "Latin"). *Don Quixote* is a chivalric romance because the seedy Don upholds courage, idealism, loyalty, dedication to his quest, and devotion to women in a century of hard nationalism, colonial exploitation, Inquisition, and continual wars of conquest. The emaciated, ridiculous Don tilts earnestly with windmills until he lies prostrate. The lesson taught is that of the sincere if deluded individual confronting a cruel society. It finds him ludicrous and slightly touched in the head to uphold chivalry while he starves for it. The conflicts are double: one man alone versus the whole nation, and his impractical idealism and love of another, long lost age of chivalry: King Arthur,

Merlin, Perceval, and Lancelot. The lone reader will not allow Don Quixote to give up, however. It is not possible to live enclosed in a materialism that heralds the death of the soul. The world has therefore cheered for him like a new Lancelot.

Saint Theresa too will answer and support Don Quixote: follow the gleam. "In my Father's house are many mansions." Así, *Las Moradas.*

In 1923 a scholar named Barto believed that two chapters of *Don Quixote* depicted the Grail Castle as it was envisaged in the popular mythology of lower-class, average Spaniards, of whom Cervantes was one of the poorest. Entwhistle disagreed in his book *The Arthurian Legend* (1975): "What the Knight of La Mancha saw . . . does not correspond with any of the Arthurian novels of Spain or Portugal, nor is it easy to follow a recent American critic [P. S. Barto]" (p. 61). This interchange of opinion between two scholars of repute is what will interest us here. Worship or celebration of the Holy Grail has always, up until Cervantes, been considered an enterprise undertaken strictly by personages of royal birth. It has furthermore always been considered a kind of state secret available only to initiates at the highest level, also at the end of their quests. But Don Quixote sees it halfway through his.

Don Quixote's experience does not originate from some courtly Spanish romances read and translated by and for Spanish royalty and then English queens. Quixote's is the common man's perception, precisely what opens Spain of the Golden Age to our profane eyes that might otherwise never have glimpsed it.

In the beautiful edition entitled *El Ingenioso Hidalgo,* the Accomplished Nobleman *Don Quijote de la Mancha,* a book written in Madrid in 1782 and published in 1833 as Part II of the first Mexican edition ever printed, the Don's most Arthurian adventure commences. One can hold this marvelously small book in one hand and read from this delightful, leather-bound volume, beginning in chapter 22, p. 5: "Here is recounted the great adventure of the Cave of Montesinos, which lies in the heart of La Mancha, which the valorous Don Quijote de la Mancha, brought to a felicitous conclusion," we translate as we read.

The Don had heard reported all around La Mancha that there was a wonderfully deep underground cave belonging to Montesinos, and that it would behoove him to dare descend into this cavern. Inside, he was told, were such sights to be seen as would stop the heart and chill the blood. The Don, Sancho Panza, and a poor author called "Cousin" took the road to the cave. They spent the last night at some little village where they purchased enough rope to hang the Don even were the cave's bottom as deep as hell.

Thus, we have even before the Don's descent into darkness two of the most prominent clues as to the whereabouts of the Grail Castle: (1) the cave where Mary Magdalene was buried and where she levitated and appeared to worshipers after her death, and also Merlin's burial cave on the Rhinns of Galloway, Scotland (or Merlin's birth cave, near Glastonbury, on the seashore at Tintagel, Cornwall, in England), and (2) the double allusion to the fact that theologically Hell lies before Paradise, i.e., the Purgatory that Queen Guinevere had successfully crossed extended before the Grail Castle named Joy, Eden, Paradise, and Castle of Souls.

Sancho protests mightily, arguing that the Don has no business whatsoever poking his nose into matters theological, and certainly no permission to dangle underground on hundreds of yards of hempen rope. But the Don is the hero; he knows how adventures are won. He prays for divine guidance before dedicating life, love, and limb to his sweetheart Dulcinea. His Banner, he says, will be Beauty. So he roped up and then sat down on the lip of the funneled entrance, which was overgrown with brambles. Nothing daunted, he slashed at the underbrush with his sword, thus disturbing flocks of crows, bats, and jackdaws that flew screeching out of the cavern's mouth. Because the Don was a good Catholic, he adamantly refused to consider black birds an ill omen even though the night birds had knocked him flat. While Sancho prayed to the Virgin and King Fernando of Aragón, the Don descended the rock funnel.

When a half hour later he and the scholarly cousin hauled the Don back to the upper world, they saw he had his eyes closed. They awoke him only with great difficulty. He cried, "No. I was so happy there!"

At this point Cervantes demonstrates his genius by putting his reader also through a harrowing series of interpolated first-person accounts that draw him too down through time into one descent after another, the Don telling his dark tale, in the course of which he meets dark Montesinos who tells his tale in the course of which a dark, dead knight also comes back from the dead to tell his tale, and so on. The reader is supposed to experience the Don's vertigo.

One fails to comprehend in what ensues how critics can ever have stigmatized Cervantes as unskilled and unlearned. The Don's account is no less than a review of Plato's *Republic* complete with the vast green meadow that always in such accounts or descents into hell lies this side of paradise. In his cavern sleep the Don crossed the meadow or demarcation line between this world and the Otherworld. In the distance he saw (Glastonbury's) crystal or "glass" castle of the Holy Grail and met its aged keeper who was named Montesinos, he said.

The French illustrator of Viardot's French translation (Paris, 1837) knows better, of course. He draws Montesinos as described, but adds Merlin at the end of chapter 23 garbed as usual like the Grim Reaper, Father Time, with his scythe across his shoulder. Quite clearly, Montesinos is Merlin. The cave of Montesinos is Merlin's Cave, and Cervantes must have read it in Old French by Richard of Ireland. In Cervantes, Merlin wears royal purple for his Roman blood, a green satin hood for green is the color of the Gaelic Grail Castle, and a black toque to signal his academic prestige. He is again a Christian prelate, visibly so, holding a rosary of beads as big as ostrich eggs.

"Ah," cries Montesinos, "we have dwelled here enchanted by Merlin, you see, while awaiting your arrival."

Why had the Don descended there? For the sake of Cervantes, of course, so Cervantes would write this Arthurian tale. The Don was escorted into the crystal castle and saw its alabaster walls. There he also saw Charlemagne's nephew (Roland in France, Durandart in Spain) laid out dead on his coffin lid. Durandart came to life to inquire if his heart had been sent after his death to his lady Belerma. Yes, he was told, Montesinos himself said he had cut it out and sent it safely away.

At this point the French translator Viardot (vol. 2, pp. 242–43) suffers a panic attack. Cervantes errs, he objected. Not Durandart, but Roland. Not Charlemagne but King Arthur. Not Montesinos but Merlin. In other words, Cervantes has caught him in his trap, for the doubling and the Don's resultant confusions are all phenomena common to sleeping versus waking states, reality versus dream, enchantment versus the hunger, war, poverty, wounding, slavery, and misery of Cervantes's daily life in Spain.

In Montesinos's Cave Don Quixote fell into a time lapse of a half hour that lasted five hundred years. He had gone underground, writes Cervantes, just like the rivers and lakes of La Mancha, which ran over ground and dropped under ground out of mortal sight. The Wise Merlin, *El Sabio Merlin* of the Spanish life of Merlin, will one day end all their enchantments. Or, in Arthurian terms, Mer-

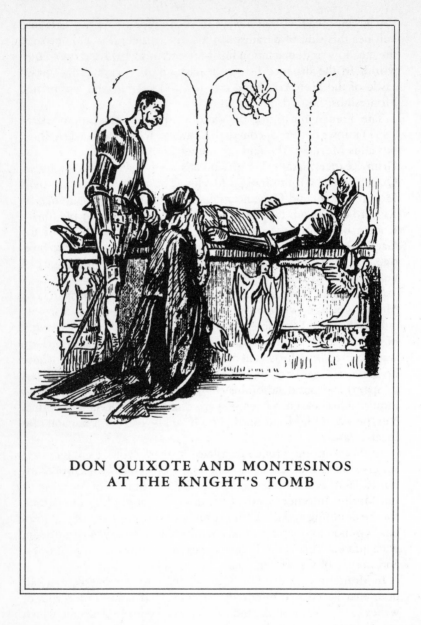

**DON QUIXOTE AND MONTESINOS
AT THE KNIGHT'S TOMB**

lin's pupil Perceval will end them at the collapse of King Arthur's reign.

Then the Don heard loud wails and the sobbing of women, for, as we know, there are priestesses at the Grail Castle. He turned to see the Grail Procession enter the castle hall: a double file of the loveliest maidens in the world, dressed all in black, with huge, oriental, white turbans on their heads. They were followed by their majestic queen, Her Majesty dressed also in mourning but wrapped from head to foot in a long, diaphanous white veil.

Cervantes has the Don continue in almost the same language and details used by the poet of the English *Gawain and the Green Knight* to delineate the physique of King Arthur's youngest half sister, Queen Morgan le Fay. In her hands she held the knight's mummified heart, and rightly so, for she is queen at the western necropolis. She must be related to the Loathly Damsel, so alike are they in appearance: shaggy black eyebrows, splayed nose, huge mouth, very red lips, gaping white fangs for teeth, and a mottled complexion. She was introduced to the Don as the Lady Belerma. Don Quixote gallantly compared her lost beauty with that of his peerless Lady Dulcinea.

The half hour Sancho said the Don had spent underground was really three days and nights, argued Don Quixote. He knew it was so for he had counted them dawns to dusks. Also, he was starved, for he had eaten not a single morsel of food during all that time. And like the persons there who never sleep, said the Don, he too was weary of looking and watching. He had recognized Queen Guinevere, he added, for she was among the residents there. He also recognized Lancelot's butler.

"You have been enchanted by that devil Merlin," Sancho told the Don.

"Not so," the Don replied, and Merlin was not the son of the devil (despite Robert de Boron's life of Merlin, which said he had been conceived by the devil upon Merlin's future mother's sleeping body).

"I pay no attention to you," said Sancho. "I know you."

"I know you too, Sancho," the Don replied, "so I pay no attention to what you say."

"You are crazy," said Sancho.

"I am not crazy," said the Don. "You are crazy."

The Don said that the proof of his being down there was that he had even met his Lady Dulcinea, and she was dancing with some girls. Dulcinea was a little short of cash to buy herself a new petti-coat, and the Don gave her what few coins he had left in his purse. And he was certainly in possession enough of his faculties to be able to understand whether it was a poniard or a dagger Montesinos had used to carve out the knight's heart, and smart enough to realize it could not have been made by one of the armorers of their ac-quaintance.

"Come out of it," pleaded Sancho.

I know you talk this way because you love me, concluded the Don. I know you have my best interests at heart, but you lack my experience of the world. So naturally, you think such difficult ad-ventures are impossible. But time does march on, as I have told you countless times. Some day I will tell you more about the marvels I saw down there, and then you will be forced to believe in the truth of what I just told you. That truth admits neither reply nor argu-ment: *"cuya verdad ni admite réplica ni disputa."*

In *La Ruta de Don Quijote* (The Route of Don Quixote) the author Azorín explains in chapter 10, on the Cave of Montesinos, that the lesson taught by Cervantes was enchantment by and in Spain itself. In very romantic Spanish with its beautiful, extended vocabulary he says that the chronicler traveling across La Mancha to the Cave feels himself oppressed, repressed, exasperated, nervous, desperate, hal-lucinated by the monotonous landscape, continuous, intense, line after line of plains covered with a dry stubble and a dull, impercep-tible hue of green. Then appears the hamlet where the Don, San-cho, and the cousin spent that last night before the descent. Then comes a new panorama of small hills, canyons, ravines, zigzagging off into infinity until the traveler comes to the place Cervantes envisaged as the Cave of Montesinos.

Whether Spain could have boasted a Grail Castle in La Mancha before Cervantes told it so is a moot question, indeed.

THE GRAIL BEARER BELERMA

The "Cave of Montesinos" story by Cervantes leaves the reader as entangled in mystery as does any Gothic novel where a white-clad maiden ventures alone, perhaps with a flickering candle, into the haunted depths of a black castle. There she may meet the famous enchanter Merlin. There she might even see a dead warrior lying upon his funeral slab of stone, and coming back to life again as any wronged hero or heroine might hope to do. The "Grail Bearer" Belerma whom Don Quixote reports he saw below in his cave resembles all the other white-clad priestesses in their hidden temples. Without this central figure Cervantes had no tale, and the Gothic charmer, no novel.

Nobody can argue either that Cervantes is unaware of his plot and characters, for he and Sancho Panza had already exhaustively argued the case of famous heroes and heroines (book 4, chap. 22). You may as well, says the Don, try to persuade somebody that the Sun does not light our world, or that Frost does not cool us, or that the Earth does not hold us up, as to try persuading someone that "King Arthur of Britain" never lived or that the "Saint Grial" is fictional only.

And yet Cervantes leaves his reader decompressed here, before and after Don Quixote allows himself to be hauled out of Montesinos's Cave. In the first instance, how does the Don know he should descend into a hole in the ground in order to discover, in the depths of the shaft, that an aperture in its side leads to a superb castle? How was such a concealed castle built? How is it maintained? How was the wounded warrior conveyed there?

Azorin, the scholarly follower of Cervantes, reported as he tracked the Don that this hole in the ground was merely "an excavación somera," a shallow ditch (p. 128). And yet Azorín felt the same unquiet. The "Cave of Montesinos" passage seems to haunt all readers alike. It disturbs the sleep. Its poetic qualities themselves, adds Azorín, are disquieting: "la poesia inquietadora."

After the troubled sleep that the lady Belerma also causes in her readers, another most disturbing facet in Cervantes's account is this castle itself. How can such splendor lie buried deep underground and be entered only through a side shaft of a narrow, vertical tunnel? Who told the Don about it? Was such a castle, or palace, not world famous? How could it be hid or protected if such golden splendor once existed? Where are its ruins today? Have they not been located?

It seems just as obvious in Cervantes that Montesinos was a real and celebrated prelate officiating in some religious establishment. And then Merlin, by Cervantes's own logic, was also once an Archbishop officiating, as Geoffrey of Monmouth testified more than once, at King Arthur's coronation, which was also his queen's coronation, but in a separate church. And Grail Castles were often said to stand on summits, like Tannhäuser's Venusbergs. Thus, we like the very name of our dignitary: *Monte Sinos* (Mountain of Destiny?).

Nor is Don Quixote the only person reported to have seen a dying knight upon his slab in the Grail Castle. The only known female Arthurian poet is Marie de France, unknown still except for her texts. In her most haunting, mysterious *Yonec* poem the lady heroine runs from her home downhill to the isle where the Grail Castle stands on its mound *(motte)*. She crosses the arm of the sea and reaches it. Don Quixote too hears or sees underground waterways. In the great hall the pregnant lady finds her dying lover whom their yet-to-be-born son Yonec will avenge. Other evidence testifies that knights killed in the Holy Land sent their hearts home to their beloveds. And such tales are always as gruesome as here, in Don Quixote's adventure.

The palace or castle which he visits is doubtless a Grail Castle. The sarcophagus and dead knight persuade us that there is necessarily a necropolis nearby. The same difficulty of entrance always occurs whenever such a hero as Perceval arrives finally, almost always by accident, like Don Quixote. And furthermore, the entrance, or last stage of this Quest, occurs suddenly, by surprise. Each stay at the Grail Castle involves the taboo against consuming food or drink in that realm intermediary between life and death, dreams and waking, sleep and consciousness. A lance or a surgeon's knife, and even cups of blood, may appear here. And here maidens weep and knights or kings are wounded yet alive while close to a death they welcome. Processions always form and re-form, pass and return, turn and sometimes pass by again. Like Perceval, the Don asked no question capable of breaking the enchantment. In fact, wordy as he usually was, here his lips remained more or less sealed.

It is fortunate that common knowledge doubtless once available to Cervantes is also available to us. Most encyclopedias will inform us that around A.D. 261, or as early as 258, the Holy Grail was in Spain. Common knowledge has it also that the Holy Grail can be seen today in the Cathedral of Valencia, Spain. Now the first question is: how did it get there? And second, did the Don see it?

Cervantes must also have known that this Spanish Grail used to be preserved in a celebrated, real cave in Spain. Why did he not reveal this to his reader? Was the subject too sacred for irreverent treatment? Or was it too dangerous a subject to be mentioned?

The real Grail Castle in Spain does not lie at the bottom of a shallow ditch, of course, nor as a lateral concavity extending from the side of a vertical tube. The real Castle is very probably the national monument called San Juan de la Peña. It is located at the bottom of the Cave of Galíon ("en el fondo de la cueva de Galión"), says the Spanish encyclopedia, which was excavated or dug under an enormous rock (pinnacle?) ("socavada en un igual peñasco") of the mountain range of the same name ("de la sierra de igual nombre"). The pinnacle or cliff is 1,168 meters high, situated in the Province of Huesca, near the city of Jaca. That Montesinos was a famous hermit at some such ancient monastery seems unlikely, but there were famous hermits there over the centuries, principally a Juan de Atarés and a Benedicto y Marcelo.

This natural cave, which had been excavated and enlarged perhaps even in prehistoric times, sheltered refugees during the Moorish invasions of the Iberian Peninsula, now Spain and Portugal. It sheltered fugitives again when Aragón fell to the African Moors. The first King of Navarre, García Jiménez, turned the first church on that site into a monastery. In time San Juan de la Peña became the pantheon of Aragón and complete in every marvelous detail of architecture, adornment, fame, and holiness.

In Paris Henri Collet, one of the most prominent of modern French scholars to become an authority on Spain, Spanish music, and the renowned author Cervantes, wrote a book (1929) about the Cave of Montesinos, which he labeled fiction. He called his book *L'Ile de Barataria* (The Isle of Barataria) because Don Quixote went there, to that "isle" on the west bank of the Ebro River from La Mancha in Castile. The quest that led him to his sacred cave commenced there. (*L'Ile de Barataria* won the 1929 French National Literary Prize.)

Collet adapted the old theory of Wolfram von Eschenbach, that the Grail was of Arabic and Jewish origin, that it dated from the conquest of Spain by Semitic peoples from Africa. Spain only continued the "great medieval tradition" (p. 60) of Jews and Arabs, who in turn had borrowed it from Hinduism. In modern dress Cervantes's lady love named Dulcinea became Collet's Spanish lady named Doña Aldonza. The lady has fled. She must be rescued.

To please his lady Don Quixote also had journeyed to the grotto of Montesinos, which turned out to be at first sight only a small ditch filled with black birds and brackish water. What did Cervantes mean?

The Cervantes passage, says Collet, concealed a deeply buried meaning: it was Merlin's Cave, and far from the "Merlin's Cave" at Tintagel, Cornwall, which floods at high tide twice every twenty-four hours. This Merlin's Cave in Cervantes was a Grail Castle of crystal where the Grail Bearer Belerma walked in procession, carrying the mummified heart of her lover. Don Quixote was the lover returned to life on earth, and another Knight of the Lion like Lancelot. When the Don required one hundred lengths of rope in order to reach the shelf in the rocky tube, he was probably, decided Collet, repeating local legend.

Why did Cervantes disguise his cave, then, its entrance, the personages he met there, and the Grail? By so doing, argued Collet, he protected not only the legend but also its practitioners. Scholars, as Cervantes knew, argued Collet, have "geometrical minds." Those contemporary scholars, who were recognized as superior in intellect and geometry, detested Merlin the astronomer, as they suspected of heresy all mystics, alchemists, necromancers, magicians, and searchers for the ideal Grail Castle. They were the Inquisition.

In that Grail Castle the inhabitants worshiped queens like Guinevere who were goddesses of eternal beauty. They were black-clad or white-clad priestesses hiding in a secret world because in the real world priestesses had been outlawed for ages. In the Cave of Montesinos they sang archaic hymns to Guinevere, or to Dulcinea del Toboso, or to the fleeing Doña Aldonza: Diamond crowned . . . Sweet shadow . . . Ray of light . . . Strange power of woman . . . Beautiful gypsy.

The real monastery, San Juan de la Peña, lies in northeastern Spain, in the distant and secret mountains of Aragón. At the dawning of the Middle Ages, it is alleged, this sanctuary received the Holy Grail that is venerated today in the Cathedral of Valencia. This Grail is held to be the very same holy vessel saved by Joseph of Arimathea. Like the heroes in King Arthur's day the inhabitants of these secret mountains thought to preserve in its purity this one relic of Christ from Jerusalem.

Entering this circular Grail Castle of Cervantes, searchers turned the copper handles of great doors, and entered the grand hall where precious gems glinted in tessellated floors, amid lofty columns of porphyry and gold that rose like massive tree trunks in an otherwise dark forest. Here Arabic scrolls *(azulejos)* of turquoise decorated the walls. The dome overhead was open to the stars—so many diamonds overhead. This castle was an immense rotunda, a pantheon of crystal. The persons present looked to Belerma, the Grail Queen.

Or, it could have been that the newest and youngest emerald-eyed Grail Queen was called Aldonza. She had been held at the Grail Castle so that the learned ancients resident there could study prophecy by observing this gifted and beautiful maiden. The Grail Procession entered, maidens two by two, each wearing an enormous, Arab turban over her head. Damsels performed ancient, liturgical dances. Belerma entered. She was carrying the heart of the dead hero. She was clad in black like Morgan le Fay. All the persons present had fled from the real world into this paradise of dreams.

The Holy Grail at the Cathedral in Valencia, says Collet, is a copy of the original Grail kept for so many centuries at San Juan de la Peña. The Valencia chalice is a simple cup made of an agate called "Oriental cornerine." It is semispherical and about the size of a large orange. The chalice stands on a foot made of seashell. It has handles and gold appliqués set with twenty-six precious pearls and two emeralds. The whole at Valencia rests upon a pedestal with four supports, all made of silver.

Henri Collet gives the history of this Spanish Grail as follows: (1) it was the Cup of the Last Supper as described in the Gospels of Matthew, Luke, and Mark; (2) it is also the chalice that Jesus described as the New Testament; and (3) it is the cup or chalice of the Eucharist. This Holy Grail stands as one of the most venerated of Christian relics, like pieces of the Cross, or of the Crown of Thorns, and like the Holy Shroud of Turin. These most venerated objects were probably taken to Rome originally by Saint Peter.

The Holy Grail itself was probably carried into Spain by Saint Lawrence, their San Lorenzo, around the year 261. Pope Sixtus II would have sent it for safekeeping into Spain during the persecutions of Christians under Valerian. Lorenzo was a native son of

Huesca in Spain. Then, according to Collet, Bishop Audebert of Huesca in 713 carried the Holy Chalice to the monastery of San Juan de la Peña because even during fresh, Moorish invasions it would be safe there in high mountains that were not easily penetrated even in peace times. In 1060 the nearby Jaca became a Bishopric and King García Jiménez made his famous defense of the Rock. The monastery was the key to the Cluniac Reform (Glastonbury was a Benedictine or Cluniac House) in the eleventh century, and the Chalice or Grail was still there in 1134, at that time housed in an ivory arch ("une arche d'ivoire"—Collet, p. 166).

Collet concludes in full power of scholarship that the legend of the Holy Grail originated there, at San Juan de la Peña, Aragón, now Spain:

Grail in the Provençal language = *grasal,* a cup, vase, or chalice
Grail in the Limousin dialect = *grial,* a cup, vase, or chalice
Grail in the Catalan language = *gresal,* a cup, vase, or chalice

We recall that Cervantes wrote "Grial," as in Limousin, the area of central France near the city of Limoges.

On April 13, 1399, the Holy Grail was removed to Valencia for use during the coronation ceremonies of Don Martin as King of Aragón and Sicily. It was placed in the Cathedral at Valencia in 1437.

Collet adds that Wolfram von Eschenbach portrayed Parzival as King García Jiménez, who was also a valorous warrior of universal appeal. Furthermore, he believed that the legend of the Holy Grail spread across the Oriental Pyrenees into southern France where it surfaced with aplomb in the religion of the Cathares there, at their Grail Castle of Montségur (Mount of Security or Salvation).

One peculiarity in Cervantes's account remains to astonish us, and it concerns not Belerma personally but what she bears. The Grail Bearer ought to walk in procession last and bear the Grail in her upraised hands. That she bears the hero's mummified heart departs from the circumstances as reported generally elsewhere. This is sufficient cause for alarm. When the first red alert is compounded by the even more alarming circumstance of the knight speaking after his heart has been cut out of his body, then the red

THE GRAIL BEARER BELERMA

flag flies high. The reader accedes to the ascription of "Gypsy" for Belerma.

Perhaps the gypsies really did come from South America or from the Aztecs or from their ancestors, the Maya. Everyone knows how the sacrificial victim there was laid on a stone tablet and how his heart was cut out with an obsidian knife, and how the priest then raised it up as an offering to the Sun. Was this the possible origin of our Grail Bearer Belerma and her mummified heart? And could the victim have spoken after this surgery? Certainly a human being can utter many words in a few seconds.

With such horrors to ponder, one inclines to sympathize with the waning and disappearance altogether of savage priests and priestesses.

Since English, Spanish, Portuguese, and French nobles translated and broadcast Arthurian material during the Middle Ages, 1170 to 1200 or 1230, they have directed us to study them and these authorial voices.

Medieval authors lead us directly to one of the world's first authors, Cervantes. It must amaze us to realize how uncannily Cervantes selected from medieval manuscripts his crucial points: Merlin's Cave, for instance, the Grail Bearer Belerma, the Grail Queen Aldonza.

In so doing, we have also come across, finally, our first, excellent etymologies for *Holy Grail.*

Saint Theresa of Ávila

What has made Cervantes's account of Don Quixote's underworld adventure so Arthurian in character is its assimilation, firstly, to Merlin's Cave. Not only was Montesinos intended to name Wise Merlin himself, but the cave of Montesinos also reproduced Merlin's Cave. That earlier cave in Britain was, as in the case of Montesinos's in Spain, a death cave. By death cave, one understands it as a burial place of honor. Merlin had foretold his death, hour and minute, for September of the year 536. It was a ritually ecclesiastical death that would take place ceremoniously at his prepared site, a cliffside cave on the north shore of the Solway Firth, near the village of Whithorn.

According to the poem *Yonec* by Marie de France, the Grail Castle also either was a necropolis or it was situated beside a cemetery. The lady's lover lay dying, where she saw him, inside the Grail Castle itself.

When the Grail Castle was referred to by name as Avallach's Isle, Avallach being a missionary from Jerusalem, the name was shortened into "Avalon," or "Isle of Avalon." King Arthur was transported by barge to the Isle of Avalon after his fatal wounding during the Battle of Camlan. Therefore, according to these witnesses as by its correspondence to Aliscans at Arles, Merlin's Cave was another death cave.

King Arthur was therefore not born in the tidal "Merlin's Cave" at Tintagel, Cornwall. The necropolis cave is a feature common to Arthurian texts because they bear witness to the practices and customs of early Christianity in which a few primitive traces linger. The Christian cave itself derives from the burial of Christ, and is reinforced therefore by the cave of his apostle Mary Magdalene, repeatedly so by his prelate Merlin, and now the latter's double, Montesinos in Renaissance Spain.

The castle rises to the forefront, however, as perhaps the prime symbol and chief structure originally housing the Holy Grail. It was the sort of castle that included within it a chapel, church, or temple. If we look briefly at three works by castle specialists, one from Scotland, a second from Spain, and a third from England, we learn that before 1066 in Scotland "castles" were timbered earthworks. W. Douglas Simpson, long a royal historiographer at the University of Aberdeen, says no census of such prototypical structures in Scotland is available. Proprietors of said constructions often lost ownership after the Norman French penetrated Scotland by peaceful means following the conquest by their Duke William of Normandie in 1066; the Norman married Celtic heiresses. This had been Lancelot's maneuver too in setting himself up in the world of landed estates inherited by women and girls according to Scottish matriarchal law.

The earliest Norman castle consisted of a moated mound encircled by a palisade, including a wooden tower, a banked and palisaded courtyard, and enclosed household buildings made also of wood. In the Norman French language, which is properly termed Anglo-Norman, a castle mound is a *motte*. The courtyard is a *bailey,* which constructions give the castle its generic name: motte and bailey. The Anglo-Norman clergy soon built churches in conjunction with the castle, and beside it. The "most impressive" examples, adds Simpson, are perhaps Duffus Castle near Elgin, Scotland, which once belonged to the Morays; Huntly Castle in Aberdeenshire, which was built by the Gordons, the "Cocks of the North"; and the well-known Castle Urquhart on the even better known Loch Ness.

In his book of 1982 (*Barcelona*) Paluzie de Lescazes lamented that the Iberian Peninsula of Cervantes and Saint Theresa of Ávila, despite its peninsulation on three sides plus its protection on the north by the dangerous Pyrenees Mountains, was frequently invaded from Europe as well as from Africa. The Romans had annexed Spain *(Hispania)* to their Empire by A.D. 200. Then around 400 the barbarians arrived in force. These were chiefly the Visigoths, Germanic tribes who founded a Spanish kingdom with its capital at Toledo. They held their kingdom in Spain and then expanded their holdings northward, evacuating the Vandals, conquering the older Roman Aquitania, and occupying its capital of Toulouse. The Visigoths had been more or less converted to Christianity by 475, when King Arthur was born in North Britain. By about 700 the very civilized and very cultured Moors from Africa commenced the conquest of Spain, which, finally, they almost entirely captured. Then ensued seven hundred years of conflict between Christianity and Islam for possession of Spain. By 1492, when both Moors and Jews were expelled from Spain, the shrine of Saint James in the northwestern corner of the peninsula had become what it is today, one of the most popular shrines for Christian pilgrims from throughout Europe: Santiago de Compostello. Saint Theresa was born in 1515, in the very land of the chief castle in Spain, Old Castile, and she was herself perhaps of Jewish blood. Cervantes too was born in Castile, but near Madrid, or in New Castile, in 1547.

Both authors wrote Castilian, which is the very beautiful but difficult written, or literary, language of Spain. Saint Theresa was born in Ávila, in the arid tableland of Old Castile, famous, before she made it immortal by her career in the church and by her books, for wool and the silk manufacture she talks about in her book *Las Moradas*, also entitled *Interior Castle*. The province where she lived as a little girl includes Segovia and its castle, called in Moorish "Alcazar." Cervantes's province of La Mancha includes a part of Moorish Toledo on its high, barren plateau. In his essay on the land of Don Quixote, Manuel Ugarte describes Castile (*Castilla* in Spanish) as a colorless monotone of crosses, death, fatality . . . sleep . . . where the wind sings like violins wailing through the bare branches of dry trees (p. 45) . . . far from Merlin in Britain.

The English scholar of military architecture Charles Oman (1978) decides that the English word *castle* dates from the *Anglo-Saxon Chronicle* entry of the year 1048. In Roman times the old structure was a prehistoric earthwork ringed, like the ramparts of Hadrian's Wall, with banks and ditches. The Romans earlier referred to a Celtic hill-fort by the Latin word *castella,* however, as in Juvenal, circa A.D. 120. Juvenal was speaking of a *castella* in Yorkshire: "castella Brigantium." In that case the word is plural, like the original Roman word Caesar used for the fortified camps his legionnaires dug each night: *castra.* His *castra* formed a legionary square, a camp surrounded by a ditch and also a palisade perhaps. In the fifth century when King Arthur was born, Saint Jerome in Jerusalem used Juvenal's word in the singular: a camp = *castellum.*

Oman adds that there is no use looking for King Arthur's camps or forts at Tintagel because that castle site on the Cornish coast dates from King Henry III (reigned 1216–72) rather than from the days of King Arthur (475–542). A superb ruin of a Celtic hill-fort such as was used in the Dark Ages of King Arthur is Dinas Bran near the Welsh town of Llangollen, not far west of Chester. Chester is, like York, but not like the greater but ruined Carlisle, a Roman fort still fairly intact. Geoffrey of Monmouth had pointed to Dinas Bran as an unforgettable example of truly ancient, military architecture. It is a steep climb to a breathtaking structure.

Nothing equals the sky-high castles in Spain, however, which medieval writers, like modern writers now, longed to see. It is no wonder that the Grail Castle, which is always described as being the most beautiful marvel of architecture in all of Europe, and which still remains the most mysterious, should swing as pivot of Arthurian narratives.

Through Gothic fiction the castle winds its way down the centuries in Scotland, Germany, England, Spain, and Italy especially— Glamis, Siegmaringen, Kenilworth, Udolfo, Otranto—as the dread abode of ancient evil.

Saint Theresa's mansions or her "interior castle" is itself immune, and only surrounded by paper dragons. Her book very much recalls the fifteenth-century French-Italian poet Charles d'Orléans. He prayed to God that the Castle of his heart might be defended against its chief foe, Danger, who prowled about it looking for a weak point where he could force the bailey and overwhelm the chatelain.

Saint Theresa of Ávila (1515–82), born Teresa de Cepeda y Ahumada, became not only a principal saint of the Catholic church but also one of only two women ever to be recognized a "Doctor of the Church." As "Teresa de Jesús" she became a Carmelite nun in 1536. She founded the convent of Saint Joseph in Ávila and collaborated with her friend and fellow religious, Saint John of the Cross, to reawaken Spain to religious enthusiasm. Spanish writers today call her simply "Madre Teresa." She addresses her *Interior Castle* to those nuns under her care: "Sisters." She is a principal saint because she led Spain to a remarkably just and peaceful religious reform. She was a tireless worker, after long bouts of severe psychosomatic illness in her young days, a gifted administrator, and, what interests us most here, a rare spiritualist. She stands deservedly at the very apex of the mystical school of religion, Spain's greatest female literary figure.

All in all, Theresa founded thirty new convents inside Spain and completely reformed her Order. She wrote four marvelous books, all of which she subjected tirelessly to the best Catholic critics of her day so that they would be acceptable and certified holy and orthodox:

1.   1565 *Camino de perfección*
     (Road to Perfection)

2. 1573 *El libro de las fundaciones*
   (The Book of the Foundations)
3. 1577 or 1588 *Las moradas o (El) Castillo interior*
   (The Mansions or [The] Interior Castle)
4. 1588 *El libro de su vida* (or *La Vida*)
   (The Book of Her Life)

She wrote the *Interior Castle,* translated into English by E. Allison Peers, to fulfill her vows of obedience. In Spain her book is called *Las Moradas,* which seems to me to come from the words of Jesus: "In my Father's house are many mansions."

Her castle of the heart and soul resembles the Grail Castle, which, of course, she never would have mentioned because it was neither rejected nor accepted by the Catholic church. In fact, without her book one might never have realized the mystical interpretation she offers for this castle symbolism. It so truly suits both her turn of mind and the Grail Castle.

Mother Theresa goes right to the matter of this castle imagery in the first two pages (pp. 697–98) of her book in *Obras* (Works), as edited in Barcelona by Antonio Comas. Our soul, she explains, resembles a Castle made all of diamonds, or the clearest of crystals, where there are many facets just as in Heaven there are many Mansions. This Castle holds in it many Mansions, she means to say, some of which are high up while others are lower down, and still others are situated to the sides; and in the very center of the very middles of all these Mansions there lies the chiefest of them all, which is where there take place many things that are of deepest secrecy between God and the soul.

Persons who saw Saint Theresa as she wrote her *Mansions* with a quill pen on parchment marveled at the speed of her hand across the pages and at her rapt concentration. If that sort of report is at all valid, then she must have possessed an intellect quite beyond modern comprehension. Ethnologists have pointed out that human intellect has dimmed constantly over centuries because of the millions lost from each generation to warfare. It may be very true, as a teacher over a lifetime has also observed first-hand, that intelligence today is far inferior to that of decades past. Saint Theresa's grasp of her material astounds us today, and especially her interweaving of symbols and themes: castle, diamond, mansions, waters, fire, temple, body, and soul.

While it is difficult to sort out one symbol from another, so deftly has she interwoven them, the castle is her principal metaphor. First of all, she shows us directly that the castle is the human soul in exile from Paradise, but close enough to Heaven that it must never despair of being able to enter it through the doorway of prayer. There one speaks freely of internal, spiritual matters alone.

The soul resembles in lucidity an Oriental pearl, or it is like the young and verdant Tree of Life planted in the springtime. But the castle itself is the diamond because it shoots white fire and is harder, brighter, more powerful than mere glass, or brightest crystal. The sun shines through its walls like the light from God that drives darkness out of the castle. The gold in the castle walls and ceilings figure as divine wisdom. The sun beams also from the very center of all the mansions, for it is God who is both sun and center of our lives and of our world. The castle therefore has the doors of prayer by which one enters freely. In contrast, the sepulcher has no door at all.

There are seven mansions in all, and the Mother gives specific directions to her daughters as to how to proceed. Their bodies are its outer walls. Their senses are vassals to the will. In the castle center they will find the precious spring of pure refreshment, and the highest mansion. Meditation will lead them safely there.

The castle also resembles the human body where the rooms one comes to know are called self-knowledge. What else is meditation but a slow reasoning with the self? Thus, the castle interior is open and close at hand. Our own interior is the castle of our souls, and similarly, another celestial building. Each mansion requires us to know our hearts. Humility is no excuse. Apology is no excuse. Why? Humility may be defined as the refusal to know oneself, or as a total lack of self-knowledge.

What of the castle's exterior? Do not poisonous vipers and other dangers lurk in wait for us around the perimeter? Where are our vain thoughts not unlike crawling lizards? Who stands guard in the outer courts but reptiles and malodorous vermin?

But over the interior castle stand the good shepherd and such guardians as Saint Augustine. Far from the sunlight of the Lord the outer limits creep in darkness and devilry, loom black with the pitch of sin; they are so far from the cleansing waters of life. Waters and the sea symbolize spirituality. To Saint Theresa, as to Queen Guinevere along the Marches into Ireland, the sacred spring dilates the soul as if bubbling from the earth it had no way to drain away so that, explains the Saint, the faster the pure water bubbled the larger the pool expanded. It is the same with the soul, which prayer enlarges, and especially if the flow of springwater comes, without conduits built to drain it away, from God alone. Thus, the element water symbolizes spirituality.

The incident at the spring in Arthurian literature, and especially in the *Lancelot* by Chrétien de Troyes, depicts Lancelot weeping and almost fainting away when he finds beside the spring the queen's royal comb, which she has left for him. Seeing it lie beside the font makes him almost collapse. Why? Because he understands that the queen has gone to the Grail Castle now, and that he is to follow. Once there, he will undergo an ordeal of initiation, which will perhaps be the Eucharist. Therefore he faints at the thought of receiving from holy hands new power, new authority, inner tranquillity, and the spark of true conviction.

Signs of fire proceed throughout *Las Moradas* as the Christian proceeds via prayer and meditation from the first to the seventh and central hall in that castle. The sun of deity will shine in the central hall as its ray, falling upon the high altar of the new cathedrals still being built in Saint Theresa's days, impregnated the Virgin Mary. The French poet Rutebeuf, who had been commissioned by the Archbishop of Paris, explained this in the piece he wrote for the opening ordination of Notre-Dame de Paris. As fire awakens the worshiper, says Theresa, it comes in the form of a comet, or as thunder and lightning from the zenith, or like the red phoenix bird that catches fire, is consumed, but arises young again, each time, from its black ashes. Only the devil dwells forever in darkness, but the sky-blue Virgin Mary crushed him with her gigantic cross on the very altar of Notre-Dame during the first performance of Rutebeuf's *Miracle* play. Just as running or living water represents life in the *Interior Castle,* so black pitch upon clear crystal shows up as sins upon the soul. Every person must strive for knowledge of the soul, which is the castle, as well as for knowledge of the self, which is the outer person. Perfect knowledge, one learns in the Sixth Mansion, is triple knowledge: (1) knowledge of the majesty of God, (2) a knowledge of the self, which will make one listen, and (3) a realization of the little worth of everything usually considered valuable on earth. Having arrived at these realizations, the soul *(alma)* scorns the world, preferring the jewels of her wedding in Seventh Heaven. What was life in the world but a long exile and descent ultimately into purgatory?

Purification there, after he had negotiated his passage across the

Sword Bridge, led Lancelot to the last degree of initiation, of which he was at that time worthy. Death was to claim him before he could proceed further.

The soul is a butterfly one has seen fluttering about a castle garden like some lost soul that cannot decide her true way, carried up and about by every willful gust of summer wind. The soul is a poor stranger on this earth. . . . This unforgettable metaphor recurs throughout the terrible religious wars in France during Saint Theresa's own lifetime, the sixteenth century. A butterfly worn as embroidery on clothing, as a locket about the neck, or in silver filigree on the lapel of one's jacket was then also a secret sign of fraternity: "I am a Protestant."

The Arthurian hero Perceval comes instantly to mind in the Saint's use of a second, even more commonly understood symbol— the dove. The dove also is a symbol of the soul ascending to heaven, or descending, as Richard Wagner saw it in his opera *Parsifal,* with manna for the hero Perceval. Like the hero, the white dove also is a stranger in the world, appearing at one holy shrine after another as it (he) seeks instruction from royal uncles who are King Hermits, as from King Arthur himself. It was the latter, but in underhand fashion, who had called up and dispatched Perceval on his seemingly endless quest in the first place. More specifically, the dove represents the final triumph of Easter Sunday when the darkened church on Good Friday blazes forth in beauty, organ music, and flowers. On that day Perceval becomes the last King of the Grail Castle in Britain. . . .

In Perceval's earlier shrines, even though they were replicas of Solomon's Temple, says Theresa, his soul slumbered. Then he could not speak. Therefore he could not advance into another, higher Mansion.

How must the soul be like the humble bee, she thinks, going erratically about to test each pretty flower for its perfume and color and nectar? How small and busy it is, and how very puny in this trackless wilderness that dwarfs it immeasurably. What pitfalls lie below and over its bursts of tiny energy. Let us too be not proud, but modest, and hope to reach our goal, which is knowledge in three parts. And when we reach it, what shall we remember then of the kaleidoscopic world we left behind? When we shall have reached the Seventh Mansion, what shall we remember from this other world we shall by then have put aside? Shall we not say then, "What nothingness we have given up"?

The humble bee is our model, to be sure, but then how much more should we, my Sisters, writes Saint Theresa, long to resemble the silkworm? She has not seen them personally, she says, although we know her native Ávila in Old Castile was in her day a center of the silk industry. Let me make a comparison, Sisters, she says, between the Mansions we build for ourselves and the silkworm's cocoon. This worm came from a tiny grain that looked dead, as our souls once looked. Then, as soon as the warm spring sun, our Lord, warmed their cold, dead kernels, they became little worms feeding busily upon the leaves of mulberry trees. When they were fully mature, the little worms accepted twigs people offered them and spun their cocoons about them. Think how they labored to make this silk in tightly wound whorls. Was not the silkworm's house one of our Mansions? Let us therefore spin our prayers. . . . Likewise, the soul will emerge from its earthly house . . . a white butterfly.

Therefore build your castles in the air and inside build its many mansions. In *Walden* our Henry David Thoreau must have recalled the *Interior Castle,* for he concluded Theresa's thoughts that castles in the air are where they should be. One has then, principally, to place the foundations underneath them, he added.

Scores of books old and new understand the fame of Saint Theresa as belonging not to her alone but to thousands upon thousands of the earliest converts to Christianity who, theologians claim, were women. Robert Kress (1975) has persuaded us that among the Jews there was no female superiority except during or until the life and teachings of Jesus. Toward this religious leader men and women acted alike so that both actually deserved the same fair dealing, which is not usually true, of course, in most areas of life. Women were present, Kress notes, at the miracle of the loaves and fishes. They shared Christ's mission. Everywhere they recognized Jesus earlier than did men. When men deserted Jesus, the women stayed. The importance of women converts is hailed, he recalls, in Acts (5:14, 6:11, 18:18). A woman named Priscilla, with her husband Aquila, accompanied Paul on his voyage. Women rushed to Jesus' side; John Stuart Mill argued that, being weaker than men, women continually cried for protection by law and therefore would just naturally have rallied to Jesus as an innovative lawgiver. Their pleas of liberty, noted Mill, always have gone unheeded by rulers such as U.S. presidents and senators, who perforce champion power. Thus, to women, law opposes the rule of evil, but only when there is no female Supreme Court justice, and not when the Justice is Jesus himself. Otherwise, there never could have been a Catherine of Siena or a Theresa of Ávila.

Two prominent historians of religion, Renan (1866), who was a Celt born in France, and Adolf Harnack, who was a German theologian, translated by James Moffat of St. Andrews, Scotland, in 1908, very astonishingly wrote massive proofs and accumulated volume after volume, stating in effect that Christianity was at its inception *a woman's religion* spread by women and supported theologically and financially by women.

One's astonishment at such an argument increases in direct proportion to the weight of the first and the length of the second proof. Persons who have thought themselves fairly informed Christians for their lifetimes recoil in disbelief. They all know Christianity as the religion that refuses women in its schools of theology, and that considers them what John Stuart Mill said they were raised to be: drudges to husbands, fathers, brothers, and especially to sons.

Renan sought the reasons for the success of any religion and found them in its social program, such as, for Buddhism, in the abolition of the caste system. By A.D. 36, he noted, Christianity had already established itself as the movement of poor people toward this new cult, which promised to raise them, and which offered to them resources that to them were priceless as well as boundless, notably, assistance and pity. During Christ's lifetime there lived in Judea alone huge numbers of indigent people, and many holy men oppressed by a Roman rule that they abhorred. The strength of community attracted converts, for the early Christians were poor brethren and poor sisters, who pooled their resources. Thus, to such as them, receipts poured in commensurate with need. All each group really needed was first a burning faith in Christ and then a solid ideal to guide them. Gradually the small groups acquired administrators, advisers, leaders, teachers, others who also rose to become their deacons. Theirs was, concluded Renan in his book of 1866 on the Apostles, a political economy based upon religion. The deacons moved up to become evangelists and missionaries. Thus was Christianity created.

Another surprise comes in learning that women were among Christ's original deacons. Those who first filled such posts of great honor were initially widows, women apt to starve in any society. Then later, only virgins were sought to perform, as they had always done in the pagan temples of Diana and Hera, Artemis and Medusa. The first years of the dawning Christian religion demonstrated that it could establish and also maintain a program of public welfare and reciprocal assistance. There both men and women could and did work side by side to relieve human misery. Such was Christ's immediate impact and such was the immediate result of his presence on earth: not war between the sexes, but peace; not hatred of women, but harmony; not fear and mistrust of each other, but respect. One can see today how and why the Holy Grail could not only derive from such days, but remain in the mind as the hope and consequence of Christ's teaching, a natural progression, in fact.

The good works of these first years, said Renan, were the result of Jesus' ministry and of his personal commandments, the consequences of his reasoning and of his love for people of all sorts and all degrees. Women flocked (p. 121ff.) quite naturally to groups that guaranteed security to such underprivileged humans as themselves. Where they came from in their society was often among the lowest of the low, like women deserted today and left with the entire care of minor children. Widows sat begging all over the streets of Judea, sights one sees in all our Western cities today. The great educated men of their day fulminated from their pulpits against allowing education for such human brutes as these women were, and also their undernourished children. Such helpless women, say those men, are considered beneath contempt, no better than receptacles, no better than plagues or scourges. Two types stood then as now for all women: gossiping widows and praying maidens.

It is easy to see how the new religion offered a refuge and a new way of life to both groups, and also a permanent asylum (Acts 6:4). Wealthy women opened their homes to converts (Acts 12:12). A female presbytery was established to shelter abused and homeless women. There alms and donations of all amounts and kinds were gratefully accepted.

Thus, the little sisters of the poor started practicing Christianity. They inaugurated it. They founded its famous institutions: congregations made up of women and self-rule, presbyteries made up of older women who ruled whole foundations, creating a new power in the world that demonstrated the Christian spirit put to the test. Thus, hundreds of lonely, footloose, widowed and unmarried women gathered together under a systematic discipline: congregationalists and presbyterians. There a woman like Mary Magdalene who gave her fortune to the poor and who spent her life ministering to her sisters became a minister and even a deacon. In this eastern climate, wrote Renan (p. 123), where a wife of twenty-four was already withered by exposure to that terrible Mediterranean sun, where for a woman there were no middle years between little girl and wrinkled crone, the new religion created an entirely different, desirable, and respectable career for that half of the human race which at least is always found capable of unselfish devotion to others, even to animals.

It should surprise nobody that priestesses continued as late as 542 to perform sacred rituals at the Castle of the Holy Grail in Britain. There according to the texts written in French and German those priestesses were not rejects from among the poor, but noble ladies, who followed and deferred to their betters, the royal ladies. Saint Theresa of Ávila herself also came from a fine family who placed her properly and safely in a convent of women, the only place where she could have been educated.

Saint Theresa's habit and head coverings as a nun also derived, Renan thought, from the costumes of early women in the first Christian centuries, immediately after the death of Christ. Then even a contemptible widow could wrap herself in a large, black shawl to gain respectability, take up employment in some Christian shelter or orphanage, rise to the rank of deacon, and eventually become equal to the esteemed men about her. Records show that even then, even a childless, middle-aged woman could rise from ignominy and become a holy figure. Thus, even the widow, if she was Christian, became, say early records, equal to the ancient, virginal, pagan priestesses. The early Christians bestowed a title on her: "Beautiful Oldster," and called her "Mother," as Saint Theresa was called centuries later. Thus, Mary Magdalene, after she gave all her fortune to Jesus, rose to become an Apostle teaching his Apostles. Christianity early learned the value of socialism, which is also known as monasticism.

Because of Christ an ordinary woman acquired what she had never before been allowed to possess: a conscience, a religion, a personality, a voice, an opportunity to serve a cause, a personal dignity, and encouragement to resist humiliation and oppression. Thus, in King Arthur's day Queen Radégonde of France escaped to a convent from the barbarities of her cruel Frankish master, the king, and was sanctified.

At one blow Christianity allowed freedom to Radégonde as it

would allow freedom to the young Castilian girl who became Saint Theresa.

The death blow was struck against the ancient idea of family because Christianity considered the soul, even a woman's soul, to be higher than paternal or spousal authority. Thus, Christianity opposed the narrow constitution of the family by quietly demoting its head. Not only was the father demoted, but he was thereafter declared answerable for the murder of his wife and daughters that previously he had been empowered to commit. Henceforth he had to answer to God for such capital crimes. Suddenly the household doors opened to the daughter, to one such as the future Saint Theresa, as to the future Saint Radégonde, and Saint Brigit of Ireland also in the Dark Ages. And to Saint Geneviève of Paris.

Such wives and daughters could be claimed by the Church as members of an elite caste exempt from the ancient necessity to bear and rear children, or live with a spouse, or even maintain a family. Such holy women in large numbers became first of all exempt from menial labor and family duty. Society respected them as freed expressly for higher tasks. They could love God by the hundreds, in their own institutions, and not by ones and twos. All this was innovative only as far as women were concerned. They too followed the examples of the Jews, their scholarly male teachers.

Women were present in the early Church, according to Harnack, whose two volumes were translated at St. Andrews in Scotland (see vol. 2, pp. 64–85). Ministers in Gaul preached in Celtic and by the year 300 were leaving Saint Theresa treatises on spirituality for her to follow in her books. Britain was meanwhile more a military province of the Romans where by the year 200, he says, there may have been a few resident Christians. No sources for Church history survive through A.D. 300. At the Synod of Rimini (A.D. 359) three penniless bishops from Britain appeared among the other four hundred delegates, who found their impecuniousness unbecoming. While the Germanies remained pagan into the 400s, Britain became rapidly Christianized in that century. Saint Patrick preached at the old Grail Castle on the Isle of Man, it is said, in 444.

Harnack agreed completely with Renan (p. 64ff.) that the New Testament documents, in the apostolic and subapostolic ages, women playing crucial roles in early Christianity.

When Galatians (3:28) pronounced men and women equal before God, that liberated all Christian women. The very solidly academic scholar proceeds to list Saint Theresa's predecessors: Priscilla, the minister and patroness Phoebe, the missionary Prisca, the women Saint Paul saluted, Mark's mother Mary who opened her home to daily meetings, the four daughters of Saint Philip, the procurator's Christian wife Gabia, who was a pillar of her Church, the woman to whom John wrote the second epistle, the female ascetics Pliny wrote about, the prophetesses in Corinth, the missionary Thekla who baptized herself, Justin's pupil Charito, Ptolemaeus's Flora, wealthy women or hostesses named Tatiana, Julia, Marcella, Marcellina, and the Roman noblewomen named Domitilla, Juliana, Marcia, Victoria, Lucretia, Secunda, Restituta, and Lucina. Tertullian wrote of them, calling them "most famous women" and "Roman matrons" of the aristocracy, as their names attest.

Stories were told of these "most famous" women like the story Matthew tells (27:19) about Pilate's wife, who warned her husband not to condemn Christ. The number of prominent women who converted to Christianity was, concluded Harnack, "extremely large" (p. 78). The number of women who suffered martyrdom, he added (p. 80), was by comparison "very significant." Girls and women outnumbered men many times over in the early Christian communities. It was truly a woman's religion, one must also conclude.

In the *Bible Review* of April 1990, William E. Phipps offered his opinion on the question of women and Christianity: "A Woman Was the First to Declare Scripture Holy" (p. 14ff.).

Meanwhile Saint Theresa has written what nobody before her wrote, about such a castle as might have suited the Castle of the Holy Grail, a work so profound and so beautiful that the Grail Questers could not have failed to agree. Thus, Saint Theresa closes here the first part of our journey, which has taken us from Jerusalem to Marseilles to Glastonbury and to Renaissance Spain.

We now turn to France and Germany, where resided the masters, the greatest authors specializing in Arthurian literature only and its Holy Grail.

Chapter
V

LANCELOT
IN FRANCE

EMPIRES

The history of France as well as the history of her greatest medieval hero, Lancelot, involves the slow rise and rapid collapse of many empires. Lancelot both rose like a bright star and vanished with hardly a trace from King Arthur's final attempt at an empire of his own. Like a red meteor Lancelot stands characteristically under the flaming July heat of Leo. He was himself thought to be a French lion, wrote the Anglo-Norman authors of his huge biography, a tale of combats and victories that lists the champions he slew. At one count there were over sixty-five heroes whom Lancelot vanquished. Because the French-writing authors worshiped Lancelot as the strongest, the handsomest, the boldest, the gentlest, and the best of all military men they could ever have held up as model, they allotted him several empires also, such as Heaven, Earth, Love, and War. The only one Lancelot failed to storm successfully was the first.

There remain today also three chief ways of considering Lancelot's career in the military. He is almost always seen first as lover of Queen Guinevere, and that adulterous love was graphically de-

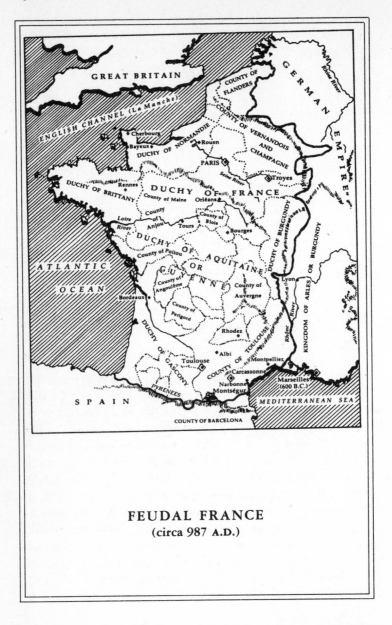

FEUDAL FRANCE
(circa 987 A.D.)

scribed by Chrétien de Troyes, himself often accepted as the greatest of French Arthurian authors. One may just as validly read Chrétien alongside the *Prose Lancelot,* however, which is several hundred pages longer and a more detailed treatment, and conclude that Lancelot was not Queen Guinevere's lover at all, but her *cavalier servant.* His nobility obliged him to serve his sovereign queen during his warrior's career in arms, and to his death. Thus, Lancelot served love in a courtly style where no adultery should have raised its criminal head. The lovers could have been innocent. Defamers also cast by means of the legend other aspersions on Lancelot, charging he betrayed Arthur, which accusation perforce attracted other allegations, such as that he left Britain for France, that he slew Gawain, that he and Guinevere, because they had committed adultery, caused the collapse of Arthur's kingdom, which, being evil, therefore deserved to collapse.

Such charges have also been seen as politically motivated. Willis Cunning, President of the Clan Cunning, in his new history of his clan in Scotland explains that since, in Arthur's case particularly, the victors wrote the history books, they tended to flatter themselves and denigrate Lancelot, Guinevere, and Arthur. Historians of Scotland have said no less: that Lancelot was slain at the port where King Arthur attempted to land after his successful campaign in *"Galles"* (not northern Gaul, which was in Arthur's day called "France," but more probably North *"Wales"*). Lancelot still looms, tarnished or not, as the greatest military man of the Celts in Dark Age Britain, as second only to King Arthur, as General after the wounding of Gawain, and as hero nonpareil.

As far as ladies are concerned, Lancelot slain is no less beloved than when alive. There can be no question at all here but that he is from the ladies' point of view perfection, the ideal of manhood. This is true to such a degree universally, century after century, within country after country, that one's suspicions are aroused. The modern gentlemen and matinee idols—such as the gallant John Wayne from California and the gorgeous Sean Connery from Edinburgh—do not even begin to capture the total appeal of this Lancelot, who was so supremely able, so courteous, and so totally unafraid. The suspicion lingers only to recur in force that the author of the *Prose Lancelot* was itself a woman. That author must have been either a woman or a Cistercian monk.

Lancelot failed only twice. He did not succeed in conquering heaven, which is to say he failed to become heavenly king at the

Grail Castle, and likewise he never became immortal.

Lancelot's life was written by these two principal texts—Chrétien's and the *Prose Lancelot*—and a third time in the *Lanzelet,* a Swiss translation of an English text traded off by King Richard I during the Third Crusade. All three texts hail from the twelfth century where love as an endearing way of life, and as the literary stylization called "courtly love," derive from the leading intellectual of the age, Saint Bernard of Clairvaux. Since Bernard was the second founder of the White Monks, or Cistercian Order, it is obvious that Geoffrey of Monmouth also revered Lancelot as hero and king characterized not only by his royal blood, but also by his holy blood. Lancelot and Perceval, the chief Arthurian heroes of France and Germany, respectively, undertook the Quest of the Holy Grail. Both men devoted their lives to the love of their ladies, the Queens Guinevere and Blanchefleur. Lancelot became the father of holy Galahad. Perceval fathered Lohengrin, the Swan Knight. Geoffrey of Monmouth in his pioneer *History,* which he wrote in Latin, refers to Lancelot by his Latin name: *Anguselus,* which translates as "Lancelot" in Old French, and as "the Angus" (Clan Chief) in English. This removes Lancelot from the Black Monks, or Benedictines, in Glastonbury and southern England.

The story of Lancelot, as even the etymology of his name attests, derived not from France in the Dark Ages, however. It unfolded in Britain and in the history of Britain. Lancelot under King Arthur fought invading Saxons, there also termed "Saracens," or heathen folk. His story was written both in Old French and in Scottish. One of the greatest historians of ancient France, François Guizot (Paris, 1872), marveled that it should be so.

Why, asked Guizot, were the barbarian invasions chronicled only in Britain? What hero opposed them on French soil? He replied: *only the Celts resisted the barbarian invaders inside Britain.* The Gauls in what soon became France offered no resistance, and neither did the Italians nor the Spaniards. They therefore left no story worth telling either, but continually mocked the British Celts for having done so, and for having complained to Rome: "Come back and defend us." Why so? Because in France, Spain, and Italy the resident Celts had already become Roman; or the middle classes had been, as Guizot put it (essay 1), "swallowed up" by the Romans. The middle classes there accepted their new barbarian conquerors and taught them both Latin and Christianity.

The Franks appeared on the frontiers of eastern Gaul around the year 200, and they were superior to the Romanized peoples chiefly because they were "free men," says Guizot (essay 2), superior because they were alive, energetic, athletic, and active. By King Arthur's day their King Clovis had renamed the country "France." He was, adds the French historian caustically, just "another scourge who founded a nation." The Franks over a period of two hundred years entered the country freely, conquered, pillaged, divided the spoils, returned home, and did it all over again the next summer. Their kings were: Clovis I (511), Clotaire I (561), Clotaire II (628), Dagobert I (638), Clovis II (656). Two realms survived all this turmoil: Neustria of the Romanized Franks and Austrasia of the eastern, or German, Franks.

The center of power gradually moved east after the Carolingians conquered the Friesians, Thuringians, Bavarians, Danes, and Saxons adjoining their realm. Charlemagne himself with his nephew Roland halted later barbarian invasions. The last Norse comers into Normandie easily operated their conquest of the Saxons in England (1066). Lancelot and Arthur had been dead for five hundred years by that time. They still remain famous even among the Franks today, who still admire resistance successfully performed.

Whereas medieval writers scoffingly portrayed Alexander the Great as a loutish sort of crude baboon, they fell down in absolute and total admiration before Lancelot. His every move charmed them to tears. And they wept when he failed the second test at the Grail Castle and turned away, himself in tears.

King Clovis rose to prominence in 481–86, wrote the Swiss historian (not of France but "of the French") Simonde de Sismondi in 1837. King Clovis was only twenty in the fifth year of his reign. Thus, this contemporary of King Arthur took command, as did Arthur also, at age fifteen. When he was twenty years of age, Clovis wedded Clotilde at Tournai, and the queen was already Christian. In Italy Theodoric of the Ostrogoths was, as of 493, also another renowned leader in Arthur's century. When King Clovis was converted to Christianity by Saint Rémi of Reims, on Christmas day in 496, he was hailed, like Arthur, as a new Constantine the Great. King Arthur, after his coronation at Carlisle, declared himself a direct descendant of a Constantine. Between 497 and 500 Clovis, who is Arthur's *alter ego,* had established the Frankish monarchy. By the time of Lancelot's death, probably in 542, King Arthur had halted the Saxon invasion of Scotland, for which reason the kindly English historian John Morris termed Arthur "the last Roman Emperor" in the Western world. Theodoric was another such.

By the year 500 Clovis's neighbors were Alaric and his Visigoths in their new capital of Toulouse, King Trasamond and the Vandals in Africa, the Burgundians on the Rhône River, and the Germans on the Rhine. But Clovis was like King Arthur not so much a king of a country as a king of men. He successfully defeated the Burgundians who had governed Burgundy, Switzerland, Dauphiné, and Provence. He had his heirs marry the Visigoths, gave them his word in a peace treaty, and then fiercely attacked them in force and drove them all the way south to their fortress at Carcassonne. He took from them Auvergne and Angoulême plus the city-states of Toulouse, Bordeaux, Rodez, and Albi.

The Frankish church assisted Clovis because he consistently conquered southern realms that were and that remained for centuries centers of what the Church recognized as heresy. The Church writers assured the world, as they borrowed Arthurian terms from Celtic heroes like Arthur, Gawain, and Lancelot, that heaven helped the Franks as the Holy Grail had helped the British Celts. At the crowning of Clovis, Perceval's dove flew down to bring him holy ointment. Queen Guinevere's white deer also came from God to show Clovis the ford across the Vienne River, and Clovis crossed it and was victorious. Merlin's column of fire led Clovis to the capture of Poitiers. In the year of the Council of Orléans (511) Clovis, who was then forty-five years old, died in Paris and was interred in the church of Queen Guinevere's contemporary, Saint Geneviève of Paris. Twenty years after King Arthur's fatal wounding at Camlan, King Clotaire I found himself king of almost all of Roman Gaul. Like his predecessors he ruled for two short years as a military leader of a dedicated, rapacious, and mobile army, and by virtue of a string of equally atrocious murders of friends, sons, and foes.

Contrary to the biographies of Lancelot written in Old French in the twelfth century, neither Arthur nor Lancelot entered Frankish territory, much less conquered it. Neither one borrowed from the Continental churches. None of the dozen or so Frankish chroniclers mentions either Arthur or Lancelot. But the Frankish foundations borrowed from the Celts their worship of the Holy Grail. In order to see proof of that debt to Britain, we must study the greatest of the Benedictine abbeys on the coast of Normandie. That Norman foundation, named Holy Trinity, in 1066 paralleled Glastonbury

Abbey. Both were in their heyday the glory of the Christian West. Even before the Abbot of Glastonbury, if it was he who removed to Normandie, the French establishment had tacitly patterned its characteristic and especially beautiful ceremony upon the similarly unavowed Glastonbury reverence for the Holy Grail.

The *Perlesvaus* text attests to that reverence at Glastonbury, and explains the importance of the Grail there at Cluniac Glastonbury. Both establishments were totally destroyed, but some of the Norman abbey's archives remain.

It is of utmost importance now that these French archives be scanned for traces of the Grail. Was this object transferred across the Straits of Dover to France? Or was it only the influence of such missionaries who founded Glastonbury after they passed the Straits in one night?

The questions are even more complicated than they initially appear because both King David I of Scotland (reigned 1124-53) and King Alexander I of Scotland (reigned 1107-27) filled their new monastic houses with Anglo-Norman monks from the Continent. Both kings of Scotland thus resisted any takeover by the English Archbishop of York. The famous abbeys in Scotland, and especially Melrose, where the ancient records of King Arthur were supposedly housed, but also Holyrood in Edinburgh which is and was quite likely an Arthur's Seat, shared their annals and documents and records with the Continental establishments that were all, of course, closer to Rome. France has always claimed preeminence in clerical matters—that it, and not Italy or Spain, sits on the right side of the Holy Father.

This closeness between the kings of Scotland and the allied French clerics on the Continent, both countries in league against England, and both commanding scores of learned Cistercian writers, explains why Arthurian texts suddenly burst upon a world (c. 1136) that never realized before King Arthur and Lancelot had once lived and saved Scotland from Anglo-Saxon invasions and conquest. It also explains how the Normans after 1066 quietly entered Scotland to acquire vast estates peaceably—by marrying native heiresses.

A great historian of Scotland, Robert L. G. Ritchie of Oxford in 1952, demonstrated that Chrétien de Troyes was actually describing Scotland in his *Lancelot,* and not describing this apparently French hero, whose name appeared to be French in any case, as winning his victories in a France that had never heard of him. And certainly he was not describing him as having won any wars against the conquering Frankish warlords. Ritchie said we would have to look for Lancelot in Scotland, and it has already commenced.

We now doubly understand the Cistercian Geoffrey of Monmouth who in 1136 astounded the learned by placing King Arthur at Dumbarton, near Glasgow, and at adjacent Loch Lomond also. Now Geoffrey of Monmouth in Wales and his friend Caradoc of Llancarvan (Llancarfan) had both heard of Arthur presumably, and from the *Annals of Wales,* the oldest copy of which dates from the days of the Norman Conquest (c. 1100). These annals *(Annales Cambriae)* contain records of independent Wales, however, from the year 445; they therefore include the lifetimes of both Arthur and Lancelot. They provide invaluable, because written, evidence of the industry and concentration upon history by White Friars such as Geoffrey and Caradoc, both of whom came from or may have lived in the most famous Cistercian houses of Wales: Tintern Abbey (founded in 1131), Strata Florida (1164), and the mother house of Whitland (after 1140). It is the *Annals of Wales* that give us the death date of King Arthur, as of the year 542.

Holy Trinity Abbey and Church stood in Fécamp, Normandie, from their building and founding around the year 658 until their destruction by a mob during the French Revolution, 1789. Usually called Fécamp, the Benedictine abbey was constructed on the site of an ancient, Roman city facing England from the white chalk cliffs north of the Seine River estuary. The French liqueur called Benedictine originated there.

The name Fécamp is a shortened, French form for the abbey's name Fig Tree Field, *Fici Campus.* One story attributes the name to the Gospel of Luke where Jesus tells the parable of the barren fig tree that the Master wanted to cut down (Luke 13:6–9). The gardener begged for another year's grace; there is, in other words, a final chance before the sentence of uselessness becomes irrevocable. Or, as Luke makes clear again (Luke 13:18, 19), the tree is a cherished symbol of empire where nations and peoples seek and find refuge; it must be spared. Or Jesus reads a lesson in history (Luke 21:25–37) that just as one sees in the fig tree the coming of the fall harvest, so similar indications point certainly to the approaching Kingdom of God. . . . The monks at Fécamp will connect the fig tree to the Holy Grail and to a King Arthur alive in Scotland not much more than a hundred years earlier than themselves.

The Norman scholar Leroux de Lincy published at Rouen, Normandie, in 1840 a treatise from the surviving records of this great French abbey and church. He discovered that it had been dedicated under King Clotaire III around the year 664, and ruled by three hundred nuns and an Abbess named Childemarca until 841 when it was destroyed by the Norsemen. Its second founding was undertaken by Richard I, third Duke of Normandie, because his birthplace was Fécamp, and dedicated by him in 990. Two Norman Dukes, Richard I and II, were interred at Holy Trinity.

The first Abbot arrived from his native Lombardy in Italy in the year 1000 or 1001. His pregnant mother Perinza had dreamed of her son's eminence. In the twelfth century a Cluniac Abbot named Henri de Sully (d. 1187) took up the rule for forty-nine years. He was angered, it is said, because he had failed to receive a similar appointment at the Benedictine house in Salisbury, England. But perhaps he has been confused with the Abbot of similar name who exhumed Arthur and Guinevere in Glastonbury. The new French Abbot, however, was also reportedly a relative of the Angevin King Henry II, thus a member of the Angevin royal family. He hastened at Fécamp to exhume and reinter the two Norman dukes and hastily to bring in to Fécamp many precious relics that could be widely venerated. He intended to attract hundreds of reverent tourists.

It was he who discovered what became Fécamp's most prized possession: the Precious Blood of Christ as usually contained in the Holy Grail. Immediately many miraculous happenings took place at Fécamp. For instance, after total darkness had enveloped the abbey, suddenly brilliant lights flashed through it and lighted it completely. At other times, choirs of heavenly angels burst into song from an empty choir loft. Then at odd times the sacred relics changed places. Sometimes a huge cross descended over the high altar. Tourists rushed to see such sights.

One date mentioned attests to the antiquity of the Grail legend at Fécamp: Bishop Baldric from Dol de Bretagne saw the Precious Blood at Fécamp Abbey in the year 1120. Its presence as thus established, argued Leroux de Lincy, must have predated 1120 by a rather long time.

Leroux de Lincy also traced the Grail from medieval works like *The Golden Legend* to medieval writers who had their information from a British hermit of the eighth century. He called the Grail a large, silver, shallow bowl, or platter, or tray. The monk Helinand also referred to this early text retranslated in the *King Arthur* Appendix (pp. 356–57). Leroux de Lincy concluded (p. 104) that a Latin Grail text certainly existed well before the twelfth century, perhaps written from the biblical accounts of Joseph of Arimathea and Nicodemus. This hypothetical British monk or hermit would already have known that King Arthur, Merlin, Morgan le Fay, Perceval, and Lancelot claimed descent from Joseph of Arimathea and his missionary son. Joseph had journeyed to Sarras, thence to Corbenic, the Palace Perilous, and to the Castle of the Holy Grail.

The Fécamp variant was not called the Holy Grail, however, but the Precious Blood. Leroux de Lincy (in his chapter 5) decided that the latter derived directly from earlier British versions of the Round Table and was the Fécamp monks' Holy Grail. Those Arthurian memories were so strong and so universally beloved in Brittany and Normandie both that some sort of extension to them was created at Fécamp. The Fécamp monks wished not to be completely outdone by the likes of those at Melrose, Holyrood, and Glastonbury. The Fécamp tradition secretly borrowed the British material, and was most probably entirely indebted to it, said the French scholar. The Fécamp monks never admitted it, however. The line of descent commenced with the Book of John, he agreed, and passed to the apocryphal Nicodemus, then to the Arthurian corpus, to emerge subsequently onto the Fig Tree Field at Fécamp, the founding of that Holy Trinity Abbey, and triumphantly into the Precious Blood contained in the earlier British Holy Grail.

The monks at Fécamp did not admit the borrowing, or the term "Grail," even though it is pretty obvious. They posited a tradition of their own which dated back to even before the first years of the sixth century, they said. Then a respected nobleman named Anségise, they said, ruled the area of Caux in Normandie, which he endeavored to protect from barbarian invasions. Anségise was, in other words, a minor, Continental King Arthur, and like him, a Christian. Early one morning Anségise summoned his escort and set out to hunt in the very valley where Holy Trinity Abbey would one day proudly stand. The party rode hard in pursuit of (Guinevere's) lovely, pure white deer. The faster they drove on horses and hounds, the farther away they drew from the lordly deer. They finally caught up, however, and encircled the beautiful creature at the very spot where the Abbey "stands today." The creature halted before a tree trunk that had sprouted several branches. First the deer ran in a circle about the trunk. Then it raised its head and stared at the company. Then calmly it again walked about the tree trunk.

Duke Anségise dismounted and signaled his party to follow suit. All awaited his (Arthurian) explanation. They knew it was a prodigy. At that moment the white deer ran quickly in a circle about the tree trunk. Duke Anségise understood that God had spoken to him, instructing him to erect on that very spot a wonderful church to the glory of God. The Duke had the branches cut from the trunk. Laying them on the ground he formed the lines of the foundations of his basilica. After this was done, he noticed that the horses and hounds had awakened from their strange sleep. In this way were the foundation stones of Fécamp Abbey laid out. The poor Duke died before he could proceed further in his project (Leroux's chapter 1).

Decades passed. Huge trees covered the valley. The lines of the temple were hidden under the forest. During all this time God found no man worthy of undertaking such a massive building project. Finally, however, during the reign of King Lothaire III, around the year 662, the king's secretary Waninge inherited the lands of Caux in Neustria, including the forest. The new administrator loved to ride through this beautiful forest. He enjoyed hunting as much as he loved solitude under the huge trees, and lying in their shade. He had no idea that he had already been chosen for a tremendous undertaking. Had he known, he would certainly have cleared the forest of dangerous animals and the underbrush from beneath the taller trees (Leroux's chapter 2). The conclusion follows:

When Waninge fell gravely ill, he saw before his eyes Judgment Day and heard the doom pronounced upon him for not having understood that the forest covered the site of Holy Trinity Abbey!

In the same way, King David of Scotland had followed the White Stag to the foot of Arthur's Seat, the volcano in the city of Edinburgh. There he too learned that he should build the Abbey Church of Holyrood because King Arthur had received a piece of the Holy Rood that he had centuries earlier donated to Melrose Abbey on the Tweed River. Thanks to King David the True Cross came to take its place of honor at its own church, Holy Rood. Ancient Welsh authors in the *Mabinogion,* a collection of Druidical tales, told how Queen Guinevere also took part in an earlier, successful Hunt of the White Stag.

Waninge's defense was pleaded by Saint Eulalia, whose hymn of praise is the oldest poem in the Romance language of French. It commences: "Eulalia was a good maiden. Hers was a lovely body, an even more beautiful soul" (Buona pulcella fut Eulalia, / bel auret corps, bellezour anima [v. 1]). This reference places Waninge's illness and dream around the year 881, when the poem was composed, and not at the year 304, when at age twelve little Eulalia suffered martyrdom for her Christian faith.

Holy Trinity Abbey was finally ordered constructed by Waninge after his recovery. He was also able to call from distant Burgundy the famous Abbess Childemarca, who would bring to Fécamp three hundred holy nuns. The abbey was built on the very lines traced by the white deer as it trod its perimeters around the tree trunk.

Soon after the nuns' arrival a marked improvement in manners was observed throughout the whole area. The nuns brought in famous confessors, who were also an example to people, from northern Normandie above the Seine River. They were able to shelter the wounded and not only protected but also healed the terribly tortured Saint Léger. A bishop ruled formerly at the palace of King Thierry I; that prelate had been deposed, blinded, and his nose and tongue had been cut from his face. The nuns disapproved. Queen Guinevere also had once been doomed to a similar disfigurement but was rescued by Lancelot. The resident nuns at Fécamp heard of Saint Léger's return to health and repeated what Childemarca decreed: that no human person should fail to worship where God had by divine revelation instructed him to do so.

The Precious Blood arrived at Fécamp in this way, said the monks there, who apparently enjoyed refuting the Glastonbury version. When Joseph of Arimathea took down from the cross the lifeless body of Christ, he noticed a great deal of blood that had coagulated around five wounds. So Joseph took his knife and scraped off the blood into his metal gauntlet. As soon as he arrived home, he put this sacred relic into a precious coffer. When Joseph felt his own death draw near, he entrusted the coffer and relic to his nephew Isaac. Isaac prospered greatly after this relic came into his safekeeping. But Isaac also incurred the suspicion of his own stupid wife and of others who denounced him to the court. He barely escaped a sentence.

Realizing how vulnerable he had become, Isaac secretly left Jerusalem and took up residence by the sea in the city of Sidon. He might have lived quietly there except that he was warned in a dream of imminent danger that would destroy or kill all life thereabouts. He dreamed that the Roman Emperor Vespasian would "pacify" Judea, and that his son Titus would in the year 70 entirely ruin Jerusalem. Isaac realized the next day the enormity of his problem.

Searching for a solution he came upon a fig tree of about the right size. He suddenly realized that he could excavate the trunk and hide the Precious Blood inside it. But would the humidity not damage it? He returned home and found a lead *pipe,* which he cleaned and prepared as a safe repository. In another of the same size he hid *Joseph's knife,* which still bore traces of congealed *blood* upon it. And he still had the iron tip from *the lance* that had pierced Christ's side. He cautiously worked all these hallowed objects inside the hollowed trunk of the fig tree. No sooner had he completed the task than the bark drew together and closed up the cut he had made in it. . . . Here appear, unadmitted by the narrator, four hallows of British Grail reverence: platter, blood, knife, and lance.

In a second dream Isaac learned that the kingdom of Judea was about to be destroyed. Immediately the next day Isaac cut down the fig tree. He lopped off its largest branches and tore off most of its leaves. He watched over the trunk and the few twigs left on it, but worried all the same because a higher-than-usual tide occasionally lapped around its roots. He could see that sooner or later the sea would not only uproot it but carry it quite away. Therefore he finally decided that this must happen because apparently it was God's will. He therefore cut down the trunk, and separated it from its roots. Then he himself cast it into the sea. It disappeared almost immediately from his sight.

Some time later an old man journeyed to Sidon from Gaul for the express purpose of giving a message to Isaac. The trunk of the fig tree, he said, had been carried by the sea all the way to the coast of northern Gaul. There finally it received from the Normans its due, which was every honor that could be bestowed upon it.

It was the Jew Isaac himself, we now learn, who became the original author of this Norman-French history called *The Precious Blood.* He first told his history to his wife and then to all the Jews. They in turn spread the history of the Fig Tree Field in Gaul to everybody else who desired to learn it. The fig tree had come to rest along the water's edge. When the ocean withdrew from what became the valley of Fécamp, it partially uncovered the trunk, and left it sanded in. Years later it was found in the valley which it named.

Actually, it was Saint Denis from his future Montmartre, said the author, correcting himself, who sent a Roman evangelist to discover the miraculous fig tree there. The Roman bravely overthrew the pagan idols and called the place the Fig Tree Field, which is Fécamp in French, and *Fici Campus* in Latin.

The Precious Blood was kept sealed in a crystal vial, and preserved inside the sanctuary of Holy Trinity Abbey. Even so, once during the Crusades an unscrupulous fellow there stole a drop of the Blood, which was a great crime against God, because he had permitted the abbey to preserve it. This was in the year 1200, says a *Poem* found by Leroux about the Blood. Not only did the robber steal a part of this most holy relic. He also robbed the abbey of another relic, a bone from the forearm of Saint Mary Magdalene.

The monks were aghast. They had expected their new recruits to be angels, not larceners. The robber was planning to go overseas with a few noblemen of the area who had taken the Cross. In order to reach the Holy Land, they had to go *outremer,* across the sea. It was to have been a holy voyage.

The sea voyage almost killed them all. The sea rose thunderously high. The wind hurled their ship repeatedly into the trough of the waves. They all almost died. In this extremity the thief finally broke. He confessed it was due to him. He admitted his guilt, for which all agreed he deserved death.

Almost at once the wind died down, and the waves grew calm. This is how the Precious Blood saved all from peril of the sea: "del peril de la mer."

After their pleasant trip back to France they returned the stolen Blood. That was publicly performed during the course of a grand procession through the streets to Holy Trinity Abbey. It was a true jubilee celebration. The knight recited his *Poem* about their voyage, the robber's confession, and the power of the Blood.

The Precious Blood was then placed in its crystal vial under the altar. After the arrival of the Abbot Henri de Sully, or around the year 1171, it was suspended on a silver chain.

The bone of Saint Mary Magdalene was also ceremoniously returned to its reliquary. Two relics from the body of Saint Geneviève were displayed beside it over the centuries at Fécamp Abbey.

They also preserved there the bones of Saint Frotmont, the son of King Offa of Mercia. The bones of Saint Vuilfrede, Bishop of York, reposed there too. Fécamp in addition treasured *two relics of John the Baptist,* and one of the Prophet Daniel. They showed relics of the Apostles Philip of Gaul, John, and Andrew, and of Paul, Stephen, and James. Among their prized relics were body parts of Saint George, Saint Martin of Tours, and Saint Ambrose of Milan (for whom Merlin may have been named Ambrosius). They also treasured a relic of an otherwise unknown holy man named Blaise, who is widely reported in the *Merlin* manuscripts to have been the confessor of Merlin's mother named Nonne (nun); and he was Merlin's teacher also.

Among these relics are four objects vaguely resembling those described in Arthurian texts as the Grail or as being a part of the Grail ceremony: a chalice of silver gilded with gold, a flat tray or platter, a lamp, and the Book of Jesus Christ. These particular objects do fit among the usual hallows present during a ceremony involving the Holy Grail. They fit so well, in fact, that the English scholar Jessie Weston in her *Quest of the Holy Grail* (London, 1913) became convinced finally that Fécamp was the original home of the Grail, and that worship of the Grail originated there, and not among the Celts of Great Britain. Fécamp, however, seems never to have made such a claim.

Her conclusion might now be accepted except for two reasons: (1) worship of the Grail in Great Britain antedated the founding of Fécamp Abbey, and (2) there has been no mention of the "Holy Grail," or even of the word "Grail" in any of the documents, lists of relics, or in the *Poem* about the Precious Blood, which Weston mistakenly calls Holy Blood *("Saint Sang").* Weston listed in her book (app., pp. 148–54) the passages in principal texts that identify an object, or a set of objects, as the Grail or as a hallow belonging to a ceremony at the British Grail Castle specifically.

She considered two authors to be the greatest masters: Chrétien in France and Wolfram in Germany. Both faltered, however, at the word for what they thought was the Grail. Chrétien sees the word *tailloir (tailleor)* as a bowl or preferably a platter upon which meat is cut at table. Wolfram goes to the heart of the problem because the verb or root *tailler* means to cut. Therefore, he concluded logically also: *tailloir (tailleor)* is a knife, and not the platter that requires a knife, for the cutting of meat.

Weston draws a conclusion here: we need a knife. Where but at Fécamp do they speak of the knife that Nicodemus used to scrape off congealed Precious Blood? Therefore, she continues, the Holy Grail originated in Holy Trinity Abbey at Fécamp where two knives appeared during the worship service! But Wolfram never speaks of any Precious Blood, nor of Fécamp. Nor does Chrétien.

Weston turns next to the Glastonbury or *Perlesvaus* text which puts Gawain present at a Grail Ceremony. There he sees five hallows: (1) the Holy Grail carried aloft by a damsel, (2) a chalice, (3) red blood, and (4) two golden candlesticks with candles. The next text examined by Weston is the German *Crown (Diu Crône)* where two maidens bear two candlesticks, two young men bear a spear, two maidens carry a "salver" (her Spanish word makes no sense here because today a salver carries a foretaste, or hors d'oeuvre at a banquet, or visiting cards). The more correct word was golden "bowl" set with precious gems. Finally the Grail Bearer herself walked in procession, carrying a red-gold lattice-worked base upon which stood a jeweled piece made of gold worked with gems, the whole base and crown of the work forming a reliquary such as one would see on an altar.

In the *Prose Lancelot* Gawain also attends a Grail ceremony that commences when a white dove carrying a gold censer flies into the hall through an open window. Thereafter Gawain sees only the Grail Bearer, whose beauty must have overcome him. All he recalled seeing otherwise was the vessel she carried. On second thought, that was a chalice, rich beyond belief. In the *Perceval* Gawain sees his famous silver platter *(tailleor),* two candlesticks, and the Grail Bearer again. She was weeping as she passed by carrying: "one Grail totally uncovered." Last of all came a sword, which lay broken in half. Again the *Prose Lancelot* proves the better narrative. Jessie Weston cannot imagine why these phenomena occur together: (1) a weeping maiden, (2) a silver platter, (3) a broken sword, and (4) the presence of Gawain. We must therefore look at the Grail experiences of Lancelot and Gawain separately, and in detail. And yet, do not these associations already stir a memory? Does not the maiden weep because a great crime was once committed against a beloved, holy man? Was not the criminal a young woman? Was she not royal? Did she not use a sword and then a silver platter?

In an attempt to settle the question of precedence, a British Grail versus a Grail at Fécamp, let us first recall that Holy Trinity Abbey in Normandie was always an orthodox establishment, certainly so from the year 1000 or 1001 when its first Abbot arrived from Italy to take charge of that house. Therefore we should not expect subsequently, or in any narrative concerning the Crusades, to find a mention of a Holy Grail, much less any ceremony involving it. The orthodoxy from France, in particular Saint Germanus of Auxerre (c. 378–448) and Saint Lupus of Troyes (c. 383–478), were twice dispatched to Britain by the Church alarmed by peculiar, unorthodox services being performed there. Saint Patrick was one of the suspects, he says in his own writings, and he reportedly preached on the Isle of Man, one possible site of King Arthur's Grail Castle, in the year 444. Much more alarming, and actually excommunicated by the Church, vanquished in debate by no less a Father of the Church than Saint Augustine (354–430), was the notoriously learned Irish theologian Pelagius (fl. c. 410–31). The Irish and Merlin too were theologically suspect in Arthur's day.

When the Franks accepted Latin as their native language, and discarded their native German so completely that very few German words (except *guerre* = war) remain in the French language, and when they accepted Christianity with equal nonchalance, there would have been no reason for them to borrow a Grail ceremony from the British Celts overseas. Furthermore, even as Christians, the Franks remained mobile warrior bands for centuries as they collected territories by war, assault, treachery, mass murder, and torture.

The French clergy at Fécamp could accept and rewrite the stories from the New Testament so that their congregations could grasp them and understand their religion. They would eventually be enjoined to discard Nicodemus and the Apocrypha altogether. Understandably, they adored the relics of their own saints like Philip of Gaul, Denis of Montmartre where he was martyred, Mary Magdalene, and the wonderfully courageous Saint Geneviève of Paris who saved the people and Paris also from the Huns.

Aside from the overwhelmed Pelagius, who threatened to disgrace clergymen in Rome far less learned and intelligent than him, no British clergyman ever seems to have worsted early French theologians. The French, as well understood in Britain, sat on the right-hand side of the Pope in Rome. Therefore again, Holy Trinity was orthodox only.

Furthermore there is no mention in the surviving archives of the destroyed Fécamp Abbey of any one of the Arthurian Grail heroes who had all died a century or so before the first mention of Fécamp as a holy site. If anyone should have figured in their legends, that hero was Lancelot. Very early in our own century, of course, Jessie Weston had argued at great length in her biography of Lancelot that he was only a fictional hero. He was invented out of the fertile imagination of that Chrétien de Troyes, who was, almost everybody says, the greatest creative genius of the French Middle Ages. Lancelot appeared only and first, full blown from Chrétien's brain. Why was he not at Fécamp, then? Or why was he not included in one of their equally fictitious narratives? Why not? He could just as well have been the person who by one blow from his sword cut that famous fig tree stump into its four pieces and hauled them in one powerful and ready hand into the abbey.

The answer is that Weston was once more mistaken. Lancelot was, first of all, not French, and not a Frank either. He did not serve under Clovis. He served under King Arthur. He was personally ordered and raised to attach himself to Queen Guinevere, and ordered to die for her, if the need arose. He did not journey to Gaul; and there Geoffrey of Monmouth is responsible for the error, or for yielding to pressure and so saying. Lancelot journeyed to "Gallia," or *ad Galliam*, which meant he went into North Wales with Arthur and not into Frankish-held and Frankish-ruled territories on the continent of Europe. No chronicler of the Franks, and there are half a dozen whose histories survive, ever mentioned a Lancelot or an Arthur. But one of them knew of Beowulf. They were all learned and laborious. And in addition Lancelot was not fictional only. While his adventures are related as embroidered and enhanced by most talented authors, especially by those who composed the *Prose Lancelot,* he was historical. He was born and he lived most of his life in Scotland: The Angus, Clan Chief.

The great French ecclesiastics of the Middle Ages had no dealings at all with the Holy Grail. It is only modern French theologians like Etienne Gilson who accept the Grail as holy and Christian. Even if Merlin was the Archbishop Dubricius and interred in Llandaf Cathedral, Wales, he still remains excommunicated, and the same is true for Morgan de Fay, whose very name it was forbidden any Catholic to mention.

The great theologian of France in the Middle Ages was Saint

Bernard of Clairvaux (1090–1153), whom Etienne Gilson at the Collège de France and University of Wales so much admires. Bernard was a contemporary of the first, Italian Abbot of Holy Trinity, Fécamp. Saint Theresa of Ávila probably took her symbolism, the bee as the Holy Ghost, from Saint Bernard. The ideas of Bernard were easily borrowed, said Gilson in his book on Bernard's mystical theology (1947): God is love; love is God.

Lancelot would have loved the doctrines of Saint Bernard, for both underwent mystical, religious experiences, and both devoted their lives to serving a holy cause. Gilson argues also that the school of courtly love in its purer forms may have derived from the writings and preaching of St Bernard.

Virtue, said the beloved Saint, gives birth to friendship and to love. Friendship itself is only reciprocal, never one-sided. The only true love is Lancelot's love of God. That love has no limit.

Christ bestows the divine kiss upon mankind because man also is involved in perfection and in the empire of heaven . . .

The last of the great, historical Grail Bearers will be named Esclarmonde: Light of the World. She and the ancient Scot Lancelot will share that trait in common, both being perfect. Esclarmonde was a "Perfect" in her Catharist church or cult. Lancelot was the perfect knight who aspired to heavenly perfection. Having failed in his Quest of the Holy Grail, which is to say, having been deemed unworthy, Lancelot sadly died in battle.

The Cistercians like Geoffrey of Monmouth who knew Lancelot as Anguselus, and Saint Bernard who preached the Third Crusade, led the humble lives of ascetics. And, added Etienne Gilson (p. 82), they gave up everything except the art of beautiful writing.

This first approach to the problem of Lancelot has led us to France which claims him anyway, and to the French version replacing British worship of their Holy Grail: the Precious Blood of Christ. In examining the records of Holy Trinity Abbey at Fécamp, France, we have again turned to the Grail texts to list Grail hallows. In other words, we begin to see that the Holy Grail was never one object alone but a group of sacred objects:

1. platter, blood, knife, lance (see page 141);
2. gold-gilded silver chalice, platter, lamp, Book of Jesus Christ (see page 143);
3. hallows seen by Gawain (see page 144).

and we have discovered errors in Grail terminology (see page 143).

LANCELOT'S QUEST

Serious attention to Arthurian literature began inside France around the time of the Revolution of 1830, perhaps because the subject of monarchy versus democracy commanded attention. The series of revolutions inside France during the course of the nineteenth century aroused keen interest in Brittany also, with its preponderantly Celtic population speaking Celtic, thus able easily to contact other Celts across the Channel in Cornwall where men also earned their living in the navy and at sea. Two Breton noblemen, Villemarqué and Jubainville, followed their great Celtic predecessors, Chateaubriand and Victor Hugo, to study this past, benevolent monarchy of King Arthur. Thus, these Bretons turned back to Arthur, as did Jessie Weston inside Britain, for solutions to the perplexing problem of how to be liberated and yet be governed. It fascinates us today, as we labor under the same problems, to observe the political implications of Arthurian studies, as they aroused interest in France, then in the United States, and immediately thereafter in Scotland. Perhaps ten examples of scholars will suffice to demonstrate what certainly became a widespread phenomenon: Villemarqué (c. 1840), Jubainville (c. 1884), Weston (1901), Lady Augusta Gregory (1902), Rolleston (1911), Dumézil (1929), Graves (1948), Macalister (1949), Loomis in New York City (1956), and D. D. R. Owen in Scotland (1962).

Each scholar studied the mythology buried deep inside Arthurian texts; and his conclusion, certainly those of Jubainville, Weston, Gregory, Macalister, and Loomis, originated and/or ended in Ireland. During Arthur's lifetime too, Ireland, notably for its renowned, ancient religious leaders, Pelagius, Saint Patrick, and Saint Brigit, was at the epicenter of a death-dealing, religious controversy: Rome versus the Irish. That controversy resulted in the disgrace and death of their theologian Pelagius, whose intellect the twentieth century can still admire. We now see clearly, for the first time in this book, that one death will multiply into the massacres of innocent millions.

Our mythologists unite, then, in tracing Lancelot to and from Ireland, as well as to and from Celtic Brittany in France. They were, of course, greatly assisted by linguistic affinity, and most especially

by place-names. We have already noticed that place-names entrap
us all in mystery and ambiguity:

LATIN	FRENCH	ENGLISH
GALLIA	GALLES	GAUL
GALLIA	GALLES	WALES
GALLIA	GALLES	FRANCE
BRITANNIA	BRETAGNE	BRITAIN
ARMORICA	BRETAGNE	BRITTANY
DUMNONIA	CORNUAILLES	CORNWALL
DUMNONIA	BRETAGNE	BRITTANY
DUMNONIA	GALVOIE	GALLOWAY (SCOTLAND)

When Villemarqué launched Arthurian studies, at least on the
continent of Europe, by laboriously making dictionaries and grammar books, and then translating texts into French from Breton and
Welsh, also by publishing in prestigious scholarly journals in Paris,
he opened the eyes of the world and made himself another
Pelagius, a new center of a bitter, scholarly controversy. It ended
in the usual way for great intellectuals who are scholars, in his
disgrace and death, of course. But his contribution must have been
worth the price to him. As a student of both Celtic and Romance
languages, he drew the world's attention to that period otherwise
almost lost to history when Latin as spoken in Gaul was becoming
Old French.

There occurred then a peculiar reduction, Villemarqué noted, in
that consonantal group that falls in the middle of Latin words, such
as: *vigilare, regina, regula, margula, nigrum, legere.* The loss of the
middle syllable gave in French: *veiller* (to watch), *reine* (queen),
règle (rule), *marge* (margin), *noir* (black), and *lire* (to read). This
observation, reinforced by professional linguists, has since given us,
by the regular omission of the middle syllable *(gu):* Geoffrey of
Monmouth's *Anguselus* (Latin) > Chrétien de Troyes's *Lancelot*
(Old French); *Angus* in Scottish or English, from *Oengus* in Old Irish
or Gaelic. We must, thus, agree with the mythologists who arrived
before us in 1986, although by other means and longer process:
Lancelot does apparently, in more than one way, derive from Ireland.

Geoffrey of Monmouth had first named this hero. He had called
him Anguselus, or Auguselus, or Aguselus, and identified him at

King Arthur's and Queen Guinevere's coronations as "rex Albanie," which is the Gaelic "Ri Alban," King of Albany, or the White
Land, which is now Scotland. The *Prose Lancelot* from its own
sources in France followed suit by identifying him similarly: Agui-
sel of Scotland. Then Chrétien de Troyes in a poem entitled *Erec
and Enide* returned to identify Lancelot recognizably as "Aguiflez
. . . li rois d'Escoce" (v. 1918), or King of Scotland (Escoce).
Geoffrey of Monmouth's translator Wace, who was putting Geoffrey's Latin into a dialect of Old French called Anglo-Norman, also
made the hero's name clear, spelling it Anguisseaus, Angusel, or
Augusel.

Persons who love to read Old French, which Americans can do
easily since English comes largely from Old French, become used
to these variant spellings, usually to the point of their forgetting
how to spell, but, fortunately not how to use a dictionary. The
problem for Chrétien and Wace was that Old French had neither
grammar book nor dictionary, nor, luckily, copy editors. The author was free if he pleased his individual patron, the editor, and
himself. Interestingly, Chrétien de Troyes with all his genius, or
perhaps because burdened by its weight upon his shoulders, failed
in some way. He left both his *Lancelot* and his *Perceval,* which are
his two masterpieces, unfinished. This remains a mystery because
a creative artist like Chrétien should have felt compelled utterly to
finish. He may therefore have committed an offense against his
patrons and incurred displeasure; they were Angevin and French
royal persons. Or he may have suffered from poor working conditions.

The French historian Robert Fawtier who at the University of
Bordeaux studied the history of the Capetian monarchs described
the bad working conditions of their scribes who even so amassed
thousands upon thousands of documents for their monarchs. Seated
on an awkward stool before a small writing desk, writing with a
goose quill pen upon sheets of parchment that exuded grease even
at the lightest touch, toiling in small badly ventilated cabinets,
unheated in winter, uncooled in summer, with windows so narrow
that in midsummer at noon a pine torch was needed in order to see
the writing, the scribe or author suffered. Smoke filled his lungs and
the resin fumes burned his eyes. Purely literary works written for
pleasure and entertainment suffered more than the documents concerning royalty, the former often surviving in only one copy. The
number of copies is most useful to scholars because the scribes were

usually only trained copyists, themselves illiterate. Thus, as in the case of Chrétien de Troyes, whose errors betray his background, one copy leaves the reader unable to study place-names copied in error by an original scribe, but corrected later by a more meticulous copyist. The case of Arthurian texts is quite different because both copies and translations, particularly for Geoffrey of Monmouth, abound. Scholars can argue from such wealth forever.

For Lancelot, the Celtic scholar Jubainville agreed: all his hauling of cyclopean stones, and his raising of slabs from the tombs of his ancestors, and all these foundation burials were ancient Irish for certain. And all his tournaments and "tiltings" came doubtless from Taillten or Teltown on the Blackwater in Meath, Ireland. Was he not originally some son of the sea gods, some King of the Isles who chained the land to the stern of his boat and hauled it into the Hebrides? But especially with his coat of mail and his helmet and his red-and-white horse of the flowing mane, as presented to Lancelot by the Lady of the Lake, or Irish Sea, was he not another Manannan, another King Lear in a coracle that sped across the briny deep all by itself? Lady Augusta Gregory followed Villemarqué with her marvelous volumes of translations from the most pristine, ancient lore in all Europe, which is Ireland's. In her search for the origins of Lancelot's "legend," for she considered the whole Arthurian material to be legendary only, Weston also accepted Irish tradition as one possibility, but Lancelot as only a conventional character in a love story. The only truly ancient facet in his development, she argued, was the theft of a king's son, Lancelot, by a water fairy, the Lady of the Lake. She thought the *Lancelot* of Chrétien took place, and one cannot see why, in the English Dover, or Wallingford, Winchester, Windsor, Southampton, Oxford, or Shoreham. She also included "Bath" and "London," both of which occur in Celtic but are always misread as English. Chrétien's "Bade" is the citadel of Bademagus, governor of the Grail island Avalon. It is not Bath in England. "London" is customarily misread for "Lothian," the Edinburgh region of Scotland. Such custom dies hard.

Robert Graves from his poet's eye identified Lancelot's Irish progenitor as the primordial, red-hot, Irish King Lugh, who first used the horse in battle. Look for Lancelot at tournaments held on the solstices and equinoxes: Midsummer Days, May Days, Easters, Christmastides, Hallowe'ens, all horse races, Tailltean or tilting games, and Lugh-mass/Lammas celebrations. Look at Lancelot, urged Graves. He and his cousin Lionel probably both have red circles on their bodies, signs of Leo the Lion. They were royal and Christly, some people today believe. Lady Gregory had already pointed to these Ascots and such other games and horse races. Lugh, she said, is older than all the other heroes of Ireland, even older than Finn, certainly older than Arthur and Lancelot. There was *no greater loss,* she added, than the disappearance of Lugh from our world!

Lugh Lamfada was, indeed, the Irish god of light and life, argued Rolleston, with arms as long as the rays of the sun, rolling his own solar wheel—was it not the original Round Table?—across the heavens at high noon. Lancelot is another high-noon hero dueling in the summer sun. His mother Taltiu must have died when he was born, on an August 1; and so the races are held at Telltown to honor her name. And her tomb was shown in Ireland all through the Middle Ages. Lancelot belongs, then again, and also, to the land of the Gael or Scots who settled their western "Scotland" during King Arthur's lifetime and who brought a real Angus with them, along with their legends of Lugh. Similar horse races were probably also held at Lugudunum, the city of the Lion in France, now Lyons (Lyon in French), added Jubainville.

We should insert now certain expansions made by Henri Dontenville in France that still existed there when Chrétien and Geoffrey introduced the twelfth century to Lancelot/Anguselus the same initiatory routes that these heroes later trod in Quests of the Holy Grail.

The Knights Templar located their scores of French Commanderies on these same secret pathways, which went originally from one megalithic dolmen to another. When were these roads first used? Dontenville replied: before the English Channel's waters had separated Britain from Brittany. At a time when the lion was still a domestic animal, when the maned creatures, lion and horse, were worshiped as solar gods. Such roads took the pilgrims then from megalithic Carnac to the Mont-Saint-Michel where in fantasy King Arthur felled his prehistoric giant. The latter's Mont-Tombe, later Saint Michael's Mount on the border of Brittany-Normandie, i.e., once in Brittany but now, by the change in course of the Couesnon River, in Normandie, was then as now perhaps the most sacred spot in all northern Gaul. Gaul was first called Frankish and France in King Arthur's lifetime (A.D. 475–542).

Macalister put his finger on this association of Lugh and Lancelot with the summer solstice and the annual, ritual horse races then. The Irish feared summer thunderstorms dreadfully, but even worse, the birth of twins. Twins have two fathers, it was thought, one of whom is mortal, and the other immortal. Thus, we have the olden stories that lay with them the fatal charge of adultery upon the mother: Arthur and his (foster) brother Kay; Lancelot and his twin Galahad who drowned in the lake; Gawain and his treacherous brother Modred who slew King Arthur and was slain by him.

The most widely read scholar who focused upon the Celtic substratum of mythology that underlies the Arthurian material, a man who spent a long career until 1966 at Columbia University, in the City of New York, was Roger Sherman Loomis. Although he softened his opinion somewhat over the years, Loomis threw the weight of his overpowering prestige as master in the American academic community upon Arthurian literature as primarily mythological *but not historical* and as certainly Celtic in origin *but not ever set in Scotland,* said he, nor connected there really or geographically. There was certainly, he held, a genetic connection, on the other hand, between the King Lugh Loinnbheimion of Ireland and Sir Lancelot of the Lake. Both Lugh and Lancelot, concluded Loomis (1970, p. 225ff.), were raised by queens, trained by "mermen," and unnamed in babyhood (by "mermen" he must have meant sailors). Both appeared in a court where they occupied high seats of honor. Both hauled megaliths and coffins, delivered prisoners, and fathered a son clandestinely. Both wore red and carried red and weapons reddened with human blood. Both were sons or grandsons many times removed from kings of Ireland.

Dumézil frightens himself and then his reader by claiming that Lancelot's horse was originally sacrificed just like the winning horse in Rome, whose throat was cut after he won the October races. Robert Graves reported the same suspicion. Others have also supposed that Lancelot's mother, like Lugh's mother, was sacrificed also because she was adulterous, that is, because she bore twins. And, of course, Guinevere's twin sister was called a half-sister sired by her father on his Seneschal's wife—the latter probably then put to death like the winning horse. Much in Arthurian texts fascinates still precisely because it remains so mysterious.

D. D. R. Owen in Scotland finally studied these very incongruities for which no satisfactory, logical explanation seemed to him to have been made possible. He gave an excellent example (p. 295) in the incident of Lancelot's rescue of Guinevere and Arthur's prisoners: (1) no foreigner could ever return alive from that prison, (2) Lancelot was such a foreigner, (3) he traveled there and rescued the queen, (4) he liberated the prisoners, but (5) he then returned safely from that land. What has this fairy-tale version concealed? Was it not rather historical?

It seems clear that what it has concealed principally is the real horror of Lancelot's real ordeals. His adventures in a linear progression form his Quest of the Holy Grail, which he already knows is foredoomed. If we look briefly at these adventures as they appear in three authoritative texts, we see right away that they are not adventures so much as beheading games. Gawain played his famous beheading game with the Green Knight, probably Merlin in disguise. He barely saved his life, or got off with not too deep a wound in his neck. He was not slain but only scarred for life, . . . to teach him better.

Let us look first at Lancelot's three beheading games as related by the *Perlesvaus* (c. 1190) because despite its somewhat later date of composition it contains a good deal of primitive material. After a year had passed, Lancelot prepared for adventure (l. 6,633ff.) by first bidding farewell to Gawain and Arthur. He returned alone to the *Gaste Cité,* the devastated Roman fortress of Carlisle, which must already have lain in ruins. He tied his horse at the bottom of a grand marble flight of steps called a "perron de marbre," or marble perron in English also. It seems that Lancelot had come to Arthuret, or one exit from the world. A knight had him kneel. He wielded a scythe over Lancelot's head, but Lancelot winced out of the way. Then a maiden stepped forth and saved his life. She was someone he was assisting. By his voluntary return and surrender Lancelot had somehow insured the return of her property. The city then filled with people.

Lancelot approached the worst passage in the world (l. 2,714ff.). He had to pass a castle guarded by two champions defending a drawbridge and a portal hung with beards and human heads. Lancelot understood that his beard also would decorate its walls.

Lancelot slew the first knight and spared the second's life when a lady requested this favor of him. Then dinner was served, its five courses brought in by mutilated knights. Lancelot accepted to remain there only overnight. He had fought here on behalf of King Arthur in the latter's campaign against Dillus the Bearded.

Lancelot came to another castle barring his route. It was the infamous Castle of Griffons or Dragons (l. 7,381ff.). The heads of fifteen slain champions decorated its doorway. Lancelot entered. He easily drew a sword out of a copper column, which immediately crumbled away before his eyes. He knew that the lord of this castle planned to behead him.

A maiden offered Lancelot a way out. He would have to go down into an underground cistern that was guarded by a lion. Lancelot accepted this route. He killed the lion. Then he killed two griffons, which are creatures with men's faces, birds' beaks, owls' eyes, dogs' teeth, asses' ears, lions' feet, and serpents' tails. The maiden gave Lancelot a little dog. He accepted the dog but refused to carry it. When they came to the griffons, they saw a wonder, which was that the griffons let them pass quietly by. The griffons were so fond of the little dog (a Pictish totem), and so charmed that they ignored the maiden and Lancelot. The two then walked uneventfully through the dark underground until they came out in an orchard. There to Lancelot's joy he saw two maidens standing and holding his horse. He jumped on and rode away.

The *Prose Lancelot* tells at great length the story of Lancelot's heroism in battles during King Arthur's war in Scotland, where the hero obeys Queen Guinevere's commands and daily fights on the Clyde River, at Blood Ford. Such encounters were usually for sanitary reasons fought in running water. This was not part of his quest.

His adventure at the Old Abbey at Bannockburn is, on the other hand, an unforgettable adventure incurred en route to the Grail Castle. Chrétien tells this story also, but here the *Prose Lancelot* account is more complete and much more comprehensible.

At a time when there were still thirty years to go before the collapse of King Arthur's reign, Lancelot came to an Old Abbey beside a cemetery containing thirty-four tombs. As instructed, Lancelot strained until he managed to lift one of the huge slabs of stone from one sarcophagus. He thus opened the tomb of Galaad *(sic),* the son of Joseph of Arimathea. Galaad had been High King of "Galles," the country named after the king. The original name had been either Hofelisse or Hostelisse.

A second tomb surrounded by flames lay also in this underground necropolis. The flames were as high as a lance—perhaps fifteen feet high. Lancelot recoiled in fear. When he drew near again, he heard a voice warning him that he was not destined to occupy the Siege Perilous, or thirteenth seat at the Round Table. Nor was he destined to put an end to these adventurous times in

King Arthur's realm. Lancelot grieved, "What sackcloth and ashes for me, then!" Only the destined one, the voice continued, will by his presence extinguish these encircling flames. Lancelot stood there in stony silence, but he burned with desire to attack the fires before him. . . . The voice he heard, he was told, belonged to Simeon.

Another man in a tomb was Moses. He lay in the Perilous Hall. Lancelot would have to await and survive the course of thirty more years in order to witness the end of perilous times. Lancelot was then permitted to take the body of Galaad into Galles.

The hero had only recently in the Castle of King Arthur's mother survived the adventure of the Perilous Bed. There as he slumbered in the middle of the night a burning and red-hot lance was shot at him. It landed in his bed. Lancelot jumped aside, pulled the lance out of his bedding, and cut off its handle. Subsequently he rescued Queen Guinevere, which ended this Grail Quest; it resulted in an initiation there by her hands.

The *Prose Lancelot* tells also how Lancelot witnessed an actual appearance of the Grail at Corbenic Castle. As the ceremony commenced, he saw a dove enter by one of the windows. Then a damsel processed. She was bearing a vessel, "un vaissel" between her hands. It was a vessel "en samblance de calice," a vessel in the semblance of a chalice. Lancelot joined his hands together, bowed his head, and knelt down as she passed him by. Then a superb dinner was served.

That night or soon thereafter Lancelot was tricked into siring a child on the Grail King's beautiful daughter. He had dreamed that the maiden he made love to was Queen Guinevere. When next morning he learned that it had been the Grail King Pelles's daughter Helen, he first thought he would kill her. Her great beauty dissuaded him, however. This Helen was the mother of Lancelot's son Galahad.

When Perceval and Hector visited the same Castle Corbenic, they also, says the same unknown author of the *Prose Lancelot,* saw the Grail. Again it was similarly "un vaissel en samblance de calice," but this time covered with white samite, preceded and followed by two lighted candles that entered and passed without any bearers being visible. Both Questers, Hector and Perceval, were subsequently healed of their serious wounds. All heard that Gawain's test there had been to mend the broken sword and that he had failed.

We might never understand the phenomena attendant upon these adventures en route to the Grail Castle unless we read of them in the pages of Mircéa Eliade, the wonderful theologian who wrote *Myths, Dreams, and Mysteries.* These are routine experiences for any person becoming a shaman, he explained (p. 60ff.). Among many cultures the aspirant claims to fly, to ride in a chariot, to descend into hell, to pass through flames unscathed, and to wander through the wilderness. Like Lancelot, he seeks solitude, lives alone, and often falls ill and becomes unconscious. He journeys into the otherworld in order to rescue dead souls. When crossing the Sword Bridge that separates world from underworld, he may become weightless. Or he may ascend either a flight of stairs or the mountain upon which stands a Grail Castle. Or he may cross water in order to reach a holy isle and its necropolis. During his initiations, which become more arduous as he advances in power over himself and his environment, he dreams vividly and recalls each dream after awakening.

Initiations generally involve the same features, as one examines them in one culture or another, Eliade thought (p. 197ff.): a forest, a master teacher (Merlin), a hermit's hut, monsters (griffons), a deathlike trance lasting as much as three days (Arthur's experience), a secret name, a secret language, a beheading game, a duel to the death, sacrifice or murder, women weeping, and possession by devils, or disease. The young men experienced severe traumas before they were received as solar gods. Their deity himself was not of the blazing sort. He had withdrawn from human beings. He figured the most ancient of primitive gods, a do-nothing deity, whom Eliade so called: *deus otiosus.*

Lancelot experienced, as he recalled it, the ride in the cart or chariot drawn by a dwarf. Tristan knew the driver as the dwarf named Frocin from "Tintagel Castle" in Galloway, Scotland. Both survived the Perilous Bed with its flaming lance, and also Castle Marvelous with its teaching maidens. Before a crowd of people who expected him, Lancelot defeated several warriors at the Perilous Ford and an importunate damsel there who also tried to seduce him. He marveled at ceremonies held in two sacred sites. The first was the Old Abbey with its royal necropolis containing the thirty-four tombs. The second sacred site was the fountain and stone perron where he found Queen Guinevere's comb and mirror, a sign of her danger. He passed safely through the Perilous Forest, and even escaped the Boiling Fountain guarded by two lions. All here has been enigmatic. These adventures contain an unmentionable, deeper reality.

Best of all, Lancelot was rewarded by a strict accounting of things to come. This constituted knowledge commensurate with the degrees of initiation he had already passed. At this point he was informed of his thirty more years to live counting from his Old Abbey experience. His son Galahad would be able to add fifteen more years to Lancelot's allotted thirty. In all, there will have been four hundred fifty-four years to go, counting from the death of Christ, to the pure knight Galahad who, alone of all initiates, would dare to sit in the Siege Perilous. He alone would survive that dread experience.

None of these exploits seems unfamiliar to Teutonic peoples, Axel Olrik wrote in Denmark. This ride on horseback to the realms of the dead, and the final lap on foot, corresponds to the same deeply felt perception among various peoples of northern Europe. The Romans learned of it too as they gradually worked and fought their way westward to the Irish Sea. In fact, they were stupefied by the Celts who displayed singly and collectively an absolute fear of death. After suicide, individuals and clans of the Celts also, took the journey by ship down their rivers, the Rhine and the Rhône, the Forth and the Clyde, to their holy island necropolis. Poets in Britain have recalled it: Tennyson's Lily Maid of Astolat on her funeral barge, as King Arthur attended by royal Dames on his ocean voyage to Avalon, Dandrane on her voyage across the Mediterranean to the Holy Land, the Saints Mary westward-bound in earlier times. The Irish journeyed by sea toward "tu thall," the other shore.

That sea voyage, which is most famous in Arthurian lore, then in grand opera, is the one made by Perceval's son Lohengrin, the Swan Knight. Babies born to a queen, says the tale, who lived perhaps on the Isle of Man in the middle of the Irish Sea, were sacrificed to the waters because they were multiple births. Before they were cast into the sea, their mother, doubtless soon to be put to death herself, hung golden chains about their tiny necks. As soon as the babies touched the water, they turned into swans, which proudly braved the waves. . . . It is an offense in Britain today to kill a swan, all swans in Britain being the personal property of Her Majesty.

Lohengrin sailed safely across the waves of the North Sea in his swan ship to Holland/Belgium where he founded the royal dynasty there. An unknown poet celebrated Lohengrin's descendant,

Godefroi de Bouillon, because that great warrior ended the First Crusade successfully in 1099 by liberating Jerusalem.

The author who refused to recognize this Lancelot-Guinevere story as mythological was Chrétien from Troyes, France; he was a protégé of Queen Eleanor of Aquitaine and England. According to the doctrines of royal and courtly love to which this queen, who had after bearing so many children for two kings, probably subscribed, marriage is the pits. The only lover you want is a *cavalier servant* who loves you so terribly that he obeys the rules of love: "moult est qui aime obéissant." Queen Eleanor had the rules of courtly love drawn up for everybody's use by her Chaplain, Andreas Capellanus. Her protégé Chrétien was probably supposed to adopt in his *Lancelot, Knight of the Cart* the point of view of a social psychologist trained in the divorce courts. No wonder Chrétien did not finish the poem but passed it on to a collaborator, Godefroi de Leigni.

Chrétien's *Lancelot* studies the old situation of a married woman, Arthur's queen no less, infatuated with a much younger man whom she hardly knows, for he is customarily absent on quests or in war. Motivation elsewhere in Chrétien's work is uncomfortably absent also. Lancelot was not present when the queen departed for the Grail Castle; yet he knew that she had gone. Everybody else knows everything else beforehand also. They know, for instance, that Lancelot is predestined to love the queen to the point of betrayal and suicide, that he will live up to every task assigned him meanwhile, however. Lancelot possesses exquisite beauty, unwavering courage, supreme strength, plus the tranquil certitude that he will always remain victorious. And yet, he fails at the Old Abbey. His failure also is absolute and irreversible. Actually, Queen Guinevere had trouble even recognizing Lancelot when he struggled to cross hell gate, or his impossible "Sword Bridge," or Gawain's "Water Bridge" that Chrétien concocted, or wrote in error for "Draw-Bridge."

After 1155 Chrétien turned from classical subjects that were decidedly pornographic, to Arthurian subjects treated in a manner recognizable as "courtly." Each of his Arthurian texts runs about 7,000 verses of octosyllabic, rhyming couplets. He is the only Arthurian poet good enough to be quotable, with the exception of Marie de France: *Erec et Enide* (c. 1170); *Lancelot, ou Le Chevalier de la charrette* (c. 1171), which has 6,150 verses by Chrétien; *Yvain ou le Chevalier au lion* (c. 1175); and *Perceval ou Le Conte du Graal* (c. 1185). Chrétien's patrons were all royal: Count Henry de Champagne who lent Chrétien his source for *Lancelot;* Countess Marie, daughter of Queen Eleanor and her first husband, the Capetian King Louis VII of France; Count Philippe d'Alsace et de Flandre, who had just returned from Scotland when he lent Chrétien his source for *Perceval.* None of these sources has as yet been recovered.

In his *Chrétien* of 1952 the scholar R. L. Graeme Ritchie of Scotland found undeniably Scottish elements in *Erec, Yvain,* and *Perceval.* He also discovered that Chrétien had read Geoffrey of Monmouth's *History of the Kings of Britain* (1136), the *Navigation* of Saint Brendan from Ireland to Iceland, Greenland, and the coast of North America, and the life of Ireland's Saint Columba. Chrétien knew that Scotland in Arthur's time (475–542) was called "Escoce" in French and either *Albanie* or *Aubanie.* When Chrétien wrote of "Loonois," he meant "Laudonensis" or Lothian around Edinburgh, where ruled a territorial Sovereignty named eponymously: Queen *Laudine* of Lothian. Yvain married this lady under very suspicious circumstances. He first discovered that the King Aiguisians was the same Anguselus in Geoffrey's Latin spelling. Arthur's mother's Castle of Maidens was the present Caerlaverock on the Rhinns of Galloway, which was Chrétien's *Galvoie,* and Caerlaverock was situated before a White Field *(Champguin)* facing Ireland across the Solway Firth. Carduel, a castle by the sea, was the once greatest Roman fortress in Britain, and now the city and junction of roads: Carlisle at the head of the Solway Firth.

Since 1952 and thanks to this pioneering book by Ritchie, the entire world of Arthurian studies looks differently: firstly, Arthurian geography moved authoritatively to Scotland from southern England and Cornwall where Arthur could never have fought and defeated Saxons between 475 and 542 for two reasons principally: (1) the Saxons were not there yet, and (2) when they did arrive there, their *Anglo-Saxon Chronicle* positively denied any encounter with Arthur. Secondly, Arthur became credible and historical, as verified by the geography. Thirdly, Geoffrey of Monmouth could be believed when he placed Arthur in Scotland. Fourthly, the half dozen or so Arthurian scholars like John Stuart Stuart Glennie (1849) who from 1900 or thereabouts had also placed Arthur in Scotland could finally be praised. And furthermore, the vast body of mythology could be studied not as proving King Arthur never lived, that his mythology was created out of hot air, but that the mythology, by its very amplitude, tied Arthur to Celtic Britain, and not to his English, formerly Anglo-Saxon foes whom he defeated inland and off both eastern and western firths of Scotland. Then, as O. G. S. Crawford of Glasgow, who founded *Antiquity* magazine and directed it, while it was still published in Scotland, set to examining Arthur all over again; he could also be credited when he offered his proofs that (1) Arthur defended Scotland at Hadrian's Wall, and (2) Arthur died there at Camlan, which probably was the *Camboglanna* station halfway across Hadrian's Wall.

"Chrétien soars into fancy," wrote Ritchie (p. 23) "but from a broad basis in fact." As Ritchie also pointed out, a medieval chronicler named Robert de Brunne had already located Maiden Castle *(Chastel des Puceles)* as Caerlaverock, which was then insulated by the Nith River and Solway shore. This certainly was the Perilous Ford, terrible to cross for Gawain and Lancelot, impossible today and still unbridged, deep with quicksand along the Nith River banks. . . . Ritchie amazingly even found out how it happened that the Counts of Flanders and Champagne were able to pass on to their authors sources that dealt so precisely with Scotland in the Dark Ages. The sources were examined, retained, or rejected by a Church Council convened in Scotland when King David was establishing Jedburgh Abbey (1118), restoring, and reorganizing the ancient diocese of Glasgow. This must be where and how Chrétien received privileged information concerning the Scottish reigns between the years 1107 and 1185. These are the very years when both Geoffrey of Monmouth and Chrétien de Troyes wrote their first texts, which revealed on either side of the Straits of Dover that there had once lived in Scotland two magnificent heroes, religious leaders, and kings: Arthur and Lancelot.

A rapid glance now at the place-names of the *Lancelot* adds evidence that seems to corroborate in some, small degree Ritchie's large findings in Chrétien's three other Arthurian texts. There are in *Lancelot* a dozen place-names from France, as one might expect from a French writer of considerable worldliness and sophistication. But why should six of these twelve place-names be not in Champagne—and no mention of Paris—but in the Languedoc governed by Chrétien's Angevin patroness, Queen Eleanor: Lyon sur la Rosne, (Les Trois) Maries, Montpellier, Pampelune en Navarre, Poiters, and the celebrated "Tolose," or Toulouse, home of France's oldest University (then called *studium generale*).

Persons have thought Chrétien traveled to London where he met Geoffrey, but he seems not to have any such places on his mind. He mentions *Engleterre* only once. He knows the names Babylon and Arab, which is very little for a writer living under the glory of Godefroi de Bouillon. Was Chrétien not a converted Jew?

Then one stumbles across a sizable number of unknown place-names, which must intrigue the reader. These are the Arthurian names of the places Lancelot visited, or where he fought: Bade, Noauz, Mautirec, La Deserte, Estrax or Estraus, Roberdic or Roberiet or Beredine or Genedic, Gorre, and Pomelegoi or Pomelesglai. Since nobody seems to want to venture a guess, let us suppose that these names of places resemble all others preponderantly in Europe, and are therefore Celtic.

1. Bade = the citadel at the Grail Castle the governor of which is Bademagus (origin of the surname *Bald*win). The name should be Pictish and later the Scottish Mac*Beth* and Venerable *Bede*.

2. The fourth variant Genedic would give us Kennedy, which is an ancient fortress ruin on the west coast of Scotland. The name in medieval French is spelled similarly: Genedic and Quennedic.

3. Noauz from the Latin and Celtic Novias and the Celtic suffix *ac* or *as* would mean New Waters, or New River.

4. Mautirec is Celtic also: Mothar = park enclosure + ac = water.

5. La Deserte is short for La Terre Deserte or Gaste = the Waste Land.

6. Estrax, Estraus is Celtic for Water River (Exeter).

7. Gorre is Avalon, or the Isle of Man whose king was King Orry > Gorre. Gorre in Arthurian texts is often spelled Voirre if the author thinks it is the Glass Castle (Glastonbury). No one has heard of a castle there, and the *Glaston* syllables refer to a Saxon family or clan settling the area round 800: "Glastings."

8. Pomelegoi and/or Pomelesglai are by far the most interesting of Chrétien's place-names (vv. 5,626 and 5,368 of the Guiot text, which is MS fr. [French Manuscript] 794 in the Bibliothèque Nationale, Paris). Chrétien left only six copies of the *Lancelot*. It was not a popular work. Chrétien spells it Pomelegoi, but Godefroi de Leigni, who picked up the translation at verse 5,641, corrected Chrétien: Pomelesglai.

We are speaking of a place that a son of a king of Ireland came from. The Celtic etymology is fascinating:

Pomel = a piece of land cut out from a larger estate and entailed for the site of an

esglai > eccles = an old-time Scottish parish church.

Where in Scotland was there such a church built upon entailed land donated by some son of a king of Ireland? Both Lancelot and Arthur might be so construed, both figuring in the royal genealogies of Ireland.

Therefore we probably have here another reference to a parish church now called Arthuret in Longtown near Carlisle, perhaps once also called Kil Arthur or Arthur's Church. It may have been built on Arthur's tribal territory. It may now be King Arthur's burial place. A large cemetery and a baptistery adjoin this present, large church rebuilt circa 1150.

The German *Parzival* text, which is certainly the longest, most authoritative mine of odd information concerning Arthurian affairs, come in handily to confirm several of Chrétien's place-names in Scotland, notably the site called Castle Marvelous where dwelled the same four queens who probably escorted the wounded Arthur to Avalon from Caerlaverock: Arnive who was Arthur's mother (the name is an anagram for Ygerne), Sangive who is Gawain's mother, and Gawain's sisters whom Wolfram names Cundrie number two and Itonje.

Several innovations by Chrétien have made his *Lancelot* particularly preferred by French scholars. They have admired his clever verses and colorful descriptions of royal socialites partying. Most of all, Chrétien is famous for his entangled, passionate and adulterous lovers, supposedly Lancelot and Guinevere, who by their crime caused him to be disqualified in his Grail Quest. Guinevere caused Arthur's realm to collapse by separating him from his chief ally, Lancelot.

Others have enjoyed Chrétien's realism, his military terminology, his male warriors at each other's throats, the royal pageantry of his pages. Everyone has enjoyed the mysteries Chrétien makes little attempt to solve. On the other hand, nothing in Chrétien's plot or characters holds water. After wondering about all these inexplicable mysteries, one probably does well to desist. Nothing holds together. No ends mesh. Why? Because Chrétien probably had it all wrong. Lancelot and Guinevere never were lovers. Period.

Chrétien stumbles also when he tries to derive knighthood historically, first, and then to situate it in the Dark Ages. The French translator of Chrétien, Paulin Paris, noted in 1868 that one should never say "knight" in connection with Arthur or his period in time.

Chrétien claimed in his poem *Cligès* that chivalry originated in Greece, came to Rome, and flowered again in France. Or, thinking again, he derived it from Greece whence it passed directly to England, now called "Bretaigne," Chrétien assumes incorrectly again.

Paulin Paris straightened it out. The first *chevaliers* or knights were dubbed in Syria around 1100. Had Chrétien looked about him, he might have realized that Lancelot acted very much like a Knight Templar.

THE KNIGHTS TEMPLAR

When Frank Tribbe, author and editor of *Spiritual Frontiers,* writes in correspondence (July 2, 1991) that the Grail was a casket in which the folded Shroud (of Turin) "was kept in the 14th century, . . . and may have been in England for a few decades of that century, . . ." he seconds our finding that Knights Templar were dispersed, disbanded in France, and even burned at the stake there as "heretics." They were not burned in England, but pensioned off only and dispersed.*

Our original suspicion, or hypothesis, has by now been reinforced by analysis of Grail texts. Tribbe's suspicion comes as further reinforcement. Thus, we have already seen in these pages, and by induction, that Lancelot was not so much a military hero as he was a religious hero. For that reason he was himself so shrouded in the very ancient envelopes of mythology.

Both Lancelot and Perceval, who thus far we assume are our premier Grail heroes and Grail initiates, emerge from their trappings only momentarily. We have long suspected they were revered when alive as noble and holy men. White doves, chalices, white samite, candles, and broken swords, or lances, await their entrances into Grail Castles. These Grail heroes have now led us inescapably to the Crusades, *during which our Grail texts were written,* and in fear and trembling on our part, to the two, most awful massacres of the Middle Ages.

We always see Lancelot, and Perceval also, by indirect lighting, never lit clearly even by a flash held in hand, always through the mirror darkly. That barrier is the twelfth century when all the greatest texts concerning these two prime questers after the Holy Grail flowed from brushes and pens onto parchment. And furthermore, a renowned historian of France as well as England, François Guizot (1787–1874), held specifically that history depends not entirely upon external evidence such as these texts, nor visibly upon expressions of any such sort. The historian studies his written evidence first, perhaps; but he also examines institutions, habits, objects dug up, agencies, and all archives. But finally, claims Guizot,

*See chapter 3 and notes to his *Portrait of Jesus* (New York, 1983).

it is the intellectual and moral qualities of human beings that make any civilization. It was, even after all that, the spirit that animated Lancelot and Perceval and which their authors caught like germs in their proximity.

The greatest Arthurian text, which is the German *Parzival,* was written by the Knight Wolfram von Eschenbach, who declares himself a Templar. Wolfram died before he could have been burned at the stake, before the Templar massacre, and, fortunately for him, outside France in any case. Lancelot had been dead for five hundred and more years before the Knights Templar were even instituted, and yet he might be mistaken at any page for such a Templar. Like them he tried and tried manfully to storm heaven. Like them he failed, but still labored with might and main to found Arthur's empire on earth. And just as the crusading Templars for centuries kept open the routes to the Holy Land, so Lancelot by the force of his will, and the gleam of his knighthood, kept ajar the gates of Galloway, the ports of the eastern and western firths, Forth and Clyde, and passed back and forth from the Galloway coast of Scotland to the Isle of Man, thence into North Wales. Like a Knight Templar Lancelot was both martial and priestly.

The Order of Knights Templar was founded in 1119. Chrétien wrote his *Lancelot* around 1177. Nowadays we listen to Vaughan Wiliams's lark-ascending music. The twelfth century heard readings in Wolfram's Grail texts of a dove descending. It was the Templar insignia. Lancelot is in more ways than one strangely contemporary with the twelfth century.

The Third Crusade saw 600,000 brave knights, who were like Lancelot the flowers of chivalry, mass against Arab armies, at Acre in the Holy Land. In that one battle alone 120,000 European knights from the only families who could afford to educate them, furnish them with horses, weapons, squires, grooms, travel expenses, food, lodging, and pocket money, died wretchedly far from home at Acre. Some had arranged for their hearts to be embalmed and sent home to their sweethearts. As far as any good show was concerned, the Third was the last Crusade. Guizot agreed: Europe had found Asia invincible. And vice versa.

Lancelot reminds us somewhat today of that universally acclaimed hero who emerged spotted but still alive from the Third Crusade. Another of France's most renowned historians, Jules Michelet (1798–1874), termed that tainted hero, Richard Coeur de Lion, the most formidable "war machine" of his century. So was

THE CONFERMENT OF KNIGHTHOOD

Lancelot of his, a survivor of hideous blood baths, at one time victorious against the best sixty-five enemy champions, said the tally. That "wicked" Richard, said Michelet, "that son of wrath," won for himself even among Muslim or Saracen foes a peerless reputation for "valor and cruelty." Lancelot, unlike Richard, dropped dead somewhere, or within a couple of days vanished at some port, said early historians in Scotland, where King Arthur was attempting to effect a landing. Richard departed by ship and died of blood poisoning in France from an arrow shot by an eight-year-old boy. Both had undergone long incarceration. King Richard somehow accumulated honor. You have to give the devil his due, argued Michelet. Richard I willed his pride to the Templars, which was only just, for he escaped from the Holy Land disguised as a Templar and on one of their huge vessels. He got all the honor, concluded Michelet, but the French king got all the profit from the Third Crusade. Richard then merely rang in the knell of the Angevin Empire, which Capetian France picked up, chunk by chunk of priceless real estate.

A third, marvelous nineteenth-century historian, this time not native to France but born in Switzerland, was Simonde de Sismondi (1773–1842). The face of Europe changed during those first three Crusades, he wrote, because it emerged from a centuries-long barbarism, the barbarian invasions commencing in King Arthur's and Lancelot's century (475–542). Europe subsequently entered a period of development. Its ever more martial nationalism lasted from 1191 to 1830 and still continued at the time of Sismondi's death. For reason of this other, cruel nationalism Sismondi refused to write a history of France. He chose instead to write *the history of the French.* The Crusades, as he saw them, were not only a war and a religious movement. They caused a renewal of commerce between Europe and Asia, with old barriers down, old prejudices disproven, relations much improved by travel and acquaintance.

On the debit side, observed Sismondi, Christianity itself suffered a severe loss. It became what it had been in Lancelot's hands also, a military religion. Christian virtues most sought then were bravery, constancy, and prowess. Christian knights were encouraged to make larger and larger blood sacrifices of Muslins called "infidels" and "nonbelievers." Even the Knights Templar forgot their Order had been constituted as priestly warriors for the defense of routes to and from Jerusalem, and defense of the Holy Sepulcher Church destroyed and rebuilt by French royalty. Even the Templars, who were as an Order sworn to celibacy and poverty, became bankers and treasurers before they lost Jerusalem again. Like Lancelot, only longer, they fought until they were drained. Less than the kings from France and England, they too lost sight of the tomb of Christ. All forgot to guarantee access to the millions of devout pilgrims thronging the ships, crowding the ports, and dying along the stony roads into Asia. The German Emperor Frederick had drowned near the border in the Saleph or Salef River.

The twelfth century that discovered King Arthur and Lancelot also seemed to undergo three movements it could neither alter nor stay: (1) France and England held each other by the throat; (2) England under King Henry II for the first years of his marriage to Eleanor of Aquitaine seemed to claim ascendancy; but (3) the Capetian kings of France continually outmaneuvered their rivals until they, by hook and by crook, deprived the Angevins of their Continental empire.

As the Third Crusade gave evidence of catastrophe, King Philip Augustus of France, when he was yet only a boy aged fourteen, gave ample demonstration in 1179 of his temper. Between that year and 1182 he summarily expelled the Jews from France after he had preempted and confiscated all their goods and possessions. King Henry's nasty son John acted likewise in York, England. And yet, to this day, his brother Richard I represents the ideal warrior just as he did in the twelfth century. Like his brother John, Richard was violent, prodigal, impetuous, callous, and almost as brainless. His dying father turned his face to the wall, knowing a bitter death at these sons' hands, July 6, 1189. . . . That year disasters in the Holy Land magnified. Thus they continued, getting worse and worse, for the next forty years until Europe was really drained of masculine blood.

It was, as far as Europe can boast, the direct result of a "diabolical generation," Jules Michelet argued in his *Histoire de France* which he commenced in 1830 (vol. 1, p. 250). This may seem a wild exaggeration, but teachers over decades have also noted the numbers of "difficult" students in certain years, "difficult" being a euphemism for intractable or uneducable. Both Richard and John Plantagenet came by their devilishness honestly, concluded Michelet, being sons of Eleanor of Aquitaine and her second husband, King Henry II, who decayed markedly after he had his Archbishop Becket slain. For whatever reason, King Henry II became more and more dissolute and debauched as he aged, his appetite for sex equaled only by his gluttony for more and more food. His repudiated Queen Eleanor was herself half woman and half snake, Michelet said, like the queen that Gawain to his horror saw once in a dark castle hall. Eleanor was probably less than that, Michelet also suspected, and a murderer too.

How strange a dream she dreamed, then, in exile watching husband, sons, and Templars all go down into bitter failure and death because of the Holy Land toward which she had twice journeyed and which she thus knew firsthand. Hers was the wildest dream, of a courtly love, where lovers are always young, handsome, courteous, courtly, and true—where neither age nor depravity furrows their sweet, rosy cheeks. And so she paid her Chaplain Andreas and her poet Chrétien to celebrate love and a doting Lancelot improbably in love with King Arthur's Queen Guinevere. The pregnant Eleanor lived for years under the shame of her husband's open adultery. Then he expelled her as her first and French royal husband had done so many years earlier. We also see Lancelot through her tears.

This Grail Quester Lancelot might be taken for a Knight Templar, so many similarities are there between him and his quest, them and theirs. It is no great task to list them briefly before we turn specifically to the Templar Order itself. There is the question of a lost and unimaginably precious treasure in both cases. The Grail itself puzzles us today and breaks our hearts, so great immeasurably is this lost treasure. The vast treasure and fleet of the Knights Templar similarly have not yet been traced or recovered. Contemporary historians will struggle to shed light here. The Grail Quest operated under an identical symbolism, that of black-and-white, which were also the colors of the Templar banner called Baucéant. This diagonally colored flag was piebald in memory of their first horse, which the first Templar Knight had to share with his first squire. The Templar emblem shows the two thus mounted. Black sheep and white sheep leaped the boundary between Christian and Muslim in the Perceval texts. That hero's brother was half black and half white. No wonder. The Crusaders left children in Syria and brought others home. King Richard I struggled mightily to wed his royal sister to the Sultan Saladin. He failed and had to have her escorted back to southern France. Having lost England on his way home from Acre, he could not send her there.

Arthurian commanders also died in battle, uncomplainingly disappearing like Arthur himself, Lancelot, Gawain, Guinevere,

King Loth, and Modred. In his trial the last Grand Master of the Temple, Jacques de Molay, told of the magnificent courage of an army of Knights Templar in the Holy Land. They were once assigned to an imbecilic French Count of Artois whose battle plan the Templars tried to persuade him was not so much a strategy as an invitation to mass suicide. Their commander insisted upon his orders. The Templars accepted to go die. They all died in that way and on that day. They had taken an oath to die in battle anyway, at their investiture. They died willingly therefore, testified Molay. Their life resembled a quest. Molay himself died after years of the most unspeakable tortures in prisons. He was then publicly burned at the stake in Paris. That sentence was illegal on the part of the French king. Molay's death was not an execution, then, but an assassination by another Capetian king's terrible hand.

Then too Lancelot's failure to achieve perfect holiness, by succeeding to kingship at the Grail Castle, resembled the mass failure of the Knights Templar to die all in odor of sanctity. All surviving Templars who returned from the Holy Land suffered expulsion at the cancellation by the Pope of their Order. Some French Templars escaped, it is true, to starve to death in the woods. The French king killed all he could find, thousands of penniless, returning veterans, inside France. Nobody will ever know why Molay returned to France, or how he figured it would be a triumphal return. He must have considered the French king's enormous debt to the Temple some sort of security for Templars defeated in Jerusalem and obliged to come home. Any other man would have understood that the French king's debt guaranteed, instead, the death of the lender. Or is it only the nineteenth-century historians who centuries later correctly judged the morals of the Capetian kings and the extent of their impecuniousness? What are the "religious fervor and military prowess" that characterized the age, asked Frank Tribbe (p. 57), when they meet royal greed? The collective aspirations aroused by the early Crusades collapsed as millions died for them. The twelfth century, like King Arthur's, which looked open-eyed upon countless barbarian invasions, was no century in which to live.

The Arthurian material is related to the Knights Templar furthermore by the person of Saint Bernard who wrote their Rule and who also inspired Cistercians like Geoffrey of Monmouth to bring into public attention the lives of the great Arthurian heroes, and the life of their Grand Masters, King Arthur and his cousin, Wise Merlin. Thus, nothing about Arthur's reign is actually secret if one ponders that vast body of literature long enough. Even the Grail ceremony as practiced by royal persons is no more secret than any Mass or Holy Office. The Templars too were accused of being pagan, and are still so accused despite efforts by such great scholars as Malcolm Barber (p. 243ff.) to clear their name. In the case of the Templars also, says Barber, "no idols have been found, nor a secret rule." The finding of sacred relics, and the trade in relics by Saint Louis of France, and probably also by King Arthur's acquisition of the Holy Rood, is another matter altogether. The "face" that the Templars allegedly kissed in their investiture ceremonies might well have been the Shroud of Turin, scholars like Frank Tribbe think today.

The Knights Templar like King Arthur were and are devoted to the Virgin Mary. The king bore her image on his shield. The Templars adopted her as did the Parisian scholar Abelard:

> You are our only hope. You stand as our advocate. We who tremble, all of us, under the wrath of our judge, fly to the protection of his mother. She must logically sue for us, and stand beside us in court.

The Templars daily prayed:

> Our Lady, who was there at the beginning of our religion, in Her, and in Her Honor shall be, if it pleases God, the end of our lives and the end of our religion, whenever it shall please God that they end. . . .

Last of all the mysterious routes of Arthur's Questers as they cross the Waste Land and start downhill to the lake and Castle of the Holy Grail are so many itineraries, theorized Louis Charpentier in his conclusions of 1967. Both Wolfram in Germany and Chrétien in France will eventually lead us, he thought, one day, to the lost Templar treasure. It will finally be found, probably under water. In Charpentier's opinion the search for the Templar treasure should begin near Troyes in Champagne where a chain of lakes lies between a series of Templar Commanderies mapped by himself (pp. 272–73). These forests are called *Grand Orient, Petit Orient,* and *Forêt du Temple.* Accordingly, the "Orient" here, says Charpentier, was Perceval's ultimate destination; or it would have been except for a discrepancy of almost a thousand years between Perceval and the first Knights Templar.

There is no anachronism present if one examines the writing of

Grail texts in the twelfth century and the political events that then stunned the western nations of Europe. It is most interesting to consider action and reaction here by the major intellectuals of the twelfth century, and no wonder at all reconsidered in the light of twelfth-century upheavals that our authors, first, turned to the Dark Ages for the explanations to be drawn from history. Nor is one surprised any longer to find that these authors, always excepting Chrétien and Wolfram, otherwise chose anonymity.

It has been argued in the case of the fifteenth-century French poet Charles d'Orléans in France, but Charles of Orleans because he was an English poet also, that the many early writers who preceded Charles remained anonymous because the cult of personality had not yet developed, that a poet had as yet no idea of his distinctive individuality. This may still be tenable in the case of royal person-ages who could at any moment wear the crown, and who, as in Charles's case, fathered the future king of France Louis XII.

A study of simple chronology for the Crusaders, for the tide of battle in Jerusalem, for the reigns of our Capetian and Angevin monarchs, and for the Grail texts as we reconstruct theoretically their dates of composition, may therefore prove enlightening. One suspects that anonymity served our authors well. One also suspects that Chrétien lived precariously firstly because he depended upon patrons, secondly because he was a converted Jew in Western lands where Jews were expelled at any drop of the hat, and lastly because he struggled a little uncomfortably in the toils of Christianity and the Holy Grail. Let us take a closer look at the same chronology we first saw in chapter 4, concerning Spain.

CRUSADE I
(1095–99)

The First Crusade was a war successfully concluded at the capture by the four noble leaders, notably, by their Commander-in-Chief Godefroi (or Godfrey) de Bouillon, of Christ's tomb, which is the Holy Sepulcher in the city of Jerusalem.

The original church had been constructed by the British-born Empress Helena Augusta and her British-born son, the Emperor Constantine the Great. Here one is already treading the sacred ground of King Arthur in Scotland, for these are his venerable ancestors. We are also in full Christianity, the Emperor Constantine having declared for it as henceforth the sole religion. Therefore Godefroi de Bouillon seized Jerusalem in 1099, and his brother Baldwin was rightfully crowned King Baldwin I of Jerusalem.

Again we are by extension in King Arthur's realm; the Baldwins of Belgium are direct descendants of Perceval's son Lohengrin, the Swan Knight. Nobility also obliges them to hold Jerusalem; the doctrine is called noblesse oblige.

Twenty years later, in 1119, the Sovereign and Military Order of the Knights Templar of Jerusalem was founded in Jerusalem for the express purpose of escorting pilgrims to that city and other shrines in Syria, and to keep safe and open the routes to and from western Europe and the Holy Land. The Templars had also perforce to become bankers, pawnbrokers, tour guides, and financiers. They were not supposed to let a million tourists, all well connected back home, starve to death, freeze, or die of sunstroke or fatigue. Meanwhile their grateful pilgrims, the royal and reigning monarchs included, bestowed estates back home upon the Templars. Counties, duchies, and even an entire kingdom in Spain were given as unrestricted donation to the Order of the Knights Templar.

CRUSADE II
(1147–49)

The Second Crusade involved an unsuccessful war to capture Damascus from the Saracens. Its leader Conrad III abandoned the effort in 1148. The Capetian King Louis VII of France, and his Queen Eleanor of Aquitaine, who accompanied him overseas *(outre-mer),* followed suit in 1149. Louis VII hurried home so he could divorce Queen Eleanor on grounds that she had failed to produce a male heir to the throne. The divorce was granted by the Pope in 1152.

Saint Bernard of Clairvaux, who gave the Knights Templar their Rule and his blessing, had preached this Crusade. The Capetian kings realized here how very profitable it was to tend to business at home and entice the Angevins into the Holy Land.

The excitement aroused by the departure of King Louis VII and his heiress wife, the richest woman in the world of her time, fell all the more bitterly upon contemporaries. Authors were spurred on to elevate Christianity higher and higher in the face of this defeat. But neither the self-styled Robert de Boron or Borron, supposedly from eastern France, nor Marie de France, has been either located or identified. Authors are vulnerable by temperament and also by their impecuniousness. Here comes a new crop of Arthurian works:

(c. 1160–70):	the "Robert de Boron" Grail romances
(c. 1160–70):	the Tristan and Isolde romances
(c. 1170–89):	the "Breton" or "British" poems of Marie de France
(c. 1170–85):	the Arthurian and Grail romances by Chrétien de Troyes

They are followed shortly (1174–86) by the laws of love as drawn up by Andreas Capellanus.

The appalling tragedy in Western eyes, which was this Second Crusade, was successfully aggravated by King Louis VII who, despite efforts to waylay her permanently, let his divorced wife fall into the stalwart embrace of the red-headed, future King Henry II of England. That setback could, of course, be countered shortly, as reigns go; for Henry and Eleanor bore such children as Francis Bacon later termed "hostages to fortune." The sons Henry had counted on died early, leaving two handicaps no father could deal with anyway: Richard and John.

By the years 1173–74 King Louis VII was supporting both ingrates with arms, money, and propaganda aimed at Henry II. As a result, by 1190, Henry had lost Normandie, always the star in any monarch's crown because immense, rich, fertile, beautiful, and strategically placed. He died of wounds received in battle against his own son Richard. Dying, Henry II turned his face to the wall. He was glad to die.

CRUSADE III
(1189–90)

Three royal chiefs this time—King Richard I of England, King Philip I of France, and the Emperor Frederick I of Germany, set out magnificently appareled, superbly attended, for the Holy Land. Their reason compelled them to hasten, for the brilliant Saladin had in 1187 reconquered Jerusalem. What a blow!

Pope Gregory VIII therefore urgently and personally preached the Third Crusade upon which all Christendom depended. Now it was chiefs against chief, the best against the very best. The Western world hung upon Richard Coeur de Lion. He had all Europe flat at his feet. Instead of hastening, however, he wintered in the western Mediterranean, his mother and her would-be daughter-in-law making all possible haste in pursuit. Richard must father a son. Fortunately, the English king had allowed his mother to post down from the north into Spain's Basque country in order to pick up their Princess Berengaria.

Sir Walter Scott tells the tale in some detail in his novel *The Talisman* (1825). There Saladin generously heals King Richard. In Guizot's *History* also the difference is brought out in two pictures it seemed too cruel to present in this book: Saladin seated on a high throne calmly allowing Christian priests and beautiful, half-naked, Western girls to file past him among other crestfallen, sad prisoners. This picture presents a damning contrast to that of the huge Richard Coeur de Lion. The latter on his gigantic war horse towers over his Crusaders in the middle ground of a picture. Behind him is massed a multitude of noble followers. In the foreground the sands are piled mounds high with dead and decapitated Muslim prisoners. Richard's mailed fist is raised in the fateful command: Kill them all! Authors cannot allow such a merciless massacre to stand unchallenged. Therefore Sir Walter's novel is by way of mild reproval.

Eventually the Kings Richard and Philip arrived safely into Syria, having lost the German Emperor in 1190 to an Asia Minor river usually considered of little import. They actually managed to capture Acre—by starving it out. Richard occasionally performed great deeds of personal heroism and ordered acts of utter cruelty and unbelievable barbarity. In 1192 he finally accepted Saladin's kind offer of a truce. It was another appalling loss to the Crusaders, of course; for they retained only a coastal strip of what had been the proud Kingdom of Jerusalem. Saladin very generously allowed all pilgrims permission to enter the Holy City henceforth, and to worship there securely in peace. By October of 1192 Richard felt free to abandon the Holy Land at Acre, and to give up his life of ease in Oriental silk gowns, which were so comfortable in the burning sands of Syria. He and Saladin had met frequently and gamed amicably. The Sultan was curious. He could simply not understand Richard's mean streak. Thus, the English king left the Holy Land forever. At that point in his life he was considered by western Europe the greatest hero of his century, a Lancelot, a nonpareil flower of chivalry.

Again, authors corrected history and rallied to the Holy Grail and a humiliated Christianity:

1190–1216: the *Didot-Perceval* text, which is anonymous, was composed from a very old, primitive and superb source. It is also from the point of view of structure, a marvelous telling.

1197–1218: Wolfram von Eschenbach, a Knight Templar from Germany, who was a literary genius no less, composed his *Parzival*. This work is universally hailed as the most authoritative and by far the most glorious of all Arthurian romances.

Between the years 1199 and 1216 King Philip Augustus of France, whose sobriquet is "the Conqueror," finally crushed the foolish sons of the dead King Henry II of England, and annexed the rest of their vast territories on the Continent. He then proceeded to defeat the Emperor Otto IV of Brunswick and annexed his territories. The much adored Richard I, who still disguised as a Knight Templar was taken prisoner in Italy and held for that huge ransom which purchased his release, yielded his realm of England. Richard died ignominiously in his war against the victorious, conquering, Capetian king in 1199.

His tomb, alongside those of his parents, may be seen today in the French royal necropolis of Fontevrault, near Tours, France. In the fifteenth century Fontevrault was ruled by the older daughter of Princess Isabelle de Valois, widow of King Richard II, and Prince Charles of Orléans. She was, curiously, named Jeanne d'Orléans. The other Jeanne of the same age but allegedly from Champagne had come to save Charles of Orléans. She saved him also, plus France once more: Jeanne d'Arc.

CRUSADE IV
(1202–04)

This time the Crusaders unfortunately turned their war machine against an ally, the city of Constantinople. Unbelievably, they sacked the city of their own Christian coreligionists. The results of this utter insanity rang with devastating results throughout the world. It seemed a prelude to the real bouts of mass insanity that were to occur in the fifteenth century. Then masses of people went totally insane. Walking across Europe, they threw themselves by hundreds at a time into the Atlantic Ocean. From the beginning years of the thirteenth century, however, the west of Europe, it would seem, could stand no more tragedy.

One rumor continues today. It was whispered that the Knights Templar absconded with mule-loads of precious relics and objets d'art from the once-splendid Constantinople. One such priceless relic, it is also thought now, was the Shroud of Turin.

THE ALBIGENSIAN CRUSADE
(1208–71)

The Albigensian Crusade was proclaimed by the Pope in 1208 against the so-called heretics of southern France, including those discovered living in northern cities. They were hunted, trapped down, interrogated, and burned at the stake. This Crusade was launched against heretics, defined as people whose beliefs and practices differed from orthodoxy. Several million people were accused, tried, and burned at the stake while the rest of France looked on.

In actuality, this Crusade appears now more like a Civil War, like the one fought in the United States with such a huge loss of life, honor, property, pride, and confidence. The scars of empty French villages where all died legally, men, women and children alike, remain desolated today, especially down toward the foothills of the Pyrenees where people had been herded. Signs in such mountain hamlets alert the traveler: name, date, time of day, number of dead. The barns and stone houses stretch along tree-lined roads—decaying and empty.

This Crusade was called "Albigensian" from the "White City" of Albi, which was and is a center of this deviate religion, a kind of ancestor of Puritanism. The heresy is usually called "Catharist" and its branch of Christianity called "Catharism" followed by "Catharists," which are Greek words for the Latin equivalents: Puritanism, Puritan, and Puritans. The last Puritanical heretics refused to be saved. They insisted upon being publicly burned.

This was a Crusade open to volunteers from anywhere who were invited to devastate the Languedoc in exchange for whatever they could carry away. Those who accepted to go on raids or to serve under leaders were promised forgiveness for all sins, and certain paradise thereafter. There was neither an organized army nor an organized defense that lasted very long. The Counts of Toulouse did what they could until the Pope stopped them.

By 1271 the unification of France was completed. The North won the war. The South lay in ruins. The literary languages of the South were virtually obliterated. The troubadours became a despised memory. The Languedoc, including all the former domains of Eleanor of Aquitaine, passed into the hands of the victorious, very able Capetian kings. The Angevins were ousted from France. All Gaul had become France. The Capetian kings appeared to have won, hands down.

One thorn remained in their sides, however; and the Capetian kings who had each future sovereign carefully trained from childhood by his father to assume the power gradually, step by step, never forgot their royal policy: *all Gaul will become France.* The immensely wealthy, landed Knights Templar had refused absolutely to attack or in any way damage the Catharist South of France.

The Capetian kings looked for a chink in the Templar armor and finally found a large crack: the fall of Jerusalem. Was not the purpose of the Sovereign and Military Order of Knights Templar to defend the Celestial City? Had it not suffered defeat? Therefore were they not unworthy, perhaps also un-Christian?

The chink in the French king's armor was a treasury flat broke from the Albigensian Crusade, which he had supposedly onlooked only. Where was the greatest lot of bullion, property, real estate, treasures, relics, objets d'art? Was it not spread across all Europe in the Templar Commanderies, manors, counties, banks, treasuries, breeding farms, estates, churches uncountable, barns, stables, livestocks, armories, chapels, servants, grooms?

Now the authors of Arthurian material have good cause to remain all anonymous, or else they reside safely outside northern France. In such times authors go to ground or live abroad, or hide. In any event, they do not remain silent. All art rises from an urgent sense of mission. That mission lies over the urgent necessity to make this a wiser and happier world for other people.

c. 1191:   The anonymous Benedictine monk at
           Glastonbury wrote *Perlesvaus*, a brilliant
           work characterized by the extreme sadism
           and cruelty of his contemporaries.

c. 1193:   Ulrich von Zatzikhoven safe in Switzerland
           translated a *Lanzelet* text into German. The
           text had probably been traded by Richard
           I. The original has not as yet been found.

1205–10:   Gottfried von Strassburg wrote a lovely *Tristan
           and Isolde*. He too resided safely in
           German-language territory.

1210–40.   The German Heinrich von dem Türlin wrote
           the superb *Diu Crône (The Crown)*, which
           contains a magnificent defense of Queen
           Guinevere, and an equally magnificent
           Grail episode featuring Gawain as
           candidate.

1220–30:   Seven Old French volumes of the *Prose Lancelot*
           were written anonymously. This is the vast
           compendium from which Sir Thomas
           Malory borrowed so heavily two hundred
           years later his *Morte d'Arthur:* eight
           hundred pages of English prose. Only
           Malory's title is French. He wrote the most
           gorgeous English.
               The *Prose Lancelot* constitutes vast
           volumes of praise for chivalry, Lancelot's
           especially, and for Arthurian nobility and
           high aspiration.

c. 1250:   The *Sone de Nansai* text was translated in Cyprus,
           which Richard I had villainously conquered
           and plundered in order to enrich himself
           and delay his arrival into the Holy Land.
           The translator turned this account of a
           Manx Grail Castle into a very awkward sort
           of Old French. The original text, known to
           have come from Carlisle on the west coast
           of Britain, has not as yet been recovered.

1118–1314

Twenty-two French Grand Masters of the Knights Templar ruled this Order until the Pope dissolved it in 1314. The rank and file Templars took vows of chastity, absolute poverty, piety, and obedience, and swore willingness to die on any field, at any time. Anyone expelled from the Order was sent to a work battalion or labor camp. The rank and file were illiterate, destitute except for their gear, and never paid. It was a lifetime sentence and dedication. They were aptly called the Poor Soldiers of Christ. One cannot but see them as Lancelots, sacrificial victims, men perpetually on the march, questing, all sons of the greater or lesser nobility.

In 1244 the Capetian kings of France found the second chink in the Order's armor, a quarrel between them and their rival Order, the Knights of Saint John of Jerusalem. They were also called the Hospitalers or in French *Hospitaliers*. This quarrel and rivalry for some reason tarnished only the good name of the Templars. The Hospitalers gratefully turned over their treasury to the Capetian monarch, thus insuring their continuance, as Knights of Malta also, down the centuries to today. The Templars haughtily, it is said, refused to bankroll the Capetian king. They thought themselves his army and his beloved sons. They were very wrong.

As one result the Capetian king thought that since they had failed to defend Jerusalem, which had been their raison d'être, they could be cashed in and their hundreds of Commanderies inside France alone could easily be seized, their vast estates easily handed over for resale to the Hospitalers, or otherwise liquidated.

King Philip IV of France laid his plans carefully and quietly. The last Grand Master walked into the trap, open eyed, innocently or arrogantly, as you will. Nobody approaches a study of these events without rancor, dismay, and outright prejudice. This history is unbelievable at best.

The Capetian monarch had Templars inside France seized overnight, incarcerated, held incommunicado, stripped naked, and tortured in ways that pass belief. No woman, it is certain, can believe that any man alive would torture another man in such ways. The Dominican Order performed the torture. Each individual Templar was made to believe that he alone had been arrested. He had no idea why nor where he was, nor what he was supposed to confess, nor if he was to be rescued or simply mutilated sexually beyond recognition.

This affair was successfully concluded on March 18, 1314, before the assembled populace in the city of Paris, France. On that day at least two Templars, and perhaps fifty-four others also, were publicly burned at stakes: the Grand Master Jacques de Molay, aged seventy-one, and the Templar Preceptor of Normandie, Geoffroi de Charney, also aged seventy-one.

King Philip IV is said to have ordered the stakes to which the Templar executives were bound to be soaked beforehand in saltwater so that the agony would last longer. He is also said to have watched it all from a lower window of the Louvre Palace.

At the last moment two Templar leaders recanted their confessions made after years of solitary confinement and sustained torture. As the fire was being lit, each proclaimed his total innocence of all charges. They died calling upon God as their witness.

It is also said that the crowd of Parisian spectators stood mute and stunned. Of course, King Philip had beforehand assembled all France in groups and read them all the charges: heresy and homosexuality. He had also notified all other crowned heads. But on March 18, 1314, *he had neglected to procure from the Courts an order for executions.* The Templars were that day *assassinated* by their lord and master. Cowed by the savage Capetian king, the Pope dissolved the Sovereign and Military Order of Knights Templar.

Some French Templars hid in the woods until they starved to death. In Spain they simply changed the name of their Order, and the same in Germany. In England they were pensioned off by the king. Their fleet disappeared, as did their treasure. The Grand Master of Auvergne is said by French scholars to have escaped to Scotland—but there seems to be no record in Scotland of his arrival. Some Templar volunteers later fought there at Bannockburn, it is said. Eventually, their Order was revived and reconstituted in Scotland, and also later in Nova Scotia, which is New Scotland.

Before the fire was lit under the Grand Master on March 18, 1314, his Preceptor Geoffroi de Charney cried out two prophecies: that the Pope and the Capetian king were guilty, and that both would die within the year. In fact, Pope Clement V died a month later, on April 20, 1314. King Philip IV died suddenly on November 29, 1314, but not because he was less guilty.

The Crusades continued sporadically on through 1371–72, the year of the Ninth Crusade, but always unsuccessfully. The Saracens won in their own homelands where some of their descendants still reside today.

Both the Papacy and the ideals of chivalry survived these disastrous foreign wars called Crusades. The word comes from the Cross of Christ. That the ideal of chivalry survived seems due in large measure to the authors of Arthurian texts, ultimately to the heroism of Gawain, Lancelot, Perceval, and King Arthur in defense of their own homelands in Scotland. That it survived and prospered is also due to the losing Angevin rulers. The Papacy increased in power and prestige and continued to employ Inquisitors to stamp out any last remnants of heresy. It increased in prestige because of the early success in the Holy Land, more so because of the successes of the Capetian monarch seated on its right side, specifically because of the victory won by King Philip IV, called "the Fair."

A French proverb advises that calumniators have only to multiply their charges for some of them to stick permanently to the accused. The Jews in France were charged with various crimes in 1306, and expelled destitute from the country. The secret order went out in 1307 to arrest all the Templars. Nobody in Jerusalem could even have heard this news in less than the thirteen weeks it took for a dispatch rider to arrive there from London or Paris.

There were at least seven principal accusations laid against the Templars inside France: (1) they denied Christianity and the saints, and they spat on the crucifix; (2) they adored idols such as cats, a head, and three faces; (3) they did not believe in the Mass or in the sacraments; (4) their Grand Master could hear confessions and grant absolution; (5) their investors (receptors) kissed new members on the mouth, navel, stomach, buttocks, and anus (or spine), and encouraged homosexuality; (6) a Templar sought gain by all possible means; (7) chapter meetings were secret, held at night in order to remain so, in short, proving that the Order was a secret society. The church forbade secret societies.

Cardinals heard these charges and the Templar executives who could not answer them satisfactorily at Chinon Castle in 1308. The Grand Master also appeared before them in 1309, offering likewise no defense. The first group of fifty-four Templars was publicly burned to death in Paris in 1310. In 1313 the Hospitalers offered the French king two hundred thousand pounds of gold as compensation. Pope Clement V died after having a nightmare that his golden palace had been set on fire, with him in it. The Italian poet Dante, who hated King Philip IV unmercifully and who accused him personally of having dirtied man's finest Order of heroism and chivalry, launched the rumor that King Philip had been gored to death by a bull. Ah, well, cried Dante. What can we expect? In this world legalese prose kills poetry. It kills beauty too, descending doves, arks of the covenant, holiness everywhere. It even kills truth. And finally, chivalry.

The voice of Eleanor of Aquitaine's Chaplain Andreas still is heard over the world, however. Chivalry, he cried, posited an ideal of manhood like that of Sir Lancelot. From King Arthur's day the code of chivalry worked a fusion between Christian, religious teachings, and idealism. The Holy Grail gave generations an idea of purity and holiness to strive for and die for. The chivalric virtues Gawain held dear as he sallied out to meet the Green Knight's perhaps fatal beheading blow formed a pentagon: liberality, loving-kindness, continence, courtesy, and piety. Andreas added: love ennobles a person. Deference to women becomes a noble man. Character is worthy. Therefore follow the thirty-one Rules of Love.

The Knights Templar have not lacked defenders over the past hundred years: Henri de Curzon, Michelet, Guizot, and Sismondi before 1900; Reinach, Melville, Oursel, Daraul, Hays, Charpentier, Bordonove, Barber, and Chevalier Brydon, who is currently writing in Edinburgh, Scotland. Barber and Bordonove stand out as great and compassionate scholars eminent for their nobility of feeling as for their impeccable research and beautiful prose.

In Paris (1886) Curzon gave us the Rule of the Templars, only three copies of which have survived: sixty-three articles inscribed and presented before the Church Council of Troyes in 1128, the Templar founder, Hugues de Payen, present. Only the three copies survive perhaps because no brother was ever allowed to possess one—only superior officers. The laws as encoded were, says Curzon (p. xiij), "irreproachable, truly monastic, and even very severe." Both Church judges and Church executioners searched them in vain for deviations. Each poor brother, for instance, was allowed in his trousseau a total of two shirts, two britches, one paneled doublet, one fitted jacket with split skirt front and back, one cloak and mail tunic, one leather belt, and two head coverings (one cotton bonnet and one felt hat). No hoods were allowed. Knights alone wore the characteristic, white cape or mantle, red crosses on all mantles. Chaplains were to wear black, closed gowns. Bishops might wear white robes.

The many Fast Days were rigorous. Each Templar was expected to leave a large part of each portion he was served for the poor. He attended eight church services each day. He remained illiterate. He was never allowed to handle money except when needed for expenditures. He returned all sums left over. If even one penny was found on his corpse, he was refused Christian burial. Open confessions were encouraged at all services. Accusations at chapter meetings were also encouraged. Templars were expelled for the least infraction of the following crimes: simony, breach of confidence, theft, escaping, plotting, treason (which meant fleeing from an Arab warrior), heresy, desertion (for fear of an Arab warrior), sodomy, and lying. Any Templar expelled was obliged to appear before his brothers naked except for underpants, and with a halter about his neck. If sentenced, he was forced to enter for life one of the hardest-working and most severe Orders, such as Saint Augustine's or Saint Benoît's. He could not be received into the Hospitalers or by the Order of Saint Lazarus.

The commission of lesser crimes could earn him only the loss of his habit for a year and a day: beating a brother Christian, being caught in a woman's company, accusing a brother falsely, asking to leave the Order, dropping the pennant in combat, breaking a seal or a lock, lending his horse, losing the money he had been given, or hurting either a slave or an animal.

The Templars were obliged to swear that they would live henceforth as "serfs" and "slaves" of the Order. The case of one Templar remains on the record; he was driven from the Order for forgetting to count a jar of butter. Their punishments included being loaded with irons, being confined in solitary for life, being deprived of food and water three days each week, washing dishes, eating on the floor, and not being allowed to dress.

At his investiture each prospective candidate must answer "No" to the following questions: married? engaged? belong to another Order? indebted beyond resources? anything to gain? ordained priest? ever excommunicated? He must answer "Yes" to the following: of knightly family? legitimate? healthy? The following promises were exacted: to obey commanders, to remain chaste, to live without property, to obey the rules of the Order, to help conquer the Holy Land and safeguard Christians and their possessions, never to desert the Temple for another Order, not to allow any crime against a Christian to stand unredressed.

His reception into the Order was pronounced "by God and by Our Lady Saint Mary, and by his Lordship Saint Peter of Rome, and by our father the Apostle, and by all brothers of the Temple." The white mantle and red cross of the Order were robed about him as the candidate knelt before the altar upon which lay the Sword. Rule 71 enjoined him: "We believe it a perilous thing to all religious belief to look upon the face of woman."

The liberal historian Jules Michelet looked back on the Templars with considerable alarm, for liberalism meant to him mass liberty, laissez faire, life under as little government as possible. Michelet was for his liberalism twice suspended at the august Collège de France. He noted first the power of that Order, which had occupied one-third of the city of Paris, and owned dependencies in Portugal, Castile, Léon, Aragon, Majorca, Germany, Italy, Sicily, England, and Ireland. A Templar's life consisted of danger and abstinence, exile, and Holy War to the death. He was never to decline battle even of one against three, which was to follow Lancelot's example. He was never to cry for mercy, never to accept ransom, never to own an inch of land, never to ask to rest, and never to change Orders. Saint Bernard had recommended glory as conqueror, happiness as martyrs. He had supplied this noble image for the Crusades, that it was a grand adventure and an eternal quest. Therefore Templars, like Lancelot, took the vanguard at Mansourah knowing they would die, and they died there.

People during the Crusades daily saw the Templars, who looked so much alike; their short haircuts of serfs, uncombed locks, bodies begrimed with sweat and dust, faces and arms black with rust and iron, skins weathered and sunburned. They were dirty, unwashed, and unshaven, but all astride fiery horses. Their investitures were held ceremoniously in dark chapels at night, as are some in Rosslyn Chapel today. Had the King of France himself intruded, observed Michelet, he would never have been seen again.

It constituted a real danger for them to lodge in Solomon's Temple stables and ruined plaza, and to hold these places superior to all others. It proved equally dangerous to keep their investitures secret, to let their worship remain mysterious like a Masonic Order, Michelet added, or the rites of Rosicrucians. Why were their temples decorated by Perceval's symbol of a descending dove? Why did they replace the greater festivals of Christianity with King Arthur's Pentecost when he always held a crown-wearing? Michelet would have liked to have known this: what remains today of King Arthur's ancient sects? What remained of them throughout the Middle Ages?

Was the Templar's Quest heroic, and also pious in search of the Grail? Why was their ungovernable, martial spirit so indestructible? Why were Templars still forbidden to wed on the one hand but on the other hand devoted to chivalry toward women? We must wonder whether the Templars were not in reality guardians of the Cup of the Last Supper. Could they not also have been keepers and bearers of the Grail? Did all this sacerdotal writing of King Arthur's inspiration really dwindle off and expire with Galahad? What became of it all? Was that not sadness and death? But in the case of the Knights Templar, did it not rather lead to massacre?

"The most tragical part of all this," concluded Michelet, "is that the Church is slain by the Church" (p. 391). When the Crusades commenced, all men everywhere believed in it, in chivalry, and in the Papacy. At the end the Church committed suicide. The Holy Land was lost. The weary Templars who had so unselfishly fought for centuries, let their arms drop by their sides. They made no defense. They, who had purchased Cyprus without the blink of an eye, who ruled nine thousand manor houses, who accepted twice all the Counts of Provence had to offer, who were given the kingdom of Aragón as a free gift, who were also given seventeen fortresses in Valencia, congregated once in Paris to present a defense. There were 546 Templars who came to court. The Capetian king promptly ruined them all by charging them ruinous fees even for the air they breathed and the stones they walked over. Thus, this great quarrel over ideas, religion, honor, principles, heroism in war, service to Christianity dwindled down to sums of money. The Parisians watched it all happen, stunned and silent.

But, some historians believe, no king of France from that day forward was ever respected by the French people, unless it was their only Protestant king, Henry IV (Bordonove, p. 239ff.).

French historians have by and large proved unable to explain why the Templars did not defend themselves. Louis Charpentier (1967) believed that they had possession of the Holy Grail, and furthermore that their Priors and Grand Masters, all French and all serving for life as they do in Scotland today, were none other than the Grail Kings. His guess was that the Holy Grail would one day be found *in a Templar chapel,* and that their treasure would be found too, even if submerged in a lake.

The reason the Templars did not defend themselves in court, said the formidable Hebrew scholar Salomon Reinach in 1911, is that they were allowed only to answer questions. The prosecutors used a questionnaire prepared especially for their interrogations. The questions were for the most part inappropriate, even nonsensical, such as: "How many times did you kiss the head? What head had three faces?" The interrogators were dumber than the Greeks, scoffed Reinach. Even the Greeks understood what was folklore and rubbish only. By referring to this "head" as Baphomet, they were trying to extract an admission that the accused was a Muslim.

Before 1265 when the Templars began to lose their forts in the Holy Land, their Grand Masters alerted western Europe that Syria was in addition to their usual warfare being invaded by Mongols from the original hordes of Gengis Khan. Is it God's will that we die here? cried the Masters; for truly it has become beyond our will to halt these catastrophes that lay us down in the sands (Bordonove, p. 186). Fifteen thousand Templars died one way or another in the last year alone: 1314. Bordonove's conclusion reads like a precept in ancient Greek democracy. In his opinion, after examining all the evidence that has survived in France, Bordonove believes that the people of a nation are more equitable than all their magistrates put together.

History has certainly proved it over and over again; the only and ultimate judge is people, average people themselves. It was Bordonove who informed his readers that Pierre d'Aumont, the Templar Master from Auvergne, had fled safely to Scotland where he met other fugitives from France, and that Scotland remains the true heir to the Knights Templar.

Chevalier Brydon, friend and correspondent from Edinburgh today, supposes that the Grail Temple was a replica of Solomon's Temple. So was Mont Salvat, or (we add) Montségur. The trials or Quests were allegorical. The Grail was also a chalice, which represented the Celtic cauldron or vessel of resurrection. The Templar gospel was in part secret. Their tradition exalted a spiritualized knighthood that was supposed to remain incorruptible. A high conscience characterized their chivalry. Nobility there was inborn, ergo natural and personal. These modern Templars, Brydon says in interviews, are still mystical guardians of these concepts: sacrifice, courtesy, duty, care of the poor, and the ideal of womanhood.

By following our priestly Lancelot, and those who wrote the Grail texts, we now see perhaps why they were written in those troubled years of trials and massacres.

Chapter
VI

PARZIVAL
AND GERMANY

PEREDUR

Since not Lancelot but "Perceval" is considered, up to now anyway, the most important initiate or Grail hero, he and his experiences at Grail ceremonies inside Grail Castles confront us now.

It would seem logical to clarify his narratives in order of their composition, as much as possible chronologically, one by one. We must realize first of all that "Perceval" goes by four chief names, and that he performs his exploits in four, chief languages and/or in four countries chiefly:

1. *Peredur*—Wales and/or Brythonic Scotland
2. *Perceval*—northern or Capetian France
3. *Parzival*—Germany and France
4. *Parsifal*—Germany and Spain

Probably the oldest surviving account of Perceval's quest for the Holy Grail comes from a Welsh collection of ancient, Druidical tales called the *Mabinogion.* The collection has been translated several times since the pioneering work of Lady Charlotte Guest in 1838. It is generally agreed now that *Peredur* is not actually native to Wales, did not take place inside Wales, but is a retelling made during the Middle Ages there of an even more ancient genealogical and heroic exploit from "the North." Glenys Goetinck of the University of Wales has said this (1975). In her introduction to the *Histories* of Geoffrey of Monmouth, Lucy Allen Paton had observed too: "Plainly the primitive traditions that are characteristic of Wales and her early mythology have become connected with the British hero [Arthur], whose victories in war Nennius recorded" (p. xiv). An authorship by Nennius is attributed to the very ancient *Annals of Wales,* which, in fact, even predate King Arthur by a few decades. From the first words of this *Peredur* text, nobody doubts for a second but that it is primitive. Most important of all, however, is the very great possibility that a translation of this *Peredur* text was Chrétien's source for his more famous and French *Perceval* text.

The Welsh text offers no genealogy for the hero Peredur, noting laconically that he is called "Longspear," that his name is Peredur, that he is a son of "York" and "from the North." The "North" he comes from is much more probably Stirling in Scotland, the real center of ancient northern tribes, and the place where Perceval's mother in the Glastonbury or *Perlesvaus* text owns vast domains between Stirling, Alloa, and the North Sea. Peredur's (Perceval's) genealogy would have been well known to all British listeners of this ancient tale. Only he and Lancelot claimed both royal and sainted ancestors. The Welsh text does therefore not bother to tell us Peredur is King Arthur's last, surviving nephew. Every listener would have known that too.

The tale appears to derive from oral tradition memorized originally and handed down for hundreds of years before being committed to this permanent, written form. The narrator hesitates at the commencement of his story, wavering between knowing and not knowing, explaining and not explaining. He was probably trained to know and not explain. Only initiates were meant to understand fully. The rest is myth, and therefore ritual, and therefore to be experienced directly. Myth is always upsetting.

The *Peredur* narrator goes through fourteen or fifteen episodes during which his hero Peredur is gradually admitted through an inner circle of elders to the vengeance he seeks and the kingship his birth merits. How many generations of bards must have recited these same units can only be imagined. The Welsh narrator has it all pretty well by rote. Nothing is described, commented upon, or fleshed out. He is reciting a learned lesson, an arcane ritual. The *Peredur* comes to us as naked myth only: episodes 1–15. This morphology establishes once and for all the hero's conquest of kingship and his vengeance upon the slayers of his father and of his six (or eleven) dead brothers. Every succeeding Perceval hero, including Perlesvaus and the English Percyvelle too, follow partially or wholly this identical pattern, embellished or not according to each author's capability and talent, either entire or abridged.

Seventh son of seven sons Peredur, we know from elsewhere, is the last of King Arthur's nephews to be summoned for inauguration as last king of the Grail Castle. Arthur's emissaries, whom the boy Peredur mistakes for angels, set him in motion. Peredur's mother dies from shock. One of the "angels" was another of the most ancient heroes of Scotland, Owain, son of King Urien from Moray. Peredur belongs to this generation of heroes, all like the MacArthurs, older than the hills.

Episode 2 brings the hero to Arthur's court. Here each narrator omits what the reader is never supposed to know: King Arthur personally programs Peredur, who is henceforth expendable. That knowledge has already caused the mother's death, and not her boy's departure; sons always leave their mothers. Arthur is seated at the head of the Solway Firth, at Carlisle, his western Camelot, called "Caer Llion" or castle of the waves, in Welsh. The point not stressed but avoided is that Arthur is the Master of this initiation game, and furthermore, that he is its secret but presiding Master. His presidency, like that of the Templar Grand Masters, will be for life. Lesser dignitaries might be reassigned. There is another one, another secret Grand Master, however, who lurks about but who is totally unidentified here: Merlin. The author of our next-oldest text will produce him too, but the *Peredur* narrator has prudently missed his presence.

Peredur now calls at a second uncle's castle, a visit he has deserved by having already overthrown sixteen champions in desolate forests, beside a lake with a castle on the opposite shore. There prophecies are given by a male and a female dwarf: Peredur will succeed. Riding the Templars' piebald nag, Peredur visits the Fisher King's castle, that hoary-headed, lame brother of his mother Eccles from her eastern Camelot. Peredur receives this new teacher's instruction. Then in a third castle he proves his present strength by cutting an iron column in two with his sword.

In this Castle of Wonders he witnesses a rite consisting of two (Grail) Processions, which horrify only the reader: two youths crossing the hall, bearing a huge spear streaming blood on the floor. Everyone present cried aloud and mourned. Meanwhile Peredur and his uncle conversed quietly. Then two maidens entered carrying a salver (or platter, or shallow bowl) in which sat a man's severed head soaking in blood. . . . It could not be more gruesome. The horror is multiplied by the traditionally laconic ending: Peredur arose early next morning. . . .

Thereafter follow three bitter adventures, which Peredur brings to satisfactory conclusions, ordering each conquered vassal to report back and surrender personally to King Arthur.

Here one begins to understand the dynamics of these very antique musical chairs games: instructions followed by martial accomplishments, followed by further accomplishments, followed by further instructions. Peredur must avenge his father's death, his brothers' deaths, his mother's death, his foster sister's injury, and safeguard and enrich Arthur at each turn.

By episode 8 he presents himself at the Witches' Court for military instruction, which again attests to the extreme age of this material. Women teachers of warriors stretched back into the extreme antiquity of both Ireland and Scandinavia also, but by Arthur's time priestesses were being phased out by the Christian church. It is very surprising to meet them openly admitted, as if priestesses were a regular phenomenon, preaching to and teaching a great hero how to kill more expertly.

Precisely after his lessons at the Witches' Court, Peredur experiences that seizure or trance which has been hailed, and justly so, as one of the most startling and revealing passages in Arthurian literature (*The Mabinogion,* translated by G. Jones and T. Jones, p. 199): "At the close of a day he came to a valley, and at the far end of the valley he came to a hermit's cell." Peredur, always an early riser, looked out to see a fall of new snow covering the ground.

There before the hermit's cave (cell), Peredur saw that a wild female hawk had brought down and killed a duck. The clatter of his horse's hooves on the rocky earth disturbed the hawk from her meal. She flew up in the air. Immediately a raven dropped down on the bloody carcass.

Peredur fell into a trance. He stared open-eyed at the red blood, the black feathered raven, and the white snow all round. They reminded him of his beloved (usually named Blanchefleur, or

White Flower) whose skin was as white as that driven snow, whose curls were as black as the raven's jet plumes, and whose cheeks had the same two red spots, as red as the duck's blood.

Having just ridden out from Carlisle, Arthur finally brought Peredur to his senses again, but not before the hero had unhorsed dozens of messengers from Arthur, and the foster brother Kay also. Arthur finally had to have Peredur literally carried in a litter to his own pavilion and revived professionally.

There at Arthur's court Peredur becomes engaged to his red-black-and-white sweetheart, here named Angharad Goldenhand. After Christian baptism they will be wed, which makes one suspect that the baptizing Archbishop Merlin is also hereabouts. Peredur is still victor; but his conquests after the trance become more and more unreal, like lions who are porters and gray men who reside in round valleys. The hero is still hallucinating, it would appear. In the hunt for the magical stag that locates the sites of future abbey churches, whether for King David of Scotland, Queen Guinevere, or the Norman founder of Fécamp Abbey in France, Peredur's dog kills the lordly creature. That upsets every reader, to no end.

Several even more terrible adventures remain. He must vanquish the Black Oppressor at the Black Barrow, or prehistoric chambered tomb under which, even today, few British persons will ever venture to set foot. He must at this barrow slay the Black Worm, or the Dragon that has a magical stone in his tail. He must correctly choose between the three paths (of the ancient goddess Hecate). At the issue of the third path he must kill the murdering, prehistoric Monster (Addanc) which builds dams under a black lake, and kills heroes with a stone spear at a stone pillar. A beautiful fairy lady gives the hero another powerful stone, or talisman, because of which he ultimately triumphs even over these neolithic peoples. Memory in literature is uncannily accurate.

Peredur emerges ultimately into a more real world ruled by the lovely Empress of Constantinople, whose ancestor must also have sired King Arthur. There (with Blanchefleur, of course) he ruled peaceably for fourteen years, probably then fathering the Lohengrin who was born with a golden chain about his neck, but thrown into the "Lake" to die, as Lancelot or his twin also was thrown there to die. After his inauguration at the Grail Castle, Peredur will have to repudiate his dear wife. He will remain celibate after that ceremony. His wife will then probably retire to raise her surviving children, as did Peredur's mother, into his or her earldom in the North.

All these myths appear to us today as genealogical records from such as the Gododdin, or from another such ancient people inhabiting eastern Scotland before they emigrated into Wales. Just as the Welsh *Peredur* narrator substitutes the familiar "York" on the east coast of Britain for the more ancient northern capitals of Edinburgh and Stirling on the east coast but farther "in the North," so he routinely substitutes the familiar old western, but small Roman fortress of Caer Llion on Usk in South Wales, for the immense Roman Fortress, Caer Llion-Carlisle, in the North, on the western or Solway Firth. Thus, the geography of the *Peredur,* unlike that of the voluminous and multiple texts in Old French, is so old it must be unscrambled.

One has merely to scan the *Perlesvaus* from Glastonbury where Perlesvaus or Peredur, Arthur, and the mother of the hero are all nicely settled in much more believable sites. But Arthur happened to be, recites the *Peredur* narrator, at one of his castles, the one at Caer Llion on the Usk River in South Wales. The author of the long *Perlesvaus,* where Peredur is always called Perlesvaus, straightens out the geography for us. The hero was born on one of his mother's thirteen valuable farms, or estates near Camelot. The estates stretched across the rich bottom land of a river that formed huge loops before it passed into the (North) Sea. From the westward-facing, granite cliff on which the fortress of Camelot stood (stands) the boy could look down on the Old Abbey with its sacrosanct tomb where Joseph of Arimathea once lay buried. Lancelot himself had worshiped there and heard the voice (Merlin's?) from the tomb. Perceval had been taken there by his young father, and there he had heard his father recite his genealogy and also calculate how many years had passed between the death of Christ and that day when the two also stood reverently at the tomb. Chrétien agreed; Camelot was also called "Senaudone," or Snowdon (now the fort of Stirling). Since she was King Arthur's very vocal sister, to whom especial respect was due, Peredur's mother was called *the* Widow Lady of Camelot. She was also called Yglais or Eccles because she had reendowed and rebuilt the Old Abbey Church below her fortress. That church is presumably the Saint Ninian's that stands today on the Bannockburn battlefield. The rich estates of *the* Widow Lady of Camelot lay along the celebrated loops of the Forth River. Where this queen lies buried, nobody has said as yet. Queen Guinevere lies buried to the north of Stirling, in the village of Meigle, beside its village church door. She probably died there in the gorgeous farm-lands, along the warm, sunny vale of Strathmore. Thus, Perceval's mother probably lies interred at her church, Saint Ninian's.

Before he can end his *Peredur* story, our narrator abruptly remembers that each Grail hero has an alternate who usually pre-cedes him until he abandons the quest entirely in favor of the second, or real, hero. But here a very curious lapse of memory occurs. Instead of giving us the alternate hero's usual unsuccessful attempt and withdrawal episode, our narrator gives us a selection we remember from the celebrated *Gawain and the Green Knight* poem. He tells how Gawain undertook to woo a lady, how he found her and fell in love, but how her cruel husband, who was the Green Knight, almost killed Gawain in a jealous rage. Catching himself up short, the narrator halts the episode at that point. His memory had slipped a cog.

Gawain probably was Peredur's alternate or secondary-track hero, just as he was Lancelot's in Chrétien's *Knight of the Cart.* Since Gawain is the eldest hero at Arthur's court, he will eventually be found closest to Arthur himself in the matter of the Grail Quest. The Welsh narrator drops him abruptly in order to finish with Peredur, but not before he has presented the Loathly Damsel to us.

Cundrie herself emerges amusingly from the Welsh text her usual repulsive, scolding self, a curly-haired spinster maiden on a yellow mule, who reproaches Peredur for having failed, by not asking about the marvels he saw at the Grail Procession, to save the Fisher King and his realm. She is here plainly described as a dwarf, and so is Gawain, occasionally, so described. The *Peredur* author himself fails to realize that Gawain will in Arthur's stead wed this Cundrie. Here she only sets adventures for King Arthur to under-take. With her long yellow teeth, her prominent abdomen and splayed nostrils, Cundrie comically resembles Madame Bovary, who also had eyes of two different colors. One of Cundrie's eyes is green, the other, black. Short-legged, hump-backed, broad-hipped, sagging-fleshed Cundrie always dismays of finding a hus-band. She makes up for it by the depth of her knowledge and her prowess as a linguist.

An old English ballad printed by Thomas Percy among his *Reliques* is entitled *The Marriage of Sir Gawaine;* it supplied Chaucer with the plot for his "Wife of Bath's Tale." The ballad tells how King Arthur was caught on the road from Penrith to Carlisle and forced to discover what it is women most desire. In perplexity, he thought to ask Cundrie, and saw that

> *Her nose was crooked and turned outward,*
> *Her chin stood all awry:*
> *And where as should have been her mouth,*
> *Lo! there was set her eye:*

> *Her hair like serpents clung about*
> *Her cheeks of deadly hue:*
> *A worse-formed lady than she was,*
> *No man might ever view.*

What women most desire, Cundrie told Arthur, is to have their will. As Chaucer expressed it, a woman wants mastery over her own life. Because of her correct answer, Cundrie won Gawain for her husband. She consoled him beforehand with the facts of the matter: that his love would make her beautiful to him. The episode of Arthur, Gawain, and the Loathly Damsel Cundrie brings the *Peredur* text to its climax.

A year has now passed, and it is Good Friday again when Peredur receives his final directions to what the author knows as the Castle of Wonders: cross the mountain, come to a lake, find a castle beside the lake, and ask for the next directions.

When Peredur finally arrived at what we know is the Grail Castle, he found the gate open. He entered. As he reached the hall, again he found the door ajar. In other words, the castle anticipated his coming and knew him for the victorious warrior who would assume the reign. . . . Ever since *Peredur* the Gothic tale and Gothic novel has followed this identical tradition of castle gate and door that open of themselves to the second, or winning hero.

When Peredur entered, he found two lads playing chess. Angrily the hero threw the pieces and the board into the lake; they had been gaming for his soul. For this infraction of the Empress's rule, Peredur was twice obliged to rid her realm of a giant. A further test still awaited him: to kill a devastating stag that disturbed her fish and browsed on her trees. This time the hero was lent Lancelot's magical talisman, the lady's yapping lapdog. His third trial was to raise a champion from under his stone sarcophagus and then defeat him thrice.

The last two paragraphs of *Peredur* stump the reader, so awkwardly have they dared to contradict all theory and all logic. Peredur arrives again at the (Grail) Castle where he is greeted by his uncle (the Fisher King) and by his cousin Gawain. Then he is told by an unnamed youth that he, the youth, had played the major roles in Peredur's adventures: the maiden, the black giant, the chess player, the stag, the (Grail) bearer of the bleeding head, and the spear that gushed blood on the hall floor. He confesses to being another of Peredur's cousins.

One youth assigns Peredur a vengeance to exact: he must kill his women teachers, now again called Witches. They had lamed the Fisher King. They had cut off the head, which was also that of a cousin of Peredur.

Peredur summoned King Arthur and they slew all the Witches. At the end "the mystery," said Meic Stephens (1986), "is cleared up in a rather offhand way"; or it is not cleared up at all.

Two points remain thorns in the flesh: (1) Whose was the head in the dish or platter? (2) What is the significance of this pupil's turning upon his teachers, and Arthur's battle against them? In this oldest Grail Procession, it is surely paramount in our minds to discover whose head is being carried in a solemn ritual performance, and why the persons present should all weep and lament loudly. Immediately after the second reference to this bleeding head, we are diverted to a battle against Peredur's teachers "of martial arts." Thus, it was a woman or women who cut off the victim's head, we may certainly assume. Our task now as we follow the longer Perceval texts and subsequently move to Gawain, and finally to Arthur, will be to look for further knowledge concerning this severed head. All this has been left unclear.

It has been widely assumed that the head was that of an ancient king named Bran (King) or the Blessed Bran in Wales, whose worship consisted of warriors feasting about him and taking his embalmed head out often and allowing it to feast along with them. But if we considered the Grail as quite another sort of worship, with a program and performance unique to itself, and its own Questers, bearers, kings, and devotees, then that would leave Bran long back in the forgotten past, or down south in Wales only. Therefore our search continues.

The French scholar Jean Markale (1971) offered several theories to explain *Peredur:* that it illustrated a conflict of two differing religions during King Arthur's reign; that it told a simple story of vengeance on the hero's part, or of his revenge on the Witches; that it recounted magical rites of initiation where Arthur appeared personally three times; or that it purposed to figure the "Rich" (Worthy) Fisher King as Christ before a disciple Peredur. In any case, he thought, the *Peredur* constitutes a Grail Quest, even if the word "Grail" never appears in this text of "incredible celebrity" (p. 183). He also felt confident that the account originated in the North of Great Britain whence it was carried during the Anglo-Saxon invasions by British immigrants into what became the kingdoms of Wales. If it recalls a conflict of religions, as seems true, then the victory went to a central, new religion that here vanquished a peripheral and demonic cult represented by the Sorceress Cundrie. This proud princess will be renamed by Wolfram: "the Proud," or "Orgeluse" (from the French adjective *orgueilleuse*). Under an invasion by demonic powers, Peredur cries "Kill!" The prophecy of the dwarfs is fulfilled: a hero kills in war. Peredur rushes about responding to adversity while the lame Fisher King fishes for Christian souls. *Perlesvaus* will make it very clear that Arthur and Perceval (Perlesvaus) re-Christianized the Grail Castle Corbenic.

We have seen in *Peredur,* then, at least ten instructors who teach and sponsor this last nephew of King Arthur. The movement fascinates the reader, taking him in discontinuous progress forward with halts called every two or three progressions. Peredur is stopped by three elders, by Sigune's reproach, by the Witches in their court, by King Arthur outside and inside Carlisle, and by Cundrie once again.

No literary critic makes this text as doubly significant as does the English social anthropologist I. M. Lewis (1971) when he describes a typical case of trance and possession. Applying his criteria, we could say also that Peredur experienced a trauma before he even left home, that his sighting of what he identified as angels on the path recalls Paul's blinding light on the road to Damascus. Even that was an instance, Lewis might agree, of trance and possession characterized by dissociation, hypnotic seizure, mediumistic behavior, and hallucination. It resembled histrionic snake-handling accompanied by the usual properties of river water, dark forests of the world, and the presence of animal masks and spirits such as lapdogs, deer, stags, and fish. Whereas witchcraft subsumes a power to harm, Peredur's power will reside, when accumulated, in his high office at the Grail Castle. This site he must find and reach and enter once and for all after his sexual function has been performed and abjured. Therefore he acquires meanwhile the techniques of sorcery.

Like all ancient shamans, Siberians, and Eskimos from the Far North, Peredur also accumulates multiple personalities, which is how the social anthropologist would probably identify his second-track, powerful heroes: Gawain, Owain, and most of all, King Arthur. His authority will also be reinforced by peripheral but imposing women, who are in their own spheres or real properties "omni-competent leaders" (p. 34). He learns from the hermit how to perform a blood sacrifice: red blood, black bird, white snow. Lancelot also learned it from Queen Guinevere, as he approached her altar in dark of night, with bloodied right hand. Because these women are pure, which is to say, childless, Cundrie, Sigune, and Guinevere reinforce his final vocation of celibate priesthood.

All in all, *Peredur* presents a view of the world gone to war where males triumph and women become downtrodden. Sex has become unnecessary. Women are pushed out of the circle of power. From occasionally dominant, they are relegated to always submissive, or pregnant, or killed. Frightening them all with her ugliness, Cundrie speaks for the old, anthropomorphic, totemic gods of the northern clans. The Empress whom Peredur weds tells him to kill and gives him the old, old talisman: a stone from Neolithic times. Thus, even though Merlin who died in A.D. 536 could not have built Stonehenge in 1750 B.C., a great priest like Merlin probably did design and live to build something like it. Thus also, Queen Guinevere is slapped on the face at the beginning of *Peredur,* to awaken her prophetic powers, doubtless, and make her orate somnambulistically.

There is a statue of the enraptured Mother Theresa sculpted by Giovanni Lorenzo Bernini (1598–1680), who was a chief architect of the piazza of Saint Peter's in Rome. Lewis reproduces it in his 1971 book, *Ecstatic Religion.*

Peredur and his relatives in North Britain lived in the most perilous times, when their government by Rome had collapsed, when huge migrations of footloose people were overthrowing their settled lives, when they were diving literally into dark forests to starve. Saint Gildas described the chaos then in such graphic terms as live forever in the terrified memories of his readers. His personal response was a towering, vitriolic rage, an absolute frenzy of howling anger.

The poor Witches must have clutched their little lapdogs to their bosoms. Each was her sweet familiar. As they stroked their pets, like us they lowered their blood pressures. As Markale pointed out (p. 200, n. 1), they had performed for Peredur's education "magical warrior rites in Scotland." Experience shows that the killing of one's women teachers is usually a deeply repressed desire, but usually the females' wish, and not the males'. One therefore again finds it most strange in Peredur, more so in King Arthur. On the other hand, the latter's youngest half sister was probably the Witches' leader, Queen Morgan le Fay, reportedly all shrouded and swathed, like any other Witch, in midnight black.

Great respect is due the Welsh scholar Goetinck, who has been not only the most brilliant, native critic of *Peredur* but also its prime textual scholar. He underlined again what he saw as the Celtic origins of the Grail, an Otherworld talisman, he decided, given to the future sovereign by Sovereignty herself, who here was openly named Empress of Constantinople, no less. Ancient Irish heroes like Finn and Conn. had earlier quested for this majestic donor called Sovereignty because she, like Queen Guinevere, owned the kingdom by inheritance. During a formal repast served by her, the sacred object that will after *Peredur* be named a "Grail," contained blood or wine, indifferently. Thus, it was both Druidical and Christian at the same stroke of a pen. Both a Perceval/Peredur and a Lancelot/Angus were once, like Lugh, rulers in Tara. Peredur's ancestors, and Perceval's, were said to have been hereditary Lords of the Isles, probably meaning the Hebrides, just where the Mac-Donalds reigned in later, more historical times. His uncles were "Otherworld enchanters," agreed Goetinck. Their talismans were the Thirteen Treasures of Britain (which I have listed in *Merlin*). Perceval's sword was forged on the Firth of Forth, near his birthplace in the rich Vale of Camelot. Iron works continued there along the Carron River until a few years ago.

These legends of Peredur/Perceval originated, agreed Goetinck, in "the Old North, and later in Wales" (p. 284), for which reason the bloody spear that passed in the Grail Procession was claimed able eventually to destroy the new Ogre Land of England: Logre.

Peredur, Chrétien, Helinandus (see *King Arthur* Appendix), and the princely historian Gerald of Wales all agreed that the Grail was a shallow dish *(escuele)* or platter that held the head of a man. In *Perlesvaus* also a Grail maiden carries a king's head. In Welsh also the Grail was a shallow dish *(dysgl)*. In Chrétien, as perhaps in the hypothetical translation of *Peredur,* which was his source, the Grail becomes, it is generally thought, a Christian symbol: dish, cup, or chalice of the Last Supper.

The problem of whose head rested in the platter still seems open for now.

PERCEVAL

Two Perceval texts come between the Welsh *Peredur* and the German *Parzival:* the so-called *Didot-Perceval* (one owned by a person named Didot) and Chrétien's *Perceval* called *Conte del Graal* or Tale (Account) of the Grail. The textual scholar of the *Prose Lancelot,* H. O. Sommer, explained why the *Didot-Perceval* must be interposed: "As Chrétien's elegant poems were for obvious reasons not suitable to be united to Robert [de Boron's] *Joseph* and *Merlin,* the unknown compiler joined them to the *Prose Lancelot"* (vol. 1, p. xiv).

To put it plainly, the *Peredur* underwent a Christianization, which was supported in every way by the later Glastonbury *Perlesvaus,* but not by Chrétien de Troyes. Chrétien halted his composition of *Lancelot* after he interpreted, or misinterpreted, the altar scene between Lancelot and Guinevere as pagan idolatry and adultery. He translated her "altar" as her "bed," which is to say, he had Lancelot go not to her altar but to her bed. Similarly, he did not complete his *Perceval.* Nobody as yet knows why.

Our unknown author calling himself Robert de Boron (or Borron) would not allow the pagan *Peredur* to stand as a true representation of King Arthur, much less as a true depiction of a Christian Merlin whom he adored. The French scholar Gaston Paris, who first edited the *Merlin* texts (called *Huth Merlin* because once owned by an Englishman named Huth) called Robert a great problem solver. The same goes for the Glastonbury author of *Perlesvaus* who must, like Robert, have had access to a vast library like that of a Benedictine Abbey.

Robert de Boron takes us all the way back again to Jerusalem and to *Joseph d'Arimathie* (Bibliothèque Nationale MS fr. 20047), which is the story of Christ's death followed by 502 verses of a life of Merlin. This text was edited recently by W. A. Nitze (Paris, 1971). Let us understand once and for all, writes Robert authoritatively, that the Grail originated not in pagan Wales, Ireland, nor any other Druidical religion, but in Jerusalem. Christ descended into Hell, as will Lancelot, Guinevere, Gawain, and Perceval. The Grail was "le vase," the Cup of the Last Supper, given to the Grail Keepers Joseph, Bron(s), and Alein. Grail means Holy Blood as symbolized by a chalice (*calice,* vv. 901–09). Those who see the Grail, stand in the very presence of God.

Where Robert showed himself most original, said Nitze (p. xi), was in the following passage (vv. 960–2,256): After the destruction of Jerusalem, Joseph went into exile as the records show. His sister married a Jew named Hebron. This man Hebron or Bron(s), who was Joseph's brother-in-law (let us be clear about this, and we have now been told so twice), became next "possessor of the Grail." The Grail was kept in or on a Grail Table, alongside a cup and a book, which was the New Testament. A certain Petrus revealed its name: "Graal!" (v. 2,657ff.). That man Moise (Moses), who talked about a Siege Perilous at a Table, was a false prophet. Ignore him. Thus, concluded Nitze (p. xiii ff.), Robert de Boron invented his variant, "Hebron" for "Bron(s)," in order to nullify the Celtic-origin theory and return the Grail worship to its point of origin, which was Christ and Jerusalem. Thus, he accepted Luke's Gospel: Chalice, New Testament, and Christ's book. The author of *Perlesvaus* at Glastonbury would support Robert by further adducing the doctrine of transubstantiation as approved by the Lateran Council of the Christian church in 1215. Hebron was one of the Rich Fisher Kings at the vales of Avalon, and from him descended Alain (Alein) and finally Perceval. The secrets of the Grail, and in particular the secret words of Christ, were all written in Jerusalem itself.

The verses about the birth of Merlin and the trial of his mother accused of intercourse with the devil follows this first, or Robert de Boron's, *Joseph* text. Merlin is saved, of course, and his mother is released, supposedly not executed, in the custody of her confessor Blaise. This same Blaise functions as guarantor of the *Merlin* story, which probably was in actuality written in Jerusalem because it comes largely from a life of Solomon. Blaise has not as yet been located, unfortunately. The verses end with a reference to a Great Grail Book, source of all the knowledge available. That Book has also never been located, but Robert de Boron claimed he had it, and he swore by it: "et par son livre le savons nous encore" (and by his book do we know it still). Some have thought this Great Grail Book was Wolfram's *Parzival.* Robert concludes his *Merlin* verses with a prophecy concerning King Arthur, that he who draws the sword from the stone shall by election of Jesus Christ be the King of the Earth.

What happened after the rule of several Grail Kings in Britain, wrote the anonymous Benedictine author of *Perlesvaus,* was this (branch 8): one of the Grail Kings died and his castle and chapel both were seized by the King of Castle Mortal, who was an uncle of Perceval. Then the Grail, other relics, *and the sword that had beheaded John the Baptist,* could no longer be seen there. The New (Testament) Law was abandoned. Perceval's sister mounted her mule and set off for her mother's estates in the Valley of Camelot. Her mother's estates, she found, had been stolen from her. Perceval then showed evidence of his future mastery by being able alone to raise the lid of a huge sarcophagus. It contained the body of that person who took down the body of Christ from the Cross, plus the bloody nails too.

Perceval then fought this Lord of the Moors, who upheld Judaism against Christianity. First he vanquished his chieftains whose severed heads filled a bucket with their blood. Then he hung this lord upside down until he had drowned, and then threw him in the river (the Forth). Perceval recovered his mother's dozen or more estates. Many of his subsequent adventures in *Perlesvaus* duplicated those of Peredur, Arthur, Lancelot, and Gawain, which suggests that each followed at one time or another the same Grail Quest with halts at the same locations.

After these preliminaries, which Robert de Boron prepared, we come to the *Didot-Perceval.* For several reasons, each emotional as well as logical, this must be one's favorite Arthurian text. The *Didot-Perceval* is a masterpiece, were one to argue simply that structure is the prime component of a literary work—its one, most unforgettable component, Victor Hugo used to assert. Secondly, this telling of a familiar Perceval story descends into pure mystery, which enchants the reader more than he can say. Thirdly, the *Didot-Perceval* or *Boron Continuation,* if one prefers to think of it thus, brings Merlin to life again before one's eyes.

It is a very real possibility that what the *Didot-Perceval* claims is really true: Merlin dictated this text himself to his confessor Blaise who had raised him from babyhood. Therefore what we read as *Didot-Perceval* really is an oracle written by the greatest of all Dark Age prophets, Merlin himself.

What we learn in the *Didot-Perceval* cannot be learned elsewhere, and it changes our whole perspective: the Grail was with Bron or Brons on an island off Ireland—ergo, on the Isle of Man in the middle of the Irish Sea. Its castle stood beside a river (the Neb) that flowed at that point into the Irish Sea. Perceval saw three men in a boat fishing there. As he approached the castle, he saw its drawbridge lowered. Chrétien's information about a "water bridge" and a "sword bridge" proves incorrect. Perceval entered and was robed in scarlet. The lame Fisher King Brons, who was then carried into the hall, turned out to be Perceval's grandfather. They sit down for supper.

The Grail Procession crossed the hall: (1) a squire bearing a lance in both hands, and one drop of blood on its tip; (2) a damsel bearing two silver platters and white towels; and (3) a squire carrying the Grail, which now becomes a vessel containing Christ's blood. Perceval asked no question. Had he asked, he would have received custody of this blood.

When Perceval returns to the Grail Castle on a Good Friday seven years later, the Grail and the same relics reappear. Then he asks for explanations and is told: (1) the lance is that of Longinus, who pierced Christ's side on the Cross; (2) "Grail" means "agreeable" to worthy persons because none can sin in its sight; (3) Brons will teach Christ's secret words spoken on the Cross to Joseph of Arimathea; (4) these secret words cannot ever be told henceforth, and are not ever to be told; and (5) Merlin here completes his dictation to Blaise. Merlin then, one regrets to hear, retires from the world.

Perceval was supposed to have asked, his first time at the Grail Castle hall: What has the Grail served? What does the Grail serve? The secret words that will ultimately be told to him will pass from his life into death. He would never reveal them to his wife, who would be Gawain's sister Elaine (a second Cundrie). His adventures here followed familiar tracks: (1) the Perilous Seat, or Seat Perilous, where the earth quaked and a voice from the tomb admonished him; (2) the meeting with the Lady Orgueilleuse de la Lande; (3) the Chessboard Castle, White Stag Hunt, and lady's lapdog; (4) the Waste Land of Camelot and Perceval's trance; (5) the handsome coward whom he vanquishes; (6) Perceval's combat at the Perilous Fort; (7) visit at the Grail Castle; (8) return to the Chessboard Castle; (9) return to the Uncle Hermit's cell on the day of Holy Cross; (10) tournament at the White Castle where Perceval surpasses Gawain; and (11) return for coronation at the Grail Castle. This time Perceval is granted a meeting with Merlin himself. This day that High Priest is dressed as Death the Grim Reaper, a scythe in his hand, perhaps the same scythe he used when as the Green Knight he scarred Gawain for life. Merlin warns Perceval to ask the meaning of what he sees during the Grail Procession. The

Grail, he says, is the cup of blood from the crucified Christ.

Once Perceval asks the proper questions, he is accepted for ordination as the future Grail King, or new Fisher King. The stone that split beneath him at the Round Table, or the Perilous Seat, was at that time mended. Once Perceval was inaugurated, he freed Merlin from all his responsibilities forever. The beloved sage then retired to his eyrie, or cage, or dovecote, from which he never again emerged except to die.

Chrétien de Troyes's sophisticated and dramatic *Perceval* poem has the hero witness an illuminated and blinding Grail Procession dominated by whiteness and dazzling white light. The Procession passes in four parts: first, a youth bears a gleaming lance, which has one drop of blood on its blade point; second, Perceval sees two servants carrying lighted, golden candelabra, each with ten lighted candles; third, a young, beautiful, and clearly noble maiden carries between both hands a Grail, her person flanked by servitors; and fourth, Perceval sees a second equally beautiful maiden who carries a silver platter ("tailleor d'argent"). Chrétien makes no mention of a severed head, or of blood in the silver platter, certainly no mention, then, of a head of either Brons, Bran, or John the Baptist. Nor does he talk about Good Friday.

As much for what Chrétien does not say, he was as early as 1948 recognized as a Jew by Urban T. Holmes, and again in 1959 by Holmes and Sister Amelia Klemke at Chapel Hill, North Carolina. Holmes painted a picture of Chrétien living in the wealthy Jewish quarter of Troyes, a friend and perhaps a pupil of the Solomon ben Isaac, who was the greatest Jewish scholar of his day, and also of the Christian theologian Peter Comestor. He knew the Countess Marie, daughter of King Louis VII and Eleanor of Aquitaine, whose Chaplain was Andreas Capellanus. He frequented the Abbey library at Beauvais, he says, was employed by Count Philip of Flanders, and knew Henry of Blois, Abbot of Glastonbury Abbey from 1126 to 1171. Therefore Chrétien preached "charity" in his Grail text, say Holmes and Klemke, whereby Jews would all be converted to Christianity (v. 6,292); they damned themselves when they crucified Christ, says Chrétien.

Those early critics who believed this interpretation agreed that the Grail Castle was intended as a replica of Solomon's Temple, both having an outer portico, lofty towers, bronze or copper columns, a Holy of Holies, golden candlesticks, a fire or fireplace for sacrifices, manna for the worshipers, angels ascending or descending like doves, and a sacred rock. It was Christianity personified by Ecclesia (Perceval's mother's name was Eccles) versus Synagoga, an equally beautiful, young Jewish lady. All faith stems from Charity, says Chrétien (v. 43), which or who never boasts of her good deeds . . . God is charity . . . and Saint Paul maintains that this is true.

Klemke added in 1981 that in her opinion the Grail in Chrétien was the Chalice of the Last Supper; the Lance was that of the Passion; the first maiden represented Ecclesia; the Lance-bearer was Longinus; the blood was Christ's Precious Blood; the silver platter was the paten or communion plate; and Perceval was an incarnation of Saint Paul. She derived the word *graal* from the *Gradual* (or steps) of the Mass. Chrétien's hopes lay in conciliation by the Jews, their conversion, and success in Jerusalem for the Knights Templar. Or that is how Klemke saw it, and perhaps unrealistically.

In the years 1975–76 at Chapel Hill and then at Bar-Ilan University in Israel Eugene J. Weinraub drew up what appears conclusively by far the best interpretation of Chrétien and Chrétien's *Perceval,* so much, in fact, does it alone address the thorny problems raised by this brilliant French author of the twelfth century. Weinraub lists in his introduction the well-known names of the principal adherents to each side of the Chrétien controversy of origins, which he also recognizes as one of the most hateful and acrimonious of all modern, scholarly disputes, the two sides having most adherents being the Christian/liturgical and/or the Celtic, the least number of champions, the Judeo-Christian (Holmes, Klemke, Goodrich), with Weinraub entering the fray for a totally and purely Jewish interpretation. His work is nothing less than brilliant also. One hastens to change sides and adopt it.

Weinraub entitles his chapter 3 "A New Judaic Interpretation." He explains that for three thousand years Jews everywhere have celebrated a family banquet called a *Seder,* and that Chrétien betrays his intimate knowledge of both Ashkenazic and Sephardic customs. Weinraub himself also consulted the Aleppo Syrian Jewish community in New York City (1968) to be sure of his facts.

His proof goes down the motions of the Grail ceremony in Chrétien, which he finds perfectly orthodox, and only Jewish orthodox: (1) the (four) questions always asked by the *youngest son,* i.e., Perceval; (2) the unleavened bread of affliction covered and uncovered, which is Chrétien's *gastel (matzah)* tasted by his weeping family members; (3) the reclining position at table of the Fisher King, and occasionally of Perceval; (4) the maiden or Jewish daughter carrying the *Seder* plate; (5) the sacrificial blood smeared (as Lancelot did) on threshold and lintels; (6) the lighted candelabras; (7) the washing of hands and drying with white towels; (8) the gleaming, white tablecloth; (9) the Passover or *Seder* plate; (10) Perceval's questions establishing and rehearsing before his family members the history, lineage, and identity of the Fisher King, which would ritually recite the Exodus story.

Chrétien lived at Troyes in eastern France, adds Weinraub, where the rabbinical academy flourished from about 1040, where famous Jewish scholars studied peacefully in an extremely prosperous market town attracting merchants and artists from Provence, Spain, Anjou, the Orient, and especially from the Holy Land. One of the two main roads into Troyes commenced in Narbonne, the very literary capital of the older Roman Empire, and the other in Toledo and Old Castile.

Perceval, concluded Weinraub, is nobody other than the Wandering Jew, to whom the Grail Bearer Cundrie, who reads Arabic, is a Goddess Fortuna always either *bona aut mala*—a good or a very bad girl, indeed. . . . As we know, Fortune is variable, fickle, and unpredictable. Her adherents are besotted who depend on her. . . . Chrétien did not finish his *Perceval*. Scholars believe he must have been interrupted by death. But he had not finished his *Lancelot* either, which becomes more and more puzzling as one ponders the recurrence of what is for an artist most incredible—and Chrétien was a brilliant author, no less, instantly world famous, instantly recognized as such by Wolfram von Eschenbach.

His continuators, we must say, quite reversed Chrétien's interpretation and his religious inclination, treading uphill immediately into a properly Christian and liturgical stance. Could the noble patron have canceled Chrétien's contract?

Instead of Chrétien we now have a "Manuscrit de Mons," and authors named Gerbert de Montreuil and Wauchier de Denain, and a Pseudo-Wauchier, edited by William Roach in three volumes. Immediately we are taken back to Celtic Merlin building the copper columns Guinevere stood between at the Grail Castle, to the huge, Celtic, stone crosses Merlin erected in Edinburgh, to the Arthurian Church of Saint Aaron in "Galles," which Geoffrey of Monmouth said was in Carlisle. He knew the churches of Julius and Aaron were there because Arthur and Guinevere were crowned in those very churches, of which there is elsewhere no mention except in Gerbert, who claims Perceval's bride Blanche-fleur endowed or reendowed the Church of Aaron. Other than in Geoffrey and Gerbert one has found no mention of Saint Aaron.

The Mons manuscript places Arthur back in Scotland, and clearly identifies his residences and that of his mother Ygerne as at Caer-laverock, at Stirling, at Edinburgh, and near the firths of Forth and Clyde just as Chrétien had located them, and just as the much more detailed *Perlesvaus* also located them.

Thus, Chrétien's text can no more be ignored than his thought can any longer be misrepresented. And Judaism, unlike Christian-ity, is an exclusive religion. For his part Gerbert de Montreuil prophesied that Jerusalem would be conquered by the Crusaders and that all would henceforth be well there forever.

Chrétien's continuators are totally overshadowed, of course, by the brilliant, worldly Chrétien de Troyes himself; but we shall come back in more detail to examine Gawain's first Grail experiences. They are the first in line, before those of Lancelot, Bors, Galahad, and Perceval, which come last.

Our Perceval texts have conducted us from the pagan interpreta-tion of the Grail in the Welsh *Peredur* to a Christian reworking done first by someone calling himself Robert de Bor(r)on, and finally to Judaism in the text of Chrétien de Troyes. We shall have to consider the possibility that the Grail came from many lands and many faiths to appeal eventually to so many people in these same lands and faiths.

PARZIVAL

Wolfram von Eschenbach (c. 1170–c. 1220) wrote his verse epic *Parzival* to admire the chivalric virtues of his hero and idealize his many heroines in this glorification of happy, married love, and successful, martial victories. The poet Wolfram himself became a hero in Richard Wagner's opera *Tannhaüser* about such a medieval poet and Crusader. Wolfram was also a Knight Templar, and as such vowed to the service of God and women.

German literature has always looked upon *Parzival* as the moral story of a young man's spiritual development from the foolishness of puberty to the full consciousness of manliness with its accompanying masculine obligations of husband, father, and in Parzival's case of kingship and guardianship of the Holy Grail. Through humiliation, blunders, discomforts, and hardships Parzival wins his way, loses it again and again, until he finally understands the responsibilities of marriage, kingship, and the high priesthood.

The German developmental novel, or Bildungsroman, very early adopted this plot or format: a young man slowly becoming mature and wise and beloved. The German *Parzival* is a very happy romance in every sense of the term. Its author's genial optimism shines through every page. For the hero, as for everybody else about him, all is brightly lit, all is pleasant or soon will become pleasant, and all is well and ends well.

The *Parzival* is readily available in two English translations done twenty years apart in 1960 or thereabouts and 1980, the first by Helen M. Mustard and Charles E. Passage and the latter by A. T. Hatto. Passage also did excellent work on recovering the German place-names used by Wolfram and retranslating them into the more familiar French names and places of Arthurian geography. He and Mustard point out at once that by the breadth of its canvas Wolfram's *Parzival* can only be compared to Dante's *Divine Comedy*. Both portray and study huge panoramas, and both are spiritual in nature and by intent. Both Wolfram and Dante dare to take a lofty, moral view and maintain it in the teeth of a materialistic, sometimes scoffing public. Both endorse and defend the lofty ideals of the Knights Templar as exemplified in the careers of Lancelot and Parzival/Perceval.

The English translations are printed in sixteen chapters, both editions furnished with long introductions, notes, indexes, and genealogical tables. There are even more proper names in *Parzival* than in Tolstoy's unabridged *War and Peace,* these two works also being panoramical, historical, and epical. It takes a little extra work in reading Wolfram to relocate the sites, his geography being as much as possible designed to flatter and praise Angevin royalty.

Whenever he describes a site with persons we know present, we almost immediately transfer this scene from North Africa or Anjou to Scotland east or west. One good example is King Arthur's western citadel of Carlisle, which was located at the head of the Solway (way > *wath* = ford) Firth, at or adjacent to the latest and by far the largest of the older Roman military command centers. It is well understood and perfectly understandable that Arthur's grandfather, the Celtic Commander who stepped in to fill the vacancy created by the Roman withdrawal from Britain, would have occupied the greatest and most strategic of Roman forts because it anchored the western end of Hadrian's Wall, firstly, and then offered its huge bulk and curtain walls as face to any aggressors penetrating the Irish Sea via the Solway Firth and St. George's Channel. The peoples in the North had to hold Hadrian's Wall, which stretched seventy-five miles across the narrowest part of Britain, east to west. It had been for centuries Rome's defense against these same, unconquered northern peoples. When Arthur's Celtic grandfather, the British Commander Amlawd Wledig (Wledig = Chief) took charge of the Wall and its chain of seventeen forts, he guaranteed in effect the border between the future kingdoms of Scotland and England. The textual scholar Rachel Bromwich from Wales traces King Arthur's pedigree through his royal mother Ygerne, whom Wolfram by anagram calls Arnive, to her father Amladd Wledig.

Queen Ygerne resides just outside Carlisle, we have to remember also, which today would be the west road toward Dumfries from the junction of the M6 freeway on the west side of the city of Carlisle. Arthurian texts speak constantly of this road junction, today a prominent railway hub also, where seven ancient roads came together from Penrith and York, to Glasgow, Edinburgh, and Carlisle, or west into Ireland. It was a famous rendezvous point for Arthur's warbands.

When Queen Guinevere was abducted and her husband the king called up his warriors, Lancelot, Chrétien narrating, almost arrived last. That Celt who answered last the call to arms was condemned to death. The call summoned warbands by a shout and/or by smoke signals, both calling them instantly to the nearest Assembly Castle, called in Celtic "mustering point," or *maidan*. Not reading Gaelic nor Old Brythonic, translators like Chrétien thought it meant "maiden." Therefore King Arthur's royal mother resided, they said, at "Maiden" Castle. The rush was, of course, for the translator then to surround her with maidens, who had to be, in this case rather awkwardly, her five married daughters.

Despite such complications the reader recognizes the place without much trouble, especially if he has already enjoyed Chrétien's *Lancelot,* which Wolfram concedes is a major source, and which it may be, of course, or may not be. This celebrated Castle of "Maidens" lies on the north shore of the Solway Firth today also, on the east bank of the River Nith as it descends south through Dumfries and flows into the Solway. The only bridge over the Nith is at Dumfries itself, and so it is important there to take the road down the east bank, without crossing the bridge.

Before reaching Caerlaverock Castle, one finds the river bank posted: Caution! Quicksand! This was probably King Arthur's Perilous Ford where a crowd of adoring, young ladies waited days to see Lancelot pass, where another enchanted throng watched Queen Isolde fire-walk, where Gawain followed Cundrie's demand that he jump his horse and pick some Druidical holly or mistletoe for her use, presumably as medicine. The olden castle site probably lay on the Solway shore and not uphill where the medieval castle is being repaired again today. In the Middle Ages, the Scottish chroniclers Robert de Brunne and Peter de Langtoft also discovered that Caerlaverock was the Arthurian "Maiden" Castle as situated and carefully described earlier by Chrétien de Troyes and then by Wolfram von Eschenbach. One has only to follow their lead, translating backward from the Latin *album campum,* to the French-Celtic *Champ guin,* to the Gaelic *Mag find,* to understand we are to recognize this castle as: (1) to the west one day's march from Carlisle, which puts us starting from the Carlisle junction, direction Dumfries, (2) a castle located before a sand shore, a *white field,* English translation, facing across a body of water, Solway Firth, as one looks in the direction of Ireland. The only obstacle between that body of water and Ireland itself is the Isle of Man lying exactly in the middle of the Irish Sea. Conclusion? Queen Guinevere was being taken captive to the Isle of Man in the Irish Sea.

Our polar flights, Los Angeles to London Heathrow, let down

over Ireland every time and cross the mainland coast of Britain either northerly, directly over the coast at Glasgow, or southerly, directly across this lovely Isle of Man. Either route brings one within sight of this Solway Firth, Merlin's Cave, and Caerlaverock Castle behind its white sand field. The major problem in orientation was in presuming that King Arthur's defensive positions were so many needles in haystacks, when they were, to the contrary, the principal mustering points in a military, all-out defense of the coasts of northern Britain. Had there been no defense, it has already been pointed out by others, there would have been, as in Gaul, no story to memorize. When that defense was engineered by King Arthur, whom the London historian John Morris called the last Roman Emperor inside Britain (475–542), no poet could help being thrilled beyond words.

Chrétien lay prostrate before Lancelot: there comes he who will this day set the standard of manhood for every other male alive beside him. Wolfram was thrilled by Parzival who to him represented every Knight Templar ideal: courage, nobility, honor, gentility, reverence, generosity, respect for women, defense of the poor and the oppressed. So in Wolfram we have come a long way from the awkward, brutal Peredur who after he had made his first kill could not get the armor off the corpse of the Red Knight without cutting the body itself out of the gear. Gawain had to ride out to the tilting ground and show the boy how to unbuckle the metal suit. In Wolfram Parzival represents the height of chivalry, *Wunsch,* says the German, or a *summum bonum,* the Romans would have said.

Following the Mustard and Passage translation now as easy reference for readers, some of whom may have met it in the New York City Rudolf Steiner School, where it has always been an assigned text for high school students, we come to the first Grail episode, book 5 (pp. 123–51). Parzival arrived finally at the Grail Castle, for which no preliminary directions were ever given any of the Questers, in the dusk of evening. . . . All Gothic fiction from Edgar Allan Poe, or its inception in the eighteenth century, rises to this tremendously terrifying moment: the first sight of the four-sided castle. Parzival's route drops suddenly down to the water's edge. Looking out over the "Lake," Perceval sees three men in a boat. They are fishing where the River Neb flows into the Irish Sea. Even today, little boats are tied up all along this riverbank. Perceval asks directions to the Grail Castle.

The problem here has been that the Grail Castle towered there right in front of him on an islet just offshore. Therefore why did he ask direction of his grandfather, the Rich Fisher King and his body servants in the little fishing boat? . . . One has to go there to find out. He had to ask because he couldn't get there from there. He was told to go back up the glen and come back down on the other side where he could cross the water via the drawbridge.

Parzival rode back up the cliff, turned right, saw no house or building within thirty miles behind him, and came back down what is now the main road to the beach in the town of Peel, or palisade, which once surrounded, says the *Lanzelet* text, the approaches to the Grail Castle as reconstructed to house King Arthur's treasury plus the Holy Grail itself. Parzival arrived at the castle (p. 124) where all awaited him sadly; for he had taken such a long time to find it, and it could only be found by chance.

He entered the Great Hall (p. 126) with its one hundred couches and its three huge fires burning red in the fireplaces. Then he witnessed the Grail Procession, the four lovely maidens wreathed in flowers, and the passage of the lighted tapers in golden candlesticks. The table was set upon a tabletop of garnet covered with a gleaming, white tablecloth. Eight maidens served the Fisher King. These ladies wore gowns of green silk from Azagouc in North Africa (?). Two princesses carried silver knives sharp enough to cut steel, and laid them on the table (p. 128). By now there were twenty-four gorgeously gowned ladies present, some dressed in gold brocade from the Middle East.

Last of all entered the Grail Queen Repanse de Schoye, who bore the Grail. Queen Repanse was the daughter of the royal Frimutel, the granddaughter of Titurel, and the sister of Schoysiane, who was Sigune's mother. Her brothers were Parzival's uncle and teacher Trevrizent, and Anfortas, who is the present Grail or Fisher King (called Pelles in French, earlier). Her other sister is Parzival's mother, Herzeloyde, Queen of "Wales" and "North Wales" (called Eccles earlier). The very complicated Grail/Arthurian genealogy established by Wolfram presents these among its many generations:

Generation 1 = The Grail King Titurel
Generation 2 = The Grail King Frimutel, son of the
                preceding
Generation 3 = The Grail King Anfortas (Pelles, or

Brons or Bron), son of the preceding
The Hermit Trevrizent, brother of the
preceding
Queen Schoysiane, sister of Anfortas
Queen Herzeloyde, sister of Anfortas
Generation 4 = Sigune, daughter of Queen Schoysiane
Prester John, son of Repanse de Schoye
and Parzival's twin brother Feirefiz
Parzival, son of Queen Herzeloyde
Generation 5 = Loherangrin (Lohengrin), son of Parzival
(Perceval, Peredur) and Condwiramurs
(Blanchefleur)

King Arthur and family would be, according to Wolfram, related
by marriage to Frimutel's line, from which both originally descended. Their common great-grandfather was named Mazadan,
and he also sired the Angevin lines. Arthur's father Utepandragun
(Uther Pendragon) would have belonged to Titurel's generation:

Generation 1 = Utepandragun, King of Britain (a noble
Roman elsewhere)
Queen Arnive (Ygerne), Arthur's Celtic
mother
Generation 2 = King Arthur
Queen Ginover (Guinevere)
King Arthur's (half) sister Sangive
married to King Lot(h) of Norway
(Lothian elsewhere)
King Florant, Sangive's first husband
Generation 3 = Sangive's daughter Itonje
Sangive's son Beacurs (Gareth)
Sangive's son Gawan (Gawain) who weds
Orgeluse
Sangive's daughter Cundrie
Arthur's son Ilinot (Lohot)

Having rehearsed the royal genealogy of the Grail Bearer Repanse de Schoye, we glance again at the Great Hall where she
walked as bright as the dawn in the eastern sky, said Wolfram. She
was preceded by sweet incense burning in glass vessels. She placed
the Grail on the jeweled table before her brother, the Grail King

Anfortas. Servants brought in one hundred tables, water in basins or finger bowls, and towels for guest and host. Bread was broken. The Grail provided food in abundance. Parzival's tutor, Prince Gurnemanz, had cautioned him to keep silent. A squire brought him a sword set with a priceless ruby, which the Grail King Anfortas had carried before his wounding. Parzival remained mute. Then the host recommended he retire to bed. Dessert and cordials were served in the bedroom. . . . Parzival suffered nightmares of sword thrusts and rushing horses. He awoke late, drenched in perspiration, dressed in solitary haste, ran through the deserted castle looking for someone, found it cold and empty, and finally mounted up. As he rode back across the drawbridge it rose behind him so fast it almost cut his horse in two. A squire yelled hateful taunts at him from the wall, but refused to acknowledge Parzival's demands for an explanation. "Goose," he was called.

In book 6 the learned maiden Cundrie, who is described as the Grail Messenger, chastises Parzival who has just recovered from his trance in the snow. According to Wolfram, Cundrie, who spoke Latin, French, and Arabic, had been trained in rhetoric and also in astronomy. Wolfram apologized for describing such an ugly, young lady. Her black braids grew coarser than a pig's bristles. Her eyebrows were so long she had to tie them up out of her face. Her eyes protruded from her skull like a bear's. She was bearded. Her hands were brown, her fingers ending in the claws she used to clutch her riding crop. Why did you not solace the suffering Fisher King? she asked Parzival. You could have ended his pain once and for all. Thus, the "Sorceress" Cundrie induced Parzival to acquire a singular virtue, a capacity for shame.

Wolfram reaches the apex of his story in book 9, which separates past from present time as the hero meets Sigune, declares his goal to be the Grail Castle of Munsalvaesche (the Mount of Salvation), and then tries unsuccessfully to follow Cundrie on her mule. In so doing he experienced three important adventures, which confirmed him in his goal. First he met a Knight Templar who had come from the Grail Castle on its Mount of Salvation, and who attempted to bar the way. He failed, and Parzival pressed on. Second, he met a gray man who bent Parzival's thought toward the seriousness of his quest. Finally he turned to the Fountain of Salvation and its hermit Trevrizent, who was also his uncle.

Trevrizent lectured to Parzival (p. 243ff.) concerning the Grail legend. It was found written in Toledo by Kyot, a famous master, he said. The original had been written by a Jew named Flegetanis who compared human destinies to the courses of the stars. All mysteries can be understood by studying the heavens. Flegetanis first read the name "Grail" in the constellations whence angels brought it down to earth. It has since their departure remained on the Mount of Salvation guarded by a race of royal Grail Kings, each one of whom was called, as Parzival was being called, to its service.

The only way to win the Grail, continues the uncle (p. 251), is to be known by name in heaven, and to be summoned to Grail service by name. At the Grail in Munsalvaesche reside many brave Templars who live by virtue of a stone called *"lapsit exillis,"* the stone that burned the phoenix to death and brought it back to life from ashes. This stone has the power to endow us with eternal youth despite our hair, which may turn white. *This stone is the Holy Grail.*

Every Good Friday, he continued (p. 252), a white dove flies down from God, as in the east window of the Arthuret church, to leave a white communion wafer upon this stone (altar) whence result all the delights of Paradise and food for the Templar guardians. Those who have been called to serve the Grail have their names and pedigrees carved on the base of this stone, man and maid alike, all brought into service as Merlin brought the girl Niniane/ Vivian there in childhood. Those who have devoted their lives to service at the Grail will be advanced after death to *perfection* (p. 252). The stone always remains pure.

Those brothers and maidens who serve the Grail form a secret company unknown to the world at large. When the knight comes to ask unprompted the proper question, he will release Anfortas from his kingship and his suffering. Future kings of the world (King Arthur?) are sent out secretly from the Grail Castle. Maidens to wife are dispatched openly. All were trained from childhood at the Grail Castle so that they would bear noble children to follow them in service. Open your hearts, Trevrizent enjoined Parzival as after penance he forgave the youth his sins.

After Gawain's adventure at the Ford Perilous, where he finally jumped a second horse across the river, he learned of the four generations of fathers and sons who were called to Grail service: (1) Rivalin and his son Tristan, (2) Utependragun and his son Arthur, (3) King Lot and his son Gawain, and (4) Gahmuret and his son Parzival.

As the day of his investiture approached, Parzival drew near King Arthur's Court where a Round Table ceremony was being held. Parzival's Angevin brother was present, half black and half white like a Templar. The company saw a gloriously dressed maiden approach them. She was clad splendidly in a hooded mantle of black velvet (p. 404ff.) embroidered in the gold *turtledoves* that were the cognizance of the Grail Castle. Queen Guinevere was preceded by four white doves at her coronation, and Gawain's red-and-white horse was branded with the turtledove to show he also served the Grail or was educated there, and Queen Guinevere also. Similarly the Lords of the Grail wore the turtledove on their garments as their insignia.

At this Round Table ceremony, which is a circle or concentric circles of table linen laid on the ground, Cundrie officiated. It was she who announced Parzival's forthcoming ordination, and who delivered the speech of official congratulation to him as he wept. The connection between Round Table and Cundrie's list of planets, or her speech, must be made. The two must indicate a star map laid out on Earth, as follows: Saturn, Jupiter, Mars, the Sun, Venus, Mercury, and the Moon. Cundrie recited these names and gave them Arabic names also.

She lists Saturn, Jupiter, and Mars first. She should have said Jupiter, Saturn, and Mars in that order, which would have given us the three outer planets that make revolutions around the Sun in 29.5, 11.9, and 1.9 years, respectively. She claims these three and the Sun bring good fortune. Then she names the two innermost planets, Venus and Mercury, thus naming all five that are easily visible to the naked eye. The other bodies she mentions are the Sun and then the Moon, which is the Earth's satellite. Her five planets, if represented on an Earth map, would give us five concentric circles around the Sun with Mercury closest, followed by Venus, then by Mars, Saturn, and Jupiter. This does not work well, however, for it leaves the Moon unrepresented, which is a pity; for an Earth map of our solar system has been suggested as the original Grail Temple constructed by Merlin. Perhaps Cundrie was pointing out that these five planets plus Sun and Moon have named or would name the days of the week.

The Merlin *Prophecy* corresponds somewhat to Cundrie's lecture. Saturn, for example, would be Cronus with his crooked sickle. Mars is the helmeted man of whom Merlin speaks. The Crab devours the sun, he says. Mercury glows close to us afire with amber rage. The chariot of the Moon disturbs the Zodiac. What Merlin meant here is that the Moon seems to wander through the sky, crossing it much more slowly than Sun and stars. It rises almost an hour later each day of its cycle, rising when the Sun rises and setting when sunset occurs. The Moon appears to drift to the east while generally moving regularly west.

Both Cundrie's lecture and Merlin's *Prophecy* are astonishingly accurate, even so. They do make sense, but it is not clear why at this time Cundrie wants to lecture on astronomy and use Arabic terms. Therefore, making another attempt to follow her thoughts, one begins to list associations such as the days of the week, the tree alphabet and corresponding sacred trees, the houses of the Zodiac, and the Arthurian personage each might bring to mind. The chart that follows has been altered by this author over the years, but, generally speaking, it is much indebted to the many, excellent works on the ancient world by Georges Dumézil (1929).

Perceval belongs to Pisces and the twelve epigomenal days of Christmas misrule when the old pagan god was birched and the sun remained hidden below the equator. By his spirituality he belongs also to those days of devotion. Queen Morgan le Fay, as her Castle Chariot represents her, figures another Moon goddess Diana whose willow tree was a sacred analgesic for screaming women in travail. Gawain is more than any other hero the dark-haired lover Aries who picks holly for his beloved and who was worshiped in spring festivals throughout the Middle East and into the West. Merlin is Mercury, the Roman escorter of souls after death, and the Wise Medicine Man; and like the ash tree he stood an *axis mundi,* or Tree of Life, rooted in hell and crowned laureate in heaven. Lancelot is the flaming, solar hero par excellence, the red lightning, winner of all fiery contests, and the tall oak that rises, said Vergil, above all other trees like a chief over his clan. Guinevere is the virginal priestess to whom the apple is allowed but forbidden to all other harrowers of hell if they wished to return to life on Earth again. With her doves seen as Roman symbols, she is Venus in all her pink, sea-born beauty. King Arthur finally is King Bran, Saturday's oldest of gods. The alder branch in his hand is the chief of trees, the first tree ever to grow after the last Ice Age. Arthur is the Celtic king called Bran, and in the Glastonbury Earth map or Zodiac he rides like Sagittarius astride his horse, along the ecliptic. The learned Cundrie knew much more, surely, but either she forgot Capricorn, or it was unknown to her.

Cundrie's Seven Planets in *Parzival*

PLANET	DAY	TREE	LETTER	ZODIAC	ARTHUR-IAN PER-SONAGE	ASSO-CIATE DEITY
Sun	Sunday	Birch	B(leithe)	Pisces	Perceval	Quirinus Vishnu Oannes Attis/ Adonis
Moon	Monday	Willow	S(ail)	Cancer	Morgan	Diana Matrona Demeter
Mars	Tuesday	Holly	T(inne)	Aries	Gawain	Cuchulain Amon-Ra Marduk Ares Tiw
Mercury	Wednesday	Ash	N(ion)	Gemini	Merlin	Woden/ Wotan Odin Asclepius
Jupiter	Thursday	Oak	D(uir)	Leo	Lancelot	Thor Baal Helios Shamash
Venus	Friday	Apple	Q(uert)	Virgo	Guinevere	Freia Isis Eve
Saturn	Saturday	Alder	F(earn)	Sagittarius	Arthur Bran	Iao Cronus Chiron Allfadur

Not to be outdone by the likes of Cundrie, Wolfram shows his own mastery of science in the construction of *Parzival,* which is as arcanely built as Dante's *Divine Comedy.* Parzival's life story takes him six years to fulfill—from the angels seen on the forest path to his inauguration at the Grail Castle: Pentecost to Pentecost. The Arthurians do smack of heresy; Pentecost is not the first and most important holy day of the orthodox, Christian church. His adventures in books 2 through 7, Mustard and Passage calculating (p. 48ff.), take him a year to accomplish, from March 20, which was a snowy Good Friday, through spring to his first visit at the Grail Castle, which he leaves on a September 18, book 6 unrolling on the following day, that autumn stretching until the end of October. Youth always passes slowly. Happier days hasten by later. He remains fifteen days at Trevrizent's hermitage over a Good Friday, the fifteen representing a pentenary system of numbers. Book 10 brings him to April 3, and by the end of book 22 into May. The Round Table on the meadow where Cundrie lectured so mysteriously on what could have been intended as an Earth map of the planets, took place on May 10, the Pentecost Sunday.

Wolfram's century, says Runciman (1947), was the great age of heresy, and Wolfram composed this monumental *Parzival* between the years 1198 and 1212 perhaps, just at the turn of the century. His contemporaries were the eminently successful conqueror, King Philip Augustus of France, and the beloved losers across the Channel, the Angevin King Henry II and his last, disastrous sons.

By the year 1160 the Catharist church, or notorious, Catharist heresy in the Languedoc, was in full cry. The Templars, who had been founded by 1118, refused to suppress Catharism, which probably helped seal their doom. One cannot, absolutely not, imagine a sweet man like Wolfram cutting heads off little babies, or massacring an entire village of kneeling, weeping people.

By the year 1200, and Wolfram was still buried in work composing the 24,810 verses of *Parzival,* five men and three women were denounced, caught in Troyes, France, and burned at the stake for heresy. Legal denunciation is an awful system of law to live under, today as in the year 1200.

Esclarmonde took the *consolamentum* in 1206, which made history because she was a much greater princess than Eleanor of Aquitaine, and beloved to this day. This great lady thus publicly announced her heresy before the world. By 1208 Saint Francis of Assisi was preaching a doctrine suspiciously Catharist. On July 22,

1209, occurred the awful massacre of a whole city, Béziers near the Mediterranean coast. The South of France was stricken with terror. . . . On June 18, 1209, their greatest, richest, most noble prince, Count Raymond of Toulouse, no less, had been publicly scourged in full view of the thousands of citizens of Toulouse for the charge of heresy. The huge walled city of Carcassonne, also near the Mediterranean coast, and also a center of learning and commerce second like Béziers only to the university city of Toulouse, was captured entire by the dread gangster operating with the blessings of the Capetian king of northern France, the hideous Simon de Montfort, and put to the sword, men, women, and children alike. No mercy at all was given. . . . Wolfram probably lived to rejoice at the death of Simon de Montfort in a siege operation on June 25, 1218.

It is no wonder that numerology enchanted Wolfram as he plunged deeper and deeper into Arthurian mysteries that around him seemed revived by the suffering, massacred Catharists, or Puritans. Parzival's penance of 15 days gives only a glimpse of the complications in Dante and Wolfram. The Book of Apocalypse, or Revelation, was based upon 666, the number of the Beast, which is the sum of all numbers 1–36. Cicero called 7 and 8 the *pleni numeri,* or full numbers, in his *Scipio's Dream.* Vergil bowed before 3, 7, 12, 30. Aeneas reigned 3 years in Rome, Ascanius ruled 30, the Alban kings, 300 = 333 years. Jesus lived 33 years; Dante's *Divine Comedy* has 1 + 33 + 33 + 33 cantos = 100. The cosmic Order contains 10 heavens, which constitute Paradise. Saint Patrick's Purgatory in Ireland functioned for centuries requiring the same 15 days of penance as did the British hermit Trevrizent of Parzival. Simonides is supposed to have said: "It is difficult to become a superior man, tetragonal in hand, foot, and spirit, forming a perfect whole." Our American redmen fasted, mourned, and performed acts of penance for 4 days, that being the period required for the spirit to voyage from the point of its liberation to eternity.

Wolfram commences his conclusion (book 16) with the terrible cries of Anfortas who begs to be allowed to die. The suffering from his putrefying wound is more terrible to him than the stench that arises from its pus. Parzival and his brother are led to Anfortas this time by Cundrie. When the outer troop of Knights Templar recognizes the golden turtledoves embroidered on her cloak, they dismount before the three. Cundrie leading, they pass the portal and enter the Great Hall where one hundred carpets have been laid (as in a Muslim mosque) upon the stone floor, and cushions scattered about over all. Refreshments are served in gold goblets.

Anfortas requested Parzival to allow him to die, which meant, to permit him not to have to look upon the Grail for seven nights and eight days. That would suffice to let death take its course.

Parzival wept and prayed on his knees that Anfortas be released from his agony. He asked him: "Uncle, what troubles you?" At once, Anfortas's face relaxed into softness, for he had been released by Christ who brought Lazarus back from the dead. Anfortas came forth beautiful again, all pain removed.

Parzival became Lord of the Grail, as it had already been written on the stone that he would become. Meanwhile Queen Condwiramurs was notified. She rode by stages toward the Land of Salvation (Terre de Salvaesche) and was royally escorted. Parzival went to her and found her in bed with her boy children. Their reunion was a joy. Outside the queen's tent the battle-scarred Templars mounted guard. Later that day they escorted Queen Condwiramurs and her son Lohengrin to Munsalvaesche. On this last return journey they detoured past the cell where Sigune had shut herself away from the world, and were grief-stricken to find her dead inside, still on her knees in prayer. Parzival ordered the cell broken into and her body entombed. The party entered Munsalvaesche that night.

In preparation for the Grail Ceremony forty more carpets were laid on the floor, and three enormous fires were again lighted in the fireplaces.

Twenty-five maidens entered. They were followed by the crowned Grail Queen Repanse de Schoye since only she was allowed to carry the Grail. The service proceeded, says Wolfram, as follows (p. 421): (1) cupbearers poured water, (2) tables were carried in and laid, (3) wheeled carts were rolled in laden with a gold service, (4) meats were served with three kinds of wine. Anfortas asked Parzival's brother if he saw the Grail set before him.

The black-and-white brother Feirefiz had fallen in love with the Grail Queen. He grew pale. Then he listed his martial exploits for Anfortas's approval. He admitted he had not seen the Grail. When he heard of this, the father Titurel sent word that Feirefiz's heathen religion was the barrier.

Next morning in the presence of Knights Templar, Feirefiz was baptized before the Grail. Upon emerging from the water in his baptismal gown Feirefiz saw the Grail. He then wedded Queen Repanse de Schoye. The words the bridegroom saw on the Grail said that no foreign person under a Templar's command should ever ask the Templar's name or his race, that he should be expressly forbidden to do so. If any foreigner asked this question, he would forfeit that Templar's service and protection. In fact, questioning was to be from that point on banned at the Grail Castle, and this in deference to the prolonged suffering of Anfortas. All Grail bearers and keepers would afterward desire to hear no question from anyone.

Repanse de Schoye journeyed to India with her husband and there gave birth to Prester John. Lohengrin the Swan journeyed to Antwerp where he founded the royal dynasty of Brabant.

Wolfram concludes: Master Chrétien de Troyes was misinformed. My source, which came from Provence into Germany, was the correct version of Parzival and the Grail. I wrote this poem for a woman's sake, and hope she will thank me sweetly.

In a reconsideration of Wolfram's *Parzival* we need not be any longer disoriented or stunned by the long, strange personal names in this poem, while recognizing from the Knight Templar oath in its final verses that in early times, perhaps universally, personal names were tabooed until the third generation. This is probably why we have Lancelot's name, for he was Lancelot III or Anguselus III or Angus III depending upon whether we are writing Old French, or Latin, or British. Charles E. Passage in his study of proper names in *Titurel* fragments (1984) really unveiled the long association between Knights Templar in Scotland and their new name, Teutonic Knights in Germany. Chevalier Robert Brydon in Edinburgh has also written brilliant articles in Templar publications (1990) concerning this old and close relationship.

Anfortas is not a proper name of any Grail King, proves Passage, but simply a contraction of the Latin word for infirm: *infirmitatus.* Perceval's father's name of Gohmuret is the Norman French Gomeret or Montgomery. Ilinot is Arthur's son from a strange land named Bertâne, which is merely Britain. Llacheu is Arthur's son Loholt who died in battle at Arthuret in 573. Queen Ampflise means *afflicha,* Widow Lady. The fourth nobleman named Gornemant comes also from the *Mabinogion,* as did *Peredur.* Wolfram's Karidoel is only Arthur's Camelot at Carlisle. Schamilôt is Camelot. Brizljân is the forest of Brocéliande (Bro + llan = Land of the

Great Temple). Arnive is Ygerne, Sigune is *cousine*, Iblis is Sibyl, Tantris is Tristan, and Orgeluse is Cundrie.

There appear at least seventeen prominent maidens and ladies in the *Parzival*, which makes it very amusing for women to read. All, even the minor ones, are characterized in enough detail to be recognized and remembered: Queens Belacane and Herzeloyde, King Erec's royal sister Jeschute, Duchess Cunneware, Queen Ginover, Obie, Obilot, Antikonie, Bene the ferryman's daughter on the waters of the underworld, Gawain's sister named Itonje (and not Cundrie), Arthur's mother Arnive, and the Duchess of Logres Orgeluse. There then remain the women who are major and recurring personages in the poem. The first and most adorable is Parzival's Queen Blanchefleur or White Flower, whose beauty made the Grail Castle glow. Here she is called Condwiramurs, which has to be French for *Conduire Amour(s):* Lead to Love. She is the royal mother of twin sons: Lohengrin and Kardeiz, which sounds like Cardiff in Wales. Another is the lady Sigune, who was daughter to Duke Kyot of Catalonia and Parzival's cousin. The lady suffered a terrible tragedy in the death of her beloved, for which reason she withdrew from the world and had herself immured in a tiny cell. There she was found dead at the end of the poem. This story was so popular that Wolfram rewrote it in *Titurel* (Hatto, p. 11). Wolfram writes several passages where he openly praises such women, celebrates all women, and explains rules of conduct toward them. He argues the power of love versus reason (books 2, 3, 6, and 13), and love wins the day. Therefore Wolfram, and not his predecessors, concludes Nutt (p. 259), must be hailed as having solved Parzival's riddle: "Above all, he [Parzival] must give reverent yet full expression to all the aspirations, all the energies of man and of woman."

In Irish folklore (Curtin, p. 139ff.) Parzival is the Fisherman's son (or grandson) who survives twelve initiations (or who survives the deaths of eleven brothers) on his way to become King of Erin and husband of Her Majesty: dove, horse, hound, eel, salmon, otter, whale, swallow, golden ring, spark, fox, and cock. Trevor Ravenscroft (1982) counted in *Parzival* several medieval metamorphoses: lion, raven, knight, peacock, swan, pelican, and chariot, ending with the crown of kingship at the Grail Castle. Parzival was a lion or solar hero; a raven typifies the oracular three legs of the sun in a wheel or tripod; a warrior knight, which was his third degree; a peacock represents the eye of heaven; a swan drives the sun's boat during the night hours; a pelican, which, like Christ, sacrificed itself for mankind; and the chariot as victorious hero riding in the vehicle of the sun, as recalled, says he, in the seventh enigma of the Tarot pack.

Wolfram commenced his masterpiece with an enigma, a riddle of black and white. All men, he said, wish to know the source of this *Parzival,* and by what authority it exists. All women wish likewise to know it. It is a story of distress, of sorrow, of joy, and of delight. The hero is a brave man who slowly becomes wise. He is at this beginning as yet unborn. He will exemplify great faith. He will be supported by women. He will become the model of manhood, a man of steel.

Parzival was composed during the great age of heresy (1198–1212). Wolfram says it came first from a Jewish scholar in Toledo, thence to Provence, and then into Germany and his hands as Knight Templar. The influence of Islam upon Western culture shines through the lecture on astronomy by the erstwhile "Witch" Cundrie. It is amazing how educated the women are in Arthurian literature, which is supposed to depict Dark Ages.

PARSIFAL

One more great work of art from Germany, this time spelled *Parsifal,* has attracted the world's loving attention. We left Wolfram's *Parzival* shortly before the expulsions of the Jews from France in 1306, which was followed in 1307 by the secret order, again by the Capetian king, to arrest all the Knights Templar. The trials of the Templars, who remained obdurate under questioning, or uncooperative, or obtuse, as one prefers to understand their inexplicable behavior, dragged on secretly from 1308 to 1314. Their executions by burnings haunted all France from 1310 to 1314, at which latter date both King and Pope died suddenly.

Through all these horrifying events, the mystery of Perceval refused also to get solved. The thorny questions that intrigue us today haunted the fourteenth and fifteenth centuries up to Sir Thomas Malory, who collected those translations called in English *Le Morte d'Arthur* from these same Old French texts that we have been studying. For Malory also, with all his genius, and he is usually called the inaugurator of English prose, everything led to this death of King Arthur. With Arthur's lips sealed, one can only go back and forth from the *Annals of Wales* around the year 450 onward, to Saint Gildas who was Arthur's contemporary, to Geoffrey of Monmouth (1136), who was his first historian, and back to the Old French manuscripts.

Archaeology has found nothing at all, for which reason archaeologists shout with absolute certitude that *Arthur never lived.* And Sir Winston Churchill quipped: "Then he should have." We have adopted Churchill's words as our modus vivendi.

The opera *Parsifal* was composed by the German Richard Wagner (1813–83), as a message for mankind from a genius like Victor Hugo and his other Romantic predecessors, who also claimed prophetic prerogatives. Wagner spelled the hero's name as *Parsi-fal,* and not in French as *Perceval* (Perlesvaus, Parzival, Percyvelle, or Peredur) because, says Wagner's biographer Ernest Newman, he accepted what he said was *the Arabic derivation* of the name: *Fal* (fool) + *Parsi* (Pure). The "Poor Fool" legend or folkloric version appears to be worldwide, most prominent in Ireland, however, where a fisherman's youngest son undergoes various animal metamorphoses, or passes school grades 1–8 or 1–12, to marry the

LEADERS: THE FIRST CRUSADE

Sovereignty of Ireland finally. Even so, even agreeing that the medieval, learned version, or romance, because written in Old French, which is a romance or Latin language, is usually doubled by the popular or oral folkloric version, one must quarrel with Wagner's unnecessary search far afield in Arabic or Persian.

The same phenomenon occurs in Arthur's name, which unfortunately predates history in Great Britain for at least his generation. The name "Arthur" shows up in the royal line of Dalriadic kings of western Scotland a generation later, but never before King Arthur himself. Edmond Faral (1929) wrote magisterially on the etymology of the name Arthur, concluding that it was not even Indo-European (Aryan) in origin. He reasoned as follows: no personal name that can be derived in all Indo-European languages irrespective of geographic area can be firmly, narrowly assigned to any one of them. Our own findings again bolster Faral: this is true for the Perceval name also, and accounts for the six, common variants of this hero's name. The corollary diverges, however, failing to accept unconditionally either Wagner's conclusion of his Arabic or the Poor (Pure) Fool theory of origin.

The French name "Perceval" does not mean "Through the Valley" or "Valleys" (Per-les-vaus) either. Like "Arthur," "Perceval" is non–Indo-European. Why go into the Holy Land for a Semitic etymology when we have, close by the Celtic Scots, the Picts of Scotland at whose Camelot and Firth of Forth Perceval was born? Pictish is also, like Aramaic and Hebrew, a non–Indo-European and non-Celtic language, few words of which have survived in any case. Both "Arthur" and "Perceval" could very well be Pictish survivals.

By curious chains of affiliation Richard Wagner chose *Parsifal (sic)* as the crown of his long creation of musical masterpieces, many of which are Arthurian and/or mythological: *Tannhäuser* of 1845 with its sacred mountain of Venusberg, which endorses Wolfram's idea that the Grail Castle was on a mountaintop; *Lohengrin* of 1848 whence Perceval's son in Brabant would by a process Sigmund Freud named reduplication lead the composer eventually to Lohengrin's father; *Tristan and Isolde* of 1850 with its *Liebestod;* the four Ring operas, *Der Ring des Nibelungen* (1852–72); and *Parsifal* in 1877–79. As early as 1872 Richard Wagner had chosen Bayreuth as the home of his own, future operatic theater, for which in that year he laid the cornerstone. He knew it would be the festival center for his own "music of the future": *Parsifal.*

As a "savage" anti-Semite Richard Wagner tied his star to the cruel, medieval Capetian king, to 1306 and to 1492, when the Jews were expelled from France and then from Spain. As an admirer of Wolfram and of the Order of Knights Templar, he thus became posthumously the official composer of Adolf Hitler and his National Socialist or Nazi military regime. Richard Wagner's genius directly linked Wolfram's *Parzival* to his *Parsifal.* Ernest Newman proved in Wagner's biography that Wagner was a demigod to the Nazis, and a master of the mythology they absorbed from him and turned into politics.

Wagner in *Parsifal* created a new musical genre called variously: a religious ceremony, a festival-drama, an opera, or as Thomas Mann decided (Cerf, 1990), a "music drama." Because Parsifal also becomes King of the Grail Castle on an Easter Sunday, the opera (Peltz, 1940) is "a stage consecrational festival play" (p. 182). Not that Wagner's opera is all that Christian.

Richard Wagner wrote the music of *Parsifal,* but he also wrote the libretto with its six main characters from Arthurian texts: Gurnemanz (Parsifal's teacher), Kundry (Cundrie), Amfortas (the wounded Grail King Anfortas), Parsifal, Titurel, and the evil Klingsor. These are surrounded by other Grail Knights and Squires, Flower Maidens demoted from Grail Bearers, and a chorus of choirboys. The time is the Middle Ages. The place is Spain, and the castle is not Wolfram's Munsalvaesche but Wagner's Montsalvat. These places are controversial, Passage not believing Wagner ever wrote "Spain" in his libretto, and nobody able for sure to decide if Montsalvat means Mountain of Salvation, or the Mountain of Security, a Refuge.

The three acts of *Parsifal* are introduced by a prelude, which is often admired more than all the music that follows. In the prelude in the first leitmotiv, or musical theme of the Eucharist, Wagner introduces the other principal musical motives of *Parsifal:* the Anguish, the four notes of Lance, the three, ascending bars of the Grail theme, and the triumphant, final theme of Faith. Act 1 takes sixty-two minutes of stage time, beginning with the bass voice of Titurel, former ruler of the Grail Castle, who narrates the exposition.

In the northern mountains of Visigothic Spain, he sings, Titurel found the apparently lifeless body of Kundry in brush where he later built his Grail Castle. The heroine Kundry (soprano) had come bringing healing balsam from Arabia for the suffering Amfortas. The sacred Spear of the Grail Castle has been lost to the demonic Klingsor (bass voice), whose castle lies on the southern slope of this same Pyrenean mountain chain, but overlooking Sephardic or Moorish Spain. Titurel had received in trust both the Cup of Christ's blood and the Spear to guard, for which he built a hidden sanctuary for their preservation. This is why no directions to the Grail Castle were ever allowed, and why no road or traceable path lay to it. Only a pure hero, pure in heart, could ever, and then only fortuitously, find the Grail Castle. The Grail was shown only to those who worked the will of Heaven. Klingsor had failed to see it.

Because he was scorned, Klingsor built his own rival castle where he made a wilderness bloom, and where, even now, he lies waiting. He is surrounded by devilishly lovely women who will lure innocent men into the harmful joys of sex, Wagner's idea taken, it would seem, from Wolfram's Grail Bearer Repanse de Schoye understood as *répandre joie* (spread joy). These women plan to turn men into pigs, like Circe on her holy island, become here a hell of masculine defilement. Amfortas has lost the Spear to Klingsor, alas! However, the wounded Grail King still saw the Grail in radiant light and heard it announce the coming of the "blameless fool" Parsifal, slowly becoming wise through pity *(Mittleid)*.

We then hear faraway voices and the cry of the dying swan (not Peredur's raven), which now Parsifal himself has pierced by his fatal arrow. . . . In the burst of a stunning high tenor voice, we hear Parsifal's first words:

> *Gewiss. Im Fluge treff ich, was fliegt!*
> *(For sure. In flight I shoot everything that flies!)*

At this right time Gurnemanz shames the hero. This is his first lesson: In this peaceful wood? You kill gentle, tame creatures? Have they harmed you? Do you see this poor, dying bird? His broken eyeball (gebrochen das Aug)? Are you not heartless and cruel? Do you not regret this, and repent?

Parsifal stands confounded, knowing nothing at all, not where he comes from, whose son he is, what he seeks in the forest, or what his name is. He vaguely recalls his mother Herzeleide and his home in some meadows, and that he made a weapon for the killing of eagles. Gurnemanz thinks the lad is probably himself a young eagle.

Knowledgeable as in the old days when she was the honored Grail messenger, our soprano Kundry explains that Parsifal has been a fatherless child; since the death in war of Gamuret he has been raised in secret places by his mother. Then Parsifal sings about his meeting with the knights (formerly angels). When Kundry tells him his mother is dead, Parsifal shows his first manly emotion. He faints, because he has been touched by the Grail's compassion. Kundry hides in dark shrubbery where she falls asleep. The soprano is only half human, we see.

Then Parsifal asks his first question: "Wer ist der Gral?" What is the Grail? . . . The scene changes to the vaulted Grail Castle Hall and Feast Chamber where the Grail Procession passes: knights at tables, squires singing, Amfortas borne in on a litter, an oblong stone altar covered with the shrine of the Grail placed upon it by squires. . . .

We have no more Grail-bearing priestesses here, in other words. Instead, we see youths advancing to offer their blood as Christ offered his, ready to live by death as he did. The Grail is his blood and the bread of his life.

When from the tomb Titurel prays to see the Grail once more, he is denied by Amfortas: No! Its *burning sight* must not be seen. The blood in the Cup glows and shines as its covering falls. The vile blood of Amfortas recoils before it. His wound reopens. The boy choir sings: Wait for the pure fool. Take my blood! Drink my blood!

They serve the Eucharist that Amfortas had blessed. The knights sit at table.

Parsifal stands alone on stage. A Grail Procession escorts Amfortas into the wings; end of act 1.

A person first hearing *Parsifal* is marked for life by that memory. I first heard it with my language majors whom I had gathered around my small radio in Newport, Vermont, on the afternoon of April 13, 1949. It was broadcast by the BBC from London, the BBC Symphony Orchestra, as I recall, conducted by Sir Adrian Boult. What struck me most unforgettably then was the music Wagner wrote for Amfortas, as sung by the wonderful, bass voice of Harold Williams.

After a reverent intermission, the audience springs to attention on the battlements of Klingsor's dread and hideous castle. Violently a demon awakens Kundry from her enchanted slumbers. There she springs, that Loathly Damsel, whose pedigree is far worse than one had ever thought. She is now the very Rose Queen of the Dead in Hell.

She is the medieval Herodias in love with John the Baptist. She anticipates Oscar Wilde's *Salomé* (1894) infatuated with John the Baptist. She deferred to her mother's counsel (Matthew 14:16ff.) and demanded the head of John the Baptist on a (silver? gold?) platter.

The *Salomé* opera by Richard Strauss adopts Oscar Wilde's view: that Herodias was besotted by John the Baptist. *Wagner says Kundry was Herodias.* She was also the pagan, Germanic goddess Gundryggia. Kundry hovers on stage over her enchanted, blue fire, brooding gleefully how she once seduced Amfortas, how he had sex with her, how she now will corrupt Parsifal, how then Klingsor will succeed in grasping their Grail.

Then we pass to a magical garden where thinly clad Flower Maidens perform their pretty dances and sing plaintively how Parsifal has wounded their lovers. Kundry drives them away. To implement other, foul plans, she has changed costume. When Parsifal looks toward her, he sees an almost naked Arabic, harem maiden lying in wait for him on her Oriental, silken couch. She calls him endearingly by his Arabic name. She offers him sex.

The frightened Parsifal draws back, alarmed by the pull of her foul mesmerism. Standing there he: (1) feels the pain of the Spear's wound, (2) sees the Cup filled with its sacred blood, (3) hears the Savior's cry: "Rescue me . . .", (4) falls to his knees in prayer, and (5) pushes Kundry away from him. The lusting maiden pleads for his love, over and again; for Parsifal was sent, she cries, for her salvation too and grace ("das Heil"). Parsifal asks her to lead him to Amfortas. He screams at her: "Begone, accursed woman!"

Thus, the Nazis condemned woman to wander forever a darkened earth, forever inconsolable at the loss of man's love. . . .

Then Klingsor appears on the battlements of his fearsome, black castle as he prepares to hurl the Spear at Parsifal. But the hero seizes the Spear from him and raises it aloft, above his fair head.

Thus, Parsifal vanquishes both the enchantments by Kundry and those of Klingsor, heals the wound of Amfortas, and condemns Klingsor's castle to darkness and decay. Both Spear and Cross are metamorphosed. The castle crumbles, its garden turning into the Waste Land, its flowers blighted and dead. As she falls back into Hell, Kundry screams in agony. So, let her! For his part, Parsifal pauses only momentarily to look back at her. Act 2 ends in the real darkness of Nazi Germany.

The curtain of act 3 parts to show us Wolfram's Fountain of Salvation, the Arthurian sacred spring. It is an early, bright morning in the Grail domain. Now an aged hermit Gurnemanz overhears Kundry moaning in a wintry bramble thicket. She is now gowned as a Christian penitent. Parsifal then enters. He too is clad in black, in armor with helm closed and Spear lowered. No weapons, Gurnemanz tells him, are here allowed on this sacred ground. It is Good Friday.

Parsifal prays before the Spear, saying he has brought salvation for Amfortas. He has broken the curse. Titurel has died. Parsifal blames himself for having taken so long to bring salvation to the Grail.

The audience is then surprised to see Kundry reenter the drama as another persona, *that of the beautiful Mary Magdalene.* Taking water and cloths, Kundry washes Parsifal's feet and bathes his face. . . . We have understood whom she has really become. She has been saved. She has become virginal.

Then Gurnemanz anoints Parsifal's head, after which Parsifal bends down to take springwater, which he pours over Kundry's bent head. After he baptizes Kundry, he kisses her on the forehead.

Invested with the holy, white mantle of a Knight Templar, Parsifal takes the Spear. Bells of the Grail Castle are heard, as in the French texts rehearsing Perceval's (or *Sone de Nansai*'s) coronation there.

Then lights on stage bring up the Grail Castle itself, in all its towered beauty.

The Grail Procession forms offstage, but visible in the wings. Warriors enter first, slowly and solemnly bearing Titurel's coffin. A second band of armed warriors carries in Amfortas lying in his litter. As he passes center stage, he tears open his robe to display his wound to the audience. . . . Solemnly Parsifal advances, approaches Amfortas, leans forward, and touches the Spear to the side of Amfortas. Immediately the wounded king is not only healed but free from all suffering. Parsifal cries:

Be healed, forgiven, and atoned!
Now I shall undertake your task!

Blood flows crimson from the Spear's point. Parsifal ascends the stone altar. He removes the Grail from its shrine. Then he kneels before it and prays.

Brighter and brighter shines the Grail. It is the highest, the holiest, the wonder of the world, which brings redemption.

A beam of white light searches across the darkened stage until it finds the Grail and streams down upon it. In its beam a pure, white dove descends, fluttering from darkness above upon the very holy head of Parsifal. . . . At that moment Kundry falls lifeless at his feet. Amfortas and Gurnemanz kneel reverently in homage to Parsifal.

The curtains close upon Parsifal holding the Holy Grail extended in blessing over the audience.

Wieland Wagner, who produced the *Ring* tetralogy at Bayreuth in 1951, made a cruciform design of a cross with five vertical bars, the tallest in the middle flanked by the two next tallest. The central stem represents Parsifal's union of Grail and Spear, his crux or kiss on Kundry's forehead, descending to his mother, the dying swan. The nearest bar to his left figures Kundry representing the sinful nature of woman, her bondage, misery, and salvation by death. The farther left bar represents total evil itself in Klingsor's absence of faith, lust for power, and terrible need. To the right of Parsifal's central column is Amfortas whose encounter with Kundry brought loss of the Spear, his wound, his misery, and absolution finally by the hand of Parsifal. Titurel at the far right stood for pure faith, for the Grail Castle of Montsalvat; and he died when he could no longer see the Grail.

Parsifal was first presented in Wagner's new theater, the Bayreuth Festspielhaus in 1882, as Wagner and his wife Cosima intended it should be produced, and only there, forever. In 1903, however, the Metropolitan Opera House presented it in New York City, over the legal objections of Frau Wagner. The lady lived until 1930, unable legally to stop the presentation of *Parsifal* elsewhere than in Bayreuth.

Jessie L. Weston followed this first Western presentation in her book (1904) on the legends that Wagner used as plots and characters in his dramas. His *Parsifal* is Kymric, she maintained, or a close variant upon the Welsh *Peredur,* in which the hero murders his women teachers. His talismanic Grail is both pagan and Christian,

Weston thought. Wagner took his genealogies from Wolfram, and his personages are maybe actually historical, she thought. She could not see why he situated his Grail Castle in Spain. What reason could he have had, Weston asked, except Wolfram's ascription of source to an Arabic manuscript in Toledo? Her question has already been answered differently here, of course, by the presence of the Grail in San Juan de la Peña.

A far better reply and an analysis of *Parsifal* came from Spain ten years later by Manuel Abril and A. Bonilla y San Martín. Wagner's art cannot be understood without reference to Schopenhauer's philosophy of the will, they said, a will to live understood as a blind force, an imperious will to strive, and in art or science, the will to escape pain. Wagner's original conclusion was: great is the power of the will, but greater is the power of renunciation. Thus, Amfortas = pain and suffering; the Grail = the castle of the free will ("voluntad libre"); the Lance = the enslaved will; Kundry = the will to live; and Parsifal is, in effect, the Redeemer. Wagner spent twenty years, concluded Abril (p. 43ff.), meditating "upon this drama about Jesus of Nazareth." Then he presented a Buddhist resolution of salvation by the annulment of the will and Parsifal's consecration to asceticism, all of which will result in liberation from torment. Wagner's ideas came not from Wales, but from India.

Never trouble about all that when you see and hear *Parsifal,* counseled the wise Ernest Newman (1949); for it is a work of art. As such, *Parsifal* appeals to us as artists irrespective of our religious beliefs. Newman informs us that Wagner took his spelling, Montsalvat, of the Grail Castle on its mountain in the Pyrenees between France and Spain from his own theory of its etymology, Mont + salvat = Mountain + savage, i.e., wilderness, or Waste Land.

As we have seen, however, there is another powerful reason why Richard Wagner should have pointed to the Pyrenees Mountains as a location for a Grail Castle, the first being the Spanish San Juan de la Peña. The second reason would be the two authors, Cervantes and the Sephardic Mother Theresa, who continued this Grail lore. There is another, even more powerful reason, however, which is the Catharist Grail Castle at Montségur in the Oriental Pyrenees. It is still standing there today.

As Ernest Newman expressed it so clearly, the Grail hero who was Wagner's ideal Parsifal, searched for this treasure that his heart sought; and it was both Christian, or the blood of the Eucharist, and pagan, or Wolfram's stone (altar), which in the latter's cryptic phrase could have fallen from heaven. Other sacred stones in ancient Rome and in Asia before that had fallen from heaven and were worshiped. The phenomenon is widespread, one may say, or this belief in holy stones is quasi-universal.

The popularity of *Parsifal* has represented a powerful force in the history of the twentieth century, which has given us another reason for having summarized Richard Wagner's libretto. His opera continues to be popular in opera houses worldwide because it is undoubtedly a great and shattering work of art: great theater, great music, shattering to the individual psyche. Music usually destroys the book from which it is supposedly derived. This has not been the case with *Parsifal*. Therefore one must accept Wagner's libretto as an ongoing force that has shaped, and continues to shape, our thoughts.

Parsifal was to some degree responsible for the success of Adolf Hitler's National Socialism from 1933 to 1945; thus, for World War II. Nowadays it is rather difficult to find this evidence in the pages of many respected historians; but the search still uncovers evidence of this influence, particularly in the authoritative pages or words of Thomas Mann (1933), Edmond Vermeil (1938), William Shirer (1960), Walter O. Langer (1972), Joachim Fest (1973), and Steven R. Cerf (1990).

As for myself, I was a first-hand observer of these events in world history, in place in France from September 1938 to the outbreak of war between France and England against Germany in 1939. In 1938 my honors and my majors in history and languages took me as Fellow of the University of Vermont to graduate study in History at the Université de Grenoble, France, and also to the Université de Paris. A few days later while Mr. Chamberlain went to appease Adolf Hitler in Munich, the banks were closed in France, Americans were ordered home, and France mobilized. Penniless I returned from the American Embassy in Paris to join my Czech and Yugoslav friends in Grenoble in time to raise funds for them as Hitler invaded Czechoslovakia and Poland. I also wrote several articles claiming that France would not choose to fight Germany to the death, but by surrendering would attempt to save the country, the army, and the greater part of its civilians. Only one of my papers, fortunately, was published, in the *Burlington Free Press* back home, which instantly brought down upon me a gag order from my mother. But my reading of the above historians is certainly colored, hopefully reinforced, by eyewitness testimony.

For one thing, any eyewitness will be haunted until his dying day by the sight around the American Embassy, 2 avenue Gabriel, Paris, of the lines of weeping Jewish people begging for visas to the United States. There stretched the Middle Ages all over again, and the worst, we graduate students all agreed, was yet to come.

The core of Hitler's policy, we also agreed then, was to found a secret society of SS warriors who would think themselves a sort of Grail brotherhood, a sort of Knights Templar vowed to use maidens, like heifers in pens, for breeding purposes. Their male initiations proposed to release unconscious forces that turned this master race into killers, sadists, torturers of Jews and women in unspeakable crimes that bound them together. The Nazis made good, ritual use of the gamma cross, or swastika, which allowed them the right to conquest under this emblem figuring the wheel of the world. Their reverence for *Parsifal* brought them Hitler in a silver suit, the falling dove, and the mountain hideaway or Venusberg castle of revelry. The Black Shirts recalled the ancient Manichaean heresy, black magic, and mesmerism, all giving unrestricted power to crush Poland and France, and prepare to invade Britain. In Germany they founded the ultra-secret Thule Society of *herrenvolk* allowed to search for the ultimate and lost Aryan Paradise, where once supermen reigned aloof and untainted with any of Kundry's dark, female blood.

Wagner's ideas of honor and knighthood, said Alfred Rosenberg (1893–1946), the Nazi editor and racist leader from Estonia, have raised German legend to the rank of a philosophy and a religion. We shall be guided by the inner beauty of our pagan god Wotan, he said, or of the Arthurian King Mark. And so, noted Alan Bullock, on May 10, 1940, the Germans attacked France, thrusting through the Ardennes where so many died in World War I and our fathers and uncles fought, in an armored column one hundred miles long, and reached the coast in ten days. Paris they entered on June 14.

The French historian Edmond Vermeil then kept close watch, publishing in 1938 his own evaluation: Rosenberg, he said, had to separate men from women because the latter would not succumb to the Nazi myths he was exalting. Women live more spontaneous, deeper lives, he noted. Only men fall prostrate before their so-called, chivalric, and grand Orders. Hitler carefully indoctrinated German youths with the Nordic Siegfried, the *pagan* Parsifal, and the savage Kriemhilde. He fulminated against a France that had opened her doors to immigrants of the non-Nordic races, and especially against a Paris that was always an enemy of racism and religious bigotry.

Women Hitler condemned personally for their ancient heritage of a matriarchy, which, he believed erroneously, served only inferior, distant peoples when, in fact, in Druidical Germany it probably lasted longer than anywhere else. We must regain, screamed Hitler over his loudspeakers, the domination we as the Nordic race maintained throughout King Arthur's fifth century and the sixth when we invaded and conquered England. Let us not allow Christianity, or Parsifal's renunciation, to weaken us again. As our historian Oswald Spengler first wrote in 1918, Christianity alone is responsible for our present, racial chaos. He also advised us, screamed Hitler, to keep all women *out of politics.* Their only role must be breeding, in a home. They serve only to perpetuate life and our race. Men will meanwhile restore the Teutonic, or Templar, Orders.

William Shirer (1961) recorded Hitler's "passion" for the music of Richard Wagner, equal only to his "passion" for history. From other eyewitnesses Shirer picked up someone who actually saw Adolf in the fall of 1936, actually dressed in the silver garment supposedly once worn by the knight of the Grail Castle in *Parsifal.* The American correspondent Dorothy Thompson reported that an American inside Germany at the Passion Play said Hitler was generally believed by German people to be Christ returned on earth (*Harper's Magazine,* December, 1934). Hitler is reported to have claimed that Wagner was a god, that his music was godly, and that it replaced churches and the church. His music was German only, was to be confined to Germany, and was in no way either cosmopolitan or international. Even the national colors of the Third Reich, black-red-white, had come from *Parsifal.*

Germany was the Sleeping Beauty whom Hitler awoke, he believed. It was also Snow White. "Somebody get me," Hitler is said to have cried at a meeting of his staff, "the address of the Brothers Grimm" (died 1859 and 1863). We must steep ourselves in our own literature, as we keep our heroes healthy, our women pregnant, our farmers on the soil, our workmen in the factories, and our soldiers in battle. We must conquer France but not become corrupted by the French. Hitler was not totally cynical, reported Alan Bullock (1962). He felt himself exempt from all commonality because he alone was marked by the very hand of Providence for a high mission (p. 384).

Joachim C. Fest wrote (1973) that Hitler actually identified with Wagner's early disappointments and his lack of early recognition. Wagner bequeathed to Hitler, the latter believed, his "granite foundations" (p. 48). As Master of Bayreuth Wagner set the program Hitler adopted: (1) Darwin's theory of natural selection, (2) anti-Semitism, (3) adoration of German barbarism, (4) the blood purification of *Parsifal,* (5) Manichaean opposites (black-white, good-evil, ruler-ruled, purity-defilement), (6) women as an inferior species to be relegated to grubbing underground, (7) the grudge against the metropolis (Wagner's 1913 grudge against Paris, and Hitler's grudge against Vienna), and (8) the populace lulled by a series of gigantic funeral celebrations where like Wagner, Hitler sold death.

Fest recalls what everyone has seen in the old Pathé newsreels and later on television, Hitler's magnificently staged celebrations of death. In his ceremony of November 9, 1935, he commemorated the Nazi dead. "National Socialism," Hitler said, "is a religion." On the Munich Königsplatz, under the Golden Banner of the Fallen, Hitler and the German people reverently received the Exhumed Bones of their fallen soldiers, which were laid then in sixteen bronze sarcophagi. Coffins were decorated with flaming braziers. An open-car cortege passed. Arm raised, Hitler ascended a red-carpeted staircase, dialogued mutely at each sarcophagus, upon which he then laid a wreath. Then six thousand uniformed troops goose-stepped past his salute. Then sixteen salvos thundered over Munich. Then rose the funeral dirge: "Germany! Germany over all!" Then came the roll call of the names of the dead. As each name was called, the crowd howled "Present!" That day the stage manager Hitler triumphed; for, as Fest reminded us, the Führer feared exposure, ridicule, horses, water, and boats most of all.

In preparation for that November celebration of Hallowe'en, Hitler had checked every detail personally: scene, music, marching men, flags, banners, torches, flowers, seating plan, guests of honor, and podium. . . . Fest wrote (p. 528) that Hitler's architectural sketches for the remodeling of Berlin very much resemble Cecil B. deMille's movie sets. He concluded that despite the "enormous terror," and it was, indeed, an enormous terror up until the day he invaded Russia, when all French graduate students of Napoléon Bonaparte knew they were seeing the beginning of Adolf's end, nothing of Hitler remained except a hideous memory. His was, said Fest, a "dead end."

The celebrated Nobel prizewinning novelist Thomas Mann bravely refuted Hitler publicly in a lecture he gave in Munich in 1933, pointing out that Richard Wagner's music was not the personal property of Germany alone, but the property of all people everywhere, reported the scholar Steven R. Cerf (1990) in *Opera News*. Wagner was precisely the cosmopolitan Hitler scorned. His music dramas were taken from and inspired by a worldwide literary heritage, which in the case of *Parsifal* came from Wales, France, England, Spain, Scotland, and the Languedoc. "National Socialism," said Mann, "is also a filthy barbarism." Its fairy tales, politically speaking, are "lies." As "music drama" *Parsifal* is nonetheless superb.

As a problem solver, like Robert de Boron before him, Richard Wagner worked interesting wonders in his libretto for *Parsifal*. Having earlier reviewed the careers of Peredur, Perceval (Perlesvaus), and Parzival, we find it most interesting to watch Wagner figure out answers. For example, what is one to do about Arabic imputations of origin? Answer: have Kundry bring balsam for Amfortas because, as everyone knows, Jewish and Arabic women were healers renowned during the Crusades. Why was the Grail Castle built? To house King Arthur's treasure? No, says Wagner, it was built to house the Spear and Lance sacred from the days of the Crucifixion. What bird did Parsifal really kill? The dying swan, of course, which was his own mother. Was that not a crime? No, because he was so very young, foolish, and therefore blameless. And, in any case he responded at once to Gurnemanz's teachings. How to explain Wolfram's choice of the fallen stone from Heaven as the Grail? Solution: an altar in olden days was a series of stone levels upon which the Grail was to be set. If the stone remains pagan, the blood and bread make up for it by being the Eucharist.

In act 2 Wolfram's Clinschor becomes Wagner's Klingsor, who awakens Kundry. There Wagner inserts his solution for the damsels who traditionally wept floods of tears when the silver platter was borne past them. It contained the head of John the Baptist, which, according to Matthew, Salome had been instructed beforehand by her mother to request as a reward for her dancing. We still have not seen any such connection of severed head of the prophet and the Grail Castle's silver platter. Such corroboration does not lie in the Perceval manuscripts where Wagner alone has inserted it. Everywhere Wagner simplifies those earlier tellings, going so far as to suppress Gawain, who is that Grail hero's second-track Quester.

At the Castle of "Maidens" Wagner finds another solution. These maidens are not held hostage and forced to embroider like poor women in a garment industry. They become Wagner's corps de ballet, dancing in pretty flower gardens before Hitler shuts them in dormitories where they remain prisoners awaiting fertilization by Nordic, Nazi supermen. Parsifal refuses Kundry's advances, spurns sex altogether, and has therefore no happy reunion with his loving Blanchefleur and sons either before or after his coronation. Parsifal finds Kundry accursed, which is woman's rebellious term for menstruation. She can only find "grace" if he makes love to her. In French literature heroines like Manon Lescaut are either born with grace or live forever deprived of it, irrespective of sex.

Wagner's happiest innovation, Passage notwithstanding, was his decision to locate the Grail Castle, and Klingsor's also, in the Pyrenees Mountains between France and Spain. Or as Churchill might again have observed, if he did not situate the Grail Castle in Spain, he should have.

In fact, the only real Grail Castle standing in the world of Richard Wagner, aside from San Juan de la Peña in Spain, was and is also located in the Oriental Pyrenees of Catharist France.

A rumor circulating among graduate students at the Université de Grenoble, 1938–39, held that the Grail was a fabulous emerald and that Adolf Hitler dreamed of it each night after he put aside *Parsifal,* which we heard was his nightly bedside reading. Rumors during the German occupation of France claimed Hitler had sent archaeologists into southern France to dig up the Grail. It was also widely reported then that the Grail treasure still lay undiscovered in the Languedoc.

The saddest innovation that Wagner used effectively in *Parsifal* was his borrowing from *Peredur* of the decision made there by King Arthur and Peredur to kill the latter's women teachers because of alleged witchcraft. Six million women were murdered during the Renaissance in Scotland and in Germany principally on charges of witchcraft. That charge is tantamount to saying all educated women are witches who now also deserve death.

How could Richard Wagner love his wife and still advocate the rejection and casting into hell of Parsifal's loving Kundry? How very far had Cundrie sunk since the days when as the royal if loathly damsel she had proposed marriage, which meant handing over her real estate, to King Arthur on the road from Penrith to Carlisle! How much farther than that had she sunk from the learned astronomer, or astrologer, who spoke Arabic and lectured to the court on the planets, Sun, and Moon, or the seven days of the week.

As first-semester graduate students at Columbia University in the fall of 1959, we were assigned our first research paper by Professor Jean-Albert Bédé of the Universities of Paris and Toulouse. We were given that semester, while listening to his two-hour lectures every Saturday morning (and no absences allowed ever), to discover when and where the ancient harmony between the sexes had turned first into unease, thence into discomfort, and finally into the Battle of the Sexes. The wisdom and kindliness of this most brilliant of all brilliant teachers at Columbia lightened the task and brightened the writing of our answers limited to eight pages double-spaced, and not a line more or less. "I am here to train you," he promised us. "I intend you to feel the full weight of the academic yoke."

By 1879, when Richard Wagner completed *Parsifal,* the Battle between the Sexes had in France already been fiercely waged for at least sixty-three years. Wagner's treatment of Kundry is a disgrace to women everywhere, and perceived as an undeserved insult, therefore a masterpiece unforgivable.

Chapter
——— VII ———

Esclarmonde
in the Pyrenees

Viscountess Esclarmonde

Three women famous in the thirteenth century were named Esclarmonde: the heiress Esclarmonde de Niort, who was the mother of three sons and who took holy orders at their majority; Esclarmonde de Perelha, daughter of the Lord of Montségur Castle, who refused to survive the surrender of her father's command, and who was burned in an auto-da-fé; and the Viscountess Esclarmonde de Foix, one of the most worshipful great ladies who ever lived in the Languedoc.

France in the thirteenth century was governed by Salic Law according to which French or Frankish women could not inherit property, could not rule, and could not therefore inherit the throne. The Languedoc, or what is now southern France far below the Loire River, was governed by Gothic Law according to which women were equal to men and possessed equal rights before the law. Esclarmonde de Foix, who was the wife of Jourdain de l'Isle and the mother of six children, still ruled her own property, which was a viscounty. Her domains extended down the deep river valley to the south of the fortress of Foix and included to the east the high and sacred mountain of Montségur with its dilapidated, ancient, Visigothic fortress hung like a stone cradle on its rock cap.

One can see Montségur today from everywhere in the eastern Pyrenees, and not get there from anywhere in under two days. Montségur is the most awesome sight in the world, but to find it a detailed map is necessary. Nobody gives directions to Montségur. Why? Because it is a sacred shrine and a necropolis? Montségur is also a sore subject, almost too sore still to mention. Like the old woman's name: Esclarmonde, Viscountess of Foix. Nobody wants to talk about her either.

Because of her, when the Protestants who had survived several massacres were finally allowed to emigrate, largely into Germany, England, and the Canadian wilderness, they were even then again severely punished. In fact, a worse punishment could hardly have been devised for a people suddenly stripped naked and allowed to leave their ancestral homes empty-handed, to save their skins. Each family was obliged to hand over to the French government all minor children who were female, and all other unmarried females. Why? The question deserves an honest answer.

French colonial policy did not want French Canada to become a Protestant colony that would be hostile to the fatherland, *la patrie.* In matters religious, it seems, women are to be recognized as more unshakable than men, more determined, and more resolute. Furthermore, women as the bearers of culture are the more dangerous sex. When Esclarmonde de Perelha refused to give up her Christian faith at Montségur Castle on March 16, 1244, she defied the king's officers not to burn her to death. That day a grandmother also refused not to die. Her daughter took her hand, walked down the cliff side with her and stepped into the bonfire. Then her young daughter, who was still only a girl, reached for her mother's hand and her grandmother's hand, and also jumped into the flames. Today there is a stone plaque where the refugees from Montségur were supposedly buried, but nobody dares ask if that is where it happened, and nobody looks in that direction, toward the Field of Ashes.

All France now recognizes March 16, 1244, as one of the Thirty Days that made France the country that it is, of freedom and liberty for all and a shining light of the world. That light especially warns a backward country like the United States. Here in America women were granted the vote long after those in European countries, and here, in 1990, women are considered minors, not equal to men before the law.

Zoé Oldenbourg's excellent book on Montségur and March 16, 1244, which belongs to the Series of the Thirty Dates which made France what it is, was originally published in Paris by Gallimard. The English translation contains the same chronology (pp. 390–95) of these historical events from the year 1002, when the first Protestants were burned because of religious beliefs, at Orléans on the Loire River, and at Toulouse in the Languedoc.

What is most unfortunate is that we do not have a record of the arguments advanced by the Viscountess Esclarmonde de Foix during a public debate between Protestant and Catholic prelates and theologians at the convocation of Pamiers around December 1, 1212. The occasion held great significance for several reasons aside from the fact that a noblewoman, who was an ordained theologian, was delegated to defend her religion against foremost Catholic prelates again convened, as they had been for two hundred years, in patient attempts to stop what they considered a Catharist heresy. Catharism was sweeping through all France, to be sure. Secondly, it furnished another opportunity to a few different scholars from the new and extraordinary Toulouse *University* to dispute for a first time the many Catholic theologians trained in the older monasteries. Until recently the monasteries had been the only seats of education in the Western world.

This ongoing debate also centered upon the principal ideas of the Capetian monarchy: (1) one nation indivisible, (2) doctrinal unity as a necessity, and (3) the sacrifice of liberty and freedom of thought and of belief to unity. The one nation would become France. The doctrinal unity would be legislated by the Catholic church, on whose right hand sat and would sit the French, more and more absolute monarchy. Until mountains began to attract climbers in the late eighteenth or early nineteenth century, French scholars even resented uneven land. They actually desired a world that was level, a nation that was harmonious, and a literature and art that were classical.

But the puritanical Languedoc remained resolutely a nation apart. Nobody has ever denied it, then or now. As John Herman Randall wrote in 1926 at Columbia University, if it is given that the church is the sole arbiter of Christianity and its only truth, then the Inquisition follows necessarily.

Saint Bernard told the Count of Toulouse that falling into the hands of the only, living God would be, for him also, perilous to the point of death. God's very mercy demanded the death of all heretics, it was decreed by the greatest theologians of the thirteenth century; and the Catharists in the Languedoc, as at Troyes and Oxford, were by any definition non-Catholic, and therefore legally heretic. Thus, Albertus Magnus, Alain de Lille, and Saint Thomas Aquinas also, says Randall, accepted the dreadful power and terrible judgment of the Inquisitors. Unity, Randall concluded, "can be purchased at too great a price." He drew strength from Bertrand Russell's *Why Men Fight.* Men fight, said Russell, because they fear free thought more than they fear ruin or death: "Thought is great and swift and free, the light of the world. . . ." (Randall, p. 680).

That was the name in Provençal of our Viscountess Esclarmonde: "the Light *(Esclar)* of the World *(Monde),*" which was also the title of Aimee Semple McPherson (née Aimee Elizabeth Kennedy, born 1890, Ontario, Canada), an American evangelist who once preached in her own church in Los Angeles (*TV Times, Los Angeles Times,* November 11–17, 1990).

Esclarmonde de Niort took the holy vows of Catharism or Puritanism and was protected subsequently by her noble husband and his men. In Catharist terms she became a "Perfect." The Viscountess Esclarmonde realized very early that war would be declared by the Capetian king, and that he would win it. In 1204 she prepared to devote her old age to her religion. In that year she renounced her heritage and all rights to her property, goods, possessions, belongings whatsoever. After becoming a widow, and with her children grown, in 1206 she also took the fatal step, received the Consolation *(Consolamentum),* and was ordained a Perfect. Thenceforward, as a poor Christian evangelist, she would care only for the poor until she became too feeble to be of service. Then she would withdraw from the world into a cell, ask to be walled in, and remain there, as did Sigune, in prayer until her death. Of all Catharist dignitaries this brilliant old lady Reverend was the most respected and the most deeply venerated.

Viscountess Esclarmonde foresaw the worst. Born to vast wealth and power, safe in the fortress of Foix on its peak overlooking wild canyons, she could have ruled Foix as the Viscountess Ermengarde was to rule Narbonne from 1134 to 1195. She saw what her fate would be were she to be captured alive. An even greater lady in the world's eyes, Countess Geralda de Montréal, had been driven from her luxurious chambers, stripped naked, thrown to drown in a well in her own courtyard, and then crushed with boulders for good measure. In 1232 Esclarmonde de Foix and the Catharist Bishop Guilhabert de Castres asked Raimon de Perelha to reconstruct, fortify, and provision the Lady Esclarmonde's most lonely fortress on the heights of Montségur. Only Narbonne and Montpellier would escape torture and death, they realized, as long as both cities avoided falling under Capetian rule. Neither city, despite Montpellier's famous Jewish medical school, could rival Toulouse. If Toulouse fell, the Languedoc would fall. No person there would remain alive. Millions faced death, as did the Viscountess of Foix doubly, by her investiture also as High Priestess of this early Protestantism.

Writing from Toulouse in 1926 Alex Coutet told the heroic story of the seven Counts of Toulouse who ruled that Visigothic state from the year 861 to the peace treaty with France on April 12, 1229, after which Count Raymond VII took the Cross and died in Tunis, thus allowing Toulouse to become French by default. The landmark year for the Catharist was 1213, when at the battle of Muret on September 13 the French Commander Simon de Montfort defeated Count Raymond VI and killed his second wife's brother, the King of Aragón. Simon de Montfort and his volunteers from France occupied Toulouse, slew all, and laid waste the county. The volunteers had been promised absolution plus all the spoils they could carry off. They could serve at their own pleasure and under their own terms against Toulouse instead of against the Muslims in the Holy Land. After Count Raymond recaptured his capital in 1217, the King of France declared total war on the whole Languedoc.

The Viscountess of Foix remained in safety in her own city where the high fortress of Foix was completed by 1002 with its two large square towers and its last defense of a round tower six vaulted stories tall, the whole overlooking the confluence of the Ariège River and tributary, from atop a huge cliff. Both Simon de Montfort and the royal forces after him failed to conquer Foix. Beneath its escarpments extended a network of caves as famous as refuges as for the Roman antiquities found there. While all the old feudal families of the Languedoc vanished in the wars and wholesale massacres of the thirteenth century, the Counts of Foix, united by marriage to the families of Carcassonne, Comminges, Narbonne, Béarn, and Barcelona, survived: Roger I (1064), Pierre (1071), Roger II a Crusader (1095), Roger-Bernard I, Raymond-Roger a

Crusader (1190) celebrated by Troubadours, and victor over Simon de Montfort (1223), Roger-Bernard II the Great who was excommunicated in 1229 and again in 1237, Roger IV who capitulated momentarily to the Crown, and Roger-Bernard III (1265–1302) who found himself hard pressed by the Regent Blanche of Castille. Nevertheless this long-lived family of the Viscountess Esclarmonde were still active in their illustrious descendants—the royal lines of Albret, Bourbon, and Vendôme, in 1589.

In 1589 a grandson of the Viscountess Esclarmonde who united the House of Foix to the families of Albret, Bourbon, Vendôme, and Navarre was crowned King Henri IV of France. As King Henri III of Navarre before he went up to Paris, this descendant of the celebrated Viscountess would have known that her name and fame were closer to the Pyrenees than to France: *esclarecer* = to clear, to illuminate, to make noble. The Viscountess was *esclarecida* = famous, illustrious, and distinguished. In her old age she shone with great luster—*con grande lustre*—as her people awaited death.

How does an entire civilization await certain, mass death? The outer world reacted. England, for one, cut off all relations with the Pope from 1208 to 1214. The august Count of Toulouse was scourged publicly at home in that masterpiece of medieval architecture, Saint-Sernin de Toulouse. Then he was ordered to Paris and publicly scourged at Notre-Dame. After the Christian Crusaders laid waste Christian Constantinople, observed Michelet (vol. 1, chap. 7), they followed this precedent and gladly laid waste southern France. The war against Béziers and Carcassonne was led by the Archbishops of Reims, Sens, and Rouen, and by six other Bishops and Counts, plus His Grace, the Duke of Burgundy. Saint Bernard is falsely reported to have coined their dispensation: "Caedite eos novi enim Dominus qui sunt ejus" (Kill them all, for God will know who the elect are). At the surrender by the city of Béziers, fifty persons were hanged, and four hundred, burned.

Since the Counts of Foix had sheltered the assassin of a Papal Legate, and since his countess and the Viscountess Esclarmonde, his sister, were admitted heretics, the Count tried a desperate measure in the hope of obtaining peace from the Pope himself. He went personally to Rome, pleaded the case of the Languedoc, and threw himself on the mercy of the Vatican. He remained there from 1209 to 1210 still hoping for peace. The Papal Court delayed giving him any reply. It kept him there month after month, thus depriving the Languedoc of its one leader second in energy and influence only to the Count of Toulouse. Finally, the answer was negative. All must die in southern France since there is neither time nor method to separate true believers from heretics. When he heard the court's decision, the Count of Foix burst into tears. The chairman mocked him: "Water may run and still not reach the Lord," he said.

In the Languedoc the mood then turned to desperation. When Minerve Castle fell, the survivors threw themselves into the fire that had been lighted to burn them. Many who died there were Elders of the Catharist church. Lord Aimeri (Emery), named for one of the oldest heroes in any Romance language because he was the epic hero of Narbonne, almost survived. The gibbet built to hang him collapsed under his weight. But the nobleman was caught below and his throat cut instantly.

Michelet's verdict carries great weight: "Mankind are not immolated to an idea with impunity. The blood that is shed finds a voice within your own heart that shakes the idol to which you have offered sacrifice . . . leaving one certainty: that you have sinned for it" (pp. 87–88).

The answers made to Michelet repeated the court's findings in the thirteenth century, and are repeated again today by defenders of the Papacy: (1) the people executed were heretics, (2) they refused to submit to orthodoxy, which made them foes of the Frankish state and church, and (3) they were neither Puritans nor Protestants, but descendants of older, detestable heresies such as the Manichaean and/or Arian.

However, the greatest of French theologians to address the subject was Charles Schmidt, Professor of Theology at the University of Strasbourg, who found in his magisterial work (Paris and Geneva, 1849) that the so-called heresy of the Albigensians or Catharists was a Protestant religion sui generis, not derived from those preceding heresies called Manichaean and Arian. Scholars in the Languedoc today, and there are countless of them writing volume after volume on this same subject, continue also to claim originality *and worship of the Holy Grail.*

The quarrel goes back to our starting point: Jesus, Jerusalem, and the Third Gospel, of John. Deviation from Roman Christianity, they still believe along with Schmidt, occurred during the lifetime of Christ and the Apostles as the latter journeyed spreading the new religion into the western fringes of the Roman world. The Gospel according to John was supposedly brought into the Languedoc by Saint Bartholomew directly from Persia and eastern Europe. Therefore while the Franks believed that the diffusion of Christianity followed this route: Jerusalem, Greece (Gospel of Luke), Rome (Saints Paul and Peter), and into France, the Languedoc testified that the route to them was: Jerusalem, Greece, Bulgaria, Provence, and into the Languedoc. Thus, they continued to accept priestesses in the very ancient image of Saint Mary Magdalene, and the Saints Mary of the Sea, all these women and their evangelist fellows buried then and now, visibly, in the south of France.

The best support of Charles Schmidt and of other modern scholars in the Languedoc was made in 1987 by Dr. A. Barthélémy. The best attack on Schmidt was perhaps Pierre Belperron's exhaustive *La Croisade contre les Albigeois et l'Union du Languedoc à la France (1209–1249)* published in Paris in 1942 and 1946 and still in print. Belperron has no patience with heresy. He believes that the crusade against the Albigensians and their union with France occurred legally and rightfully, and was limited to the years from 1209 to 1249. His book is a reply to Zoé Oldenbourg and also to the radical German Otto Rahn, whom we shall soon encounter. Belperron found heretics in southern, high places, and Jews close beside them, which was certainly true in the Languedoc and in Spain also. Belperron's method demonstrated his own intolerance, however. First he found out if an author was Protestant. He then announced this lamentable fact before denouncing the author as bigoted and prejudiced.

There is a "whole literature" that Belperron relegated to footnote 2 (p. 449) about the treasure of Montségur. He wrote that it was in all probability Albigensian sacred books; but numerous scholars of the Romance languages, he continued, have wished to see in all this the Holy Grail, Perceval, and the romances of the Round Table, which they would recognize today even as Montségur and the Wolfram's Monsalvaesche which inspired Richard Wagner.

"Let us hope," prayed Barthélémy in 1987 at Toulouse, to the contrary, that some bits of spiritual nourishment have survived these Catharist massacres, and that some fallen debris has floated down to today, to nourish our sufferings and light our way (p. 253). Let it be the Holy Grail, he prayed.

There are easily a hundred books on the subject in the bookstores of Albi today, and Albi is the small mountain city the name of which gave the Languedocian heretics their title of Albigensian. Signs all over Albi today warn the residents to remember that all the foreign

(American and German) visitors who throng there every summer are not only their patrons and benefactors, but their "Friends," descendants, and their very welcome guests. The small blue sign "Culte" at street corners directs both visitor and native to the nearest poor, Protestant church.

Walking the streets of Albi, crossing the square to the very thriving bookstore crammed to the ceiling with new history books, or hunting for one's professor's family through rose-colored Toulouse, now a center for aircraft manufacture, one is reminded of Rome.

In fact, here as in Great Britain in more or less the same centuries, Celts were subdued and adopted into the Roman Empire. No more proudly than King Arthur and Queen Guinevere, the highest aristocrats south of the Loire River also claimed noble descent from patrician Romans who were firstly their conquerors, secondly their governors, and finally their relatives. Ancient trading depots predated the Roman arrival in Gaul. People there say now they tried to halt Hannibal's progress. Their cities prospered greatly under Augustus Caesar.

In Britain the Romano-Celts under King Arthur fought the Anglo-Saxons and won a few battles obviously not fought in England where the later Anglo-Saxon advance was carefully dated and situated, place by place, year by year. Similarly, but centuries later, the Ibero-Romans south of the Loire River fought the Franks led by their more able Capetian kings. Did not the Angevin nobles, and especially Richard I, Eleanor of Aquitaine, attended by their public relations people, or courtiers like Walter Map and Gervase of Tilbury, not bring the Arthurian corpus and the Grail literature into medieval Provence and the Languedoc? Wolfram von Eschenbach denies it. *Parsival* originated in Toledo, he wrote, among the beloved and learned Sephardic Jews of central Spain and Toulouse.

The landmark years are not too far apart: Arthur's victory over the Saxons circa 500; William of Orange's (Orange < Aransio) victory over the Saracens at Aliscans near Arles in 793; Arthur's defeat at Camlan in the year 542, claim the *Annals of Wales*. By the year 800 all trace of Arthur's Grail Castles at Dumbarton on the Clyde River, then at Peel Castle on the Isle of Man in the Irish Sea, were obliterated by Viking conquest. William of Orange retired to his monastery at Saint-Guillaume-le-Désert, a part of which, barring error, stands today, overlooking the Hudson River, as the Cloisters Museum, Metropolitan Museum of Art, New York City. The difference is that although he bore the image of the Virgin Mary in his wars, King Arthur has not been canonized, nor has Merlin. The ancient epic hero of Provence, William of Orange, is now Saint Guillaume de Gellone. His chapel was rebuilt after William's death, but its original structure had been erected before the Virgin Mary's death, and rebuilt during King Arthur's lifetime. Christ had appeared and prayed there near Aliscans or Alyscamps south of Arles and because He had left a knee print, everyone in the North wanted to be floated down the Rhône and interred in that necropolis. William's nephew, who died in his arms, was named Vivien, which is the name of Lancelot's Lady of the Lake.

When the Angevin Richard I died in France, he was King of Arles. His courtier Gervase of Tilbury, who was an author of trifles and bits of rumor about King Arthur, was the Marshal of Arles in the thirteenth century. The connections deepen, for Wolfram von Eschenbach also made a partial translation into German of the first part of William of Orange's epic poem *Aliscans*. The original is considered, and especially its first three thousand verses, one of the world's greatest epics. The Arthurian poet Ulrich von dem Türlin also translated some ten thousand verses of *Aliscans* where similarities to Arthurian literature appear plainly, such as: the major hero Arthur and William both wed foreign brides who came from pagan peoples, the Pictish Guinevere and the Saracen Guiborc; both literatures present a defense of the homeland against invaders of another religion; the proper names of the Arthurian places and persons bear some if faint resemblance, the one to the other, as in Vivian, Cador, Blanchefleur, plus Aliscans as necropolis and Avalon as Grail site and necropolis; a similar, religious character of King Arthur and Duke Guillaume, both of whose swords are named and considered holy, horses also of Gawain and Guillaume named and precious; the young hero and heir dying suddenly on the field of battle, i.e., Vivien and Modred (whom the historians of the Scots claimed was Arthur's last nephew and heir); the Giant Renouart in *Aliscans* resembling with his primitive club swung over his head as a weapon Arthur's oldest nephew and first Commander Gawain in battle frenzy. Finally, the *Aliscans* moves the reader much as do the best pages of the Arthur manuscripts. The *Aliscans* in its first verses gives the reader's heart a thump:

> *A icel jor que la dolor fu grans*
> *Et la bataille orible en Aliscans,*
> *Li cuens Guillaume i soffri granz ahans . . .*

Americans must read the above verses aloud to catch the lovely
poetry, and they are to pronounce each letter and syllable, as in
modern English. There are ten syllables to each verse. The final
word *ahans,* which requires an exhalation, so perfectly expresses
pain.

> *Upon that day when sorrowing was great*
> *And battle horrible in Aliscans,*
> *Count William there suffered great agony . . .*

The poem is so beautiful it fully testifies to this long tradition for
great literature that under the patronage of Toulouse has attracted
and rewarded so many authors, continuing until today. Only a
fifteen-year-old French lad, of French, Catholic father and Protestant and Celtic mother, educated in turn by either divorced parent
in France or in Spain, fooled the judges of literature once in Toulouse into believing he was a mature poet and genius: the boy
Victor Hugo. But the judges from the august Academy at Toulouse
awarded the boy first prize anyway.

It was the mature and celebrated troubadour Guilhem Montanhagol, reported Jules Coutet (Toulouse, 1898), who under the
patronage of Count Raymond of Toulouse not only celebrated the
Viscountess Esclarmonde de Foix but lived a forlorn refugee in
exile later, far from home in Castile and Aragón, where he witnessed sadly the extinction of liberty and the end of the feudal lords
of Toulouse around 1242. His poems attacking the Inquisition are
still famous. Guilhem said he also lived to see the death of the
Provençal language, and therefore the last verses of troubadour
poetry in Provençal. This loss brought down in its wake the death
of a people and of their civilization. Poetry had tried in vain to
disarm both the Catholic clergy and French royalty. The native
aristocrats tried their best, argued Guilhem in his verses *(servientes),*
to remain chaste in love and Christian in their faith. They were
accused of cutting the birth rate on the one hand, and of heresy on
the other.

Stanza 6 of his poem celebrating Esclarmonde ends with a prayer:

> *N'Esclarmonda sal Dieus e gar*
> *Q'es de fina beutat ses par.*

> *May God save and guard Esclarmonda*
> *For she is peerless in delicate beauty.*

Esclarmonde appears here to have been the first of French poetry's Peerless Ladies such as the royal wife whom Charles d'Orléans later celebrated in perfect troubadour style.

In his stanza 7 Guilhem tells us Esclarmonde is so perfectly pure of life and spirit that she remains day in and day out sheltered from all evil. He ends his praise (stanza 9): Esclarmonde, your name alone truly signifies that you do light up the world and so, because you are so pure, you have never done but what you ought. You have become her as such a name should have been.

The historian Napoléon Peyrat (Paris, 1880–82) concluded his study of troubadours (chap. 7) by affirming that the two religious cycles in Europe were the Grail texts that exist in two places: *Roman Great Britain and Roman Aquitania.* The religion peculiar to Toulouse spread from there to Ireland, influenced Saint Columba, and was condemned at Oxford in 1160. It had taught: (1) follow the Apostles first and foremost, (2) refuse the sacraments, (3) refuse the Eucharist, (4) prefer virginity, (5) never yield or deny your faith, and (6) have mercy on those souls put in prison ("Aias merce de l'esperit pousat en carcer"). Those who followed these teachings were branded, stripped, whipped, and driven out into the Pyrenees Mountains. Or they were burned. These punishments dragged on, causing, after the fall of Montségur, more and more violent, general uprisings.

The last Catharist Bishops finally took refuge in labyrinthine caves, some of them as much as thirteen miles long, at Ornolac and Lombrives. The surviving mountain people followed their leaders. Dogs were sent in to kill them. The entrances finally were walled up. Among the stalagmites today, it is said, there stretch inside these last refuges mountains of human bones. Those so immured died inside these caves, today giant ossuaries. The necropolis of Ornolac holds the bones of the nobles from Foix, perhaps including those of the Viscountess Esclarmonde.

The Middle Ages, said Albert Réville (Paris, 1874), hung their hats upon their presumed right to oppress the human conscience, individual or collective, either by conquest or by anathema. The day they realized that neither method works or can be called legitimate, was the day when one could say the Middle Ages ended.

When the term "Protestant" is used here to refer to what may have been the religious beliefs and practices of this venerated old lady, who was the heiress Esclarmonde, it is used generally to mean first that she did not subscribe to or join the Roman Catholic church, nor recognize the primacy of the Pope. She probably practiced Protestantism in some form akin to what we could recognize as such, by claiming liberty in secular matters, and by exercising her private judgment rather than accepting another dogma. In other words, she would have argued against both tradition and the paternal authority of a patriarchy, feeling herself responsible primarily and directly to God. This is not to say that she nor anyone else vanquished the greatest theologians of the Catholic church in the thirteenth century.

Speaking as a student of literature and philology only, with no pretension to knowledge of theology, this author feels after reading their great arguments rather as Omar Khayyam felt, as so superbly translated by Edward Fitzgerald:

XXVII

Myself when young did eagerly frequent
Doctor and Saint, and heard great Argument
About it and about: but evermore
Came out by the same Door as in I went.

In order to convey a better notion of Esclarmonde's beliefs, we might review some points of Catharist ritual as listed more completely and explained painstakingly by the eminent Catharist scholar René Nelli (Paris, 1968):

1. *Aparelhament.* A public, monthly confession by Perfects after benediction.
2. *Ben.* Adhesion to the *Ben* (Good), or adopting Catharism.
3. *Caretas.* The liturgy of charity: sermon, service, *Consolamentum,* kiss of peace.
4. *Consolament.* A spiritual baptism by hands, similar to extreme unction. A voluntary renunciation of the material world, an entrance into the Catharist church as a Perfect, or minister.
5. *Convenza.* The "Our Father" prayer recited on behalf of the dying who were at that time unable to recite it.
6. *Endura.* The ceremony of deprivation or dieting to death permitted to Catharists during the war of the thirteenth century. Permission was also granted to

those who preferred death by cold. These permissions were expressly granted to those besieged persons shut inside the Castle of Foix.

7. *Esperit.* A point of doctrine positing a triad or three persons of the trinity, or spirit, soul, and body.

8. *Melhorament.* An amelioration, or a prayer to become a better person, addressed to a Perfect after three genuflections and a prayer for benediction.

The supplicant says: "Bon crestia balhats-nos la bénédiction de Dieu et de vos. Pregatz per nos." (Good Christian, grant us God's blessing and yours. Pray for us.)

The Perfect replies: "Ajatz-la de Dieu e de nos!" (Receive it from God and from us!) "Que Dieu vos aduga a bon fin e vos foga bon crestian." (May God assist you to make a good end, and make you a Good Christian.)*

9. *Orazom.* The Lord's Prayer.

This Catharist Ritual, of which these are merely nine points from Nelli's nineteen major technical terms, also mentions the Castle of the Horn, which may mean the Grail in Great Britain, according to Arthurian texts. It is not meant to be the Castle of St. Luke, usually represented as an ox, but the Castle of the solar and pastoral Ram, which represents the Virgin Mary, says Catharist doctrine, so figured because the horns of the Virgin drove out Satan and also wounded Lucifer the same way. Perhaps the Catharists thought of Aries the Ram (Gawain) as the Virgin's protector.

Writing on this Catharist religion of Viscountess Esclarmonde, who put on the black garments of a Perfect and after her children were raised and after she became a widow, undertook to minister only to the poor, Michel Roquebert (Toulouse, 1988) concluded that Catharism was Christian because it taught revelation, the New Testament, the Lord's Prayer, Christ as sent to earth by God, and salvation by asceticism and by baptism. It considered itself an exclusive and the best religion of all because the most pure.

The Catharists referred to themselves as "Weavers," and as "Friends of God." Both "weaver" and "butler" were secret words for Catharist. By their condemnations (1119, 1139, 1148, 1157,

---

*"Good Man," "Good Christian," "Good Woman" meant Catharist.

1163, 1165, 1179, and 1184) they finally proved to the world the disciplinary power of Church and state. They are remembered for their simple lives, their self-sacrifice, their care of the poor, their abhorrence of money and pollution, their strict conduct between the sexes, their abstinence, and their frugality. Contrary to the Catholic church, the Catharists routinely admitted qualified men and women both to the priesthood. Also contrary to the Roman church they preached in the popular languages and read the New Testament in the Occitan language of the Languedoc.

Their culture raised heroic women whose names today are all but forgotten outside their native land: Lampagie, Esclarmonde, Alazaïs, India, Mélissende.

Proof that the name Esclarmonde has been forgotten in France comes from the music of Jules Massenet (1842–1912), born in the Loire area of France, who wrote the music for his opera *Esclarmonde:* four acts and eight tableaux, 1889. Like his other music written to celebrate famous or notorious women such as Hérodiade, Cleopatra, Cinderella, Sappho, Ariadne, Thaïs, and Manon, the very productive and very successful French musician Massenet also wrote music for others: Eve, the Virgin Mary, Mary Magdalene, and Esclarmonde.

Massenet's *Esclarmonde* presents a great problem, however. It is, in fact, a real mystery. The heroine Esclarmonde, who sings the high soprano and title role, is neither the Viscountess de Foix nor either of the other two real ladies named Esclarmonde who lived in the thirteenth century.

Nor does the Viscountess Esclarmonde de Foix appear as yet in French or other encyclopedias. Nor has any of the fifty or so music reference books in the stack of our universities ever heard of a historical Esclarmonde. One lone critic in a French music dictionary (*Dictionnaire des Opéras,* New York, 1969) comments upon this unusual name, saying (p. 404) that it seems to him the name alone was the real "find." The very name, he adds, "engendered" in him feelings of love, melancholy, and poetry. That is certainly true in the French language, the two first vowels pronounced open, the *E* followed by the even more open *a,* then followed by the closed, nasal *o,* constitute very musical French, even when spoken only. Neither this more astute critic, nor anyone else, it appears, has ever questioned the name, or Massenet's opera title, further than that.

The fact that a French music critic, therefore an unusually sensitive person, immediately felt feelings of sadness at the mention of her name, seems to indicate subliminal memory.

The opera was commissioned for premiere at the Paris Universal Exposition of 1889, and was then considered extremely modern music, indeed. The title role was inaugurated by the Australian soprano Sibyl Sanderson whom her biographer called *La Stupenda* (Sydney, 1981). The role requires a stupendous virtuosity in the soprano since its high notes are said to be the highest in the register. Madame Sanderson also premiered *Esclarmonde* in the United States, at New Orleans in 1893, where again she amazed her audience. At the Metropolitan Opera premiere of *Esclarmonde,* New York City, November 19, 1976, the audience was privileged to hear one of the greatest of coloratura technicians of our century, the lovely and wonderful Prima Donna Joan Sutherland, born in Sydney on November 7, 1926.

The libretto was written by Alfred Blau and Louis de Gramont and the opera subtitled "romanesque," which is by itself alone a denial of its historicity since *romanesque* in French means merely "fabulous," fictional only. There are nine characters but two only are major: the veiled Princess of Byzantium whose name is Esclarmonde, and her lover Count Roland of Blois whom she seduces.

In this muddle of inappropriate names for the nine principals, an Arthurian scholar discards every one except Esclarmonde's title, which in *Peredur* indicated his future bride: the Empress of Constantinople. In fact, during the prologue she is so hailed by the populace: "O divine . . . sublime Empress . . . Byzantium at thy feet!" The Viscountess de Foix, pronounced "Fwa" just like "Blwa" (Blois), in real life was certainly never addressed as "thee . . . thou . . . thy"; that is not done to a great, French lady, perhaps not even by her husband. But here, the crowd addresses the princess, who is only a girl of twenty, familiarly, to express their love.

On the palace terrace in act 1 Esclarmonde announces her strategy, which will be to seduce Roland (shades of Charlemagne's dead nephew, alas!), by climbing upon her (Delphic) tripod and praying to the moon, etc.

In act 2, while the hero sleeps, Esclarmonde seduces him, praying now for dawn to hold her course and delay this precious night. Her song recalls the "dawn song" in Gounod's opera *Roméo and Juliette.* Their duet here is superb, and justly applauded. For him, *andante cantabile,* the moment of love is divine. The Chorus of Spirits praises the wedding, singing gloriously "Hymen!" Esclarmonde, and here is the crux of the drama, vows the hero to silence. He must never see her face or reveal their liaison. As reward, she invests him with the Sword of Saint George. He has sworn silence.

By act 3 Roland proves true to his name in epic poetry by fighting Saracens at the Loire River. There unfortunately the Bishop traps him into revealing his amour:

> *During the night she came*
> *This strange, sweet, unknown creature.*
> *She gave herself to me, whom my arms embraced,*
> *And who taught me what love is . . .*

But the Bishop cries, "Witchcraft!" when Esclarmonde enters, and adds: "I expel you, demon. Back!" She is led to the scaffold while Roland summons her Spirits to defend her. Curtain.

Act 4 takes us to Shakespeare's Forest of Arden where a tournament to decide Esclarmonde's husband will be held. Esclarmonde arises from the witches' smoke and flames, crying that Roland betrayed her. She vows to save him anyway, and die. He protests. She flies off in a cloud.

The tournament is held as an epilogue. Esclarmonde enters veiled. Roland wins the combat. He refuses to wed the princess until, of course, she reveals herself as his beloved.

In an *allegro maestoso* the crowd hails their "divine" Esclarmonde, and valorous hero. In fact, they say the universe acclaims them. The crowd shivers with the passion of love.

As all critics saw at once, the *Esclarmonde* has borrowed the crux of Richard Wagner's *Lohengrin,* but reversed; for in the Arthurian opera the new wife Elsa is made to swear she will respect the taboo of her husband Lohengrin's name. When she fails to do so, he leaves Brabant on his swan (ship), which causes Elsa to die, a death she has duly deserved. Massenet also borrowed Wagner's innovation of the leitmotiv.

But *Lohengrin* (Weimar, 1850) is par excellence the Grail opera, the theme of the Grail commencing the prelude in the highest register possible to the orchestra, and gradually developing into the climax of all musicians, the music written to convey to the audience the powerful, heavenly vision of a Grail blessing them like a dove descending from heaven. And *Lohengrin* ends the same way, the hero's lyric tenor voice explaining: In a far country stands Wagner's Grail Castle of Monsalvat. There pure knights guard the Holy Grail. It was brought by angels from heaven. A dove descends to them on Easter every year, replenishing their faith. These knights (Templar) become yearly strong enough to represent in their persons purity in this world. (The Grail is the chalice that holds Christ's blood from his dying hour.) If faith ever fails, the knights must leave Monsalvat forever. Elsa's faith in Lohengrin has failed. Therefore he must depart.

Lohengrin reveals his identity at the last: My name is Lohengrin. I am the son of the Grail King Parsifal (Parzival). . . . The hero departs on the wings of the dove.

Something like this *Lohengrin* plot would better have suited *Esclarmonde.* The unfortunate story used in her opera comes from a medieval "classical" romance, most of which were rather scabrous, thus dissimilar to the more idealistic Arthurian legends of the High Middle Ages. The *Esclarmonde* is actually based upon an old city myth of Thebes and Naples, actually a rewrite of the story of Parthenope. Parthenope was another name for Atalanta, and "Parthénopé" in French still means "Naples." Thus, Parthenopaeus, the son of Parthenope, founded the city of Naples.

Like Esclarmonde in the Massenet opera, Parthenope and/or Atalanta gave birth secretly to her son. Her father was escorting her out of the city to a mountaintop where he intended to sacrifice her. By losing her virginity she had disgraced him and her family. During their ascent of the mountain Parthenope stepped aside into some bushes and delivered her son, whom she abandoned there. As soon as her father noticed that the girl was not pregnant after all, he spared her life.

The son's name, Parthenopaeus, means son of a pierced maidenhead, or hymen.

Despite the glory of its music and the Oriental splendor of its set, the opera *Esclarmonde* can hardly be seen as a compliment to the puritanical, elderly priestess, Viscountess Esclarmonde de Foix.

Fortified now with our new knowledge of this great lady named Esclarmonde, who is daily becoming better and better known in the

Languedoc, we are certainly justified in believing that Arthurian personages were also equally historical. The orators Guinevere, Morgan le Fay, and Cundrie were also great aristocrats like Esclarmonde. They too were revered as scholars and holy women. We must also accept the relationships between ancient Provence and that other Roman province called Britannia by the Roman governors. Arthur's equals in military affairs lived along with him, but in Roman Aquitania and Provincia.

The Holy Grail as emblem of a primitive form of Christianity not separated from Judaism seems to have been widespread.

THE GRAIL CASTLE MONTSÉGUR

The essential aspect of Montségur, now seriously reconsidered as a Castle of the Holy Grail, retains its position on the top of an extraordinarily spectacular mountain pinnacle. Wolfram von Eschenbach, poet, and friend of troubadours in the Languedoc and Toledo, strongly endorsed the theory that the Grail Castle crowned a spectacular peak; but he did not necessarily locate that summit at a particular place. In his edition of Wolfram's *Titurel,* Passage decided (1984) that these *(Titurel)* fragments, which preceded *Parzival,* gave Richard Wagner a lead also; but Wagner's *Parsifal* too, its modern libretto to the contrary, *may never have mentioned* Spain specifically, or the Languedoc, as site of the mountain Grail Castle.

Wolfram talked about Scotland instead, and a Scot whose forces came from a "Greenland," as of a Morholt who came from a green Ireland. In his *Titurel* fragments he says Titurel was the grandfather of the Grail King Amfortas for whom other heroes built a chapel. The original Grail Castle, he says, *was located in "Bertâne," or Britain.*

This must be our conclusion also, and for the added reasons of chronology. It is not possible to believe that the massacre of the Catharists who surrendered at Montségur in 1244 caused poets in Angevin territories or in France to write new Grail legends derived from that event, however horrible and publicized. And that event was not publicized but done secretly, quickly, and ordered forgotten.

Regular soldiers who massacre large numbers of noble and distinguished women by means of a ceremonious if hasty auto-da-fé, witnessed by an entire army, in broad daylight, probably prefer to forget it even if not ordered to do so; and they were ordered to forget it by their superior officers and by the high prelates present and officiating.

An auto-da-fé such as the one at the foot of the Montségur cliffs on March 14, 1244 was better forgotten. The Grail manuscripts from Britain and France preceded this ceremony by a century, even including the *Prose Lancelot.* Furthermore, the authors of the Grail manuscripts in Old French were, anonymous or not, obviously the great intellectuals of their day. They wrote from the known monastic centers where their friends resided, ruling hundreds of scholars in their Orders. These authors lived at the center of political events of their day. It is inconceivable that such authors and prelates would not have heard of this auto-da-fé, however, which was a fantastic ceremony performed after pronouncement of judgment by ecclesiastical authorities of first importance in western Europe, followed by mass execution enacted by secular authorities, in this case by the army of the Capetian king ruling northern France, and duly witnessed by thousands of soldiers. Witnesses to this mass burning of surrendered and otherwise captured heretics, most of whom were females of all ages, properly shared the guilt, and guilt there was.

Therefore, if Montségur was a Castle of the Holy Grail, it became so after the writing of the major Arthurian romances in the eleventh and twelfth centuries. Those centuries and their authors placed the Grail Castle in Britain, and never in France. For a Grail Castle to have been in France, i.e., the region north of the Loire River, the church would have had to accept the Grail as orthodox, which has never happened as yet. France was always closest, and/or claimed to be closest, to the church.

This talk of twelfth and thirteenth centuries has not even yet adduced the really clinching argument: that King Arthur was the original Grail King, with Merlin too as his Archbishop, and that they lived in Great Britain in the fifth and sixth centuries. Thus, their Grail Castle is many centuries older as a holy place of worship than Montségur Castle and its abominably hideous auto-da-fé. Both parties, executioners and victims, outreached each other in intransigence. That is the real pity: the hard hearts of mankind.

Before continuing to look at Montségur as a possible Grail Castle after all, because perhaps so called first by English clerical scholars such as Walter Map (Mapes) from Oxford, and Gervase of Tilbury, both expert propagandists and great gossips, plus the English lords lesser than King Richard I, all highly honored if less extravagant with their money than him, plus the great ladies like Richard's sister Jeanne who finally married the Count of Toulouse, we should first examine the mountain itself. Is a remarkable mountain possible as site of a Grail Castle? Its first choice, of course, offers us the Western island of Arthurian literature, which is called Avalon, its older castle called Corbenic.

The alternate and later site, then, is a mountain. When Sir Edmund Hilary first ascended Mt. Everest, more properly Chomolungma, and was asked why he persisted in performing this great exploit, he answered: "Because it is there," which seems a dismissal and no answer at all. Many other, reasonable answers leap to mind. The mountaintop, and Chomolungma expressly, is like Nanda Devi beside it, the original home of the Mother Goddess, and therefore a prehistoric paradise. Such a mountain is anyway the nearest spot on earth to heaven. Therefore great mountaintops around the world tend to bear her name, like Mt. Gorgonio overlooking Los Angeles, which is also named for the Mother Goddess under her clan name: Medusa, the sleeping Gorgon. Her son in France is the lovely giant Gargantua, and her abode any number of Mt. Gorgons.

It follows that the Mother is beautiful, greatly to be desired as a mother of a son, and therefore seductive and/or seducer depending on whose point of view one espouses. Even in the opera *Esclarmonde* the future mother prays to Diana, Goddess of the Moon, and the black-clad triple Hecate of the Crossways where her altars stood. Her daughters are black-clad like the Catharist Viscountess Esclarmonde, and they immure themselves inside cells on the mountainside, where like Sigune they are found stiff and dead. The historical Esclarmonde could have died this way also, and also perhaps by starving herself in one of the cells constructed so as to overhang the cliff face at Montségur. Or she underwent *endura* at Foix Castle. Nobody has thought she was burned in the Montségur auto-da-fé, but that is not certain since no roll of the sentenced was kept, and nobody was asked to make one. But someone as prominent and so venerated as she was, even called by Napoléon Peyrat the "Pope" of the Catharists, could not have been ignored, and probably was not burned.

The mountain goddess's learned familiars would have been called priestesses by those who respected them, but witches by those who like Peredur decided to kill them. It is even so possible to excuse Peredur, and Arthur too, of this multiple murder because their contemporary the Emperor Justinian had just outlawed women in the priesthood and closed the schools to them. How women can become educated in any society, especially one where, unlike France and Scotland, tuition is not free, is always the graver problem. Therefore we have seen Cundrie sink abominably from the learned Loathly Damsel lecturing in Arabic on the planets, and considering herself a fit bride for Arthur, even wedding a reluctant Gawain, to the Kundry who rolls about in the shrubbery outside Richard Wagner's Mountain of Salvation unable even to come indoors. Converted, she obliges by dying at once. She has finally degenerated to a subhuman species like her contemporary Grendel's dam, who is killed under the lake by Beowulf. All such conquered, dark-skinned females are doubly outcasts, despised because displaced, then because of their gender.

Under paradise their mountain is subterranean as Don Quixote discovered when he lowered himself down the vertical shaft, or as any Gothic novelist like Jules Verne knows by counting the steps down for his hero. How otherwise can the designate save his life in purgatory, except by halting at the proper, magical number of steps, and then, like Don Quixote, proceeding horizontally? Some white-clad priestess like the traitor Ariadne had to give him directions, or at least, a ball of white twine cut to the prescribed length. The successful Gothic novelist knows the secret of his enchanting scenario: the heroine, who is a white-clad priestess, descends into darkness, holding her flickering candle bravely *because she must seek knowledge.* It is woman's modus vivendi.

Therefore Psyche must see her husband, must even ask Cupid his name, even though she has been ordered not to do any such things, and threatened with direct punishment if she defies his injunctions. Similarly, even the fictional Esclarmonde in her unscholarly opera must unveil herself and see Roland. Elsa must ask Lohengrin his name and lose him as Psyche lost Cupid. In other words, women who dare to seek knowledge are, like our mother Eve and the Greek Pandora also, considered unnatural, low-lived, and as loathly as the spinster Cundrie. Or they are to be slain as abhorred witches whose knowledge, especially if medical, is vastly to be condemned.

The lady's gift alone is acceptable, but for the duration of the hero's quest only. Cundrie advised Gawain to seek a certain branch, doubtless either the Yule holly or the more sacred mistletoe. Vergil described, and he was the best of all poets, the Golden Bough that Sybil told Aeneas he would have to find if he expected to return safely from hell. Or some priestess gave her darling a golden wand as his talisman, or a lion's skin to wear in memory of Heracles, and as guarantee the guard dog Cerberus would slink into his kennel and let the Quester pass him safely by. Queen Guinevere left by the sacred fountain her tokens, a royal comb and mirror, talismans for Lancelot to find. The priestess called Lady of the Lake gave him and Perceval also a golden ring to wear. When Tannhaüser's bare branch leafed out, he recognized it as a sign of the goddess's love and returned underground to stay her lover forever. He was an apostate.

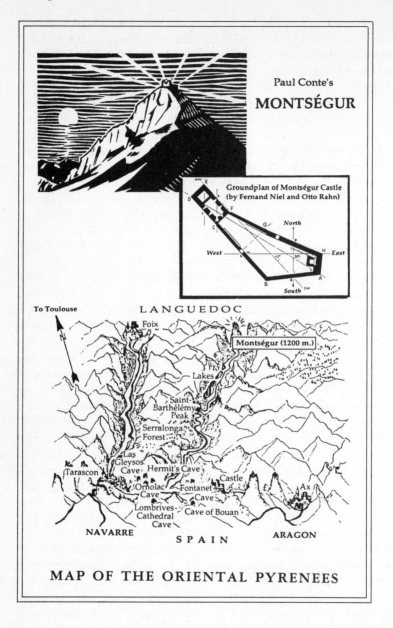

Paul Conte's
MONTSÉGUR

Groundplan of Montségur Castle
(by Fernand Niel and Otto Rahn)

North

West   *East*

South

L A N G U E D O C

To Toulouse

Foix

Montségur (1200 m.)

Lakes

Saint-
Barthélémy
Peak

Serralonga
Forest

Las
Gleysos
Cave   Hermit's Cave

Tarascon   Castle

Ormolac   Fontanet
Cave   Cave   Ax

Lombrives
Cathedral   Cave of Bouan
Cave

NAVARRE   **ARAGON**

S P A I N

MAP OF THE ORIENTAL PYRENEES

Not only is Montségur an extraordinarily magnificent mountain
that even at first glimpse sets a climber's eager eye to searching its
possible ascent routes—and all but one are so difficult as to be
impossible except to a first-class Alpinist—it possesses all the other
requirements to become a magic mountain of myth. Its subterraneans, which expert Alpinists like the famous author Fernand
Niel repeatedly reported (1954, 1955, 1962, 1967) are no longer
to be found, alas, descended by shafts totaling three thousand steps
cut into the mountain's stony heart. Its vast labyrinth of undergrounds once far surpassed Don Quixote's discoveries. They too
are no longer to be found, if one can believe it.

Furthermore, Montségur overlooks an underground river and,
more impressive even than that, a dark tarn long centuries tabooed.
Anyone who has never seen a Pyrenean underground river surge
forth at some height above a main road, pour ferociously thunder-
ing out of a lava tube to fall foaming powerful gray water under the
highway and go roaring down a vertical chasm has missed it. Local
people say the area around the holy Montségur abounds in dark,
highland lakes as black and accursed as Lake Avernus was, near the
Italian Sibyl's cell on Monte Grillo. There is another such accursed
lake under Montségur also over which no bird flies nor lives, into
which were cast objects like a dragon's hoard of ancient gold and
gems. The thunder rises from it fit to tear mountains asunder, if
anything falls into it today. The lake is therefore tabooed doubly,
because it also holds the ancient loot from Solomon's Temple and
Alaric's sack of Rome. Everyone knows better than to throw even
a tiny stone into this lake, for fear of rousing the sleeping thunder
god.

Much was always dread and perilous thereabouts, and the cliff
faces of Montségur most of all. During the final years before 1244
Montségur Castle was inhabited by refugees from all over Occitania. They hoped to survive the war on its fortified height, or hung
on its sheer, unscalable cliff faces, or crouched inside tiny huts built
on narrow ledges to which access was afforded only by means of
cordage let down from above. No sign of all this meets the eye
today from Montségur village below the summit, but Fernand Niel,
corded up with fellow Alpinists, came upon the crumbling stones
of a low, retaining wall behind which, on a ledge, some precious
person huddled for days, or weeks, or years awaiting the auto-da-fé
that all had learned to expect.

Some refugees toiled up the one access route in order to be

ordained by the Deaconess Esclarmonde or the Bishop Guilhabert de Castres. When the news flashed out that Montségur had finally, under heavy bombardment by thirty-pound boulders catapulted in from nearby, then throngs of other weeping pilgrims, especially women who were close relatives of the captured, toiled slowly up the trail from the *Pas,* or south gate to the peaks. Unfortunately they were seized too and thrust among the condemned of whom no count then was made.

Montségur's three peaks proved as perilous to them as Guinevere's altar and lintel smeared with sacrificial blood proved to Lancelot, or his Sword Bridge, or Gawain's Perilous Cemetery, or Percival's Seat of Dread. Initiations at Montségur proved fatal. The distant, inaccessible peak of Foix with its unconquered castle looked over from the west and could do no more to help. The three nearest fortified peaks of Roca, Rocafissada, and Rocotalhada collapsed and escaped siege.

Everywhere it appears in Europe, said the Reverend Sabine Baring-Gould (1873) in his chapter on "The Mountain of Venus" (pp. 209–29), the summit of the sacred mountain, and it appears everywhere, must first of all resemble "a stone sarcophagus," which is the very case for Montségur.

The story attached to it follows the same morphological pattern: (1) an underground people reside there but desire, like Kundry, union with upperworld humans, (2) a hero like the fictional Esclarmonde's Roland is lured into their subterranean where he is seduced by a dark woman, (3) he desires to revisit earth again and rejoin his old religion, and so he escapes, (4) he finally returns to his new and preferred existence underground and to the embrace of his dark goddess. To a surprising degree, this is Montségur's myth, or their truth.

Celtic Britain usually opted for the opposing theory of an icy-cold island located at Ultima Thule, in the far, cold confines of the western sea. It lay beyond dense fogs in the far isles where the white Hyperboreans dwelling beyond the North Star held power over the lost wisdom of earth. Centers of initiation, Dr. Barthélémy from Toulouse recently concluded, *lie all around us,* even today. We may even *pass them by* as we go about our daily lives, and never suspect their presence. Even so, all ordinary people become initiates at level one, or in their bodies, and are called "hylics." Initiates of the soul at level two are psychics; in spirit, at level three, are pneumatics. Hitler, Rosenberg, and Rudolf Hess had reached level three, it is thought.

The Nazi Otto Rahn, who was or who became an SS officer, seems first to have launched Montségur spectacularly as a Castle of the Holy Grail in writing his book about the Albigensian Crusade against the Grail (Stuttgart, 1933). It truly remains a wonderful book, a monument to this German idealist author, who died mysteriously during a descent in the Alps. His book was translated immediately into French (Paris, 1934) because, as Rahn observed, no person inside France can possibly look with an unprejudiced eye at this question, so abidingly does it lie close to their hearts. In his translator's preface Robert Pitrou of Bordeaux also cautioned the French reader to beware: that Otto Rahn believed with absolute conviction that (1) the Catharists were the last owners of the Holy Grail, and (2) the Holy Grail "perished" when they died at the hands of "the pope and the King of France" at the beginning of the thirteenth century (p. 9).

After offering circumstantial evidence in part 1, Rahn moves in part 2 of his German text to direct testimony from the shepherds he interviewed in the Mt. Thabor or Montségur Mountains.

As long as the walls of Montségur Castle remained unbreached, Rahn said he was told (pp. 860–87 of the French edition), the Perfects kept the Grail there. That fortress was besieged by "troops of Lucifer" who wanted to recover the lost emerald, or Grail of his crown, which had fallen during Lucifer's expulsion from heaven. His emerald was the Holy Grail. Thus, we meet again Wolfram's belief, which is labeled the "German" and "pagan" theory, that the Grail was a stone.

The French dictionary and encyclopedia *Petit Larousse* (1967) defines *Graal* and/or *Saint Graal* (p. 1,394) as "the emerald vase" that *would have* served Christ at the Last Supper and in which Joseph of Arimathea *would have* collected the blood that flowed from Christ's side that had been pierced by the centurion. Certain romances, it continues, tell the story of the quest of the Grail by knights of "the King Arthur."

The Grail spear, says the learned Barbara G. Walker in her *Woman's Dictionary,* represents the lightning of the Storm God as he impregnates the Mother Goddess on her high mountaintop. The Grail vase or chalice hides its real meaning, she adds (pp. 90–91), as the womb of the Goddess, for which reason in processions the Grail was always carried by a virginal Grail Bearer crowned with flowers, another feminine, sexual symbol. In France, we add, women wearing scentless, artificial flowers are therefore always scorned and frowned upon by *macho* men.

Wolfram von Eschenbach's idea of Grail was his cryptic "Lapis Exilis," stone or emerald fallen from heaven. In Genoa the *Sacro Catino* was also a green glass chalice called "the Holy Grail," and preserved in the cathedral there until it was shattered and proven false, i.e., not divine. This repeats the Grail of San Juan de la Peña treasured in the cathedral of Valencia, broken, but there miraculously restored without flaw or crack.

Before Wolfram's day one recalls the priestly, *green* robes and malachite eyes of Queen Guinevere herself, as she stood between malachite (copper) columns at the Grail Castle, and one also recalls verses from some Catharist troubadour that perseverate: "la robe verte des saints" (the green robe of the saints).

Otto Rahn also heard from his shepherds at Montségur that when that fortress was captured, a white dove (Esclarmonde?) escaped and flew over the walled crest, opening a chasm in the mountain's flank. This story was probably believed as a solution to the problem of Esclarmonde's escape from death there, via a fissure in the rock. Fernand Niel and his fellow Alpinists explored as many such chimneys as they could, all reported carefully in Niel's books.

Rahn was also told that the Grail Guardian was Viscountess Esclarmonde de Foix. At the very end of the siege she personally cast the Holy Grail into a black chasm below Montségur and saw the fissure close of itself. The Grail is still on one of the mountain's flanks, in a sealed crevasse, in other words. When the French "Devils entered" the fortress on the summit, they searched in vain for the Holy Grail, continued the shepherd; they were too late. Therefore in their fury, they threw the Pures into an auto-da-fé, which they had already prepared at the foot of the Montségur precipice. That place the local people still revere as the Field of the Cremated, or the Field of Fire. Visitors should respect the reverence and grief of authors like Georges Serrus, who resides there in summer, and other villagers thereabouts.

Since Otto Rahn was by profession a speleologist, he was able to write thrilling pages about the caverns of the Sabarthès south of Montségur (see page 269) and especially about the Lombrives caverns called "the Cathedral" by the local people of Ornolac. The entrance to this gigantic labyrinthine cave is between two prehistoric menhirs dating supposedly from the early, local King Heracles who sailed on his golden cup, and who founded Marseilles, if only mythologically.

Rahn charms his armchair readers by his spelunker's minute description of the cavern's gigantic vestibule, stalactites of white limestone, walls of brown marble, jewels of rock crystal, underground paths into the heart of the Pyrenees, great hall eighty meters high, water dripping from dark vaults overhead, church pews of stalactites, the whole forming the secret, hidden cathedral of the Catharists. When the storm strikes the vertical flanks of Montségur, witnesses Rahn, the din inside the cavern is deafening with the rushing of thunderous underground rivers. This can only bring to the reader's mind visions of Lucifer plunging headlong through the upper atmosphere. There white water cascades hard enough to make the whole mountain shiver. The hardier explorers come finally to the celebrated stone staircase, which pitches them down hundreds of feet with a second cavern beneath the first. There beneath a whole chain of mountains stands a club-shaped stalagmite that the local explorers call the *Tomb of Hercules!* The tomb of his wife, the native princess Pyrene who gave the Pyrenees Mountains her name, lies yonder. . . . Ancient storytellers in Marseilles during the lifetime of Mary Magdalene recorded this tale. To them the Grail was the hero's golden cup he sailed in through the celestial vault above our heads. Isn't mythology wonderful?

The Cave of Ornolac was, indeed, the last refuge for the trembling survivors of massacre and auto-da-fé, and their bones still lie in mounds there, to be sure. Only Esclarmonde escaped, said the shepherds to Otto Rahn, whom they reassured calmly: Esclarmonde flew away with the Grail into Asia. And bowed their heads in prayer.'

That last solution is all the more interesting because the priestesses of Greece and Egypt too originated from an earlier worship in both Asia Minor and India. It was first, of course, the very worshipful Princess Medea who flew off on her dragon chariot, returning from a Greece she abhorred for its mistreatment of women and mothers to an Asia that had long before revered Amazon priestesses and Mother Goddesses. Viscountess Esclarmonde was in her person *the Lord of Montségur,* Rahn reminds us, for its castle was her castle, which she deeded, probably in 1204, so that it could be rebuilt and serve as one of the final refuges for her people.

Her troubadour Montanhagol also wrote from a safer refuge in Spain:

> *N'Esclarmunda, vostre noms signifia*
> *Que vos donatz clardat al mon per ver*
> *Et etz monda, que no fes mon dever*
> *Aitals ets plan com al ric nom tanebia . . .*

> *Lady Esclarmonde, your name signifies*
> *You enlighten the world, in truth,*
> *And you are pure, only doing your duty,*
> *Also are worthy to bear so rich* a name . . .*

The Counts of Toulouse's favorite troubadour was Peire Cardenal, whose song begins, "Tartaressa ni voutor . . ."—Not a buzzard, not a vulture but can smell out carrion as can these priests who hunt us down to kill us. He ended the song with a prayer for the Catharists:

> *Save us from the tortures of hell,*
> *Safeguard us sinners from such torments.*
> *Unravel our foes from the skeins of sin*
> *Which foul their hearts and twine them round.*
> *And grant them, Lord, your pardon,*
> *Once truly they have confessed.*

Wolfram failed to say it best: "Montsalvaesche . . . Las! Personne ne te veut consoler . . ."—Alas, Montsalvaesche . . . Nobody can ever console you. "Alas," cried the troubadour. "How great you were, Montségur! And look at you now!"

For his part the mountain climber Fernand Niel set about haunting the crags and crevasses of Montségur, and hauling himself step by step up its chimneys. He reasoned (Toulouse, 1949) that occasionally local historians like himself were *called upon* to solve local problems of history that national history had perforce overlooked not only for lack of interest but also because of the impossibility of

---

*"Rich" as in "Rich Fisher King" means illustrious.

being on the sites, and lastly, for lacking the passion to pursue their infinite detail.

The details he pursued for years constituted Niel's solution of a very practical problem requiring him with endless patience to make a list of those persons still alive inside the fortress of Montségur on the eve of surrender, a second list of persons the day of the surrender, a third list of those surrendering, and a final list of those known to have been cremated in the auto-da-fé that very day.

Then Niel asked and answered the obvious questions: How many persons slipped safely in between the castle interior, the castle exterior, and the auto-da-fé? The astonishing answer was: *four persons!*

These questions followed: Who were they? Where were they before, during, and after the surrender? When did they vanish? How did they vanish? Why did they vanish? Where did they go? Why were they not stopped by the sentries? Who employed the sentries? Can the mystery be solved?

Fernand Niel pursued these questions doggedly in his own quest lasting more than a decade because of the one unexplained mystery remaining after the auto-da-fé and the deaths of the last Catharists who had escaped and fled to what would be their tomb in the southern caves: Where was the Grail? Who took charge of the Grail? How did it leave Montségur? Who carried it away? Was that not legend only? Was it not only truth?

Because the Grail was and is the lost treasure of Montségur.

Before turning to a summary of Niel's and others' findings, let us first summarize very briefly the Albigensian Crusade, as follows:

1209. Royalist Crusaders capture the chief city of Béziers within hours of their attack. Every person within the city walls is immediately slaughtered. No quarter is given to anyone, man, woman, or child. Count Raimon-Roger de Foix goes at once to Rome to protest and to plead with the Vatican. His final word to them later was: "You have slaughtered five hundred thousand persons."

1211. The French Royalist Crusader, Commander Simon de Montfort, finds himself master of four major

Catharist cities: Béziers, Razès, Albi, and Carcassonne. Civilians are all massacred.

1212. Montfort's brother seizes the weavers' village of Lavelanet on the shoulder that buttresses the Montségur peak itself. Those two, Lavelanet and Montségur village alone, lie on the sacred mountain's ascent route.*

1213. The Court of Toulouse and King of Aragón are defeated at the Battle of Muret. Count Raymond VI rushes at once to England to bring back his young son and heir, the future Count Raymond VII of Toulouse, to be called "the Great" Count.

1214. Terrified refugees escort their small children, and helpless, old people start staggering up the precipitous routes into Montségur. This exodus continued until March 16, 1244.

1218. The Count of Toulouse reconquers in lightning succession Beaucaire (of *Aucassin et Nicolette*) and Toulouse.

June 15, 1218. Simon de Montfort is killed outside the walls of Toulouse.

1220. The massive Cathedral of Saint-Sernin is completed at Toulouse. It is an architectural wonder of the world.

1223. Count Raimon-Roger de Foix escorts his sister, the Perfect and *Archdeaconess* Esclarmonde of the Catha-

*See my favorite Frédéric Soulié, *Le Château des Pyrénées* (Toulouse, 1859).

rist church, to the refuge of Montségur. Her brother, Count Raimon-Roger, whom the troubadours always referred to as "Drut," or Beloved, dies.

1229. The Count of Toulouse is excommunicated, and again in 1237. Nothing stops him for long, however, except death.

1232. The Catharist Bishop Guilhabert de Castres moves permanently to Montségur to adminster to and to assist the besieged. The Lords of the Languedoc band together to escort and help the fleeing populace find shelter up in Montségur; the mountain is declared a final refuge, a sanctuary, and a sacred site forever more.

Its necropolis will lie at the foot of the peak.

In their book *The Treasure of Montségur* (1987, 1990) Walter N. Birks and R. A. Gilbert pay tribute to this Catharist Bishop Guilhabert de Castres (p. 56). At the Council of Pamiers (1207), which was held near Foix, and where Viscountess Esclarmonde debated prelates, the Catharist Bishop was also present.

The Bishop replied, as quoted by Birks and Gilbert, in words to this effect: I left my home, my father, my mother, and my little children. You see me as I am: poor, humble, peaceful, pure in heart, weeping, suffering hunger and thirst, bearing upon my shoulders the hatred of the world, all for the sake of righteousness.

1242. The widow of King John of England attempts to bring aid to Montségur and is foiled by the Regent of France, Queen Blanche de Castille.

1243. Montségur is completely besieged and totally cut off by the royal army. By December the inhabitants are not only starving and thirsty but bombarded day and night. They are comforted by the knowledge that the Count of Toulouse is attempting to cut through the siege lines and deliver them. They expect his miraculous arrival at any moment. He fails here.

March 1, 1244. Negotiations commence finally for the unconditional surrender of Montségur. Montségur only begs to be permitted to await the spring equinox, when the sun will rise due east over the summit on Monday, March 14, 1244. During the evening of March 13 all the refugees who desire it, one by one receive the *Consolamentum* following a general assembly for confession.

March 14, 1244. Eight Inquisitors line up to receive the hostages, as they have demanded. All the young sons and younger brothers of known Catharist noblemen are taken away separately "for interrogation."

All the Catharists inside Montségur have distributed their property and signed their wills, which are notarized inside the fortress.

March 16, 1244. Three women lead the procession notably that descends to be burned: the Marchioness de Lantar, a grandmother; her daughter Corba de Perelha, and Corba's daughter, the Viscountess Esclarmonde de Perelha. Although between 210 and 215 persons are burned (Niel's estimate, 1954) only 28 of their names are known. Two others are Braïda, the sister of Count Arnaud-Roger de Mirepoix, and the Countess Ermengarde d'Ussat.

The dying women murmur: "My kingdom is not of this world."

The Grail treasure is reported, or whispered, from mouth to mouth, to be safe in her Castle Ussat.

The Grail Treasure

Napoléon Peyrat (1882) at the end of his third volume on Mont-ségur summarized the problem concerning that sanctuary to date, saying that even in his century the entrance to the stairway of three thousand steps leading down the interior of the mountain had been lost. He maintained to the end that Montségur was always John's tabernacle of God among men, and that it was dedicated to John, the Beloved Disciple. By 1882 its grottoes had long been closed and their situations forgotten. No entrance to stairs or caves or grottoes was then known. During the war of the thirteenth century, the war some people still persisted in calling an "Albigensian Crusade," the tombs of the Catharists who had died on Montségur before the fatal March of 1244, had long been so completely destroyed as to have been obliterated. The ashes of the massacred dead were cast to the winds that sweep across the Saint Bartholomews from nearby Spain before the sudden storms so common in the Pyrenees and their horizontal wild rainstorms so fierce they cast streams of rain across inside walls opposite windows. had washed them all down into subterranean rivers. And to cap it all and provide one, last sorrow, memory of Catharists was forbidden by the Inquisition. Their names were proscribed in the Languedoc as had been the names of Merlin and Morgan le Fay inside Great Britain of their day.

In 1954 Fernand Niel came back again to the problem of this forgetting. Unfortunately, he decided then, there is no surviving ocular testimony either, and he had by then combed the mountain for years at the risk of his life; for let it be understood that the cliff faces of Montségur present even to the eye unusual terrors. Niel had by then concluded firmly that four persons remained unaccounted for between the surrender and the auto-da-fé. One of them was the experienced mountain guide and expert climber Amiel Aicart, and there were missing three other known mountain men. In all, then, there were probably only these four escapees, all expert climbers, all mature men born in that proximity. Nobody around Montségur ever mentioned their names. Nobody ever claimed to know where they had disappeared to. These four men vanished.

Fernand Niel spent decades examining the evidence presented to and by the Inquisitors. Four men were, unbeknownst to the Inquisitors, missing from their count, Niel discovered. The only way these men could have escaped and also vanished permanently, was for them to have remained hidden during the auto-da-fé ceremony itself, while the hymn-singing victims were being rounded up, lined up, and watched as they filed down the mountain between the lines of royal troops. Then later, in total darkness, these men must have attacked one of the two unscalable cliff faces. Niel himself had climbed each one. And once, someone has said, an eight-year-old local girl, who had slipped from the summit onto a small ledge, all by herself came down that precipice. The same face, one hears, grows more difficult in rainy summers that cover the rock with running water, algae, and grasses. . . . Niel even calculated what lengths of rope the four men must have prepared in advance in order for them to have survived such a descent, particularly one made during total darkness.

A final problem remained for Niel, which was how the four men even then could have slipped through a cordon of royal troops who were posted as sentries on every path up or down the Montségur fortress, and in and out of Lavalenet and Montségur villages. Niel finally concluded that it must have been the Count of Toulouse who had suborned the sentries. Not only was he camped outside the area occupied by the Capetian king's army, but all the same, nearby. The Count was also very beloved throughout the Languedoc. And he had with him any amount of bullion. And he also intended to fight to the death.

When the last Count of Toulouse died, said Niel (pp. 219–26), he took with him every last vestige of independence in Occitania. Even the native language in its primary form, which is speech, vanished. Without the few poems of the troubadours and the Catharist translation of the Bible, their epics Occitanian and/or Provençal would have vanished forever too. Niel adds that not only did the Catharist church die, but that the spirit of a people died too with their rulers.

Montségur remains nothing else but jagged stone ruins on its summit, but even so, a "symbol of spiritual Light," concluded Niel (p. 226), because of its "charme étrange" (strange or magical charm). Theirs was a sincere attempt to lessen evil in the world, he thought, and that is a problem still awaiting a better or a definitive solution.

This sanctuary of Montségur and its necropolis stand there now as an example of mankind's suffering, typifying their struggle to make this a better world for all so that today Montségur still rises fractured above its deep and fearsome crevasses that are not empty but full of presences as are its summits and its slopes. The Lady Esclarmonde de Perelha, whose husband was then the Lord of Montségur, died, observed Niel, just like the Druid priestess Velleda. Montségur remains "a veritable sanctuary of the spirit," concluded Niel in 1954, his last sentence of that year.

His last sentence of 1955 sounded another battle cry: Why will not Catharism as a religion rise again (p. 123)? That year he revised his final solution somewhat, having discovered that a treasure of gold and silver was transported somehow from Montségur Castle to the fortified caves under or adjacent to Castle Usson before March 16, 1244, and that the Inquisitors burned in final count 206 or 215 heretics led by the noble Bertrand d'en Marti. In addition, four Perfects had also been lowered down the cliff that or some earlier night by means of cables, and they carried strapped on their backs the *treasures of Montségur,* which were their sacred books. Thus, the Catharist records, ritual, Bible, and other documents as studied and published by René Nelli, were among the original manuscripts also stored for safekeeping once in the Viscountess Esclarmonde's stronghold.

This sacred Temple of the Catharists was never considered a military site, concluded Niel, since it boasted no strategic value whatsoever. It resembled no other medieval castle known to man, being an odd, stone coffer, a pentagonal sarcophagus resembling nothing less than the ancient hero Gawain's pentagon of Arthurian virtues. The structure enclosed only a small surface of Montségur's summit, which made it from a military point of view totally indefensible.

The Bishop of Carcassonne, who was the artillery expert of that royalist army, built his catapult outside the castle walls whence he could easily shower the besieged with stones weighing sixty to eighty pounds. Such stones are still scattered about the summit of Montségur. Furthermore, and experience today has amply proven it, Montségur can be seen from long distances in many directions, but finding it proves awkward. It requires patience and a long journey to get only to its foot. And then one discovers that it is not one mountain with a gradual ascent like Mount Mansfield in one's native Vermont, or Camel's Hump either, but a cone surrounded by a series of precipitous valleys, dark lakes, and thunderous cataracts.

**THE DEATH OF SIMON DE MONFORT
AT TOULOUSE**

The marvel is that the Catharists, and their youngsters too, persevered in dying silently. They are said to have answered no questions, and they broke under no torture nor fear of death by fire.
Complete silence was maintained after they began the descent,
except for their continued repetition of hymns with the words of
Jesus.

For the succeeding twenty-five years the new King Jaime I of
Aragón watched the Capetian king's troops gradually withdraw
from the area. The second line of fortresses between Montségur
and what is now the Spanish border held, a line unbroken between
the strongholds of Puylaurens and Quéribus.

As late as 1252 in the Languedoc proper, however, Pope Innocent IV permitted torture of any and all remaining Catharists. In
1283 an enraged populace attacked the Inquisitor Nicolas d'Abbé-
ville inside the city of Carcassonne. In 1295 another group invaded
and laid waste a Dominican convent of the Inquisitors. Between the
years 1298 and 1309 the Minister Pierre Authier, who was perhaps
the last living Catharist Bishop, still escaped capture and still
preached to congregations there. The Church of Saint Barthélémy
still held services in those years, but in 1300 Catharists at Albi were
captured and tried. In 1320 the last Catharist leader to preach
against the Dominican Order, which had furnished so many Inquisitors, was publicly tortured to death in Carcassonne. . . . As the
French poet says so beautifully: Nobody should die before seeing
Carcassonne, the most perfect, and most spectacular of walled,
medieval cities.

In Haarlem, Holland, in 1960, A. Gadal also addressed the
position of Catharism today for Rosicrucians and others who wish
to experience this ancient religion. You must start (Route I) in the
County of Foix, valley of the Ariège River, an area known to Pliny
in Rome and bypassed by Julius Caesar, he directed. There in the
high country the Black Virgin appeared to the Franks. On September 8 each year an annual pilgrimage celebrates their deliverance
from the Saracens. Sabartez is the grotto country *where Catharism
originated in A.D. 350*: Lombrives, Ornolac, Bouan, Fontanet. There
the Perfects were initiated. On the far side of the Mt. Tabor chain
rises Montségur, called the "Lighthouse of Catharism."

Route II takes one on a tour around Mont Nègre, which was the
station for the most eloquent of Catharist preachers: Esclarmonde

de Foix, Guilhabert de Castres, Prince Raimon-Roger de Foix the Beloved, praised all by the troubadours for their nobility of person and their silver tongues. They advised meditation on these themes: Life is Death. Death is the kiss of God. Crossing the Symbolic Wall into the immense underground churches of Ussat, the future novice after a stay of four years emerges by the Mystic Portal.

This is today the Road to the Holy Grail. The new initiate of today will follow it, says Gadal. His tutor will be an Ancient One. In the churches the candidate will hear the Voice of Hours telling time. He will see Perfects clad in black. He will live under tons of stone, at an even temperature, nourished with fresh vegetables and bread, fresh fruit, and pure water. He will sleep on beds of branches and fresh leaves. Only the Pure can touch the Symbol of the Holy Grail. Novices will bake bread, spin, weave, press oil from nuts, make preserves from fruit. Former noble disciples, who are the lords of the area, donate all provisions. The first lessons teach renunciation of the world, perfect obedience, and poverty.

The Holy Grail, which is now a chalice ("un vase précieux," p. 45) is raised by the Master who says "Lapis ex Coelis" (Stone from the Skies), in the words of Wolfram von Eschenbach.

The Second Degree teaches students about the Golden Chalice and Pentacle as carved on mountains by Rama, Krishna, Hermes, Moses, Orpheus, Pythagoras, Plato, and Jesus. Our inheritance descends from Atlantis, Hinduism, Persia, Babylon, Egypt, Jesus, Mary, Mary Magdalene, Martha, Saint Trophime, Marseilles, Arles and Aliscans, the Pyrenees, and Mary Magdalene's Cave at Sainte Baume. After initiation, the ordained are finally shown Route III, which mounts to Montségur. There they will see Lucifer, Aurora's son, with the blazing emerald in his forehead, who was the once proud and ruined King Nebuchadnezzar of Babylon, of whom Isaiah spoke. Or the Cross of Light of the Catharists, as seen frequently in printers' watermarks from southern France, could have been a visualization of the angels' wings in Ezekiel.

Antoine Lévis Mirepoix (1924) in his epilogue explained that Montségur symbolized the sun, that it was constructed as a sun temple for Lancelot, which opened at the solstices and equinoxes in order to collect within its Grail the first rays of the rising sun. The Catharist Cross, thought the symbolist René Alleau (p. 90), in some, now mysterious way represented either an emerald of their Saint Bartholomew or Saint Andrew, who linked the emerald and the sapphire to man, and who evangelized Achaea and Scythia. The latter's Cross is green in Trèves and in Troyes, but red on a missal in Clermont.

Both Rahn and Niel show diagrams of the ground plan of Montségur Castle, demonstrating its alignment with the sunrise at the winter solstice where points halfway along the north, east, and southeast walls face the first beam or sword of light. The peculiar layout of its walls actually makes the outer walls of Montségur a joining of eight straight lines, each of a different length, a strikingly unusual and geometrically complicated design.

In 1951 the Grail and Montségur were treated by Honorary Professor Paul Conte of the Gers Historical and Archaeological Society of France, following the Third International Congress of Catharist Studies in September of that year. Every scholar present raised the question of the Montségur Treasure as having been either the Catharist Scripture, a book, on the one hand, or the Grail and (Cervantes's) tombs of its guardian knights on the other hand. All present agreed that Montségur, where the Congress concluded, was a historical site of singular importance.

As Wolfram von Eschenbach testified, he had his material for *Parzival* and *Titurel* from a troubadour named Guyot in French, a man now known to have translated the New Testament at Toledo. Wolfram's Grail story, in German, emerged from the Spanish Grail treasured at San Juan de la Peña and later at Valencia. Its cult emigrated that short distance to the Catharists in the Pyrenees of France, thence to Britain in the twelfth century, said Conte. It was Saint Lawrence who had originally brought the Cup of the Last Supper, and other such relics of the life of Jesus, directly into Spain.

The hero whom Wolfram celebrated as Parzival, and whose name the northern French spelled "Perceval," was based upon the Catharist noble Trencavel, Lord of Carcassonne; "Perceval" means "cut in two," as does "Tren-cavel" in Occitanian; Montsalvat = Munsalvaesche = Montségur. Perceval or Parzival halted at a fountain, and so did the young Count Trencavel at Fontanet whence a secret path leads to the peak and Montségur Castle of the Holy Grail. As sun temple, Montségur was the initiation center that the Grail Questers searched for tirelessly.

Conte believed the Grail had already been safely carried from Montségur during the darkness of Christmas Eve, 1243, and that it was hidden in the caves to the south.

It is our duty, said Conte, to search ancient history for those ancient beliefs that might draw our own dying civilization back to life.

As a historian Conte very much admired Dr. Wiersma Verschaffeld of the University of La Haye in Holland who addressed the 1951 Congress. She said that belief in the Grail revives divine forces dormant in ourselves otherwise, but suddenly awakened, suddenly inspired to create something new and splendid for ourselves and others.

If we have not found on the heights of Montségur either rich tombs, clanking armor, or new Catharist bibles, concluded Conte, we can at least grasp that here took place once upon a time a truly titanic clash of two divergent civilizations during which the courage, abnegation, and faith of Christian martyrs came close to toppling the very solid foundations of French, royal power in that world and of the Roman church in the Middle Ages (p. 345).

Still not satisfied that he had conveyed to the world all that Montségur meant and still means today, Fernand Niel returned (1962) to this impossibility for a creative artist to raise some edifice on paper. We shall have to say simply, he tried it again (p. 17), to tell readers that if Montségur was not the Grail Castle, *then no other place was.* The problems of proof stagger a searcher like Niel— nothing at all having survived the centuries, no bones either, no subterraneans, and only the recorded testimony of six women and a ten-year-old boy.

All that meets hand or eye now at Montségur is gigantic mountain and herculean stones, which even so betray their masons' attempts to build and rebuild a castle (1204). Its main doorway alone stands as a single example of architecture that appears, by its odd dimensions (six feet by ten feet), to be unique. Singular also was its surrender when not a single other Catharist castle capitulated.

Its chapel dedicated to the Virgin Mary brings to mind her cult favored by King Arthur as by Knights Templar then and now. Thousands prayed there at Montségur during the last forty years of its use. At the end some two hundred persons surrendered, refused to recant, and descended the mountain in full view of at least ten thousand besiegers. The Holy Grail was a cup, a book, or an emerald—at the least, a small, transportable object.

Niel's personal belief was then that Montségur was originally a temple to the sun ruled by Titurel *and built by Merlin* on the Spanish frontier. If he could only prove that the Grail was ever at Montségur, added Niel (1967), he would by extension have proven also that this was "truly one of the most extraordinary sites in the world" (p. 31).

Opposition to Catharism, to Montségur as Christian and/or holy, to any theory of a Christian Grail or priestesses who could be Christian has followed proponents, from Napoléon Peyrat to Fernand Niel. Rev. S. R. Maitland, for example, blasted Catharists in 1832. Peyrat's three volumes appeared in 1880. Why have we no admonitions to the poor from them? asked Maitland. Why have we none of their so-called prayers by believers or Perfects? Their rites are not scriptural. Their people lived in "outlawry" (section 12), and were maintained by followers attached to them. Their reception into this sect was merely a laying on of hands. These Catharists were correctly charged by the church with allowing women to preach: Toulouse (1056), Tours (1163), Montpellier (1195), Béziers (1233), Narbonne (1235), and Albi (1254).

The prime English authority on Catharism has been since 1947 Steven Runciman, who defined Catharism as a Christian dualist heresy, which did not have to be tolerated, tolerance not being a Christian virtue (p. 1). These heretics and associate Gnostics were generally talented writers, he admitted; but they rejected baptism, the Eucharist, marriage, a male priesthood, a hierarchy, and worship of the Cross, he alleged. Their evangelists were nothing but itinerant weavers. These people were vegetarians and ascetics who held "secret meetings in Broceliande forest" (c. 1140) of King Arthur (p. 116). Their dualist signs are to be seen still in "watermarks used in the manufacture of paper" (p. 179). Theirs was a pessimistic but not an "ignoble religion." They had so little hope they consented to die at the stake, or wherever.

Dr. Wiersma Verschaffeld attacked Runciman in the *Cahiers d'Etudes Cathares* (Catharist Studies) of 1949 (no. 3, p. 63). The English historian, she said, gives no proof that Catharists resembled such other heretics as the Bogomils and Gnostics. He ignores the Catharist veneration of the Virgin, their emphasis upon spiritual love, and their respect for the intellect and spirituality of women. He errs in denigrating their possible possession of such Christian relics as the Grail. Not only does this English scholar demonstrate his contempt for another Christian faith, but, even worse, he actually applauds the destruction of the Catharists themselves. He also rejects their influence upon both the Knights Templar and the Rosicrucians, Verschaffeld alleged.

The archivist and paleographer Anne Brenon in her book (1988) documented the true face of Catharism and located their many churches on a map (p. 113). This Christian religion lingered on until the end of the fifteenth century, she proved; but American explorers and settlers testify that it may have spread into the new world also, with its noble names that Americans also know: Montcalm, Vermont, Cadillac, Champlain, Cartier, Montreal, Thoreau, Lautrec, Bowdoin, Revere; a few of whose places also recall the south: Montpel(l)ier, Saint Lawrence, Notre Dame, Saint Bartholomew, Saint Paul, Saint Louis. In her book (1969) Dominique Paladilhe included a guide to the Languedoc and also genealogies of its first families: Trencavel (918–1269) and a second branch (1291–c. 1669), Toulouse (836–1271), Foix-Comminges-Carcassonne (c. 900–1265, main branch).

In booklets available at Montségur village, in the local bookstore owned by the author Georges Serrus, he and Michel Roquebert concluded (1986, 1988) that Catharism was a pan-European religion, which was Christian, and which spread from Bulgaria across Italy and France before being halted in London and Oxford. Persecutions of Catharists actually commenced in Champagne circa 1000 and continued for at least five hundred years in France. These contemporary scholars believe that Catharist doctrines go back at least to Origen at Alexandria in the second century. They certainly flourished in Constantinople, for its Catharist "Pope" Nicetas presided in the year 1167 at a Catharist Council in the city of Toulouse. He taught that *Christ was the author* of the book of Revelation, the authentic message of their Catharist church. During the persecutions depositions were taken by the Catholic church from seven thousand persons, professing Catharism, and forty thousand names of known Catharists were recorded.

Unsympathetic as his history of Catharism has seemed to historians writing in southern France today, the conclusions of Runciman stand the test of time. He refused to accept the modern views that related the Holy Grail to Montségur and to Catharism generally (app. 4, p. 187). His major argument was this: "The Grail story is essentially a story in honor of the Sacrament of the Communion." The Catharist church recognized only one sacrament: baptism by hands. They rejected the Eucharist.

We may add that since Catharism dated from circa 1000 in

France, any indebtedness to Arthurian literature and any similarities must be due to their importation from Great Britain and the age of King Arthur, who died in 542.

The two cultures have much in common, it is true: Dark Age Britain and the medieval Languedoc and Provence. The Catharists called themselves "Friends." Their enemies called them "Cathares," which to us means "Puritans."

The well-known, medieval theologian Alain de Lisle, who, whatever he thought of himself, was no linguist, said: "Cathare" comes from "cat" because the Catharists kissed and worshiped cats, and also Lucifer, who was himself a cat.

Prejudice aside in memory of the dead bodies on both sides of the controversy, we must still admit in conclusion that nobody as yet has tried to solve the problem left by Perceval's departure from the Grail Castle in Britain. But we must remember that he was bound for "Sarras," which probably was southern France.

Chapter
VIII

KING ARTHUR
IN SCOTLAND

THE FIRST GRAIL HERO: GAWAIN

Before looking at Gawain whom we shall see as the first Grail hero, we should recapitulate the thorny problem of King Arthur's historicity. To an American historian, the question seems foolish: King Arthur was so obviously historical. However, the controversy inside Britain seems to revolve about two incomprehensions: (1) scholars inside Britain, even the very best, are not known even by the community of British scholars, and (2) the history of the Dark Ages is not taught in British schools. As a result, nobody has looked at the evidence, and nobody wishes to do so. Exception is made always for the most learned of historians, like R. H. Hodgkin in his two-volume *History of the Anglo-Saxons* (Oxford, 1935) and The Right Honourable Winston Churchill in his four-volume *History of the English-Speaking Peoples* (1956; reprinted in New York, 1990). Sir Winston Churchill speaks of the persecution and ignominy heaped upon British scholars who over the years attempted to shake scholarly bigotry and prove Arthur historical. Those scorned scholars were such Scots as John Stuart Stuart Glennie, one supposes, and R. L. G. Ritchie, and also the late O. G. S. Crawford. Publishers say that no reader inside Britain is interested. The final word inside Britain seems to be that so long as archaeologists have found no proof of historicity, then there was no history. In other words, they offer a purely materialistic answer. And dig. Or it may be that history there is generally thought of as something that never happened, or that it is merely a fable we agree to agree upon, as Bonaparte let fall among other pearls of his wisdom.

Treated as historical, Arthurians are now about to be considered as original Questers for the Grail. Chronologically they come after our chapters 1 and 2 and probably after the arrival of missionaries into Glastonbury. They can only be seen as historical if "in the North" of Britain.

The English historian William of Malmesbury, who wrote at Glastonbury in the twelfth century, asserted that Gawain ruled Galloway in Scotland. These peninsulas, which jut out into the Solway Firth, are there called "Rhinns of Galloway," the old Walweitha, which is also Gawain's name, Walwein, or the Latin alternate spelling: Galvagin. This Galloway figures prominently throughout Arthurian texts because it was, and it still is today, the shortest route from Roman Carlisle into Ireland. Gawain also controlled the ports along those "marches," so many days' journeys into Ireland, as well as into points south: the Isle of Man where King Arthur stored his bullion, and the coast of North Wales. These places, Cumbria and southern Scotland (Borders) constituted Arthur's kingdom.

The best Glastonbury text is the *Perlesvaus,* written at Glastonbury's Benedictine Abbey, which contains some of the oldest material concerning Arthur, Perceval, Gawain, and their Grail Castle on the Isle of Man. The *Perlesvaus* author offers the solution to troubling problems: (1) What was on the platter of gold or silver that the Grail Bearers carried in procession? (2) What caused the pool of blood in the platter? (3) Whose blood was it? (4) What did the blood signify? (5) Why did the maiden(s) weep and sob pitifully whenever the bloody platter passed them?

The story is this, wrote the unknown *Perlesvaus* author: at the Grail Castle Gawain was charged to wrest the sword *that had beheaded John the Baptist* from its present owner, Gurgalain, King of *Albania,* now Scotland. Arthur's Gawain, deputized as his first Commander in Chief, successfully performed this feat. He returned home from the Grail Castle in the Irish Sea, back along the Rhinns of Galloway, which he ruled, defeated King Gurgalain, and took from him the sword that had beheaded John the Baptist. He then returned and presented it to the Grail King.

Problems remain, however: (1) To which Grail King did he offer this inestimably holy relic? Certainly not to Joseph of Arimathea and/or son, who had long been dead, in fact, for at least four hundred years. To Pelles and/or sons? To Anfortas (Amfortas)? To Titurel? No. He would have given the sword, which later figures, that is, during the lifetimes of King Arthur, Merlin, Gawain, Lancelot, Queen Guinevere, and Perceval, in Grail Processions, to that prelate whose life duplicates the life and preachings of John the Baptist himself. He would have turned the sword over to Merlin. Actually, says the text, he handed it to "the Grail King."

We must therefore suspect that Merlin was a Grail King, whose ceremonial name was Merlin's, in that holy chapel and sacred place. The celebrated novelist and medieval scholar J. R. R. Tolkien (Oxford, 1968) gives alternate names for Gawain: Gawan, Wawan, Gauvain (French), Gwalchmei (Welsh), and Galvagin (Latin). He ruled Galloway (Walweitha), agree Tolkien and Roger Sherman Loomis also. He is the same hero called Gwallt-advwyn or "Brighthair" in the Welsh tales called *Mabinogion.* Chaucer in his *Squire's Tale* (vv. 89–97) calls this hero the greatest of King Arthur's knights and once upon a time the most courteous also. R. S. Loomis equates Gawain with the older Irish hero Cuchulain, who obligingly killed the old "gray" man of winter and stole from him his young, lovely wife called White Flower, or Blathnat, or Blanchefleur (in the French *Perceval* telling). That scenario sounds like an annual December pageant.

Gawain, then, has almost as many names as the Queen Guinevere he adored and faithfully served. Merlin too is known through many names, each representing one of his prime functions. When Gawain presented this holy relic, the very sword that had beheaded John the Baptist, he probably handed it to Merlin. Therefore Merlin was probably that Grail King usually called Pelles. John the Baptist in his lifetime had fearlessly denounced King Herod, and he was beheaded by Salome. During Merlin's lifetime Saint Gildas with equal disregard for his own safety denounced five licentious rulers and all unworthy priests of the Dark Ages, in his book *The Ruin of Britain.* Gildas was a Pict born in Dumbarton, Scotland, exactly where Geoffrey of Monmouth said (1136) King Arthur won his greatest victory in the year 500.

Merlin appears, openly named, at the Grail Castle in the *Didot-Perceval* text where he acts as one of Perceval's "uncles" or hermit teachers, and where at the end he retires to his "bird-cage," by which was probably meant the observatory where he made his predictions and wrote his *Prophecy*.

Heinrich Zimmer also proposed an original reading of the best-known of Arthurian texts, *Gawain and the Green Knight,* edited by Tolkien in 1968: Merlin was the Green Knight, where originally a "Gray" Winter is overcome by the young lover Gawain. Latin literature had bequeathed to Arthurian poets one of its favorite duets: Winter versus Summer. This is the plot of this Arthurian poem in which Gawain beheads the "Green Knight," journeys through storm and snow to his kingdom, woos his pretty wife, meets an aged Morgan le Fay, offers his neck to the Green Knight's royal ax, and gets off with a permanent scar. In other words, Gawain there conquers Winter, revives the Waste Land, makes the world verdant again, and, adds the older Irish version of the play, tosses the naughty, lascivious young wife into the sea.

Perlesvaus agreed that Gawain performed his assigned task at the Grail Castle, deposited the sword, and was again allowed to depart safely without being subjected to Lancelot's lions, arrows, or Perceval's clanging drawbridge that almost cut him and his horse in two. William of Malmesbury recognized Gawain as a great warrior second only to the youngest of the Lancelot kings.

Gawain as first Grail hero became justly famous worldwide in Irish, Welsh, French, German, and English literatures. Like Lancelot, he was widely admired and studied. Unlike Lancelot, who has no death narrative or satisfactory explanation of his death except in the formal history of Scotland, Gawain possesses a complete account from young manhood to his death on an invasion beach. Sir Thomas Malory wrongly placed that shore at Dover, then the Saxon Shore, instead of on the Rhinns of Galloway where Gawain belonged.

Gawain's horse was branded with the turtledove emblem of the Grail Castle *(Parzival),* and he took another mount from a Saxon convoy *(Prose Lancelot).* Ending with Chaucer and Malory, the greatest of authors have treated Gawain. When he first pledged his allegiance to Queen Guinevere, she vowed to employ four authors full time on his adventures *(Prose Lancelot).* Since these were her first authors, they very ably situated Gawain's cycle of high adventures in close parallel to the ceremonial investitures and ritual humiliations of earlier sun gods, all solar heroes like Marduk, Son of the Sun, a thousand years earlier (c. 605 B.C.), in the *Enuma elish* from the Middle East.

Gawain's teacher in theology was said to have been Sulpicius Severus of Aquitania (fl. 360–425). He came from a distinguished Roman, consular family, and that name was offered up because Sulpicius Severus was more widely known than any other monk or bishop of his day. Name-dropping in the case of Gawain, oldest son of King Loth of Lothian (Edinburgh, Scotland), can be excused.

Malory has it right otherwise, portraying Gawain as a sweetheart of ladies, as a youthful Aries of the springtime, or as Taurus the Bull whose strength waned after noon. He was overmatched, added Malory, by six other champions of King Arthur. Gawain was born on May 1 and died on May 10, presumably in 542 when Lancelot also died, and at the same invasion beach or Galloway harbor. One thinks of it as being in the Stranraer loch, which is the closest ferry port to Larne, Ireland, and him as being buried nearby at Caer Ryan: King's Loch perhaps, and King's Burial Mound.

Before his sudden death Gawain had become scar-faced, and he had also lost a front tooth—these wounds in addition to the disgraceful, red scar along his neck. Like Perceval and his father, Gawain was depicted also as gigantic and bright, or red-haired, like the Scots who invaded Man around the year 500, Man's early historian and Governor Sacheverell reported (A. W. Moore, 1977) from Douglas.

Saint Bridgit may have founded the famous nunnery at Douglas, on the Isle of Man during King Arthur's lifetime (Moore, vol. 1, p. 69). The history of ancient Man before the general destruction of virtually all evidence by the Viking conquerors around the year 800 testifies that the resident high ecclesiastics there, the priests Pelles and Merlin into Perceval, descended, according to laws of ancient, Celtic tribes, from a single family, father to son. It was therefore the aged Morgan de Fay, of Merlin's same family and Arthur's, who in the celebrated *Gawain and the Green Knight* ordered Gawain scarred.

In the German *Parzival,* which seems equally authentic as a very primitive source rewritten by Wolfram von Eschenbach, the Grail Castle is said to have been built by an earlier pagan king named Clinschor. Thus, the Arthurian heroes conquered the Isle of Man and Christianized and re-Christianized the Grail. In order to enhance his ordination Gawain was ordered to bring there the holiest of ancient relics, the sword of John the Baptist to whom Merlin was personally dedicated. Gawain himself most resembles the later patron saint of England, the Oriental George who was also born at the spring equinox and venerated in 1098 by the Crusaders (who wore their red cross), and who rescued a princess.

Saint George was brought to England by King Edward III after his conquests in Scotland. Gawain undergoes the Perilous Leap *in Scotland,* at the Perilous Ford, where he seizes Old Man Winter's symbol of the red holly branch. Every ancient king of the Celts bore some branch in his hand so he could be recognized in battle and rallied to by his men. Each clan of Scotland still has its personal branch.

The *Prose Lancelot* (*Vulgate,* vol. a, p. 343ff.) gives a lovely picture of Gawain at the Grail Castle, where he was welcomed and invited to sit beside the unnamed Grail King. Gawain then saw a white dove fly in. It carried a censer ("enchensier") in its beak. Sweet perfumes filled the hall. Everybody knelt. A damsel then processed from the same doorway. She bore above her head "the richest vessel" ("le plus riche uaissel" or "waissail"; the word is supposed to be Norse or Saxon). Here Gawain failed to conform or bow his head. The good smell of delicious food filled the room, but Gawain was not served, and, in fact, was struck by an angry dwarf. Subsequently he was blinded. After his eyes cleared a day later, he saw a dozen damsels enter weeping and lamenting. They entered from the same doorway used before by the dove.

He then survived a nightmarish battle and a terrible storm. He thought he heard angels singing, and he saw the same damsel bring in the "vessel," place it on a silver table, surround it with twelve censers, and sing. Like Lancelot after him, Gawain was also humiliated by being cast into a cart ("une karete"). The Grail Castle, where all these events unfolded, "has the name Corbenic" ("a non corbenic"). Later a hermit explained to Gawain that he had experienced these marvels at the Castle of the Holy Grail. He would otherwise not have known it.

When Gawain first arrived at the Grail Castle in *Perlesvaus,* admittedly a text also from most ancient lore, he saw a lion chained at the gate; Lancelot would see lions in Chrétien's *Perceval.* Gawain also saw sergeants armed with bows no warrior's armor could withstand. This time he was ordered back to King Gurgalain in Albania for the holy sword. In Chrétien he was Lancelot's double, who fell in the waves when he stormed the castle's sea wall. In *Perlesvaus* he returned to find the land gate or drawbridge unguarded.

His next approach gives the long, detailed account from valley, chapel, sepulcher, three bridges, to lion, marble steps, couches, chessboard (of *Peredur*), twelve knights, damsels, and a blinding light. Gawain presents the sword and is invited to dine with the Grail's guardian knights. He witnesses the Grail Procession, is abashed at the sight of the Lance, and plays chess and is vanquished, and chastened; and he departs along the opposite shore as a violent storm whips him. His Lordship ("Messire Gawain") heartily wished that night were over. The Isle of Man still suffers these sudden, violent storms.

Gawain's son wished so too, the night he stumbled into a strange castle and saw materialize out of darkness the terrible Dragoness who metamorphosed into the Blonde Esmerée of the laid-waste city. The Storm God there at least recognized the Unknown as Gawain's son before he chastised him unmercifully too (Pernoud, 1947, p. 217ff.). The story was told by Renaud de Beaujeu in the twelfth century.

Another French poet topped Renaud with his haunted Perilous Necropolis *(Atre périlleux)* where Gawain himself comes to an abandoned chapel. He passes the lych-gate into the cemetery. As he sits there, he sees the lord of the castle come by to invite him to tie up his horse and follow him. Gawain points out that it is after dark, and that the castle is barred and closed. He refuses to abandon his horse. Then alone in that cemetery Gawain sees the slab of a sarcophagus rise up. Amazed, he watches a beautiful woman awaken from the dead and rise up. She is the devil's concubine, obliged like Psyche to satisfy his lust daily, and shut up otherwise in coldest stone. Gawain rises up and delivers her by defeating her devil.

It is well known that the medieval romance and the fairy tale also arise from a common source in legend that was once history. These oldest of Arthurian hero tales featuring this senior Gawain offer a perfect example of both literary genres. We always commence at each telling in King Arthur's Court where two heroes prepare to undertake an exploit. The date is given: December 24, April 23, some high holiday. The preferred antagonist is enough to frighten anyone, being some supernatural male from an unknown, dread land. Arthur's man accepts the challenge. A date is set. The young champion is granted a preparatory period. Rendezvous is set and mutually acceptable. The knot of intrigue is thus tied.

Gawain struck the first blow, and he must answer. His old king has chosen him. The young male is expendable, . . . always. The king has decided the departure date. Gawain's chosen horse, named Gringalet, is prepared. On the way a donor, who is usually an august lady with her lady-in-waiting, offers the hero a magic talisman, which will save his life. Gawain refused the golden ring that both Yvain and Lancelot would in turn accept. Gawain accepted the green sash of a fiancé. Like Yvain he was wounded, but in the neck instead of in the face. Thus, as hero, he was not A+. However, he managed to rid the world of that particular threat from that old, powerful antagonist; and he returned more or less whole, to King Arthur's Court.

The Gawain tales give us the same seven characters of that ancient, noble genre, which is the Arthurian fairy tale that only records the deeds of majesties and other royal personages: (1) the antagonist Gawain, who seemed like lightning itself; (2) the donor, who is a learned chatelaine, and, were one brave enough still to suppose it, a magician and one of his women teachers; (3) the hero's magical auxiliary such as the red-and-white horse he would not desert, or his shield, or his sash; (4) the fairy princess who sends him leaping across chasms for a holly branch, or who tries to beguile, i.e., seduce him in those other ways; (5) the dispatcher who remains in shadow but who must be King Arthur, really the only begetter in all this performance; (6) the young, handsome, daring hero Gawain; and (7) his alternate, second-string champion Yvain, who usually sets out first but who also first abandons the quest when the going gets hard, such as when fountains boil, or bluebirds sweep skyward in flocks, or drawbridges fall on one's horse.

When all that has been said and done, even back there, while the thirteenth century is stunned witnessing the horrors of large-scale massacre, a German scholar naming himself Heinrich von dem Türlin delighted readers everywhere with a new Arthurian text called *Diu Crône, The Crown.* An English translation, financed by the University of Kentucky and published by the University of Nebraska, has just appeared (1989). Preface and introduction are also by the translator, J. W. Thomas.

Gawain's last or Grail Quest forms chapter 12 (pp. 316–30) of this excellent work, which Alfred Nutt first summarized and commented upon in 1888 (pp. 26–27 of the 1965 edition). To a marked degree Heinrich's text corresponds to Chrétien's telling and to Wolfram's, as Nutt demonstrated; but this last or Grail sighting by Gawain is new and added to both earlier texts.

Gawain finds Kay in prison at the Grail Castle, and so one is not entirely disoriented. Lancelot in Chrétien had also found Kay there, wounded and moaning, as the hero smeared blood on casing and lintel before he approached Queen Guinevere's *altar*. It *was* her altar he approached, and not her *bed,* as Chrétien had thought. Kay lay in a bed just outside the chapel where the priestess Guinevere still officiated.

It is such a sore point that we should say it again: twice during King Arthur's reign, twice before the year 542, the French clergy inside France, which sits at the right hand of the Papacy, by edicts outlawed women priests in the Church. Furthermore, we know from French church records, from the *Annals of Wales* also, from Arthurian literature, and from the writings of Saint Patrick, that Papal Legates Germanus and Lupus, who then headed the French church, were twice sent to Britain in Arthur's fifth century to chastise prelates of the British church. The Roman Catholic church in Rome was slowly becoming organized meanwhile and soon able in the years following King Arthur's death to administer western Europe including both France and Britain. As the *Peredur* has told us, priestesses who had been teachers of young, Celtic aristocrats were murdered suddenly by Peredur *and by King Arthur.*

During Queen Guinevere's lifetime, her people, who were the Picts of northeastern Scotland, had not yet joined the Scots in their newly resettled, western Highlands of Scotland. Although two or three suppositions have Guinevere murdered at the Grail Castle, or drawn and quartered in her Vale of Strathmore, she was most probably welcomed home into Pictland at Meigle and buried there where her grave and gravestone stand today, in the lovely churchyard in the small village of Meigle (Saint Michael?). The place is just north of Coupar Angus, and adjacent to Glamis Castle.

Contemporary scholarship (1990) inside southern France at Toulouse, where interest in the Grail runs very high because the Languedoc is now disputing its earliest possession with Britain and claiming it originated not with King Arthur but in the Pyrenees, points out that the dating of Arthurian manuscripts has little to do with the manuscript. Thus, even though Heinrich von dem Türlin supposedly wrote in the thirteenth century, that supposedly proves little or nothing. This is generally true of books also, which are published only when the author finds a publisher, and thirdly, when the publisher remains solvent long enough to distribute the book. Our dating, says Barthélémy, is quite irrelevant. The German texts, *Lanzelet, Parzival,* and *Diu Crône,* may very well contain the oldest material.

British scholars generally claim King Arthur never lived anyway—and if he won his twelve victories in eastern England, which was in his lifetime held by Saxons, or against them in western England which they had not yet settled—then truly he never lived.

Scholars in the Languedoc today turn out large numbers of beautifully printed, marvelously researched books that shun Britain, and demand the Grail for themselves. They refuse to accept the outmoded ideas of Arthurian scholarship that still hang on in Britain today: (1) King Arthur never lived and English archaeologists have proven it (when all they have proven is that they have found nothing); (2) the personages at the Grail Castle were pagans because priestesses officiated there; (3) King Arthur was interred in Glastonbury Abbey, although it was not built until two hundred years after his death, i.e., by King Ine of Wessex in the eighth century and refounded by Saint Dunstan in 946; (4) King Arthur was born in Tintagel Castle, Cornwall, although that castle had not even been built yet (it wasn't built by 1066, either, when King William I commenced listing his real estate inside England); (5) Merlin was a black magician, although he was, in fact, the Archbishop Dubric or Dubricius of the Celtic, Christian church, interred since Geoffrey of Monmouth's days in Llandaff Cathedral, South Wales; (6) Geoffrey of Monmouth, King Arthur's first historian (1136) is a foul liar and a "thief outside the walls" although in truth he was named Bishop of Saint Asaph's Cathedral in North Wales; but of course he did not long survive the jealousy, hatred, and envy of his English contemporaries.

French scholars of today are correct in that the actual date when a literary work appears openly is neither proof that it had just been written nor evidence of the antiquity of its source. Traffic was intense in those Arthurian texts that, like Geoffrey of Monmouth's *History,* had become the property of Angevin aristocrats—as of the foreign princes and princesses who either entered the Church and journeyed to the Holy Land as pilgrims, or who "took the Cross" and traveled overland or overseas to Sicily, Cyprus, Syria, and Israel, by way of Constantinople, and Edessa famous for relics like the Shroud of Turin and the Antioch Cup. Every person in the world, it would seem, wants to purchase a souvenir from his travels abroad. King (Saint) Louis almost bankrupted France as he bought up Egypt to bring home to Notre-Dame de Paris or Notre-Dame de Chartres; but, of course, the Capetian Crown was just then immensely rich with the Knights Templar's fortunes. It could even afford to rebuild the Church of the Holy Sepulcher in Jerusalem, their west transept of which is supposedly visible still today.

Aristocrats everywhere in Europe who shared the crusading spirit found common bonds in Arthurian literature, which has hardly a single commoner in it. More elevated even than run-of-the-mill texts stand the thirteen or so best Grail accounts because they portray in great if conflicting detail a religion, or at least, a worship devised by and limited to the high aristocracy of Scotland. To Britain were rapidly added the larger area of continental Germany, then Switzerland, from Spain, from as far west as Iceland and as far east as the lakes and seas of Finland whence perhaps had migrated the tribes of the Picts.

Strangely or not, each area seems to have preferred one part of Arthurian archives or to have favored one particular hero above all others. Immediately Merlin appealed above all others to teachers of young warriors in Iceland. Peredur survived magnificently inside Germany as the pure-in-heart who rose to be Grail King. Lohengrin was adopted by Belgium as ancestor of their Godefroi de Bouillon who in 1095 "liberated" Jerusalem. Lancelot became so early the sole property of France that scholars continued down the long centuries to believe he was simply a French fiction, until circa 1862, when the Breton nobleman Hersart de la Villemarqué protested that Lancelot was a Celt, and in no way French, or in no way invented from whole cloth only.

Thus, wherever their stories are written and rewritten, Arthurian personages and their unforgettable scenes continue on under scant disguises into the literatures of the Renaissance: Cervantes, Madre Theresa, Rabelais the Christian Evangelist from Chinon Castle and the University of Montpellier, from Dante to Ariosto, Boiardo (translated by Lord Byron), and the noble Italian Tasso who became the beloved poet and historian par excellence, and for all time, of the Crusades.

All these centuries King Arthur himself prepared in silence to move into the heavens of grander opera, first with sweet Henry Purcell as composer, libretto by John Dryden. Their *King Arthur, or The British Worthy* was first presented at Dorset Gardens, London, in the summer of 1691. Its first performance abroad occurred on April 24, 1800, in New York City. But it was revived in Birmingham, England, on October 6, 1897; in Paris, as translated by J. Delage-Prat, on May 9, 1922; and again at Columbia University New York on April 24, 1935. Two other operas, the second an adaptation of the first, by Arne, Purcell, and Garrick (Drury Lane, December 13, 1770) and the third with music composed by Sir Edward William Elgar for a play by Lawrence Binyon, were both entitled simply *King Arthur.*

Arthurian texts, however, do not fall either into the realms of music or history, but must be classed, and studied first and foremost for what they are, which is supremely great literature.

These texts are by any definition in any century or place literature so overwhelmingly grand, true, honest, timeless, and wonderful that they have understandably earned the devotion and shaped the personalities of mankind wherever people have been so privileged as to read or hear or see them performed.

Certain contemporary scholars are trained until they recognize at first sight the voices of the world's greatest authors. One such person is the J. W. Thomas who has just translated Heinrich von dem Türlin's *The Crown,* and another, Dr. A. Barthélémy of Toulouse, who recently published his brilliant and original criticism of the Holy Grail: *Le Graal* (October 1987). When such persons are born with a great measure of literary ability, which is an inherited characteristic running traceably in certain blood lines, they alone must remain the final authority on Arthurian literature. They alone identify an author *and his text* from a mere few lines, separate Robert de Boron from Chrétien de Troyes, distinguish the *Lanzelet* from the *Parzival,* and know Marie de France from Béroul or Thomas, both of whom also wrote *Tristans.*

Such scholars, who were well tested at their graduate faculties for this innate ability and acquired skill, testify best as to the antiquity and authenticity of each Arthurian text. They agree calmly here in America that the *Didot-Perceval* and the *Parzival* contain very old material that betrays its antiquity as does the *Peredur,* which, by its support also of contemporary Church policy, authenticates as historical King Arthur's dates and lifetime: priestesses who had been teachers, had become witches, and were doubtless slaughtered.

King Arthur was born, says Chrétien, at a seaside castle before which stretched a white sandy field: Caerlaverock on the Rhinns of

Galloway, just west a few miles from Camelot/Carlisle. By consensus and predominant mentions in *108* Arthurian texts, the last and greatest of Roman forts inside Britain was Carlisle/Camelot. Just a few miles to the north of it stand Longtown and Arthuret at the crossing of secondary and Roman roads, and at green fields where very probably King Arthur, and certainly one of his sons, lies buried. Merlin's Cave, now called Saint Ninian's, on the far western Rhinns of this same Galloway that Prince Gawain once so honorably ruled, brings tears to our eyes. All hereabouts is tribal land of the Grail Kings.

Heinrich von dem Türlin now demands our close attention.

Heinrich's text: Gawain's final quest for the Holy Grail took him and his party over the Waste Land, *twelve* days out of Camelot, until Gawain led his forces to the shores of a lake. At this shore they found only a ramshackle jetty projecting into open water as far as they could see. They had by this time traveled steadily for twelve days. Their discouragement was great. They saw neither ford, ship, nor barge. Gawain told them they would have to swim for it. And so they led their horses to the beach and swam the rest of that long day and into the night. . . .

In other words, Heinrich agrees with Chrétien's *Lancelot* that Gawain and Lancelot separated, somewhere along the Rhinns of Galloway, the former choosing to go by water and Lancelot choosing to lead his party overland. Both groups had come together, and then started from Camelot in pursuit of the kidnapped Guinevere. Lancelot glimpsed her one night and day out of Carlisle at Caerlaverock Castle, it would seem.

Chrétien agrees that Gawain "fell" into the "Lake." Heinrich prefers to understand that at some point he swam. Chrétien has the better solution, if one takes into account distance and terrain, and assumes that the Grail Castle they seek stood on an islet off the west coast of the Isle of Man. This Grail Castle is elsewhere depicted thus, as facing Ireland, which would put it on or adjacent to the west side of Man, which is in the center of the Irish Sea. Ulrich's *Lanzelet* text further describes the place as surrounded by a wooden *palisade,* what is technically called a "peel" or palisaded stronghold. Today the islet in question lies off the west coast of the Isle of Man, across a channel from the coastal or beach town of Peel. The water off this shore is as deep and dangerous a sea as could anywhere be braved.

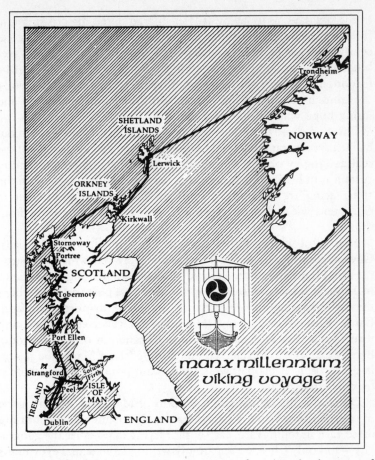

As an act of celebration, commemorating four hundred years of Norse rule of the Isle of Man resulting in a parliamentary system embodied by Tynwald, which has endured for one thousand years, a replica of the Viking Longship, known as the Gokstad Ship was built in Norway. The ship, a slightly scaled down version of the original, is 15 meters long and 3.5 meters in the beam. She was built at Onsøy near Oslo, and was named "Odin's Raven." After sea trials she sailed from Trondheim on May 27th, 1979, following the route shown above, retracing the course taken by the Vikings on their voyages of conquest and settlement. The crew, eleven from the Isle of Man, and five from Norway, was carefully selected and trained for the rigors of protracted passages in an open boat. Odin's Raven arrived in Peel on July 4th, 1979.

In the old days, as today by sail, small craft dared the crossing into Ireland not more than three days a year. Racing yachts have recently been lost in these same waters. The sight and sound of waves breaking on the southern and western shores of Man will never be forgotten. The spray rises sky-high trying to wet the rosy clouds.

Heinrich continues: They swam until they were exhausted and losing hope when a big wave cast them ashore. . . .

Chrétien chose to understand that people had to fish Gawain out by means of a grappling hook. His choice again takes account of the real geography of this islet. A stroll around its eighteenth-century curtain wall brings the curious to a narrow landing cove cut in the cliffs facing Ireland. One has to smile these centuries later at Chrétien's wit and charm, seeing Gawain's bulk being hauled out thus.

Heinrich backtracks: they separated at a junction of four roads, Gawain choosing to go the fourth alone. Kay was with their party.

Here Heinrich joins the careful visualization by Marie de France in *Yonec,* this junction still today at the central point on Man where the east–west road to Peel is crossed by the south–north road from Castle Rushen to Ramsay. Heinrich has reversed himself and thrown out Gawain's sea crossing in Chrétien in order to reroute him by Lancelot's overland crossing of the Isle of Man: Douglas on its east coast to Peel on its west. Or Gawain swam the Solway before he crossed to Man.

Douglas is the capital and chief port of Man, and also the name of one of King Arthur's twelve battles. No matter how confusing these various tellings are, each author trying to visualize the geography—and only Chrétien apparently writing from actual eyewitness knowledge—still the place itself is there and it fits the various accounts. R. L. Graeme Ritchie first discovered and corroborated this fact for Chrétien and Scotland in his formal lecture at Oxford University in 1952. We have only followed his lead from 1986.

According to Chrétien also, plus the *Prose Lancelot,* and Malory notably, Kay was lamentably a member of these parties.

Heinrich continues: Gawain was traversing a Waste Land when he encountered a ring of fire. It altogether surrounded him. He saw no possible exit. The flames encircled him tightly. . . .

Here for a second time we meet what was originally a fire-walking feat. Heinrich chose not to develop it. In other words, Gawain once walked safely through flames and, as we shall soon see, he was richly rewarded. By achieving this priestly, or kingly feat, Gawain will merit sight of the Grail. As much as one recalls such a performance in Arthurian texts, only the Irish Princess Isolde also walked through fire as a test of her superiority, innocence, and chastity. It can probably be safely assumed that Gawain has again proven his virginity as he did for the Green Knight Merlin, who therefore let him off with only a scar that would demonstrate to all how close the hero had come to yielding to the young seductress Blathnat, or White Flower. Only she was, in the Irish telling, cast into the sea for her amorous sin.

Heinrich continues: Gawain emerged from flames into a paradise ruled by a golden-crowned goddess. Her palace (the Arthurian Castle of Maidens, which certainly brings to mind the age-old, many times redowered nunnery at Douglas) was thronged with at least one thousand maidens. Two gorgeous messenger-maidens escorted Gawain to the castle hall. He saw the crown worn by the goddess. The goddess and her ladies-in-waiting rose as he approached. The goddess kissed him. She instructed Gawain to fix their likenesses firmly in mind, all six of them. If and when he should ever see the six of them again, goddess, messengers, and ladies, he should promptly ask a question about the Grail. She cautioned him not to fall asleep there and especially not to drink, if he persisted in winning his quest. Otherwise, he would fail.

In other words, we have Heinrich's directions again as seen in Marie de France's poem *Yonec* where a desperate lady actually descends the road to the mysterious islet and its (Grail) castle in order to find her beloved. She too enters a hall like this same hall that Heinrich speaks of, where she finds her lover lying on a *stone* slab, just as Don Quixote eventually found the dead knight and saw the Grail Procession of maidens.

The injunction against drink (there) proves that Gawain will soon have arrived in Purgatory, a concomitant state between life and death, an intermediate halt for expiatory purification. Some person there, Don Quixote's knight on his bier, or the Grail King Anfortas, awaits punishment there temporarily, for his unavoidable, venial sins. According to Arthurian texts the heroic Quester may return from the Grail to the real world only if he abstains from food and drink. If he yields there to some sexy, fairy creature, he will fail in his quest.

Lancelot yielded to the Grail King's daughter sometimes called Helen, which is Manx for Island; and Galahad was conceived. And so to his eternal grief, Lancelot failed to achieve the Grail, or to become despite his superior pedigree, king at the Grail Castle. Thus, Gawain *must not* make the maidens weep and he must again send gifts: gloves, gold ring, and a stone.

This Castle of Maidens is here revealed as some last step before arrival on a future day at the Grail Castle itself. Both *Peredur* and the *Perceval Continuations* testify that these are the lady teachers whom Perceval and King Arthur will come very shortly to kill. Here too they are clearly seen as Gawain's final teachers.

It is very hard, and finally impossible not to see here the olden nunnery at Douglas. Histories of Man assure us it was dowered by Irish princesses and redowered over centuries at Douglas, at Man's deeply indented, eastern harbor. And furthermore it is harder not to visualize Marie de France herself there in the twelfth century and for two reasons in particular: (1) because she knows Manx geography including landmarks, terrain, lie of the land, and distance, and (2) because she translated Henry of Saltrey's purgatory text, and he was in her lifetime a religious at nearby Rushen Abbey. One can never read the reports by scholars at the Manx Museum, or speak with the learned lady curator there, without seeing in the mind's eye the underground necropolis at Douglas with its rows of female skeletons ranged neatly side by side.

Heinrich continues: Gawain left the maidens and journeyed for six days toward the Castle of the Rich Fisher King, *which was on an Isle.* His route took him through a dense forest where he saw a hideous sight: naked maidens as lovely as anyone ever saw were being herded together and whipped by a flaming red devil of a man. The girls screamed with pain and cried out for help, but the red demon paid homage to Gawain. The hero saw the girls sink into the ground. Then he saw a second, terrible sight. There was an old woman. She held something made of glass in her hand. She was chasing a mounted warrior to whom a lovely girl clung, pitifully calling "Help!" The old woman threw her glass object against the trunk of a tree. All at once the forest exploded in flames.

After this horror Gawain saw a third spectacle. He rode past a hideous monster who held a mounted warrior captive. The warrior was old. He was chained with gold fetters. The monster was chewing on a tree branch. The warrior was tied fast to his horse. He held out in his right hand a precious casket of red zircon. It contained a solid perfume. As soon as Gawain inhaled it, he felt a surge of happiness. He also forgot his fatigue.

Gawain here is surely drawing very near Purgatory itself, for the maidens are being scourged by Satan all clad in red, as he is usually depicted, but with a whip in hand instead of a fork. The same scene is told somewhat differently in *Perlesvaus* where the hero Gawain actually rescues one maiden from her master who was whipping her, but loses her again as her master strips her naked, drives her into a pool, and whips her to death as the water runs red with her blood.

Such dream sequences again point up the findings of anthropologists and theologians who have studied shamanism and initiations, Lewis and Eliade standing out among many others. The paste that Gawain smelled or sniffed reminds us of Iran where gentlemen often offer their teacher the gift of a metal vial containing a white salve, which is the concentrated perfume attar of roses. Gawain seems to have taken a drug of some sort. A lady donor attended by a maiden gave Lancelot a similar drug, or dose of medicine, and Yvain also, when one or the other was wandering naked and mad in a forest. These recollections of initiation by trials, which included hallucinogens, are not unique to Gawain. Nor are the nightmares of women teachers or maidens called witches being tortured and killed. Did Gawain see the last priestesses in the world being slain?

Heinrich now rises to his most thrilling pages, what French scholars of literature term the passage he longed to write, *la scène à faire*. Gawain followed hoof tracks out of the forest. Soon he came within sight of a mounted party. As fast as he could urge his horse, he could not catch them up. Darkness was falling. He hurried. He came within sight of a castle. The gate stood open. The horsemen entered with a clatter of hooves. Gawain followed. He made it in, dismounted, looked about, and saw not a living soul. The courtyard lay silent and deserted. He found a room set for supper. He saw a table laden with all manner of delicacies, and provided with white table linen, hand towels, gold finger bowls, water, wine. He found the stable provided superbly for his horse. It too was empty otherwise. Through other closed doors Gawain entered chambers, and then the great hall. There was nobody there either. He reclined on a gold cushion, and dined alone. He served himself in the same way the next morning and departed. The drawbridge descended before him and rose after him. He heard a maiden bidding him farewell.

A month later he returned to this same castle.

When Gawain returned to this Glass Castle a last time he learned that both Kay and Lanzelet (Lancelot) were being held prisoner there. The castle floors were strewn with roses, which the *Prose*

Lancelot said formed a crown each day for the child Lancelot. Gawain this time saw the same two youths whom Peredur also saw playing chess. That night servants brought basins of water for washing hands, as in Chrétien's Grail Castle, and servants brought in countless candles in splendid candelabras.

Now Heinrich rises to the occasion: Gawain first sees a youth enter and lay a gleaming sword before the Grail King. Servants and cupbearers then brought in dinner, which neither the host nor Gawain touched. Stewards filed in one after another. Then processed two gem-bedecked and aristocratic maidens. Then came two squires carrying a gorgeous spear. They were followed by two more maidens carrying a golden bowl set with sparkling jewels. These were followed by the world's most beautiful lady. She was crowned and exquisitely gowned. The lady bore a cloth of embroidered silk upon which lay a gold filigreed *lattice** into which was set in red gold one single jewel. Gawain thought it was a sacred relic in a reliquary.

The lady proudly wore the golden crown. She was followed by one loudly weeping maiden. They bowed before the host. The first two maidens and the two squires together laid the spear on the table in front of the host. They set the bowl under the spear. Then Gawain couldn't believe his eyes, but he saw three drops of blood drip from the spear into the bowl, before the lord of the castle. The four stepped back. Then the lady set the reliquary down before the host. She lifted off its lid. Gawain saw that the bowl held a small round of bread. The host broke it in three and put one piece in his mouth. Gawain waited no longer, for he had recognized his teacher. She was the crowned lady.

He asked his question: "Who are these persons assembled? What does this marvel mean?"

The Grail King informed him that this service was and must remain secret. Gawain was looking at the Grail. You will never learn more than that, he tells Gawain.

Parzival has already failed to achieve the Grail, for which reason he and his whole clan have been expelled (to Sarras) from the country forever.

Only the ladies among all those present were still alive. Only these ladies and maidens had been entrusted by God with the mystery of the Holy Grail.

*Shroud of Turin?

The Grail, concluded the king, would never again be seen publicly, nor would any person ever reveal more about it, nor would any tongue tell more, nor any other eye see.

Daylight was breaking before the Grail disappeared and all the company too, except for the women. . . . The goddess thanked Gawain for having delivered her from her secret obligation. God had answered her prayer. Her task was finished.

We have now, one more time, seen the end of Grail worship inside Britain, and the departure for Sarras of the last Grail King, Perceval.

Unless the Knights Templar, fleeing massacre inside France, brought it to Scotland where it had originated.

THE GRAIL KING ARTHUR

The British King Arthur stirs the hearts in our century as he has done for fifteen centuries. To us he stands symbolically for the Alpha, the beginning, the Great A that recurs in so many other proper names associated with the Holy Grail. It has stood not only for Avalon, the Isle where Arthur housed his Grail, but also for Albania, which he ruled as Ri Alban, or Rig Albanach. The connection to Aquitania was reinforced by authors of the twelfth century, as to Aliscans, another isle that was also both sanctuary and necropolis.

King Arthur's northern origin again brings to mind the Grizzly Bear, which figures as his totem on earth as in the heavens. There the Great Bear becomes our Great Dipper circling the North Star. Merlin would have known it as he climbed nightly into his observatory. Lancelot brings to mind also his totem, the Dog Star Sirius, known in ancient Egypt too as the Key to the Sky.

What a northern folk thought of the grizzly that hunted their forests ahead of man and beside him still becomes clear to us from the Finnish epic *Kalevala* (Canto XLVI). Before he had to kill the bear Otso, because his people were near starvation in the frozen winter, and needed clothing too, the ancient hero of days prayed to him (p. 218ff.):

> Oh, Otso, with your honeyed paws and sable stockings, go into the deep forest, handsome creature, golden beauty; . . . you were made by the Forest Mother to wander in the summer marshes and sleep the winter away in a hollow cherry stump . . . Now thou must go, thou apple of the forest, upon a journey, treasured golden one . . . while I sing of thee. . . .

With the bear to personify King Arthur and the dragon to grace Arthur's pennant, which Merlin caused to streak down the sky over dark Scotland like a flaming torch, King Arthur stands and is remembered. Like Otso and Otava overhead, he has his favorite places, at least a hundred such named for him inside Great Britain alone.

Eighty some places inside Scotland recall not only his fortresses named Camelot and his twelve battle sites, but also his necropolis at Arthuret, which is now in Cumbria, on the English side of the

Scottish Border. Many such places named in Arthur's memory also figure more correctly as Neolithic monuments, which only testifies again to Arthur's ancient renown. Geoffrey of Monmouth was even mistranslated so as to make him say that Merlin built Stonehenge for Uther Pendragon, when what he really consecrated was memorials to the Celtic dead in Edinburgh. Such more recent stone monuments stand there today on Calton Hill, Edinburgh: hill of the prehistoric Royal Caledonians. This constant association of Arthur with dolmens and henge monuments from 2000 B.C. or thereabouts testifies to Arthur's antiquity perceived as both then and now. People know better, but then know better still.

King Arthur's pedigree as established by Arthur Wade-Evans in 1934 goes back to the British Emperor Maximus in the year 388. Maximus figures again in the Welsh *Mabinogion* as the husband of the Empress Helena who bore Constantine the Great and discovered the Holy Sepulcher in Jerusalem. She also constructed the first Christian church over this tomb of Christ. Thus, Wade-Evans accepted Arthur as born circa 475 and his older cousin Merlin was born circa 450. The latter died, as he had prophesied during an eclipse of the sun in September 536. Arthur, Gawain, and Lancelot died, say the *Annals of Wales,* in 542. The *Mabinogion* testifies that the last battle of Arthur took place at Camlan. The very word raises the hair on one's head. It was the most terrible of all defeats ever suffered by the Celts: a *camlan.*

The date 542 from the *Annals of Wales* has often been accepted as a reasonable *ad quem* for the disappearance and death of King Arthur's heroes, only eight men having survived the rout, their number including Arthur's successors: rulers of North Wales and Pictland both. Dalriada, the third kingdom in question, then, at Arthur's death took a daughter from among Merlin's descendants to wed so that the personal name *Arthur* survived as such in their Scottish, or western Highland, royal line. No trace of this name *Arthur* has been found prior to King Arthur.

More significantly for their worship of the Grail, Perceval too died or removed to Sarras in 542, or soon thereafter. Galahad's generation, and Lohengrin's, thus witnessed the disappearance overseas of the Grail itself. Some scholars in the Languedoc today have traced a similar worship, perhaps even of the Grail, in unbroken line from Christ's missionaries there, in France, and in Spain: Saints Philippe (Philip), Lorenzo (Lawrence), and Barthélémy (Bartholomew). In any case, the last Grail Castle inside

Britain, says the *Sone de Nansai* translation of a manuscript from Carlisle (or Camelot), stood adjacent to the Isle of Man, and facing the present Manx town of Peel.

This Grail Castle islet is today called Saint Patrick's Isle, and presumably to commemorate the year 444 when Saint Patrick preached there. Man and the Southern Hebrides constituted, in fact, the first Christian Bishopric in Great Britain. Ruins of Saint Patrick's Church stand there today. Beside them rise the larger ruins of Saint Germanus's Cathedral, and this French prelate went to Britain in 429 and again in 445–46, very probably both times to censure Saints Patrick and Dubricius (Merlin). In his *Confession* Saint Patrick hints as much. The Catholic church later took action against both Merlin and "the goddess" Morgan le Fay, who in *Gawain and the Green Knight,* as elsewhere in Arthurian lore, lived on the Isle of Man. The Church has not condemned the Holy Grail, but weighs it again today, say correspondents from Rome.

That King Arthur lived in these centuries of the Dark Ages, when seaborne invasions left nothing whole, comes again from another Arthurian genealogy drawn by the Welsh textual scholar Rachel Bromwich (1978), "Notes to Personal Names":

**Amlawdd Wledig m. Gwen
(daughter of Cunedda Wledig).***

Their five children were:

1. Dywana	2. Custennin	3. Goleuddyd	4. Eigr	5. Rieingulid
father	father	father	mother	mother
of	of	of	of	of
Huallu	Goreu	Culhwch	Arthur	Saint Illtud

Gawain and brothers, including the fatal Modred, come from the generation following Arthur's, as do Lancelot and Perceval. Arthur's five half sisters provided him with young champions while Merlin's descendants remained in or returned to Wales and the Cornwall in southern England, which they Christianized. Gawain's Galloway was originally called "Cornwall," or Dumnonia, as was Brittany in France. The entire west of Europe had ages before been

---

*The reader will recall that Wledig means Commander in Chief. The *Annals of Wales* and/or the *Mabinogion* give information concerning Arthur and these four cousins.

settled by tribes of these Celts. All those prehistoric peoples fell to the Romans—except for Guinevere's Picts in eastern Scotland, who remained unsubdued. They only yielded eastern Ireland and eastern Scotland finally under repeated centuries of invasions by Romans, Angles, Saxons, Vikings, and Normans.

King Arthur should probably be understood as a Grail King equal in majesty to Anfortas, Pelles, and Titurel, because, first of all, he functioned to dispatch heroes on the Quest for the Holy Grail. Their several names and their many but same and repeated adventures along the way are given in various Arthurian texts. In Sir Thomas Malory's *Morte d'Arthur* King Arthur sponsors what seem countless numbers of young men who by their offers to devote, and to sacrifice their lives, bear witness to the king's stature even in his lifetime. We know from the Perceval texts how Arthur received this youngest son of his royal sister, the Widow Lady of Camelot (at Stirling, Scotland), with love, but also with tears. We remember too how when Perceval sat stalled on his horse outside Carlisle he fell into the trance at the sight of red, white, and black, which were even at Rome the three, ancient and sacred colors of religious ceremony. King Arthur rode out with Gawain to Perceval's rescue. Thus, he functioned also to supervise his Quester and set him back on the track.

Arthur continually functioned as a real king interacting with armies and with these Questers in understandable ways. When Lancelot fought his final duel with Meleagant at the Grail Castle, suddenly and without either notice or explanation, King Arthur not only appeared but presided. It was not his quarrel, of course, but Queen Guinevere's. She therefore gave the thumbs-down signal to Lancelot, who then decapitated the confessed kidnapper of Her Majesty.

In *Perlesvaus* where Guinevere is said to have died, King Arthur dowered the Grail Castle with her personal treasure. He had chosen his Queen Guinevere, subject to Merlin's approval, as his High Priestess, and not as the mother of his two or three children. Arthur's queen was like himself an autonomous ruler, and an authority in religious matters; she too presided at the Grail Castle at Lancelot's second investiture there. He advanced in dark of night to her altar. King Arthur served in daylight as arbiter; he was not called upon when Lancelot fought and won his judicial combat there. The fact of his military victory had proven Lancelot just and doomed Meleagant ipso facto to death.

King Arthur's personal veneration of the Virgin Mary has made him worshipful to Knights Templar and still adored in southern France. There small sons who are dedicated to the Virgin Mary wear suits of her colors: pale blue and white. These were also the colors of the Queen of England's first College in New York City, and, thus, those today of (her) Columbia University. King Arthur, said the Welsh Bards, who had it from memory during their long years of training, wore the image of the Virgin on his *shield* (or on his *shoulder?*). The Welsh original is troublesome because of its two possible meanings, but the idea is clear: that King Arthur venerated the Virgin. He was also said to have donated a piece of the True Cross to Melrose (Abbey) in southeastern Scotland.

Arthur's Seat, which is the extinct volcano in the city of Edinburgh, has at its base Holyrood Castle still belonging to monarchy in Britain, and beside it the ruins of Holyrood Abbey. Now, Holy Rood and *Vera Cruz* are alternate names for True Cross. Here Arthur is still connected to his ancestress, Celtic tribe, Welsh Empress Helena, and the Emperor Maximus in the year 388. And he is connected here also not only to Commanders on Hadrian's Wall, but to the Emperor Constantine the Great. He first declared Christianity the official religion of his Eastern Roman Empire.

Geoffrey of Monmouth reported Arthur as saying he was descended from the (an) Emperor Constantine, which again ties Arthur to Jerusalem and to Christ. Thus, the London historian and editor John Morris rightly called King Arthur the last Roman Emperor in the West. Not to be outdone, Queen Guinevere too was descended from "noble Romans." And how after five hundred years of a Roman occupation of Britain garrisoned and provided with enormous legionary fortresses such as Carlisle/Camelot on the border of a conquered "England" and a partially unconquered "Scotland," could it have been otherwise? And Carlisle was the latest and by far the largest of these Roman defensive establishments. When Arthur seized Carlisle, it represented the last word in architecture and military technology.

The best evidence for the historical King Arthur lies in Welsh Annals such as the Nennius compilation that list his twelve astonishing victories. They were obviously not won south of Hadrian's Wall anchored on its western waters by Carlisle itself. Finally these battles yielded to research, being located for the greater part in and around the seventeen Roman forts on Hadrian's Wall, and at Edinburgh, Dumbarton (Glasgow), Loch Lomond, and Stirling/Bannockburn, which was and is the key to the defense of Scotland.

The second-best, new evidence comes from the guest list at Arthur's coronation and Guinevere's at Carlisle itself. Instead of coming either from southern England, or from fictional places altogether, or worse yet, from twelfth-century sites as has previously been argued, the guests of honor came from Edinburgh's Salisbury, from Carlisle, and much more believably, from the seventeen forts along Hadrian's Wall.

Arthur's greatest victory at Mt. Badon turns out by the independent and added testimony of Saint Gildas, to be Dumbarton (Fortress of the Britons) in or beside the Clyde River downstream from Glasgow. This situation of Mt. Badon supports Geoffrey of Monmouth's name for it: *Alclut,* fort on the Clyde, adjacent four miles down the River Leven from Loch Lomond's south shore also, as Geoffrey wrote. Arthur's final battle and death blow took place, after Merlin's death, at Camlan, which O. G. S. Crawford of Glasgow demonstrated (1935) was also one of the most striking Roman forts on Hadrian's Wall: Camboglanna > Cam lan.

This historical Arthur has, all told, a life history in six parts: Birth, Antecedents, Childhood (a lacuna of fifteen years), Kinging (Recognition, Twelve Battles, Wedding, Coronation), Peace (second lacuna, twelve to fifteen years), and Last Campaign and Camlan. His birth story derives in part from that of Hercules as per the usual, Dark Age, epic material; the birth and life stories of the hero Aimeri de Narbonne on the Mediterranean/Roman city, follow suit. Curiously Merlin's name was also "Aimeri," Emrys in Welsh, and Ambrosius in Latin. A difference is that Arthur has as yet no epic—only Geoffrey's prose history, and the major Arthurian texts in Romance languages and German. Arthur's ancestry is corroborated both by ancient Wales, as by P. K. Johnstone in Roman "Consular Chronology" (1962).

The major part of Arthur's mature life follows his recognition ceremony where, Merlin directing, he drew the sword from the stone. The period of peace he brought after his twelfth victory at Mt. Badon was followed by what has seemed an expedition into Wales rather than to "Galles" (France) as Geoffrey has led many historians to believe. His last battle at Camlan where he slew Modred is referred to several times not only in the *Annals of Wales* but also in the *Mabinogion* as well. The terrible carnage there must have brought death to all the major clan chiefs of the North, who formed Arthur's personal retinue vowed to die before he did.

Archaeological excavation continues at the Camboglanna Fort now under the jurisdiction of Carlisle City. Interest in nearby Arthuret Parish, Longtown near Carlisle, is also great; for King Arthur and one of his sons also, was probably interred there in his own tribal territory.

The question of Arthur in Scotland has always been raised in contradistinction to an Arthur at Glastonbury, England. Medieval romances including most notably the *Perlesvaus* written at Glastonbury Abbey invariably place Árthur in Scotland. Dorothy Kempe carefully noted this in 1905 as she edited the *Grand-Saint-Graal.* In this observation she followed William of Malmesbury, Geoffrey of Monmouth, and later on Renaissance historians of Scotland: Hector Boece writing in Paris in 1575, and John Major also. Kempe also noted how the Grail Kings were routinely called by different names—so that Arthur may also have once been called Bran (King) or Brons (Hebron). William Douglas Simpson as early as 1928 suspected Arthur's Camelot was the Stirling fortress, Scotland. Edmond Faral in 1929 also placed Arthur in Scotland the length of his three volumes published that year in Paris. The final blow to Glastonbury's claim of Arthur was struck also in New York in 1929 when Acton Griscom and Robert Ellis Jones published Geoffrey's Latin and Welsh texts at Columbia University, and located his place-names correctly in the North.

O. G. S. Crawford of Glasgow took up the challenge in 1931, again in 1935, and then when he founded *Antiquity* and sought scholars to prove or disprove Scotland's claim to Arthur. He was masterfully supported by R. L. Graeme Ritchie who at Oxford University in 1952 also situated Chrétien de Troyes beyond a shadow of a doubt in Scotland and his Arthurian personages there also. Others such as Peter Rickard (1956), Tolkien (1968), John Morris (1973), Rachel Bromwich (1978), and Kathleen Hughes (1980) of Trinity College Dublin all pointed King Arthur to Scotland.

With Roger Sherman Loomis leading, other scholars have stressed a mythological rather than a historical and geographically located King Arthur—a school that continued particularly strong until the death of Professor Loomis at Columbia University in 1966. In retrospect it seems now that King Arthur may be profitably recognized as mythological, but as no more so than other great conquerors, less so, for example, than Alexander the Great who on virtually no evidence broke the medieval hearts of the French literate public for centuries in competition to King Arthur. On second thought Arthur seems now most mythological when he appears as those beloved personages who recur, from ancient age to age: the King of the Gods, and the Father of His Country.

Sir James Frazer laid down a general law of mythology, that illustrious names are always tabooed, as in the case of Galahad/Lancelot. The injunction extended with especial severity to the names of royal dead, for which reason the name "Arthur" lay dormant so many centuries, known but seldom used, and not pronounced. The most renowned of Danish mythologists, Axel Olrik, endorsed Frazer's law, which he extended further: the names of illustrious dead are tabooed until their sanctity has evaporated. Then and only then may they be named, i.e., "King Arthur." This explains perhaps the widespread appearance of this king in the early twelfth century, until which time he had presumably remained unutterably holy.

The names of ancient kings could never be pronounced, say anthropologists; for such vocalization imperiled royal souls so deeply that the incautious person who had let slip a name must be put to death. This law extended even to the great figure's birthname, i.e., "Galahad." In ancient Eleusis, added Frazer, the names of priests could also be neither said nor written. To protect august personages, and to safeguard common people, these sacred names were often sealed and entrusted to the depths of the sea.

In order to avoid the taboo of names, people called their kings by some tribal totem, such as "bear," "lion," "fish," "ram," "raven," or "crow." At Delphi and Thebes, as in Britain, the king was called "dragon," hence Uther Pendragon, and Uther Vran (Raven). We err probably in presuming that great kings ever disappeared from memory or imagination. The reason is that their rites were transmitted, having been transmuted first into mythology, and then stored as pageants, stories, and tales. Modern mythology has set itself the task of reconstructing the intuitions of prehistoric periods. The Arthurians also survived in the form of planetary deities, as astral mythology. Their records are read in Wales by the young: the *Mabinogion,* and mnemonic devices, or *Triads.* Most importantly, however, knowledge of King Arthur has survived best in great literature.

Sir James Frazer laid down another law of mythology: the mightier the personage, the grander his name. Therefore, when Arthur's name could safely be uttered, he was accorded the highest and most respectful of Celtic titles: "King," and "Emperor."

That a literature honoring his presence as king of the Round Table fellowship should have followed, and not preceded his deposition and death, is also confirmed by the findings of Georges Dumézil studying ancient Rome. A great part of the Roman pantheon entered literature, he found, only at the time of its general dissolution. The Roman rulers or gods, like those of the Celtic tribes, belonged to a period that also witnessed long invasions by Indo-European peoples. We compare their words for *king:* Vedic *râj,* Celtic *rig,* Indo-European *reg,* Irish *ri,* and Latin *rex.* The highest priest in Rome was called "king of the rites," *rex sacrorum.* The name *queen* occurs also among the gods, as in Morrigan. (Morgan le Fay), whose name is shortened to Regan, or which occurs in Gaelic as *mor + rigain,* great queen.

Those gods who ruled on earth as kings were often replaced at certain fixed intervals, either by custom or because their strength and magical-religious potency had diminished. Some ruled for five years, others, for eight or twelve. Some were warned by comets or meteors that their tenures had elapsed. Funeral games, resembling Arthurian jousts and tournaments, or Irish horse fairs and midsummer horse races, celebrated and honored their passings. Their ghosts tended to return to earth on the seventh day of the week, the Saturday, which may have been dedicated to King Arthur as the Archer Sagittarius.

The magician Merlin, and the poet Taliesin, guaranteed Arthur's sanctity and his victories. Thus, his reign seemed an unbroken succession of royalty stretching from ages past into eons to come, permanent and stable. As by divine power, this weighty king sent about the business of his realm young substitute kings who by means of their fiery and heroic natures righted wrongs and personally redressed injuries sustained by Arthur's subjects. In times of peril the young emissaries suffered the perils of office, volunteering as Gawain volunteered when the Green Knight intruded upon the Yuletide festivity. At state occasions they might again replace the king in more onerous functions, such as ritual humiliation upon a chariot (Lancelot).

According to ancient laws of the North Teutonic peoples, a king was the easiest to recognize. Their ancient historian Saxo Grammaticus supplied what must be a picture of King Arthur. In his character an ideal king was generous, brave, and just. In body he was tireless, accomplished, and without blemish. Proven of royal kin, he was set apart also by the fine, fierce eyes of a falcon, by his shining, auburn or blond hair, his personal beauty, and refined manners. He had been duly chosen and formally acknowledged at the proper place, *which was a stone circle.*

A final piece of evidence that declares King Arthur to have been a king of the gods was mentioned by Robert Graves in *The White Goddess* (chap. 18). Welsh *Triad* no. 24 called Arthur a "Crimson-stained One of Britain," which meant that his hands and face had been dyed crimson in token of his sacred eminence.

Such a king might relinquish his throne by suicide, by abdication, assassination, captivity, or death. As battle leader he was usually short-lived, which Arthur was not. If he died a natural death, he was allowed burial upon his own ship, which was the case for King Arthur. It was not he but Lancelot who more than once attempted suicide.

The more one observes the gods, the more one is struck by that overlord who is their father. As Jupiter *(Zeu pater)* ruled his family on Olympus, so the ancient Irish Dagda was named Father and Horse in the same title: Eochaid Ollathair. The Norse Odin or Woden was called Alfadur, or All Father. In Sanskrit *Dyaus pitar* is again Father of the Gods. Those called "Father" were truly omniscient and tutelary deities: Dagda, Pwyll, Lugh, Merlin, and Arthur. The latter is furthermore the familiar, beloved *eniautos daimon,* or wounded god.

The name of the supreme god in Gaul and Ireland was frequently prefixed with the word "horse," as *Epo* (Gaulish), *Ech* (Gaelic), and *Eoh* (Anglian), but pronounced "Yo," as in the Marie de France spelling "Yonec."

The derivation of the name Arthur may very well be the ancient word "father," for in the cases of Gothic and Gaelic the initial consonant had already been dropped in those primitive languages. Thus, the word "father" in Gothic was "atta," and in Irish "athair" and "athir." The lengthening of the initial vowel "a" before the sound of "th" causes a lowering influence, which might easily insert the low dental "r" into the first syllable, thus, "Arthur." Then the Gaelic compounds "all" + "athair" > White Father. Thus, Arthur may have been also called Teutates = Father of His People, a name that has survived on altars and tombstones.

While Arthur was still venerated as a god, his name did not appear as that of any human being; for another rule of mythology, also according to Axel Olrik, states: ". . . no cult name of a god is ever used at the same time as a name for a human being." Thus, Arthur as a low and commonly used name appeared very late, or only in the twelfth century. What has remained of him can give only the most pale idea of what reverence for Arthur once was: temples, dolmens, cromlechs, hills, and stone circles that people lovingly claim were his.

Mourned over the centuries, revered as the noblest of rulers, loved as the dearest of fathers, King Arthur still wields a magic that will not be dimmed. How could he have been less than altogether some king of heaven, some god of war, a ruler of the seas, a god of light, a giver of venison, and a lord of the Zodiac?

More difficult to isolate than the real, historical King Arthur and the second, mythological king is the secret Grail King Arthur. Even so, the author of *Perlesvaus* points him out. In so doing he gives us the only clear notion of the Holy Grail, its ritual of worship, and its king.

Before he arrived at the Castle of King Fisherman, Arthur had already worshiped at four chapels (*Perlesvaus,* vol. 1):

1.   (l. 254ff.) This chapel lay a short distance from Carlisle. Arthur saw a dead hermit there after he had dismounted and entered. It was evening. The chapel lay in open fields. It was surrounded by a large cemetery. Arthur saw many coffins. This was not the chapel where Queen Guinevere had asked him to worship.

    We may assume that this was the Arthuret Church, still a lone church in open fields in front of a very large cemetery.

2.   (l. 272ff.) The queen had asked Arthur to worship in this chapel, to be found in a White Forest two days' journey from Carlisle. This second chapel was dedicated to Saint Augustine, says the text. Arthur arrived there and sat on the ground listening to the service. He was not allowed to enter, but he heard the sweet voice of a priestess officiating at the altar. Then we are given dates: 510–515. Arthur is now forty years old, and it is ten years into his reign. If his reign commenced after the victory of Mt. Badon, then the year is 510. If he was born in 475, as seems very likely, then the year is 515. The year 515 is probably the date *ad quem,* for priestesses were outlawed at Tours, France, in the years 515 and 520.

Arthur was told he had arrived outside Saint Augustine's Chapel in a remote and perilous place. This is not correct, and the ancient ritual Arthur witnessed here is known *and was published* in *Antiquity* (1940) by its discoverer, Wilhelm Levison.

Arthur really saw an early type of Mass involving in dramatic or dramatized fashion transformations: wafer into Christ child, into Christ embraced by the hermit, into the sacrificial bread. After the hermit recited prayers, the Virgin Mary appeared with her son. Arthur wept then when he saw Christ crowned with thorns. Son and Mother then vanished in flames.

One last error in the *Perlesvaus* must be corrected: the Chapel's dedicatory name, Augustine or even Augustinian, is in error for *Ninian.* The service Levison discovered was the very service performed at Saint Ninian's. The chapel at the "White Forest" is therefore Whithorn on the Galloway shore, a two days' journey by horseback from Carlisle. This was a famous, holy site before Arthur's day and dedicated to this earliest of Scottish saints at this earliest of Scottish churches, so holy a place, in fact, that each king of Scotland was, after King Arthur, obliged to worship there.

Saint Ninian's burial cave rises over the shore nearby. Richard of Ireland wrote that both Merlin and the Lady of the Lake Niniane were interred in that cave.

(No evidence allows us, thus far, to claim openly that the priest here and priestess, or Lady, were Merlin and Niniane.)

3. (1. 467ff.) Chapel three is visited not only by Arthur but by Perceval, Perceval's sister, Lancelot, and Gawain among others. It was reendowed by Arthur's half sister, the Widow Lady of Camelot; and either she was called Yglais *(église)* and/or her chapel on its four marble columns was called, as it was all over Scotland, an *eccles* church. It then contained the body of Joseph of Arimathea, which Perceval removed for safekeeping elsewhere as the Anglo-Saxon invasions worsened and Arthur's realm appeared unable to hold out much longer.

It has seemed, and seems likely still, that this chapel, which lay on a main road crossing Hadrian's Wall, was the

Saint Ninian's church and necropolis of Bannockburn on
the main Roman road into Stirling.

4. (l. 5,025 ff.) The fourth chapel is the one mistakenly translated as, and therefore called "Round Table," in reality,
a tabled rotunda *(rotonda)* well known to early travelers,
well studied, but now destroyed.

This very holy chapel, which once stood near the
mouth of the Carron River, at Falkirk, was said to have
been laid waste, or to be "Gaste," even in Arthur's day.
When he worshiped there, he saw an altar in the center
of its round, stone floor (the mark of which has appeared
on drawings of the rotunda). Arthur's Order convened
there as Merlin had planned for Uther Pendragon also
to do.

Perlesvaus tells us that the Shroud of Christ (Shroud of
Turin?) lay across the altar in "el saint monument"—this
holy monument. Perceval's sister Dandrane spent a night
alone in vigil here. The dome was open to the night sky.
She was very frightened.

Her fear, Arthur's tears, and Queen Guinevere's requests or
direction of King Arthur's spirituality all bear witness to the idea
that these various chapels were initiatory centers on the road to the
Grail Castle. King Arthur has by now undergone four stages, which
have put him significantly ahead of his questing heroes. He will
now undergo his final initiation at the Grail Castle.

The English branch 22 of *Perlesvaus* can be found as translated
by Sebastian Evans and called *The High History of the Holy Grail*
(reprinted in London, 1969) (pp. 266–70). These few pages give
the story of King Arthur's experience at the Grail Castle, and his
sight of the Grail ceremony. His trip there occurred after its recap-
ture and during its reorganization and re-Christianization.

First of all, then, Arthur donated Queen Guinevere's gold crown
to the Grail treasury (l. 7,175). Then he was escorted on a royal
tour through the new premises.

Perlesvaus calls the place where the Grail was the Castle of King
Fisherman, and not Avalon, because the anonymous author writing
at Glastonbury Abbey believes that his Abbey at Glastonbury is the
Isle of Avalon. Queen Guinevere is buried there, he thinks.

His "Castle of King Fisherman" corresponds in its geography,
surroundings, and construction, however, to the same Grail Castle

described by other Arthurian authors from the time of Chrétien de Troyes early in the twelfth century.

Arthur is at the Grail Castle: isle, river, sea, valley approach, white-clad hermits, drawbridge, castle windows, Grail Procession, bells, holy chapel, tomb of King Fisherman, great (Celtic) Cross before the entrance.

Arthur learns how the old chapel lay nearby, how the very sword that had beheaded John the Baptist was seized in Scotland from someone called "King Gurgalain." This name in Welsh would not have indicated a king, but rather a *gwr* (vassal) + *galan* (enemy), or an enemy vassal of King Gawain. Today the Church of Saint John lies on the same approach road: Douglas to Peel, Isle of Man.

King Arthur here attends Mass. At that ceremony he sees a chalice for the first time. He also sees the corporal, or linen cloth used in the Eucharist. He hears the story of Solomon's Ship. He understands that the Grail chalice is the only one in all Great Britain. He also understands the rite of baptism.

Perlesvaus tells us explicitly that Arthur alone, *and only Arthur,* ever saw the Grail *in all its five aspects* (manners, mutants). Arthur shared a sacrament that was secret.

We are warned too not to confuse the Grail Castle with Camelot. We too end by understanding that the Grail is not one object that the true initiate can see without being blinded or burned—but *five* manifestations or five objects seen in mutation ("muances"), as it were.

The Grail Castle was King Arthur's fifth and final place of worship (l. 7,232). He kept his pledge to remember the Grail chalice privately. He never recorded what he saw.

CONCLUSION: THE HOLY GRAIL

What was the Holy Grail? This question has finally been answered. It came through an understanding of the problem of *muances,* being a group of objects and phenomena associated with an early Christian worship. These objects were hallowed. They demonstrated changes of names. They were mutants like tied notes in music, or like cast-off garments, old coverings like skin, hair, feathers, and horns. Merlin said it best: he too was a moulting bird about to climb into his lofty bird cage and leave human society forever. We now understand his pun in the *Didot-Perceval* text. There occur in all life too changes of envelopes: *mutato nomine,* or a change of names. Merlin describes himself as one rare bird, a *rara avis* experiencing temporary blindness even as he looks for omens, prognostications, bird-signs *(auspicia), muances.* He will read auspices, flights of birds below the stars, and he will pray to heaven. Only one person saw all the manifestations of the Holy Grail, and all of them simultaneously.

Latin again described this Grail worship as *mutatis mutandis,* the necessary changes appearing in texts of the Holy Grail due to

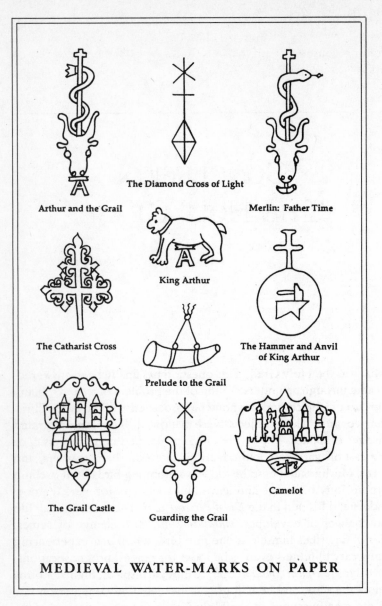

The Diamond Cross of Light

Arthur and the Grail

Merlin: Father Time

King Arthur

The Catharist Cross

The Hammer and Anvil of King Arthur

Prelude to the Grail

The Grail Castle

Guarding the Grail

Camelot

MEDIEVAL WATER-MARKS ON PAPER

several misapprehensions on the worshipers' parts, one of which was this, troubling temporary blindness. The Questers went blind from nervousness, apprehension, and shock. Their sudden loss of vision was aggravated by sudden flames, hot flares, and brilliant lights, which dazzled. They made the initiates close their eyes.

Another sort of confused, addled reporting came quite simply from dullness on Perceval's part, or Gawain's, as from a guilty conscience on Lancelot's. Thus, more than once, each candidate violated the taboo of food in purgatory, ate a good supper, enjoyed the candies afterward, and next morning found himself and his horse abandoned. It was never easy to attend services at the Grail Castle.

Hallucinogenics compounded the problem for Lancelot and his cousin Yvain. They both cringed before awful visions of boiling fountains, sudden eruptions of bluebirds, and ravening lions.

The readers' problems all along, as they have for centuries tried to understand all this prehistoric lore, have been compounded by language not only ancient and foreign to them, but also misread and mistranslated by earlier attempts. We now see perhaps that the Grail and its ancient initiatory centers lie all about us still, some on bare stones like the necropolis on Saint Patrick's Isle, others as bare, stone cradles like Montségur, others overwhelming architecture like San Juan de la Peña, and La Seo Cathedral in Valencia. Rosslyn Chapel outside Edinburgh still will show visitors its Apprentice Pillar, which contains *the* Holy Grail, they know there. Initiate Knights Templar are still invested there into that ancient, holy Order of the Grail. The worship of the Holy Grail survives, thus, in foreign parts and sites. Poor textual scholarship will be renewed and remedied as one regains faith.

Appetites cannot predominate, the candidates must learn, or suffer punishment. All will occur in darkness and by candlelight. The white of robes, the flash of gold on the sword, the low murmur of organ music, the soft sound of feet as the processional climbs the altar steps, the beating of hearts, the raising of arms before the Grand Prior or Master; and the ceremony continues under the quick, bright flashing of banners once Merlin's and Arthur's.

Other difficulties ensue. Human memory is so faulty that under the pressure of darkness and the dazzle of fires all that can be recalled are brief pictures of a white cloth, a cross, a sword, and formal, ancient words. Shadowy seniors stand mute behind the candidates, in dark side aisles. Thus, memory and eyewitness testimony both fail. Fatigue is another factor experienced by Gawain, Perceval, and Lancelot after so many months, even years, of hard, painful questing. Tension and apprehension also diminished the candidates' efforts to describe and recall. All they remembered sometimes was the clang of the drawbridge, which almost cut their horses in two.

Even the mainline heroes were invariably unable to narrate comprehensible accounts of their experiences in the Grail Castle itself. First of all, each had despaired of ever finding it. And one despairs today before finally arriving at the foot of Montségur where the road ends at its still village and few houses.

Gawain succeeded rather better by comparison, said Heinrich, but then, Gawain was a king. So, no wonder. Even Lancelot admitted failure finally, and we shall never understand the depth of his grief. Perceval claimed a success that quite possibly he never actually achieved. How otherwise can one today grasp the disappearance of the Grail from Great Britain on the one hand, and the dispersion overseas of his family and male heir on the other? Queen Guinevere, who wore a crown tattoo on her hip, and who was probably the golden-crowned goddess whom Gawain saw finally as he completed his Grail Quest, also disappeared soon thereafter and from the Grail Castle. At least, she was last seen alive then and there. Tristan apparently pleaded nolo contendere. Priestesses such as Morgan le Fay, Kundry or Cundrie, Dandrane, Repanse de Schoye, and Esclarmonde were phased out by bloodletting, marriage, or murder. Knowledge of Arabic and astronomy was no recommendation. Their archives survived, rewritten over and over, as Arthurian literature, almost worldwide by now.

Gawain must remain as the second most successful quester. Of them all, King Arthur was first. Not even the splendid victories in twelve battles followed by a sometimes estimated peace of twenty years can explain the aura of reverence and awe that separates ourselves from King Arthur. It is meanwhile perfectly true that he was so beloved by Scots and Welshmen that the Anglo-Saxons borrowed him for their very own hero and still hold him for themselves, buried beside Queen Guinevere, they say, in Glastonbury.

Surely, no victor elsewhere has been so adored for so long by the very peoples he kept back and conquered. He forbade their entry into Scotland there along Hadrian's Wall.

Its commanders witnessed Arthur's coronation and his queen's. Just north of Hadrian's Wall, but, as distance goes today, really adjacent to it, lay Arthur's preliminary initiation centers: The Grail or Arthuret Church; Whithorn Church, or the *Candida Casa,* which no longer exists except for a few stones; Saint Ninian's Church on the Bannockburn battlefield below Stirling Castle in upper Scotland, and Saint Ninian's Cave on the Rhinns of Galloway where today the Catholic church holds services sometimes on summer Sundays. Pilgrims holding the hands of lots of little children trudge up and down the forest path.

Only Arthur also survived "three days under the stone," say the Welsh annals, which must refer to some extraordinarily painful ordeal of initiation. Thus, only King Arthur, says *Perlesvaus,* saw the Grail in its five *muances.* He was, then, both king and High Priest after Merlin.

What changes of name constitute the five aspects of the Grail, or what five objects were used in worship of the Holy Grail? They are:

1. Chalice (vase, vessel, *calice, calix, calyx,* or cup); in three Romance languages the word *Graal* means chalice.
2. *Tailleoir* or *tailleor* (silver platter, or silver knives).
3. Sword and/or broken sword.
4. Spear, or lance.
5. Book, or Gospel (secret book, words, gospel). This is directly attributed to several personages: Jesus, John the Beloved Disciple, Solomon, John the Baptist, and others, such as John of the Apocalypse.

In short, every one of the five, principal *muances* or hallows derives from Jesus, his life, and his death. The chalice caught his Precious Blood, treasured it, and eventually held the Eucharist. The silver platter and/or knives, as Wolfram understood it, related to Merlin, who was Arthur's cousin and his prime minister, as to the John the Baptist, whose life-style Merlin adopted because that John heralded the coming of Christ. In the Grail Quest Gawain not only fetched the sword that had beheaded John the Baptist, but also failed to mend it when it was broken. The spear or lance appeared clearly as a dread object much to be revered because once Longinus pierced with his spear the side of Christ on the Cross.

The Book participated in order to distinguish the medieval figure of Ecclesia as she is sculpted on cathedrals, but primarily because she was Arthur's sister and Perceval's mother, Eccles (Yglais in

French). Her New Law stands then in contradistinction to the Old Law, or Old Testament, represented by the equally lovely Synagoga also sculpted and revered in medieval cathedrals.

One understands with what impact any part, pages, or book of the New Testament fell upon the far-out, pagan world of Roman Gaul, Roman Britain, Roman Spain. These were the prosperous, far distant outposts of the Roman Empire—and for much more than five hundred years. Such treasured pages, or book, set about, from their first reading, establishing the new religion derived from Judaism. This book therefore started in Jerusalem, and truly with King Solomon. It was his sword and his ship that symbolically brought the refugees flying to the western ends of the earth. Their names, lives, and teachings are as revered today as in A.D. 70—Saint Mary Magdalene, the Saints Mary of the Sea, Saints Lazarus, Joseph of Arimathea, James, Lawrence, Philip, and Bartholomew, and then Saint Dubricius, called Merlin.

This is not to deny the great importance of those supernumeraries who attended each Grail ceremony wherever it took place. One constant adjunct is light in all that night and darkness, the Grail always being celebrated in a great, dark castle hall lit by fireplaces until maidens or squires bearing superb candelabra entered in solemn procession and measured step. A procession including royal maidens always figures in this worship, as seen by Don Quixote, and the Kings Lancelot, Gawain, Perceval, and Arthur. Then a white dove flies in perhaps from the same window or doorway, so that to the seated congregants it appears to fall always, a descending dove, often considered the Holy Spirit. The most beautiful descending dove in the world flies from the heart of a blue flower in the east window of the Arthuret Church, Longtown, Cumbria. Objects such as the most revered chalice are placed upon an ark, an altar, a stone that is sometimes a precious jewel. The Grail is then called a reliquary, for it contains blood or bread. Both contents bring to mind again silver platter and knives. We go in circles, it is true.

The wounded Christ must be the sadly suffering Fisher King fishing for souls, which is Christ's name in Greek, and too it recalls his fishermen who became Apostles at their lake in Israel—to Lancelot's lake in Britain. Taking vows also the Grail heroes depart later as Dark Age Apostles to their earthly kingdoms, or abroad. Thus, a procession always occurs prior to the entrance of the Grail, and it continues a yearly tradition today among the gypsies in the

Camargue as among the Knights Templar wherever they are rein-vested now. Today the ancient ship of Solomon still also figures as the church. At its commencement in western Europe the letter *alpha* recurred for holy persons and holy places.

A second, most holy place is the Perilous Cemetery or necropolis named Aliscans in southern France, or Avalon in Britain, but in any case *Atre* perilous where a horrid ghost rises up to terrify the Quester. An ancient necropolis lies beside the ruined churches on Saint Patrick's Isle, opposite the town of Peel, Isle of Man, and around the Arthuret church. The Field of Ashes also rests some-where below the peak of Montségur, as beside the ruins of Glaston-bury Abbey, and enfolds the lone church standing high at Arthuret, near Camelot/Carlisle. Each site was perilous because it was a dread entrance into purgatory. All great heroes sooner or later braved its terrors, as did the great women of religion including the Virgin Mary and Queen Guinevere.

The first time Lancelot saw the queen in the Grail Castle, she stood between two "copper" pillars that were green like her eyes but were carved from precious malachite and topped with gilded capitals. Identical, royal columns, also reaching from floor to ceil-ing, stand today, exactly as described in the *Prose Lancelot,* in the czar's green palace in St. Petersburg, now called Hermitage Mu-seum. Copper always points the way, say folklorists, to an under-world entrance. Here and there are horrifyingly contiguous.

The British Grail Castle where King Arthur and his entourage worshiped stood on a western islet adjacent to the ancient, oracular center, Isle of Man, never conquered nor occupied by Romans.

When at the Manx millennium the King of Norway visited Man in 1979, which the Vikings began to occupy and loot around the year 800, he had a map drawn showing their route from Norway to Man (see page 303).

This Grail Castle, then, stood in that lake which was the stormy Irish Sea. Alternate Grail Castles such as Montségur, Mount of Security, in the Oriental Pyrenees, and the Spanish Montserrat, which was in medieval times also alternately called Montsalvat, Mount of Salvation, crowned high mountains. Montserrat was like Glastonbury and Holy Trinity Abbey in Fécamp, Normandie, a great Spanish, Benedictine abbey of the eleventh century. Sara-gossa in Spain is the closest rival to Rosslyn Chapel in Scotland, however, the cathedral in Saragossa conquered by the Goths in the fifth century and called El Pilar. The Apprentice Column or Pillar in Rosslyn Chapel is still today said to contain the Holy Grail inside its white, sculptured stone. That Grail is further thought to be a silver platter.

The sculptured tombs Queen Guinevere commissioned are to be seen today in her ancient Pictish land, northeastern Scotland, from Stirling northward almost to Aberdeen. Thus, a wide geographic area attests today to what may once have been a reverence for, if not a universal worship of, the Holy Grail.

In 1937 Julius Evola addressed the problem of the Grail heredity in his book on "the mystery" of the Grail, a valuable work edited for a third time in 1972. He discovered five major and very prominent heirs: (1) Knights Templar, (2) Catharists, (3) Dante and the Ghibellines, (4) followers everywhere of the hermetic traditions of occult wisdom, and (5) Rosicrucians, who champion secret learning and who meet presently in Catharist sites. These followers or heirs of Grail worship continued it and renewed it widely with no particular concern for its Arthurian, Scottish origin.

In 1974 at Paris Charles Roy addressed the dissemination question, pointing out that Grail worship spread abroad widely from six major sources: (1) from the many Benedictine houses throughout Europe, from Glastonbury and Fécamp precisely as well as from Scotland's Deare Abbey founded a few years only after King Arthur's death; (2) from ancient Christian sites that continued popular with pilgrims in large numbers: Marseilles, Aliscans, Lyons, Brittany, Spain, and Ireland; (3) from Angevin royals and nobles who traveled widely and married widely in France, England, Spain, Italy, and the Holy Land; (4) from the beloved troubadours in Provence and the Languedoc; (5) from the ten major and many other minor authors and/or translators of Grail texts at Oxford, at Beauvais and Troyes in France, at Burgundy, and at Monmouth as well as elsewhere in Wales; and (6) from the world-famous Jewish schools such as Toulouse, Montpellier, Narbonne, Toledo, and Troyes.

Three French scholars of the twentieth century have notably pushed back the dark waters surrounding Arthurian literature, so muddied, in fact, that they had virtually drowned King Arthur or proven him a myth only. The first has been the honored, French theologian Etienne Gilson, who delivered Powell Lectures at Indiana University; and they were published and widely read (1941 and 1955). "Just as the Greeks are our masters of philosophy," Gilson said, we must keep firmly in mind that "the Jews are our masters in religion" (pp. 40–41). Both Augustinians and Cistercians (like Geoffrey of Monmouth) saw in this tradition of a Holy Grail and its quest a prime instance of their belief: only love of God, and that alone, leads to beatitude. Only love works to bring man a vision of the Grail, which is God, said their old theologian Guillaume de Saint-Thierry: "In visione Dei, ubi solus amor operatur . . ." Thus, the sight of the Grail was seeing God. The Questers were blinded by it. The young priestesses wept loudly. It amounted to the highest of mystical experiences.

Such was very probably the "face" that the Knights Templar were so violently accused of "kissing." Frank Tribble has already shown that the Templars, and their Commander Geoffrey de Charny, for years may have had possession of the Shroud of Turin. The face of Jesus is seen on the Shroud. Thus, their practice was also a means to a sight of God's only begotten son. The Templars refused answers to questions; and like the Catharists whom they refused also to attack, persecute, or burn, they stood firm perhaps for their freedom to worship some world-famous relic. The Grail and its worship, continued Etienne Gilson, originated in Jerusalem. Our own search has commenced there.

In fact, he continued, in Cistercian works like Geoffrey of Monmouth's *History of the Kings of Britain* (1136), all is underlain with feeling as well as with knowledge. The central theme of such works turns out to be Grace via the ecstasies of such love as Madre Theresa felt for her sisters. Grace is the meaning of the Grail. Its first apparition therefore came in the city of Jerusalem itself, on the eve of Pentecost when baptism occurred as the Holy Ghost descended in fire on the Apostles. John the Baptist had predicted it. Thus, Pentecost remained King Arthur's principal holy day.

The Grail's origin lies in the Acts of the Apostles (2:2):

> And when the day of Pentecost was fully come, they were all with one accord in one place. And suddenly there came a sound from heaven, as of a rushing mighty wind, and it filled all the house where they were sitting. And there appeared unto them cloven tongues like as of fire, and it sat upon each of them.

And the prophet Joel said that God promised to pour forth his Spirit on all flesh: sons, daughters, young men, old men, servants, and handmaidens. Whoever calls upon the Lord shall be saved.

The reward of Questers is such an experience, an "open sight" of God, adds Gilson, or to see the Grail "trestot descovert," said Gawain—all uncovered. Lancelot failed because he was able to summon only dreams of the Grail, which constitute a low level of mystical experience. Both Perceval and Galahad—there is even more evidence—wore red to symbolize the fires of baptism, those flames always seen by witnesses and participants after the full Grail Procession.

The long-awaited Galahad performed superbly divine acts because he bathed in the Grace of God. We must understand, concluded Gilson, that theologically speaking, God's secrets like the Grail are accessible to mankind only through Grace.

Now, the Grail Quest was surely a search for God's secrets, hence a search for that ecstatic moment before the Quester was blinded. All were, like Saint Theresa and Don Quixote, searchers after spirituality. The searchers' beauty was not so much flesh as spiritual; Saint Bernard of Clairvaux might have so described Galahad: "spiritualis tamen potius quam carnalis." Thus, key words in all Grail texts are: search, ask, look, understand, be shown openly, see openly.

Dante followed another movement very discernible not only in *Peredur* but also strongly reinforced by the *Perceval Continuations,* which bear witness: the shunting aside of priestesses, or the murder of women teachers. They were queens and "goddesses": Guinevere and Morgan le Fay, Sigune, Dandrane, Cundrie, Repanse de Schoye, and Viscountess Esclarmonde. Similarly, in *The Divine Comedy* Beatrice, emerald-eyed like Guinevere, leaves off guiding the traveler. She is replaced by the silver-tongued theologian Saint Bernard of Clairvaux, who founded the Cistercian Order and also the Knights Templar.

The persistence of the Grail in ancient Christianity down the ages, even if it dwelled among such impossibly poor theologians as the Catharist Esclarmonde, tends to suggest that reverence of it indicates a religious movement that was quasi-universal. The old religion held that God was inside man, or, as Leo Tolstoy called his book on theology, *The Kingdom of God Is Within You* (1893). Like the Grail Bearers, Questers, and Templars, Tolstoy took aristocracy seriously. The Catharists brought religion down to the common man who, like the American Puritans arriving in the early 1620s in the Massachusetts Bay Colony, decided to offer education to all persons equally and free of charge for twelve years.

This heritage from King Arthur's candidature at the Grail Castle implied answering obvious contradictions apparent to all persons on earth. Why was man, who was created by God, often wretched, homeless, and prostrate? How to reconcile the majesty of the deity with the misery of mankind? How to synchronize dogma and life? Do we not need an aristocracy of the spirit? Do we not long for an end to vulgarity, and, in exchange, a nobler vision than that of war, cinema, and television? Do not our spirits require uplifting? What and where is our peace?

A history of the Grail and its inheritors leads to the knowledge that religious bigotry causes murders of the most valuable, most highly educated persons of any society: Arthur's priestesses, Catharist women leaders and ministers, Jewish artists, scholars, and doctors century after century culminating in Adolf Hitler's rule of Nazi Germany. Those massacred indiscriminately could claim high social status, but neither achievement nor position could save them. In the case of the Knights Templar, even service to the death, and poverty, failed likewise to save them. These massacred peoples have today principally only the voices of Jewish and other such authors from York, from Oxford, from Jerusalem, from Troyes, and from Toledo to narrate for them the Holy Grail ceremonies that link Judaism and Christianity, Synagoga herself to Ecclesia.

Such great authors left us, concluded our second French scholar, Charles Roy (Paris, 1974), a worldwide imagery that dreaming or awake unites all human beings. We all recognize the Grail Castle, first of all, as symbol of the human heart: "Defend, O God, this castle of my heart . . ." In my castle are many mansions, repeated Saint Theresa so sweetly, so memorably. Secondly, we all recognize the Swan Knight Lohengrin, who rescued women dispossessed, says Barbara Walker, "by new patriarchal laws" (p. 411). But the swan also bore two lovely children: Sunset and Dawn. As the Roman Cycnus, the swan symbolized the poet, who is the greatest of all literary artists, and who dying sings for us the sweetest of all notes. The dove also symbolizes the spirit, as the ox symbolizes the Grail Castle, as the bear symbolizes Arthur's courage and paternity. Woman to Catharists as to Arthurians was teacher, prophet, warrior, queen, goddess, and in Guinevere's case, angel also.

The Grail itself figured multiplied almost endlessly: cup, chalice, reliquary, ciborium, emerald, heart, neolithic stone. There were four degrees in initiation at the Grail ceremony, claims Roy, but they involved ascending approaches to holiness, such as: baptism at the spring or sacred fountain, a halt at the Arthuret baptistery, long and lonely exile from Arthur's Court, quest as instructions sought from one teacher to another more learned than the preceding, worship at a stone perron of countless ages past, and the hearing of the word *AUM* and sound of the earth's creation.

All this was passed on before memories faded by our authors of the precious, best Grail manuscripts painfully copied from abbeys and first universities such as Toulouse, and then Paris, Montpellier, and Oxford. Authors understood the Church Father Origen's early instruction, that great literature may be read on three levels, each corresponding to the reader's maturity: (1) literally according to his physical maturity, (2) allegorically according to his soul's development, and (3) mystically as the spirit apprehends the world more clearly. As always, great literature rests upon the unshakable principles of liberalism and individualism, also agrees Roy (p. 260ff.). But it may also be both hermetic and enigmatic, for which added reasons it reaches immortality as life on earth goes.

The ten or so major texts concerning the Holy Grail have long set a record of continuous popularity at home and abroad for over one thousand years by now. Their origin, however, stretches back to the lifetime of Christ, and then backward again.

The Holy Grail has become by itself a mystique of history. As we have seen by its passage from one land to another, from one century to another, from one high point of reverence to a following full massacre of millions, then history must be a perpetual recommencement (p. 265).

As they descend the eons before recorded time, the old respect and love of ancestors is displayed at each Grail necropolis. Beside each Grail Castle of the heart, stands the person of King Arthur. He is the father "figure," or metaphor, we say. He is also our *atavus,* our personal great-great-great-grandfather. This atavism on the readers' parts too makes us all sons and kings' daughters, as the Romans also knew. We were royal like Arthur, *atavis regibus,* our forefathers having been kings before us. Having heard the Acts read from the pulpit, certain young persons take happily to Latin as their truly native language, even today, fortunately and despite television.

Lancelot's extreme atavism set him to removing the graves of his fathers to places of greater safety—presumably to the eastern and always unconquered Highlands of Scotland. They stand there today.

Her equally driving atavism set Guinevere to learn to read and write, and to commission sculptures for these tombs. So justly her own funeral monument stands today in Meigle, Scotland. Both she and Lancelot metaphorically tried to ascend the mountain of their Dark Age, Celestial Jerusalem. Both sought the mystery of the "Word" from John the Beloved Disciple, and the Catharists, after them, and the Knights Templar also, and the Rosicrucians. They thus linked their Christianities to Hebrew teachings before them, as to others before even them. Their Waste Land was another Promised Land. What was their Grail Quest if not mankind waiting for Godot as the modern, beloved Irish Samuel Beckett saw it? Was it not Everyman's journey, every prodigal son in exile far from home, in search of God?

Our third French scholar is Dr. A. Barthélémy from Toulouse, who in his book *Le Graal* of 1987 opened wide the doors to a new approach to this fascinating subject (his conclusions, p. 237ff.). First, he dispelled the fear Arthurian scholars have long felt before the problem of chronology in Grail texts. Must we not study the texts in order of their writing? They have thought so.

No, answered Barthélémy.

As we know, he wrote, the major Grail texts all derive from the few years, more or less emerge, between 1170 and 1220. We have been forced to consider Chrétien's and Wolfram's first texts first. Now, if we treat them first as scholars have always done, then the Grail and its worship are pagan, or other, but in no way Christian. If they are not Christian, then what are they? Early in our century Jessie L. Weston said it for all of us: the texts are pagan and if not Celtic, then Iranian, or Arabic, or Hindu, or Yogic, and so on. No Christian symbolism was intended by either Chrétien or Wolfram, for little or none such is present, of course. Wolfram calls the Grail a stone, for instance, and not a chalice.

Then if we consider Robert de Boron as following Chrétien, he can be dismissed, as did Gaston Paris, insisting he was nothing more than a clever "re-arranger" of better men's works. But what if Robert de Boron really wrote his texts in isolation, in Burgundy, as he stipulated? What if he was, in that sense, first? Both he and the three so-called Continuators of Chrétien present deeply Christian Grail texts. Heinrich follows the First, or Pseudo-Wauchier, Continuator closely, and also presents Gawain's final Grail encounter as reverently Christian (Roach, vol. 1, v. 13, p. 141ff.).

What difference do one's dates make when (1) Chrétien's and

Wolfram's are merely the first manuscripts we have to date, not necessarily the first, and (2) their dates are only hypothetical at best or boast the weight of opinion of only certain scholars who may have been biased, or irreligious, and/or anti-Christian anyway?

Our format in this Holy Grail book has been much inspired, thus, by Barthélémy. We began with Jerusalem and sought confirmation in certain Grail texts. Then going to Marseilles we followed the Apostles from Jerusalem after the fall of the Celestial City in A.D. 70. By studying those two great centers we found our Grail themes more or less already established: John the Baptist, the necropolis, the cave, book, temple, gospel, ship, procession, reliquary, lance, vessel, goddess, and platter or knives. The Glastonbury chapter added: Grail Castle on an island, Queen Guinevere, Grail Bearers, priestesses, and broken sword. Spain seconded the earlier themes: cave, necropolis, otherworld, knife, procession, and question, and added Grail Queen. France, which was chapter 5, added the mythology surrounding Lancelot's person, Precious Blood, silver platter or bowl, and the White Deer as founder of an abbey in France and later in Scotland (Holy Rood), and corroborated Jewish authorship, chalice, relics, book, knife, and lance. Chapter 6 on Parsifal in Germany added the Grail Castle on a mountain, the severed head, the death of the witches or teachers, the secret gospel known to Merlin above all other priests, the Grail table as a garnet, and the Grail as a stone with writing carved on it, and repeated the story of the spear, the author as Jews from Toledo and Jerusalem, and the new Grail Queen as Repanse de Schoye rather than Queen Guinevere.

In chapter 7 we encountered recorded history again, as Knights Templar recurred in connection with Catharists, both perhaps worshiping a Grail-type religion, and we saw how both Templars and Catharists suffered death for their beliefs. Here again the Grail Castle and its necropolis also were located on a prominent mountain in the wasteland become a high, desolate range of the Oriental Pyrenees. Here we met a newer explanation, or an older one, connecting the Virgin Mary to the British Grail Castle of the Horn, Corbenic. Here again we met names proscribed or tabooed, sun worship by solar heroes, their treasure of a secret book, Christ's book again, and real tombs of dead Catharists in real caves where Rosicrucians worship today.

We concluded the search with Gawain's successful initiation at the Grail Castle, an investiture narrated by Heinrich von dem

Türlin and the first *Chrétien Continuation. Perlesvaus* from Glaston-bury's ancient Abbey concluded with King Arthur's sight of the five *muances,* all Christian hallows. He was the Grail King.

That King Arthur was the Grail King comes home so graphically as one enters the Arthuret Church, which stands on his tribal land, adjacent to Hadrian's Wall, adjacent also to the city of Carlisle, which more than one hundred references in Arthurian manuscripts allege was King Arthur's Camelot. Residents in Longtown, Carlisle, in which community the Church stands alone in its fields, corrobo-rate the findings here in this book. They point to the bed of the Esk River, which once flowed along the edge of the high bank, and Michael Hill, upon which the ancient churches were built, de-stroyed, and the last one rebuilt by King James VI of Scotland around 1100.

The present Church, which dates from the early Middle Ages, then, contains an older Falling Dove of the Holy Grail atop its east window. The sight of it behind the banners and ensigns of the Lords Lieutenant of Cumbria, now Sir Charles and Lady Graham, melts the heart. The white dove descends from a mandala, or blue flower with azure petals. This is in the daylight. At night the dove surges forth from the stained glass depictions of the All Angels and St. Michael and Apostles below it, like a luminous live spirit of ancient faith. Finally the rising moon behind the window shines ghostly through the blue flower and seems to urge the dove to speak in tongues to us.

From Longtown the most lovely Grail Procession started on Thursday morning, September 12, 1991, along the two-lane mac-adam road, to the Arthuret Church. The file was led by the school-teacher.

The teacher apologized: "We know," she said, "that we are not invited to come here today. We know that we were invited to come to the Flower Festival in honor of King Arthur on Saturday next. I am sorry, but *we could not wait.*"

Behind her filed first the littlest of her little children. With happy smiles they climbed at once upon the lap of the author, one after the other. Settling themselves down comfortably, with small voices they told her, "We have brought a piece of paper for you to sign." They processed after that up and down the Church aisles and smelled the flowers, and laid fingers on the feathers of the descending doves.

From September 12 to 15 the Arthuret Church was filled with flower representations, and this will be an annual event, of King Arthur as the Hammer King, of King Arthur at his greatest victory of Mount Badon, and sadly, with red carnations for his blood, of King Arthur among the broken helmets and broken swords at his final battlefield adjacent to this Church.

Residents of Longtown, for Arthuret is a parish on King Arthur's tribal land, and a lone church within the Diocese of Carlisle, had carefully prepared evidence. They supported the findings of this Grail book. "See where the Esk River used to come right up to this ancient landing place," they urged. "This very likely was where the body of the dying King was ferried downstream from Camlan to this sacred Saint Michael's Hill." They also brought with them ancient papers from their now unknown authors to prove it.

The residents have founded their own Arthurian Society of Longtown, Cumbria. They claim King Arthur as resident of Carlisle and as buried in their own and his own Church. They also celebrate his entourage, and Merlin especially, whose baptistery is also adjacent, as has long been known. They celebrated with splendid flower representations that reached from floors to ceilings in many displays—Lancelot, Queen Guinevere, and other knights of the Round Table. They remembered all the noble Questers, and their mothers who dowered churches. This Church has a tradition of placing flowers on all its graves every Sunday. Nobody knows why this has been for the ages their unique tradition. But one can guess.

At Arthuret Church, with its Cross dating back to the year 800, and its undergrounds dating back to Arthur's age, folk tradition flows in its own channels to its own glory and celebration of the ancient past. "We want our children to know their own past," they say, and the school executives and teachers agree.

Every pew along the central aisle of the Arthuret Church was decorated with the falling dove of the Holy Grail, white satin ribbons, and a white lily for King Arthur, the Grail King.

Medieval Grail Texts

This chart presents medieval Grail texts as first listed by Alfred Nutt in his book *Studies of the Legends of the Holy Grail with Especial Reference to the Hypothesis of its Celtic Origin* (London, 1888), Chapters 1 and 2.

ORIGINAL
LANGUAGE

Old French

1. *Conte du Graal,* 60,000 verses, also known as *Conte del Graal,* in four parts:
   1) *Conte du Graal* by Chrétien de Troyes (also known as *Perceval*)
   2) *Conte du Graal* by Gautier de Doulens (also known as *Continuation*)
   3) *Conte du Graal* by Manessier (also known as *Continuation*)
   4) *Conte du Graal* by Gerbert (also known as *Continuation*)

Old High German

2. *Parzival* by Wolfram von Eschenbach

Old High German

3. *Diu Crône* by Heinrich von dem Türlin (also known as *The Crown*)

Old French

4. *Didot-Perceval* (also known as *Petit Saint Graal*)

Welsh

5. *Mabinogion,* "Peredur" (ab Evrawc)

English

6. *The Thornton MS, Sir Perceval de Galles*

Old French

7. *Queste del Saint Graal* (also known as *Y Seint Graal*)

Old French

8. *Grand-Saint-Graal* (also known as *Grand St. Graal,* and as *History of the Holy Grail*)

Old French

9. *Joseph d'Arimathie* by Robert de Boron (Borron) in two parts:
   1) *Joseph d'Arimathie* or *Arimathea* (also

known as *Le Roman de l'estoire dou Graal*)

    2) *Merlin*

Old French   10. *Perlesvaus* (also known as *Perceval le Gallois*, and as *The High History of the Holy Grail*)

Checklist of Secondary Sources

The authors' names followed by a date indicating an early publication.

Paris, G.	1856	Guest	1932
Villemarqué	1862	Krappe	1933
Paris, P.	1868	Rahn	1933
Glennie, J. S. S.	1869	Johnstone	1934
Zimmer	1884	Rappoport	1934
Rhys	1891	Crawford	1935
Maury	1896	Evola	1937
Evans	1898	Jackson	1938
Weston	1901	Loomis, L. H.	1938
Nitze	1902	Newstead	1939
Nutt	1902	Piggott	1941
Kempe	1905	Belperron	1942
Maynardier	1907	Brown	1943
Waite	1909	Paton	1943
Peebles	1911	Zumthor	1943
Loth	1912	Holmes	1948
Lot	1918	Donnelly	1949
Gilson	1921	Tatlock	1950
Pauphilet	1921	Ritchie	1952
Scudder	1921	Klemke	1959
Loomis, R. S.	1926	Adolf	1960
Chambers	1927	Ashe	1960
Faral	1929	Locke	1960
Griscom	1929	Bromwich	1961
Jones	1929	Goodrich	1963
Brinkley	1932	Stoker	1963

Marx	1965	Goetinck	1975
Fletcher	1966	Weinraub	1975
Olschki	1966	Bordonove	1977
Toynbee	1969	Frappier	1977
Frappier	1972	Cavendish	1978
Gallais	1972	Senior	1979
Carman	1973	Kennedy	1980
Merriman	1973	Tolstoy, N.	1985
Morris	1973	Barthélémy	1987
Owen, D.	1973	Burks and Gilbert	1987
Alcock	1974	Currer-Briggs	1987
Roy	1974	Querido	1988
Entwhistle	1975		

Selected Bibliography

ABRIL, MANUEL. *La filosofía de Parsifal* (Madrid, 1914).
ADAM OF DOMERHAM. *Historia de rebus Glastoniensibus* (c. 1290), 2 vols., ed. by Thomas Hearne (Oxford, 1727).
ADAMS, HENRY. *Le Mont-Saint-Michel and Chartres* (New York, 1913).
ADOLF, HELEN. *Visio Pacis. Holy City and Grail* (Pennsylvania, 1960).
ADORNO, THEODOR W. *Versuch über Wagner* (Frankfort, 1903, 1969). See *In Search of Wagner*, trans. by Rodney Livingstone (London, 1981).
ALAIN DE LILLE (ALANUS DE INSULIS). *De Fide catholica contra haereticos sui temporis.* In J. P. Migne's *Patrologiae Cursus Completus*, vol. 210. Written before 1202.
ALBRECHT VON SCHARFENBERG. *Der Jüngere Titurel*, ed. by Werner Wolf (Bern, 1952).
ALESSON, JEAN. *Les Femmes décorées de la Légion d'Honneur et les femmes militaires* (Paris, 1888).
ALISCANS, ed. by F. de Montaiglon and A. de Montaiglon (Paris, 1870).
ALLEAU, RENÉ. *De la nature des symboles* (Paris, 1958).
AMADOR DE LOS RÍOS, JOSÉ. *Historia social, política y religiosa de los Judios de España y Portugal* (Madrid, 1960).
ANDERSON, FLAVIA. *The Ancient Secret* (London, 1953).
ANDERSON, MARJORIE O. *Kings and Kingship in Early Scotland* (Edinburgh and London, 1980).
ANITCHKOF, EUGÈNE. "Le Galaad du *Lancelot-Graal* et les Galaads de la Bible." *Romania* LIII (1927): 388ff.
———. "Le Saint Graal et les aspirations religieuses du XIIe siècle." *Romania* LVIII (1932): 274–86.
ANNALS OF WALES, *ANNALES CAMBRIAE*, ed. by John ab Ithel Williams (1860) and by Egerton Phillmore (1888). See also the

Welsh Triads, *Trioedd Ynys Prydein,* ed. by Rachel Bromwich (Cardiff, 1961, 1979).

ANWYL, SIR EDWARD. *Ancient Celtic Deities.* In *Transactions of the Celtic Society of Inverness* (Inverness, Scotland, 1921).

APPIA, ADOLPHE. *Music and the Art of the Theatre* (Miami, 1962).

AQUINAS, SAINT THOMAS. *Summa Theologica.* In J. P. Migne's *Patrologiae Cursus Completus,* 2nd series, vol. 3.

ARNOLD, MATTHEW. "Hebraism and Hellenism." In *The Portable Matthew Arnold,* ed. by Lionel Trilling, pp. 557–73 (New York, 1949).

ARON, R. *Les Années obscured de Jésus* (Paris, 1960).

ARTHUR (English verse from the Marquis of Bath's MS), ed. by Frederick J. Furnivall (London, 1864).

ASHE, GEOFFREY. *Camelot and the Vision of Albion* (New York, 1971).

ASHE, GEOFFREY, LESLIE ALCOCK, C. A. RALEGH RADFORD, PHILIP RAHTZ, AND JILL RACY. *The Quest for Arthur's Britain* (London and New York, 1968).

AUGUSTINE, SAINT. "Confessions" (book 7). In *The Works of Aurelius Augustine,* trans. by Rev. Marcus Dodds (Edinburgh, 1876).

AZORÍN, GARCIA MERCADAL. *La Ruta de Don Quijote* (Madrid, 1985).

BAIGENT, MICHAEL, AND RICHARD LEIGH. *The Temple and the Lodge* (New York, 1989).

BAIGENT, MICHAEL, RICHARD LEIGH, AND HENRY LINCOLN. *Holy Blood, Holy Grail* (Great Britain, 1982, 1983; New York, 1983).

BAILEY, JAMES R. *The God Kings and the Titans. The New World Ascendancy in Ancient Times* (New York, 1973).

BALCH, H. E. *Mendip—The Great Cave of Wookey-Hole* (Bristol and London, 1947).

BARBER, MALCOLM. *The Trial of the Templars* (Cambridge and London, 1978).

BARCLAY, WILLIAM. *The Mind of Jesus* (New York, 1960, 1961, 1976).

———. *The Gospel of John,* 2 vols. (Edinburgh, 1955, 1956; Philadelphia, 1975).

BARING-GOULD, SABINE. *Curious Myths of the Middle Ages* (London, Oxford, and Cambridge, 1873). See app. B (p. 641ff.), "Mountain of Venus."

———. *Lives of the British Saints,* 16 vols. (London, 1914).

BARTHÉLÉMY, DR. A. *Au XIIe siècle. Le Graal, sa première révélation* (Toulouse, 1987).

BARTO, PHILIP STEPHAN. "The Subterranean Grail Paradise of Cervantes." *PMLA* XXXVIII, no. 2 (June 1923): 401–11.

BARZUN, JACQUES. *Race. A Study in Modern Superstition* (New York, 1937).

BAYLEY, HAROLD. *The Lost Language of Symbolism,* 2 vols., illus. (New York, 1912, 1951, 1952).

BEARD, MARY RITTER. *Woman as Force in History. A Study in Traditions and Realities* (New York, 1946).

BELL, A. R. L. Introduction to *An Annotated Bibliography of the Bayeux Tapestry* (Greensbury, Penn., 1988).

———. "The Dissolution of the Monasteries." Research MS, Medievalists-at-Work Series (Slide-Tape/Video), Learning Resources Division, CSLB (Long Beach, Calif., 1984).

———. "Eleanor of Aquitaine." Script, 2 parts, Medievalists-at-Work Series (Long Beach, Calif., 1986).

———. "The Knights Templar in France." Script, Medievalists-at-Work Series (Long Beach, Calif., 1986).

———. "Our Keltic Heritage." Santa Rosa Highland Games (San Francisco, 1990).

———. "Permanent Parisians." Center for Medieval and Renaissance Studies, CSLB (Long Beach, Calif., 1987).

———. "St. Patrick." Research MS Medievalists-at-Work Series (Slide-Tape/Video), Learning Resources Division, CSLB (Long Beach, Calif., 1984).

BELPERRON, PIERRE. *Croisade contre les Albigeois et l'Union du Languedoc à la France* (1209–49) (Paris, 1942, 1967).

BENTON, JOHN. "The Court of Champagne as a Literary Center." *Speculum* 36 (1961): 551–91.

BERGOUNIOUX, FRÉDÉRIC-MARIE, O.F.M., AND FR. JOSEPH GOETZ, S.J. *Prehistoric and Primitive Religions* (London, 1965).

BERGSON, HENRI. *L'Evolution créatrice* (Paris, 1907–08, 1910).

BERNARD, SAINT. *De gratia et libero arbitrio.* See Migne's *Patrologiae Cursus Completus . . . Series Latina* (Paris, 1855–95).

BERTRAND, MICHEL, AND JEAN ANGELINI (JEAN-MICHEL ANGEBERT). *The Quest and the Third Reich* (Paris, 1971; New York, 1974).

BIRKS, WALTER N., AND R. A. GILBERT. *The "Treasure" of Montségur* (London, 1987, 1990).

BIZET, GEORGES. *L'Arlésienne* (1872).

———. *Carmen* (1875).

BLACKIE, LORNA. *Clans and Tartans: The Fabric of Scotland* (New York, 1987). See p. 67 for the Rosslyn Chapel and Grail Pillar in Scotland.

BOECE, HECTOR. *The History and Chronicles of Scotland,* 2 vols., trans. by John Bellenden (Paris, 1575; Edinburgh, 1821).

BONILLA Y SAN MARTÍN, ED. *La Demanda de Sancto Grial.* In *Nueva Biblioteca de Autores Españoles,* vol. 6, pp. 1–338 (Madrid, 1907).

BONNET, GEORGES ETIENNE. *Fin d'une Europe* (Geneva, 1948).

BORDONOVE, GEORGES. *Les Templiers* (Paris, 1977).

BORST, ARNO. *Die Katharer* (Stuttgart, 1953), trans. by Charles Roy as *Les Cathares* in the Collection d'Histoire des Religions (Paris, 1974). See Roy.

BOUCHE, HONORÉ. *Histoire de Provence* (Aix, 1665).

BRENNAN, J. H. *The Occult Reich* (New York, 1974).

BRENON, ANNE. *Le Vrai visage du Catharisme,* illus. (Toulouse, 1988).

BREWER, ELIZABETH. *From Cuchulain to Gawain* (Totowa, 1973).

BRINKLEY, ROBERTS FLORENCE. *Arthurian Legend in the Seventeenth Century* (Johns Hopkins University, 1932; New York, 1967, 1970).

BROCKWAY, WALLACE, AND HERBERT WEINSTOCK. *Men of Music. Their Lives, Times, and Achievements* (New York, 1939).

BROMWICH, RACHEL. (See Annals of Wales entry.)

BROTHERS, DR. JOYCE. *Woman* (Garden City, N.Y., 1961).

BROWN, ARTHUR C. L. *The Origin of the Grail Legend* (Cambridge, 1943; New York, 1966).

BROWN, J. A. C. *Techniques of Persuasion: From Propaganda to Brainwashing* (Harmondsworth, 1963).

BROWN, SCHUYLER. *The Origins of Christianity* (New York, 1984).

BROWNLEE, WILLIAM H. "Whence the Gospel According to John?" In *John and Qumran,* ed. by James H. Charlesworth, pp. 166–94 (London, 1972).

BRUCE, JAMES DOUGLAS, AND ALFONS HILKA. *The Evolution of Arthurian Romance from the Beginnings Down to the Year 1300,* 2 vols. (Gloucester, 1958).

BRUNS, J. EDGAR. *The Forbidden Gospel* (San Francisco, London, New York, 1976).

THE BRUT, OR *CHRONICLES OF ENGLAND* (from MS Rawlinson B 171), ed. by Frederick W. O. Brie (London, 1906). See part 1, chap. 86ff. for Arthur's and Gawain's deaths, and for how Lancelot's body was borne into Scotland for burial (p. 89).

BRYDON, ROBERT D. R., CHEVALIER. "The Germanic Tradition, The Scottish Knights Templar and the Mystery of the Holy Grail," pp. 6–10; "Stella Templum Scotorum," pp. 6–10, no dates; plus letters and conversations concerning the Knights Templar. See also Frederic Lindsay's article, "1314 and All That," *Scotland on Sunday Magazine* (August 1991), pp. 22–24.

BUCHANAN, GEORGE. *The History of Scotland,* trans. by John Watkins (London, 1831).

BUCHANAN, PATRICK J. "This Is the Battle for America's Soul." *Los Angeles Times,* "Opinion" (March 25, 1990): M5.

BUECHNER, HOWARD A., AND WILHELM BERNHART. *Adolf Hitler and the Secrets of the Holy Lance* (Metairie, La., 1988).

BULLOCK, ALAN. *Hitler. A Study in Tyranny* (New York and Evanston, 1962).

BULTMANN, RUDOLF KARL. *Die Geschichte der Synoptischen Tradition* (Göttingen, 1957).

———. *The Gospel of John,* trans. by G. R. Beasley-Murray (Oxford, 1971).

———. *Jesus Christ and Mythology* (New York, 1958).

BURDACH, KINRAD. *Der Gral: Forschungen über seinen Ursprung und seinen Zusammenhang mit der Longinus Legende* (Stuttgart, 1938).

BURMAN, EDWARD. *The Templars, Knights of God. The Rise and Fall of the Knights Templar* (Wellingborough, 1986).

CAHIERS D'ETUDES CATHARES FOR 1949, NOS. 1–4. Institut d'Etudes Occitanes (Toulouse, France). Articles by Déodat Roché, René Nelli, Th. Maurer, Simone Weil, René Lavaud, Dr. Wierma Verschaffeld, Roman Goldron, Suzette Nelli, Raymonde Tricoire, and Raymond Dorbes.

CAINE, SIR HALL. *The Little Manx Nation* (London, 1891).

CAMPBELL, GEORGE A. *The Knights Templar: Their Rise and Fall* (London, 1937).

CAPELLANUS, ANDREAS. *The Art of Courtly Love* (1174–86), ed. and abr. by Frederick W. Locke (New York, 1957).

CAPT, E. RAYMOND. *The Lost Chapter of Acts of the Apostles* (Thousand Oaks, Calif., 1982).

CARADOC OF LLANCARVAN. *Vita Sancti Gildae* (c. 1130) and *Alia Vita Gildae.* See *Historical Documents Concerning the Ancient Britons,* ed. by Rev. John A. Giles, vols. 1 and 2 (London, 1847).

CARMAN, J. NEALE. *A Study of the Pseudo-Map Cycle of Arthurian Romance* (Lawrence, Kans., 1973).

———. "The Symbolism of the Perlesvaus." *PMLA* LXI (1946): 42–83.

CARRÉ, GUSTAVE. *Histoire populaire de Troyes et du département de l'Aube* (Troyes, 1881).

CAVENDISH, RICHARD. *King Arthur of the Grail: The Arthurian Legends and Their Meaning* (London, 1978).

CÉLINE, LOUIS FERDINAND. *Les Beaux draps* (Paris, 1941).

CERF, STEVEN R. "Mann and Myth." (Metropolitan) *Opera News* 54, no. 14 (March 31, 1990): 18–19, 46.

CERVANTES SAAVEDRA, MIGUEL DE. *Don Quichotte de la Mancha,* vol. 2, trans. by Tony Johannot (Paris, 1939).

———. *Don Quijote,* vol. 4 (Mexico, 1833).

——. *El ingenioso hidalgo Don Quijote de La Mancha,* 3 vols., ed. by Luis Andres Murillo (Madrid, 1978).

——. *El ingenioso hidalgo Don Quijote de La Mancha,* part 2, vol. 4 (Mexico, 1833).

CHADWICK, NORA K. *Celtic Britain* (London, 1964).

CHANSON DE LA CROISADE CONTRE LES ALBIGEOIS, ed. by Paul Meyer (Paris, 1875).

CHANSON DU CHEVALIER AU CYGNE ET DE GODEFROID DE BOUILLON, ed. by C. Hippeau, 2 vols. (Paris, 1874–77).

CHARLES-ROUX, JULES. *Aigues-Mortes* (Paris, 1910). See Appendix for a translation of the essay on gypsies of the Marquis of Baroncelli-Javon: "Les Bohémiens des Saintes-Maries-de-la-Mer."

——. *Légendes de Provence* (Paris, 1909).

CHARPENTIER, LOUIS. *Les Mystères Templiers* (Paris, 1967).

CHRÉTIEN DE TROYES. *Arthurian Romances,* trans. by W. W. Comfort. Introduction and notes by D. D. R. Owen (London and New York, 1914–75).

——. *Christian von Troyes sämtliche Werke,* ed. by Wendelin Foerster, 5 vols. (Halle, 1884–1932). Rev. ed. by Hermann Brewer (Halle, 1933).

——. *Der Percevalroman,* ed. by Alfons Hilka (Halle, 1932).

——. *Les Romans de Chrétien de Troyes,* 5 vols., ed. by Félix Lecoy (Paris, 1975).

——. *Les Romans de Chrétien de Troyes,* 5 vols., ed. by Mario Roques (Paris, 1955–65). Vol 3: *Le Chevalier de la charrete.*

CHRÉTIEN DE TROYES. *PERCEVAL OU LE ROMAN DU GRAAL,* Preface by Armand Hoog; trans. and notes by Jean-Pierre-Foucher and André Ortais (Paris, 1949, 1974).

CHRISTIAN VON TROYES. *Sämtliche Werke,* 4 vols., ed. by Wendelin Foerster (Halle, 1884–99).

CHRONICLES OF THE PICTS, CHRONICLES OF THE SCOTS, AND OTHER EARLY MEMORIALS OF SCOTTISH HISTORY, ed. by William F. Skene (Edinburgh, 1867).

CHRONICLES OF THE REIGNS: STEPHEN, HENRY II, AND RICHARD I, vols. 1 and 2, ed. by Richard Howlett (London, 1884, 1964). See vol. 82 in the *Rerum Britannicarum Medii Aevi Scriptores,* Rolls Series.

CITY OF JERUSALEM, trans. by C. R. Conder. Palestine Pilgrims' Text Society, VI, no. 2 (London, 1888).

CLARKE, ROBIN. *La Course à la mort, ou La Technocratie de la guerre,* trans. by Georges Renard (Paris, 1972).

CLÉDAT, L. *Le Nouveau Testament* (trans. of the New Testament into Provençal, followed by a Catharist Ritual, thirteenth century). Bibliothèque de la Faculté des Lettres, vol. 6 (Paris, 1887).

CLOTTES, JEAN. *Dolmens et menhirs du Midi* (Toulouse, 1987).

COHEN, GUSTAVE. *La Vie littéraire en France au Moyen-âge* (Paris, 1949).
———. *Un grand romancier d'Amour et d'Aventure au XIIe siècle, Chrétien de Troyes* (Paris, 1931).
COHN, NORMAN. *The Pursuit of the Millennium* (New York, 1957, 1961).
COLETTE, SIDONIE GABRIELLE. See *Claudine et Annie,* trans. by Antonia White, in *The Complete Claudine* (New York, 1976).
COLLET, HENRI. *L'Ile de Barataria* (Paris, 1929).
COMPTON, JAMES V. *The Swastika and the Eagle* (Boston, 1967).
COMTE, P. "Le Graal et Montségur." *Bulletin de la Société Archaéologique et historique du Gers* (1951): 332–45.
CONNOLLY, PETER. *A History of the Jewish People in the Time of Jesus* (New York, 1987).
CONTINUATION DE PERCEVAL, 2 vols., ed. by Mary Williams (Paris, 1922–25).
CONTINUATION-PERCEVAL (DEUXIÈME CONTINUATION DE PERCEVAL, or *CONTINUATION DE WAUCHIER*), ed. by Charles Potvin (Mons, 1866–71).
CONTINUATIONS OF THE OLD FRENCH PERCEVAL, 2 vols., ed. by William Roach (Philadelphia, 1949–50).
CONZELMANN, HANS. *Geschichte des Urchristentums* (Göttingen, n.d.), trans. by John E. Steely (Nashville and New York, 1973).
COPIES DES REGISTRES DE L'INQUISITION D'ALBI, CARCASSONNE, TOULOUSE, NARBONNE (Series of 258 MSS, Bibliothèque Nationale, Paris). Copies ordered by Jean-Baptiste Colbert, Minister of France (c. 1661), ed. by Jean Doat.
CORBO, VIRGIL. *The House of Saint Peter at Capharnaum* (Jerusalem, 1969).
COTTRELL, LEONARD. *Seeing Roman Britain* (London, 1967).
COULET, JULES, ED. *Le Troubadour Montanhagol* (Toulouse, 1898). See Montanhagol, Guilhem, or Guilhem de Montanhagol.
COULTON, G. G. "The Death Penalty for Heresy from 1184 to 1921 A.D." *Medieval Studies* 18 (London, 1924).
COUTET, ALEX. *Toulouse* (Toulouse, 1926). Preface by Pol Neveux, Frontispiece by Fernand Olié.
CRAWFORD, OSBERT GUY STANHOPE. "Arthur and His Battles," *Antiquity* 9 (1935): 277–91. See also "King Arthur's Last Battle," *Antiquity* 5 (June 1931): 236–39.
———. *Topography of Roman Scotland North of the Antonine Wall* (Cambridge, 1949).
CRESTOMATHIE DE L'ANCIEN FRANÇAIS, ed. by Karl Bartsch (Leipzig, 1895; New York, 1958). See the *Cantilena of St. Eulalia,* pp. 3–4.

CROSS, T. P., AND W. A. NITZE. *Lancelot and Guenevere. A Study on the Origins of Courtly Love* (Chicago, 1930).

CURRER-BRIGGS, NOEL. *The Shroud and the Grail. A Modern Quest for the True Grail,* illus. (London and New York, 1987–88). See also Appendices, Chronology, Postscript, Bibliography, and Notes.

CURTIN, JEREMIAH. *Myths and Folk-Lore of Ireland* (London, 1890, 1975). See "The Fisherman's Son and the Gruagach of Tricks," a folklore version of Perceval/Parzival.

CURZON, HENRI DE. *La Règle du Temple,* for the Société de l'histoire de France (Paris, 1886).

CYR, DONALD L., ED. *Glastonbury Treasures* (Santa Barbara, Calif., 1989).

DARAUL, ARKON. *Les Sociétés secrètes,* trans. by Francine Ménétrier (Paris, 1970). See Templars, pp. 52–81.

DAUDET, ALPHONSE. *Tartarin de Tarascon* (Paris, 1872); and *Lettres de Mon Moulin* (Paris, 1872), which seem to have inspired R. L. Stevenson.

DAVIES, EDWARD. *The Mythology and Rites of the British Druids ascertained by National Documents* (London, 1809).

THE DEATH OF KING ARTHUR, trans. by James Cable (London, 1971, 1975).

DEGRASSI, ATTILIO. *I Fasti consolari dell' impero romano* (Rome, 1952).

DEL VASTO, LANZA. *Commentaire de l'Evangile* (Paris, 1951).

DENOMY, A. J. *The Heresey of Courtly Love* (New York, 1947).

DER PROSAROMAN VON JOSEPH VON ARIMATHIA, ed. by Georg Weidner (Oppeln, 1881).

DEUEL, WALLACE R. *People Under Hitler* (New York, 1942). See chap. 18: "The Suppression of Intelligence," pp. 260–73.

DICKINSON, WILLIAM CROFT. *Scotland from the Earliest Times to 1603* (London and Edinburgh, 1961).

DICKINSON, WILLIAM CROFT, GORDON DONALDSON, AND ISABEL A. MILNE. *A Source Book of Scottish History,* vol. 1 (Edinburgh, 1952).

DIDOT-PERCEVAL. See Del Skeels entry.

DIEL, P. *Le Symbolisme dans la mythologie grecque* (Paris, 1952).

DIGGS, DOROTHY. *A Working Manual for Altar Guilds* (Wilton, Conn., 1957, 1968).

DODD, CHARLES H. *Historical Tradition in the Fourth Gospel* (Cambridge, 1963).

————. *The Interpretation of the Fourth Gospel* (Cambridge, 1954).

DONDAINE, A., ED. *Liber des duobus principiis* (thirteenth century MS) and "Fragment of Catharist Ritual" (Rome, 1939).

DONTENVILLE, HENRI. *Mythologie française* (Paris, 1948, 1973).

DUMÉZIL, GEORGES. *Le Problème des Centaures* (Paris, 1929). See also his books of 1954 and 1966.

EDWARD, OTIS CARL, JR. *How It All Began. Origins of the Christian Church* (New York, 1973).

EDWARDS, RUTH DUDLEY. *Atlas of Irish History* (London, 1973).

EISEN, DR. GUSTAV(US) A. *The Great Chalice of Antioch,* 2 vols. (New York, 1933).

EL BALADRO DEL SABIO MERLIN, CON SUS PROFECIAS (Burgos, 1848).

ELDER, ISABEL HILL. *Celt, Druid and Culdee* (London, 1973).

ELIADE, MIRCÉA. *Le Chamanisme et les techniques archaïques de l'extase* (Paris, 1951).

———. *Myths, Dreams, and Mysteries,* trans. by Philip Mairet (New York, 1960).

———. *Symbolism, the Sacred, and the Arts,* ed. by Diane Apostolos-Cappadona (New York, 1985).

———. *Traité d'histoire des religions* (Paris, 1968).

ELLIOT, GIL. *Twentieth Century Book of the Dead* (London, 1972).

THE ELUCIDATION. A PROLOGUE TO THE "CONTE DEL GRAAL," ed. by Albert Wilder Thompson (New York, 1931).

EMERY, RICHARD WILDER. *Heresy and Inquisition in Narbonne.* Columbia University Dissertation (New York, 1941).

LES ENFANCES GAUVAIN, ed. by Paul Meyer in *Romania* 39 (1910): 1–32.

ENSLIN, MORTON S. *From Jesus to Christianity* (Boston and Toronto, 1964).

ENTWHISTLE, WILLIAM J. *The Arthurian Legend in the Literatures of the Spanish Peninsula* (New York, 1925, 1975).

"ENUMA ELISH." In *Poems of Heaven and Hell,* ed. by N. K. Sanders (London, 1921).

ETCHEGOYEN, G. *L'Amour divin, essai sur les sources de sainte Thérèse* (Paris, 1923).

EUSEBIUS OF CAESAREA. *The Ecclesiastical History of Eusebius Pamphilus,* trans. by C. F. Cruse (Philadelphia, 1840).

———. *The History of the Christian Church from Christ to Constantine,* trans. by G. A. Williamson (Baltimore, 1965).

EVANS, SEBASTIAN. *In Quest of the Holy Grail* (London, 1898).

EVANS-WENTZ, W. Y. *Fairy Faith in Celtic Countries.* Foreword by Kathleen Raine (Oxford, 1911; London, 1927).

EVOLA, GIULIO CESARE ANDREA. *Il Mistero del Graal (Le Mystère du Graal)* (Bari, 1937; Munich, 1955; Rome, 1972). See pp. 139–87 for the "Inheritors": Templars, Catharists, Dante, the Hermetic Tradition, and the Rosicrucians.

FAIRBAIRN, NEIL, AND MICHAEL CYPRIEN. *A Traveller's Guide to the Kingdoms of Arthur* (London, 1983; Harrisburg, n.d.).

FARAL, EDMOND. *La Littérature arthurienne,* 3 vols. (Paris, 1929).

FAWTIER, ROBERT. *Les Capétiens et la France* (Paris, 1942).

FERGUSON, GEORGE W. *Signs and Symbols in Christian Art* (New York, 1954).

FEST, JOACHIM C. *Hitler,* trans. by Richard Winston and Clara Winston (New York, 1973).

FISHER, LIZETTE ANDREWS. *The Mystic Vision in the Grail Legend and in the "Divine Comedy,"* Columbia University Studies (New York, 1917).

FLAMMARION, CAMILLE. *Death and Its Mystery After Death,* vol. 3, trans. by Latrobe Carroll (New York and London, 1923).

———. *Death and Its Mystery at the Moment of Death,* vol. 2, trans. by Latrobe Carroll (New York, 1922).

———. *Death and Its Mystery Before Death,* vol. 1, trans. by E. S. Brooks (New York, 1921).

———. *L'Inconnu et les problèmes psychiques* (Paris, 1900).

———. *Mysterious Psychic Forces* (Boston, 1907).

FONTENELLE, BERNARD DE. *Histoire des Oracles* (Amsterdam, 1764).

FOURQUET, J. *Wolfram d'Eschenbach et le Conte del Graal* (Paris, 1938).

FOWLER, D. C. *Prowess and Charity in the Perceval of Chrétien de Troyes* (Seattle, 1959).

FOWLER, ELIZABETH. "The Origins and Development of the Penannular Brooch in Europe." *Proceedings of the Prehistoric Society* XXVI (1960): 149–77.

FRAPPIER, JEAN. *Autour du Graal* (Geneva, 1977).

———. *Chrétien de Troyes et le mythe du Graal* (Paris, 1972).

———. *Chrétien de Troyes, l'homme et l'oeuvre* (Paris, 1957).

———. "Le Graal et ses feux divergents." *Romance Philology* XXIV (1970–71): 373–440.

———. "Sur la composition du *Conte del Graal.*" *Moyen Age* LXIV (1958): 67–102.

FRAZER, SIR JAMES. *The Golden Bough. A Study in Comparative Religion,* 12 vols. (London, 1911, 1922).

FRECULFUS (FRECULF), BISHOP OF LISIEUX. *Chronicorum libri duo,* ed. by E. Grunauer as *De Fontibus historiae Freculfi* (Winterthur, 1864).

FROISSART, SIR JOHN (JEAN). *The Chronicles of England, France, and Spain.* Introduction by Charles W. Dunn (New York, 1961).

FURNIVALL, FREDERICK J. *La Queste del Saint Graal,* 4 vols. Roxburghe Club (London, 1864).

———. ed. *The History of the Holy Grail,* Henry Lovelich's edition for the Roxburghe Club (London, 1863–64); or see EETS, vols. 1 and 2, Extra Series 20, 24, 28, 30, or 95 (1874).

GADAL, A. *Sur le chemin du Saint-Graal* (Haarlem, 1960).

GAER, JOSEPH. *The Lore of the New Testament* (Boston, 1952).

GAETANO DA TERESA. *Il Catino di Smeraldo Orientale, Gemma consagrata da N.S. Gesu Cristo nell' Ultima Cena degli Azimi . . .* (Genoa, 1726). The *catino* in San Lorenzo, Genoa, is believed to be Christ's emerald-glass dish of the Last Supper.

GALLAIS, PIERRE. *Perceval et l'initiation* (Paris, 1972).

GASTER, MOSES. *Studies and Texts,* vol. 2 (London, 1925–28). See "The Legend of the Grail," pp. 895–98.

GAUTIER, LÉON. *Les Epopées françaises,* 4 vols. (Paris, 1868).

GELLING, PETER, AND HILDA ELLIS DAVIDSON. *The Chariot of the Sun* (London, 1969).

GEOFFREY OF MONMOUTH (GALFRIDUS MONUMUTENSIS). *Historia regum Britanniae,* ed. by Acton Griscom and Robert Ellis Jones (New York and Toronto, 1929).

GEOFFREY OF MONMOUTH (?). *Vita Merlini,* ed. by J. J. Parry (Urbana, 1925). In my opinion, this work was ascribed to Geoffrey in order to defame him. The work is a vicious parody of Christianity, and an insult to a Christian Bishop, which Geoffrey was to become.

GERALDUS CAMBRENSIS (GERALD OF WALES). *Opera,* 8 vols., ed. by J. S. Brewer, J. F. Dimock and G. F. Warner (London, 1886–91).

GERBERT DE MONTREUIL. *La Continuation de Perceval,* 2 vols., ed. by Mary Williams (Paris, 1922–25).

GERVAIS OF TILBURY. *De Gervasius von Tilbury Otia Imperialia,* ed. by F. Liebrecht (Hanover, 1856).

GESTA PILATI, OR ACTS OF PONTIUS PILATE. See "Gospel of Nicodemus" entry.

GESTA REGIS HENRICI SECUNDI (HISTORY OF KING HENRY II OF ENGLAND), ed. by W. Stubbs for the *Rerum Britannicarum Medii Aevi Scriptores,* no. 49, 2 vols. (London, 1867).

GILDAS. THE RUIN OF BRITAIN AND OTHER DOCUMENTS, ed. and trans. by Michael Winterbottom (London and Chichester, 1987).

GILSON, ETIENNE. *God and Philosophy,* Powell Lectures, Indiana University (New Haven, 1941).

———. "La Mystique de la Grâce dans *La Queste del Saint Graal.*" In *Les Idées et les lettres,* pp. 59–91 (Paris, 1955).

———. *La Théologie mystique de Saint Bernard* (Paris, 1947).

GIONO, JEAN. *Provence,* illus. by Jacques Thévenet (Paris, 1957).

———. *Provence perdue,* illus. by Bernard Buffet (Manosque, 1968).

GIONO, JEAN, AND GEORGE MONMARCHÉ. *Provence,* ill. by Gerald Maurois (Paris, 1954).

GLENNIE, JOHN STUART STUART. *Arthurian Localities,* EETS 112 (Edinburgh and London, 1869).

GOBINEAU, COUNT JOSEPH-ARTHUR DE. *Essai sur l'inégalité des races humaines* (Paris, 1853–55).

THE GODODDIN. THE OLDEST SCOTTISH POEM, ed. by Kenneth Hurlstone Jackson (Edinburgh, 1969).

GOETINCK, GLENYS W. *"Peredur." A Study of Welsh Tradition in the Grail Legends* (Cardiff, 1975). See chap. 5, pp. 275–303, for Peredur and the Grail.

GOODENOUGH, EDWIN R. *Jewish Symbols in the Greco-Roman Period,* vols. 7–8 *(Pagan Symbols in Judaism)* (New York, 1958).

———. *Religious Tradition and Myth* (New Haven, 1937).

GOODRICH, NORMA LORRE. *Ancient Myths* (New York, 1960–92).

———. *Charles, Duke of Orleans* (New York, 1963).

———. *Charles of Orleans* (Geneva, 1967–92).

———. *Guinevere* (New York, 1991–92).

———. *King Arthur* (New York, 1986, 1987, 1988, 1990; Milan, 1989; Paris, 1991).

———. *"La Morte Aymeri de Narbonne." Comparative Literature,* University of Maryland (1965).

———. *Medieval Myths* (New York, 1961–92).

———. *Merlin* (New York, 1987, 1988, 1990).

———. *Priestesses* (New York, 1990, 1991).

———. *The Ways of Love. Eleven Romances from Medieval France* (Boston and Toronto, 1964; London, 1965).

"GOSPEL OF NICODEMUS" See *The Lost Books of the Bible and the Forgotten Books of Eden,* Introduction by Frank Crane, pp. 63–91 (New York, Newfoundland, London, Ontario, 1974).

GOSPELS OF JOHN (2 VOLS.) AND *LUKE,* ed. by William Barclay in the Series "Daily Study Bible" (Edinburgh and New York, 1953, 1955, 1956, 1975).

GRAFENBERG, WIRNT VON. *Wigalois,* trans. by J. W. Thomas (Lincoln and London, 1977).

GRAND-SAINT-GRAAL. See Dorothy Kempe entry.

GRANT, ROBERT MCQUEEN. *Augustus to Constantine. The Thrust of the Christian Movement into the Roman World* (New York, 1970; London, 1971).

———. *The Earliest Lives of Jesus* (New York, 1961).

GRAVES, ROBERT. *Adam's Rib* (New York, 1958).

———. *King Jesus* (New York, 1946; London, 1960).

———. *The White Goddess* (New York, 1948).

GRAY, LOUIS HERBERT. "Baltic Mythology." In *Mythology of All Races,* vol. 3 (New York, 1964).

GREGORY, LADY ISABELLA AUGUSTA. *Cuchulain of Muirthemne,* vol. 2 (London, 1902).

———. *Gods and Fighting Men,* vol. 3 (London, 1904).

GRIFFITH, F. L. *Stories of the High-Priests of Memphis* (Oxford, 1900).

GRISCOM, ACTON, AND ROBERT ELLIS JONES, ED. See Geoffrey of Monmouth entry.

GROUSSET, RENÉ. *L'Epopée des croisades* (Paris, 1939). See chap. 12 (pp. 292–325) for the Third Crusade.

GUÉNON, RENÉ. "L'Esotérisme du Graal." In *Lumière du Graal,* ed. by René Nelli, pp. 37–49 (Paris, 1951).

"GUILLAUME D'ORANGE." FOUR TWELFTH-CENTURY EPICS, Introduction and trans. by Joan M. Ferrante (New York and London, 1974).

GUIZOT, FRANÇOIS, P. G. *Essais sur l'histoire de France,* illus. (Paris, 1872).

GUYER, FOSTER E. *Chrétien de Troyes* (Bern, 1958).

HADAS, MOSES, AND MORTON SMITH. *Heroes and Gods* (New York, 1965).

HARNACK, A. VON. *Lehrbuch der Dogmengesschichte,* 3 vols. in 5th ed. (Tübingen, 1931–32).

———. *The Mission and Expansion of Christianity in the First Three Centuries,* 2 vols., trans. by James Moffatt of St. Andrews (New York and London, 1908).

HARVEY, JOHN HOOPER. *The Plantagenets* (London, 1967).

HATTAT, RICHARD. *Ancient and Romano-British Brooches* (Sherborne, Dorset, 1982).

HATTO, A. T., TRANS. *Wolfram von Eschenbach. "Parzival"* (London and New York, 1980).

HAYS, H. R. *The Dangerous Sex. The Myth of Feminine Evil* (New York, 1964). See chap. 13, "Knights without Ladies," p. 134ff.

HEATH, REV. ALBAN. *The "Painted Savages" of England* (London, n.d.).

HEAVER, A. R. *Somerset's Pre-historic Zodiac Circle* (London, 1966).

HEINRICH VON DEM TÜRLIN. *Diu Crône,* ed. by G. H. F. Scholl (Stuttgart, 1852).

HEINZEL, RICHARD. *Über die französischen Gralromane* (Vienna, 1891).

HELINE, CORINNE. *Mysteries of the Holy Grail* (Santa Monica, Calif., reprinted 1986).

HERAENS, WILHELM, ED. *Peregrinatio ad Loca Sancta* (Heidelberg, 1908).

HILKA, ALFONS. See James Douglas Bruce entry.

HISTORY OF THE HOLY GRAIL, a translation of *Grand-Saint-Graal* of c. 1450 by Henry Lovelich, ed. by Frederick J. Furnivall (London, 1925).

HOLMES, E. *The Albigensian or Catharist Heresy. A Story and a Study* (London, 1925).

HOLMES, URBAN T., JR. *Chrétien de Troyes* (New York, 1970). See p.

53 where Professor Holmes makes a discovery: that Chrétien referred to himself as "Crestiiens li Gois," which could mean "Crétien the former Jew."

————. "A New Interpretation of Chrétien's *Conte del Graal.*" University of North Carolina, *Studies in the Romance Languages and Literatures* VIII (1948): 36.

HOLMES, URBAN T., AND AMELIA KLENKE. *Chrétien, Troyes, and the Grail* (Chapel Hill, 1959).

HOOG, ARMAND, ED. *Chrétien de Troyes. Perceval ou le Roman du Graal,* trans. by Jean-Pierre Foucher and André Ortais (Paris, 1949, 1974).

HUGHES, KATHLEEN. *Celtic Britain in the Early Middle Ages,* ed. by David Dumville (Woodbridge, Suffolk, 1980).

HUGHES, PENNETHORNE. *Witchcraft* (London, 1952–70).

HUXLEY, ALDOUS. *The Perennial Philosophy* (New York, 1944).

IMBS, P. "A la recherche d'une littérature cathare." *Revue du Moyen Age Latin* 5 (1949): 289–302.

JACOPUS DE VORAGINE. *The Golden Legend,* trans. and adapted by Granger Ryan and Helmut Ripperger, pp. 355–64 (New York, 1969).

JAMES, WILLIAM. *The Varieties of Religious Experience* (New York, 1902).

JEFFERSON, THOMAS. *The Life and Morals of Jesus of Nazareth* (The Jefferson Bible) (New York, 1940).

JERPHANIAN, GUILLAUME DE. *Le Calice d'Antioch,* illus. (Rome, 1926).

JOHN OF GLASTONBURY. *Chronica sive historia de rebus Glastoniensibus,* 2 vols., ed. by Thomas Hearne (Oxford, 1726).

JOSEPH D'ARIMATHIE (LE ROMAN DE L'ESTOIRE DOU GRAAL), Bibliothéque Nationale MS 20047, followed by 502 vv. of *Merlin,* ed. by Wm. A. Nitze (Paris, 1971), and by Gaston Paris (Paris, 1886).

JOSEPH OF ARIMATHIE, ed. by W. W. Skeat, EETS, Original Series no. 44 (London, 1871).

JOSEPHUS, FLAVIUS. *Antiquities of the Jews,* 4 vols., ed. by H. Stebbing (Philadelphia and New York, n.d.). See also *The Works of Flavius Josephus,* and/or *Complete Works of Josephus.* The Temple is described in book 5, chapter 5.

————. *Contra Apionem,* ed. by Theodore Reinach and Léon Blum (Paris, 1930).

JOWETT, GEORGE F. *The Drama of the Lost Disciples* (London, 1961, 1980).

JOYCE, DONOVAN. *The Jesus Scroll* (Melbourne, 1972; New York, 1973).

JUBAINVILLE, H. D'ARBOIS DE. *Le Cycle mythologique irlandais et la mythologie celtique* (Paris, 1884).

JULLIAN, CAMILLE. *Histoire de la Gaule*, 8 vols. (Paris, 1902–26).

JUNG, EMMA, AND MARIE-LOUISE FRANZ. *The Grail Legend*, trans. by Andrea Dykes (London, 1971).

KAHANNE, HENRI, RENÉE, AND A. PIETRANGELI. *The Krater and the Grail. Hermetic Sources of the "Parzival"* (Urbana, 1965).

KALEVALA. THE LAND OF HEROES, 2 vols., trans. by W. F. Kirby. Introduction by J. B. C. Grundy (London and New York, 1907–74).

KATZ, DAVID S. *Philo-semitism and the Readmission of the Jews to England, 1603–1655* (Oxford, 1982).

KAZANTZAKIS, NIKOS. *The Last Temptation of Christ* (New York, 1960). The story of Jesus and Mary Magdalene, a prostitute (i.e., body versus soul).

KEATING, REV. GEORGE. *The History of Ireland from The Earliest Period to the English Invasion*, trans. by John O'Mahony (New York, 1857).

KELLY, AMY RUTH. *Eleanor of Aquitaine and the Four Kings* (Cambridge, 1950).

KELLY, J. N. D. *Early Christian Creeds* (London, 1959).

———. *Early Christian Doctrines* (London, 1958).

KEMPE, DOROTHY. "The Legend of the Holy Grail, its Sources, Character and Development." In *The Holy Grail* or *Grand-Saint-Graal*, EETS, Extra Series no. XCV (London, 1905), p. 37ff.

KLAUSER, THEODOR. *A Short History of the Western Liturgy* (New York, 1969).

KLENKE, M. AMELIA. *Chrétien de Troyes and "Le Conte del Graal"* (Madrid and Catholic University of America, 1981).

THE KORAN, trans. by J. M. Rodwell. Introduction by G. Margoliouth (London and New York, 1909–77).

KRAUTHEIMER, RICHARD. *Early Christian and Byzantine Architecture* (Baltimore, 1965).

KRESS, ROBERT. *Whither Womankind? The Humanity of Women* (St. Meinrad, Indiana, 1975).

KROON, REINOUT P. "A Mind/Matter Axiom." In *The Journal of Religion and Psychical Research*, vol. 12, no. 2 (April 1989): 74–84.

LANCELOT OF THE LAIK, ed. by W. W. Skeat, EETS, Original Series no. 6 (London, 1865).

LANG, ANDREW. *Myth, Literature, and Religion*, 2 vols. (London, 1887 and 1899).

LANGER, WALTER C. *The Mind of Adolf Hitler* (New York and London, 1972).

LAWRENCE, D. H. (LAWRENCE H. DAVIDSON). *Movements in European History* (London, 1921).

LAYAMON. See Wace and Layamon entry.

LEARSI, RUFUS (ISRAEL GOLDBERG). *Israel: A History of the Jewish People* (Cleveland, 1949).

LÉON-DUFOUR, XAVIER. *Les Evangiles et l'histoire de Jésus* (Paris, 1963).

LEROUX DE LINCY, ANTOINE JEAN VICTOR. *Histoire de l'Abbaye de Fécamp* or *Essai historique et littéraire sur l'Abbaye de Fécamp, par Leroux de Lincy,* illus. (Rouen, 1840).

LESTOIRE DEL SAINT GRAAL, trans. as *The Quest of the Holy Grail* by Pauline M. Matarasso (Harmondsworth, 1969).

LEVIN, SAUL. *The Indo-European and Semitic Languages* (Albany, 1971).

LÉVIS MIREPOIX, ANTOINE F.J.P.M. *Montségur* (Paris, 1924).

LEVY, GERTRUDE R. *The Gate of Horn* (London, 1948).

LEWIS, C. S. *The Allegory of Love. A Study in Medieval Tradition* (London, 1936; New York, 1958–63). See chap. 3, p. 113ff., for allegory in Chrétien de Troyes.

———. *Mere Christianity* (New York, 1952).

LEWIS, I. M. *Ecstatic Religion* (Harmondsworth, 1971).

LEWIS, LIONEL SMITHETT. *St. Joseph of Arimathea at Glastonbury, or The Apostolic Church of Britain* (Cambridge, 1922–76).

LEWIS, TIMOTHY, AND J. DOUGLAS BRUCE. "The Pretended Exhumation of Arthur and Guinevere." *Revue Celtique* 33 (1912): 432–51.

LINDSAY, JACK. *Arthur and His Times* (London, 1958).

LOISY, ALFRED. *La Naissance du Christianisme* (Paris, 1933).

LONGNON, A., ED. *Documents relatifs au Comte de Champagne et de Brie. Documents inédits,* 2 vols. (Paris, 1901–14).

LOOMIS, LAURA HIBBARD. *Adventures in the Middle Ages* (New York, 1962).

LOOMIS, ROGER SHERMAN. *Arthurian Tradition and Chrétien de Troyes* (New York, 1949).

———. *The Grail from Celtic Myth to Christian Symbol* (Cardiff, 1963).

———. *Studies in Medieval Literature* (New York, 1970).

———. *Wales and the Arthurian Legend* (Cardiff, 1956).

LOT, FERDINAND, AND R. FAWTIER. *Histoire des institutions françaises au Moyen Age,* vol. 2 ("Institutions royales") (Paris, 1958–62). A study of the French kings versus the Papacy.

LOT-BORODINE, MYRRHA. "Autour du Saint-Graal." *Speculum* VIII (1933): 415–30; *Romania* 56 (1930): 526–57; *Romania* 57 (1931): 147–205.

LOWITH, KARL. *Meaning in History* (Chicago, 1949).

LYRICS OF THE TROUBADOURS AND TROUVÈRES. AN ANTHOLOGY AND A HISTORY, ed. by Frederick Goldin (New York, 1973).

MABINOGION, trans. and ed. by Lady Charlotte Guest (London and Toronto, 1906).

MABINOGION, trans. by Gwyn Jones and Thomas Jones (London, 1948, 1949, 1968).

MACALISTER, ROBERT ALEXANDER STEWART. *The Archaeology of Ireland* (London, 1949; New York, 1972).

MCARTHUR, HARVEY K. *The Quest through the Centuries* (Philadelphia, 1966).

MCBIRNIE, WILLIAM STEUART. *The Search for the Twelve Apostles* (Wheaton, Ill., 1973, 1977).

MACDONALD, ANGUS JOHN. *The Hebridean Connection,* ed. and Introduction by Donald A. Fergusson (Halifax, 1990).

MACGREGOR, GEDDES. *Scotland Forever Home* (New York, 1980).

MCKERRACHER, ARCHIE. "The Round Talbe Was at Stenhousemuir." *The SCOTS Magazine* 131, no. 5 (August 1989): 505–13.

MACLEOD, FIONA (WILLIAM SHARP). *The Immortal House* (London, 1908).

MAITLAND, SAMUEL ROFFEY. *Facts and Documents Illustrative of the History, Doctrine and Rites of the Ancient Albigenses and Waldenses* (Bristol, Exeter, Gloucester, Dublin, and London, 1832).

MÂLE, EMILE. *L'Art religieux du XIIᵉ siècle en France* (Paris, 1928).

———. *L'Art religieux du XIIIᵉ siècle en France* (Paris, 1948).

———. *La Fin du paganisme en Gaule et les plus anciennes basiliques chrétiennes,* illus. (Paris, 1950).

MALORY, SIR THOMAS. *Le Morte d'Arthur,* 2 vols. Preface by Sir John Rhys (London and New York, 1906–61).

MALTWOOD, KATHERINE E. *The Enchantments of Britain* (Victoria, B.C., 1944).

———. *Guide to Glastonbury's Temple of the Stars* (London, 1934, 1964).

MANN, THOMAS. *Betrachtungen eines Unpolitischen (1918),* trans. by Walter D. Morris as *Reflections of a Nonpolitical Man* (New York, 1983).

MANUSCRITS FRANÇAIS DE LA BIBLIOTHÈQUE DU ROI, ed. by M. P. Paris (Paris, 1837).

MAP (MAPES), WALTER (C. 1140–C. 1210). *De Nugis curialium* or *Courtiers' Trifles,* trans. by Frederick Tupper and M. B. Ogle (Chapel Hill, 1924).

———. *De Nugis curialium,* ed. by M. R. James in *Anecdota Oxoniensia,* Medieval and Modern Series (Oxford, 1914). This author was once falsely supposed to have written Arthurian material. He is often referred to as the "Pseudo-Map."

MARIE DE FRANCE. *"Espurgatoire Saint Patriz" of Marie de France, with a Text of the Latin Original,* ed. by T. Atkinson Jenkins (Chicago, 1903).

———. *Lais,* ed. by A. Ewert (London, 1944). See "Yonec," pp. 82–96.

MARKALE, JEAN. *L'Epopée celtique en Bretagne* (Paris, 1971). For "Peredur," see pp. 182–209.

MARSEILLE INFORMATIONS NOS. 143–144 (1983). Illustrated periodical report from the Musée d'Histoire de Marseille, Jardin Des Vestiges: History and Archaeology. Courtesy of M. Jacques Arnaud, ed., and M. the Mayor of Marseille (Marseilles).

MARTIN, E. *Zur Gralsage* (Strasbourg, 1880).

MARTIN DU GARD, MAURICE. *La Chronique de Vichy* (Paris, 1948).

MARTINS, CHARLES. "Une Ville oubliée: Aigues-Mortes, son passé, son present, son avenir." *Revue des Deux Mondes* 3 (January 1874): 780–816.

MARX, JEAN. *La Légende arthurienne et le Graal* (Geneva, 1974). See Appendix for list and summary of fifteen Grail MSS.

MASSENET, JULES E. F. *Esclarmonde,* "Opéra Romanesque." 4 acts and 8 tableaux (n.d.). Poem by Alfred Blau and Louis de Gramont. Music by J. Massenet. Esclarmonde sung by Sibyl Sanderson (Paris, 1889).

MATARASSO, PAULINE. *The Redemption of Chivalry: A Study of the Queste del Saint Graal* (Geneva, 1979).

MATTHEW PARIS (MATTHAEUS PARISIENSIS). *Chronica Maiora,* ed. by H. R. Luard for *Rerum Britannicarum Medii Aevi Scriptores* 57 (London, 1872–84).

MAURY, ALBERT. *Croyances et légendes du Moyen Age* (Paris, 1896; Geneva, 1972).

MEADE, MARION. *Eleanor of Aquitaine* (New York, 1977).

MELVILLE, MARION. *La Vie des Templiers* (Paris, 1951, 1974).

MENÉNDEZ Y PELAYO, M. *Historia de los Heterodox Españoles,* 3 vols. (Madrid, 1880–81; Santander, 1948).

MERGELL, BODO. *Der Gral in Wolframs Parzival* (Halle, 1952).

MERIMÉE, PROSPER. *Carmen* (Paris, 1852).

MERTZ, HENRIETTE. *The Mystic Symbol* (Gaithersburg, Md., 1986).

MEYER, PAUL, ED. *La Chanson de la Croisade contre les Albigeois,* for La Société de l'Histoire de France, 2 vols. (Paris, 1875–79).

MICHA, A. *La Tradition manuscrite des romans de Chrétien de Troyes* (Paris, 1931).

MICHELET, JULES. *History of France,* vol. 1, trans. by G. H. Smith (New York, 1875).

————. *Procès des Templiers*, 2 vols. (Collection des documents inédits de la France) (Paris, 1841).

MICHELL, JOHN. *The View over Atlantis* (London, 1969; New York, 1972).

MIGNE, J. P., ED. *Patrilogiae Cursus Completus, Series Latina*, 221 vols. (Paris, 1855–95); *Series Secunda*, 4 vols. (Paris, 1845–46).

MILL, JOHN STUART. *The Subjection of Women* (Philadelphia, 1869).

MILLER, HELEN HILL. *Realms of Arthur* (New York, 1969).

MISTRAL, FRÉDÉRIC. *Mireille*, illus. by Frédéric Montenard (Paris, 1930). See chap. 11 ("Les Saintes") for the account of the voyage of the Saints Mary from Jerusalem to Marseilles.

MITCHELL, OTIS C. *Hitler over Germany* (Philadelphia, 1983). See the Epilogue, p. 255ff.

MOORE, A. W. *A History of the Isle of Man*, 2 vols. (London, 1900; Douglas, 1977).

MORGAN, R. W. *St. Paul in Britain* (London, 1860).

MORRIS, JOHN. *The Age of Arthur* (New York, 1973).

MURRAY, GILBERT. *Five Stages of Greek Religion* (New York, 1925).

MYERS, FREDERICK WILLIAM HENRY. *Human Personality and Its Survival of Bodily Death* (London, 1903, 1920).

NAPOLÉON III, S.M.I. *Histoire de Jules César*, 2 vols. (New York, 1865; Paris, 1866).

NEALE, JOHN MASON. *A History of the Holy Eastern Church*, 2 vols. (London, 1850).

NELLI, RENÉ. *Ecritures cathares* (Paris, 1968).

————. "Le Graal dans l'ethnographie." In *Lumière du Graal*, pp. 1–36 (Paris, 1951).

————. *La Philosophie du Catharisme: Le Dualisme radical au XIIIe siècle* (Paris, 1978).

NENNIUS. *British History and the Welsh Annals*, ed. by John Morris (London and Totowa, 1980).

————. *Historia Britonum*, ed. by Ferdinand Lot (Paris, 1934).

NEWMAN, ERNEST. *The Wagner Operas* (New York, 1949).

NEWMAN, J. L. *Jewish Influence on Early Christian Reform Movements*. Columbia University Oriental Studies no. 23 (New York, 1925).

NEWSOM, CARROLL V. *The Roots of Christianity* (Englewood Cliffs, 1979).

NEWSTEAD, HELAINE. *Bran the Blessed in Arthurian Romance* (New York, 1939, 1966).

NICOLAISEN, W. F. H. *Scottish Place-Names* (London, 1976, 1979, 1986).

NIEL, FERNAND. *Albigeois et Cathares* (Paris, 1955).

————. *Montségur, la montagne inspirée* (Paris, 1954).

————. *Montségur, la site et son histoire* (Grenoble, 1962).

———. *Montségur, temple et forteresse des Cathares d'Occitanie* (Grenoble, 1967).

———. *Le Pog de Montségur* (Toulouse, 1949).

NITZE, WILLIAM ALBERT. "The Exhumation of King Arthur at Glastonbury." *Speculum* 9 (1934): 355–61.

———. *The Old French Grail Romance "Perlesvaus": A Study of its Principal Sources.* Dissertation (Baltimore, 1902).

———. "Perceval and the Holy Grail." In *Publications in Modern Philology,* vol. 28, no. 5 (Berkeley and Los Angeles, 1949).

NITZE, WILLIAM ALBERT, AND T. A. JENKINS, EDS. *Le Haut Livre du Graal, Perlesvaus,* 2 vols. (Chicago, 1932–37).

NITZE, WILLIAM ALBERT, AND HARRY F. WILLIAMS. "Arthurian Names in the *Perceval* of Chrétien de Troyes." California University Publications, *Modern Philology* 38 (1952–63): 265–97.

NOGUÈRES, HENRI, M. DEGLIAME-FOUCHÉ, AND J. L. VIGIER. *Histoire de la Résistance en France de 1940 à 1945* (Paris, 1967).

NORGATE, KATE. *England under the Angevin Kings,* 2 vols. (London, 1887).

NORTHERN ANNALS (THE LOST). These annals seem to have been last used in the thirteenth century. See entry no. 2168 in *A Bibliography of English History to 1485* by Charles Gross, ed. by Edgar R. Graves (Oxford, 1975).

NUTT, ALFRED. *The Legends of "The Holy Grail,"* no. 14 in *Popular Studies in Mythology, Romance and Folklore* (London, 1902). This study is based upon his earlier *Studies* of 1888.

———. *Studies on the Legend of the Holy Grail* (London, 1888; New York, 1965).

O'GARA, MARGARET. *Triumph in Defeat: Infallibility, Vatican I, and the French Minority Bishops* (Catholic University of America, 1990).

OLDENBOURG, ZOÉ. *Le Bûcher de Montségur* (Paris, 1959), trans. by Peter Green as *Massacre at Montségur* (New York, 1962).

———. *Massacre at Montségur* (New York, 1961).

OLRIK, A. *The Heroic Legends of Denmark,* trans. by Lee M. Hollander (London and New York, 1919).

OLSCHKI, LEONARDO. *The Grail Castle and Its Mysteries,* trans. by J. A. Scott, ed. by Eugene Vinaver (Berkeley and Los Angeles, 1966).

OMAN, CHARLES. *Castles* (part 1: English Castles; part 2: Castles of Wales) (New York, 1978).

OTTO, RUDOLF. *Mysticism East and West: A Comparative Analysis of the Nature of Mysticism,* trans. by B. L. Bracey and R. C. Payne (New York, 1932, 1957–58).

OURSEL, RAYMOND, TRANS. AND ED. *Le Procès des Templiers* (Paris, 1955). These are primary sources.

OWEN, D. D. R. *The Evolution of the Grail Legend* (Edinburgh and London, 1968).

——. "The Radiance in the Grail Castle," *Romania* LXXXIII (1962): 108–17.

——. *The Vision of Hell* (Edinburgh and London, 1970).

PALACIOS, MIGUEL ASÍN. "Las Moradas en el símil de los castillos y moradas del alma en la mística islámica y en Santa Teresa." *Al-Andalus* XI (1946): 263–74.

PALADILHE, DOMINIQUE. *Les Grandes heures cathares* (Paris, 1969).

——. *Simon de Montfort et le drame cathare* (Paris, 1988).

PALESTINE PILGRIMS' TEXT SOCIETY (eleventh and twelfth centuries), vol. 6 (London, 1897), trans. by Aubrey Stewart and C. R. Conder. See "The City of Jerusalem" and "Description of the Holy Land" by John Poloner.

PALUZIE DE LESCAZES, CARLOS. *Castles of Europe* (Barcelona, 1982).

PARDO, P. ENRIQUE JORGE. *Poesías de Santa Teresa. Poesías a Santa Teresa,* illus. by J. Sánchez Merino (Bilbao, 1962).

PARIS, GASTON. *La Littérature française au moyen âge* (Paris, 1890–1913).

PARIS, PAULIN, ED. *Romans de la Table Ronde,* 5 vols. (Paris, 1868–77).

PARSONS, ALBERT ROSS. *"Parsifal." The Finding of Christ through Art, or Richard Wagner as Theologian* (New York and London, 1890).

PARTNER, PETER. *The Murdered Magicians. The Templars and Their Myth* (New York, 1981).

PARZIVAL by Wolfram von Eschenbach, trans. by A. T. Hatto (London and New York, 1980).

PARZIVAL by Wolfram von Eschenbach, trans. by Helen M. Mustard and Charles E. Passage (New York, 1961).

PATAI, RAPHAEL. *The Hebrew Goddess* (New York, 1967).

PATON, LUCY ALLEN. Introduction to the *Histories* of Geoffrey of Monmouth (London, 1902, 1944).

PAUPHILET, ALBERT. *Etudes sur la Queste del Saint Graal* (attribuée à Gautier Map) (Paris, 1921, 1968).

——. *Le Legs du Moyen Age* (Melun, 1950).

——. "Au Sujet du Graal." *Romania* LXVI (1941): 289–321, 481–504.

PEEBLES, ROSE JEFFRIES. *The Legend of Longinus, etc. and its Connection with the Grail* (Dissertation, 1910; Baltimore, 1911).

PELTZ, MARY ELLIS, AND ROBERT LAWRENCE. *The Metropolitan Opera Guide* (New York, 1939, 1940).

PENNICK, NIGEL. *Hitler's Secret Sciences* (Suffolk, 1981).

PERCEVAL LE GALLOIS, 6 vols., ed. by Charles Potvin (Mons, 1866–71).

PERCY, THOMAS. *Percy's Relique of Ancient English Poetry,* vol. 2 (London, Toronto, New York, 1926). See "The Marriage of Sir Gawaine," p. 195ff.

PERLESVAUS. See *The High History of the Holy Graal,* ed. and trans. by Sebastian Evans (London, n.d.); ed. by Ernest Rhys (London and New York, n.d., but reprinted under the same English title in 1969).

PERLESVAUS: LE HAUT LIVRE DU GRAAL, 2 vols., ed. by W. A. Nitze and T. A. Jenkins (Chicago, 1932–37; New York, 1972).

PERNOUD, RÉGINE. *Aliénor d'Aquitaine* (Paris, 1967).

———. *La Poésie médiévale française* (Paris, 1947).

PEYRAT, NAPOLÉON. *Histoire des Albigeois,* 3 vols. (Paris, 1880–82).

PHIPPS, WILLIAM E. *Was Jesus Married? The Distortion of Sexuality in the Christian Tradition* (Cambridge, 1970).

———. "A Woman Was the First to Declare Scripture Holy," *Bible Review* (April 1990): 14–45.

PIGEONNEAU, H. *Le Cycle de la Croisade et de la famille de Bouillon* (Saint-Cloud, 1877).

POLKINGHORNE, JOHN. *Science and Providence: God's Interaction with the World* (Boston, 1989).

POLLMAN, L. *Chrétien de Troyes und der "Conte del Graal"* (Tübingen, 1965).

POLLOCK, F., AND F. W. MAITLAND. *The History of English Law before the Time of Edward I,* vol. 2 of 2nd ed. (Cambridge, 1911).

PONSOYE, PIERRE. *L'Islam et le Graal* (Paris, 1957).

POWELL, TERENCE G. E. *The Celts* (London, 1958).

POWER, EILEEN. *Medieval Women,* ed. by M. M. Postan (Cambridge, 1975).

PROPP, VLADIMIR JA. *Morphologie du conte* (Leningrad, 1928; Paris, 1990).

PROSE LANCELOT ("QUEST" SECTION). See *The Quest of the Holy Grail,* trans. by P. M. Matarasso (London, 1969).

PROSE LANCELOT. VULGATE VERSION OF THE ARTHURIAN ROMANCES, 8 vols., ed. by H. O. Sommer (Washington, 1908–16).

PUECH, HENRI-CHARLES. *Le Manichéisme* (Paris, 1949).

———. *La Queste du Graal* (Paris, 1965).

QUEEN MARIE OF HUNGARY. See, for the Arthurian MSS in her personal collection, "Notice sur la librairie de la reine Marie de Hongrie, soeur de Charles-Quint, régente des Pays-Bas" in the *Compte-rendu des séances de la Commission royale d'histoire* 10 (1845).

QUERIDO, RENÉ M. "The Significance of the Grail Story for Our Time." *Anthroposophy Today* (Summer 1988): 68–75.

LA QUEST DEL SAINT GRAAL, ed. by F. J. Furnivall (London, 1864).

LA QUESTE DEL SAINT GRAAL, ed. by Albert Pauphilet (Paris, 1923).

QUESTE DEL SAINT GRAAL, ALSO KNOWN AS *LA QUESTE DEL ST. GRAAL;* ALSO KNOWN AS *Y SEINT GRAAL,* 8 vols., as trans. by Robert Williams (London, 1876). See also *Vulgate Version of the Arthurian Romances* for vol. 1 (Lestoire del Saint Graal), ed. by H. O. Sommer.

QUILLET, JEANNINE. *Les Clefs du pouvoir au moyen âge,* from the series *Questions d'histoire* (Paris, 1972).

RABANUS, OR HRABANUS MARCUS, ARCHBISHOP OF MAINZ (776–856). "Life of Mary Magdalen" from his *Opera Omnia* in Migne, vol. 257 (Paris, 1851–52).

RAHN, OTTO. *La Cour de Lucifer* (Paris, 1974); *Luzifers hofgesind* (Leipzig and Berlin, 1937).

———. *La Croisade contre le Graal* (Paris, 1934).

———. *Kreuzzug gegen den Gral. Die Tragödie des Katharismus* (Stuttgart, 1933–74); trans. by Robert Pitrou, ed. by Christiane Roy; Preface by René Nelli: *La Croisade contre le Graal* (Paris, 1974).

RANDALL, JOHN HERMAN. *The Making of the Modern Mind* (Cambridge, 1926, 1940).

RAPPOPORT, A. S. *Medieval Legends of Christ* (London, 1934).

RAVENSCROFT, TREVOR. *The Cup of Destiny. The Quest for the Grail* (York Beach, Maine, 1982).

REAMES, SHERRY L. *The Legenda aurea. A Reexamination of Its Paradoxical History* (University of Wisconsin, 1985). See Bibliography for *The Golden Legend,* pp. 305–11.

REIK, THEODOR. *The Creation of Woman* (New York, 1960).

———. *Pagan Rites in Judaism* (New York, 1964).

REINACH, SALOMON. *Cultes, mythes, et religions,* 5 vols. (Paris, 1908–12).

———. "Les Survivances européennes du Catharisme," Compte rendu du Vᵉ Congrès International des Sciences Historiques, p. 188 (Brussels, 1923).

———. "La Tête magique des Templiers." *Revue de l'Histoire des Religions* (1911): 25–39.

RELIGION AND PARAPSYCHOLOGY, ed. by Arthur S. Berger and Henry O. Thompson (New York, 1990). See "Religion . . . and the Shroud of Turin," pp. 191–214 (including Bibliography) by Frank C. Tribbe.

RENAN, ERNEST. *Les Apôtres* (Paris, 1866).

———. *Etudes sur la politique religieuse du règne de Philippe le Bel* (Paris, 1899). Study of Philip the Fair versus the Papacy.

———. *Histoire du peuple d'Isräel* (Paris, 1887–95).

———. *Life of Jesus* (Paris, 1895; Boston, 1910).

RENAUD DE BEAUJEU. *Le Bel Inconnu,* trans. and adapted into English verse as *Libeaus Desconus* (The Fair Unknown); ed. by Max

Kalaza (Leipzig, 1890). See also a prose translation and notes by Caroline M. Watts: *Sir Cleges. Sir Libeaus Desconus* (London, 1912; New York, 1970).

RÉVILLE, ALBERT. "Les Albigeois. Origines, développement et disparition du Catharisme dans la France Méridionale, d' après de nouvelles recherches." *Revue des Deux Mondes* (1874): 42–76.

RHŶS, SIR JOHN. *Celtic Britain* (London, 1882).

———. *Celtic Heathendom* (London and Edinburgh, 1888).

———. *Studies in the Arthurian Legend* (London, 1891, 1966).

RICHARD THE LION-HEARTED, ed. and trans. by Bradford B. Broughton (New York, 1966).

RICKARD, PETER. *Britain in Medieval French Literature, 1100–1500* (Cambridge, 1956). See chap. 9, "Scotland and the Scots," p. 206ff.

RIESER, MAX. *The True Founder of Christianity and The Hellenistic Philosophy* (Amsterdam/Uithorn, 1979). This book denies that the Gospel authors were historical and argues that Christianity commenced in Rome, not in Jerusalem.

RINGBOM, L. J. *Graltempel und Paradies* (Stockholm, 1951).

RITCHIE, ROBERT L. GRAEME. *Chrétien de Troyes and Scotland* (Oxford, 1952).

———. *The Normans in Scotland* (Edinburgh, 1954).

ROBERT DE BORON (BORRON). *Le Roman de l'Estoire dou Graal,* ed. by William A. Nitze (Paris, 1927).

ROBERTS, STEPHEN H. *The House that Hitler Built* (New York, 1938).

———. "Riddle of Hitler." *Harper's Magazine* 176 (1938): 246–54.

ROBINSON, HENRY WHEELER. *Christian Doctrine of Man* (Edinburgh, 1911–52).

ROBINSON, JOSEPH ARMITAGE, DEAN OF WELLS CATHEDRAL. *Two Glastonbury Legends: King Arthur and St. Joseph of Arimathea* (Cambridge, 1926).

ROGER DE HOVEDEN(CE). *Chronica (Annales anglicani),* ed. by W. Stubbs. *Rerum Britannicarum Medii Aevi Scriptores,* no. 51, 4 vols. (London, 1868–71).

ROGER OF HOWDEN (HOVEDON). *Chronica,* ed. by W. R. Stubbs as vol. 3 (*Rolls Series,* vol. 51) (London, 1870).

ROQUEBERT, MICHEL. *La Religion cathare* (Toulouse, 1988).

ROQUES, MARIO. *Le Graal de Chrétien et la Demoiselle du Graal* (Geneva and Lille, 1955).

ROMANS DE LA TABLE RONDE, 5 vols., ed. by Paulin Paris (Paris, 1868–77).

ROMAN VAN LANCELOT, 2 vols., ed. by W. J. A. Jonckbloet (Gravenhage, 1846–49).

ROSENBERG, ALFRED. *Der Mythus des 20. Jahrhunderts* (Munich, 1930, 1931). This book furnished Adolf Hitler's National Socialism, with its anti-Christian, anti-Jewish, and neopagan doctrine.

——. *Race and Race History,* ed. by Robert Pois (New York, 1970).

ROSS, ANNE. *Pagan Celtic Britain in Iconography and Tradition* (London and New York, 1967).

ROUGEMONT, DENIS DE. *L'Amour et l'Occident* (Paris, 1939).

——. *Les Mythes de l'amour* (Paris, 1961).

ROY, CHARLES. See Postface (pp. 233–66) in his translation of Arno Borst. See Arno Borst entry.

ROYAL COMMISSION. *An Inventory of the Ancient Monuments on Anglesey* (London, 1937).

RUNCIMAN, STEVEN. *The Medieval Manichee. A Study of the Christian Dualist Heresy* (Cambridge, New York, 1947, 1982).

RUSSELL, BERTRAND. *Why Men Fight* (New York, 1917).

RUSSELL, GEORGE WILLIAM (A. E.). *The Candle of Vision* (London, 1918).

LE SAINT-GRAAL, ed. by Eugène Hucher, 3 vols. (Le Mans and Paris, 1875–78).

SAINT-LOUP, STANISLAS (MARC AUGIER?). *Nouveaux Cathares pour Montségur* (Paris, 1969).

SALIBI, KAMAL. *The Bible Came from Arabia* (London, 1985; Hamburg, 1985). Original title: *Die Bibel kam aus dem Lande Asir.* Preface dated Beirut, 1985.

SANDERS, LAWRENCE. *Capital Crimes* (New York, 1989, 1990).

SANDMEL, SAMUEL. *The First Christian Century in Judaism and Christianity. Certainties and Uncertainties* (New York, 1969).

SANTA TERESA DE JESÚS. *Obras,* ed. by Antonio Comas (Barcelona, 1961).

SAXO GRAMMATICUS. *The Nine Books of Danish History,* 2 vols., ed. by Oliver Eaton (London and Copenhagen, 1905).

SCHLAUCH, MARGARET. "The Allegory of Church and Synagogue." *Speculum* XIV (1939): 448–64.

SCHMIDT, CHARLES. *Histoire et doctrine de la secte des Cathares, ou Albigeois,* 2 vols. (Paris and Geneva, 1849). Professor Schmidt is considered a major French-Protestant theologian. His book is a defense of Catharism.

SCHOLEM, GERSHOM. *Kabbalah and Its Symbolism,* trans. by Ralph Manheim, *Zur Kabbala und ihrer symbolik* (Zurich, 1960; New York, 1965, 1977).

SCHWEITZER, DR. ALBERT. *The Quest of the Historical Jesus,* trans. by W. Montgomery and F. C. Burkitt (London, 1926). Epigraph: "The abiding and eternal in Jesus is absolutely independent of historical knowledge and can only be understood by contact with His spirit which is still at work in the world" (p. 399).

SCROGIN, MICHAEL. "Jesus a Feminist? The Men Held All the Cards." *Spiritual Frontiers* (Spring 1986): 85–89.

SELTNIAN, CHARLES. *The Twelve Olympians and Their Guests* (London, 1952; New York, 1962).

SENIOR, MICHAEL. *Myths of Britain* (London, 1979). See "The Grail," pp. 205–32.

SERRUS, GEORGES, AND MICHEL ROQUEBERT. *Châteaux cathares* (Toulouse, 1986).

(SHAH NAMA) THE EPIC OF THE KINGS. THE NATIONAL EPIC OF PERSIA BY FERDOWSI, trans. by Reuben Levy (The Royal Institute of Publication of Teheran, Chicago, 1967). See p. 291ff. for Mani as prophet.

SHARP, MARY. *A Traveller's Guide to Saints in Europe* (London, 1964).

SHIRER, WILLIAM L. *The Rise and Fall of Adolf Hitler* (New York, 1961).

———. *The Rise and Fall of the Third Reich* (New York, 1960). Wagner took his notions of racism from Count J. A. de Gobineau and from the Englishman, Houston Steward Chamberlain (p. 103).

SILFEN, PAUL HARRISON. *The Völkish Ideology and the Roots of Nazism* (New York, 1973).

SIMON, EDITH. *The Piebald Standard. A Biography of the Knights Templar* (London, 1959).

SIMPSON, W. DOUGLAS. *The Ancient Stones of Scotland* (London, 1965, 1968).

———. *Portrait of the Highlands,* illus. (London, 1969).

———. *Scottish Castles* (Edinburgh, 1959).

———. *Stirlingshire* (Cambridge, 1928).

SINGER, SAMUEL. *Wolfram und der Gral: Neue Parzivalstudien* (Bern, 1939).

SIR PERCEVAL OF GALLES, the Thornton MS, ed. by J. O. Halliwell (London, 1844).

SISMONDI, J. C. L. SIMONDE DE. *Histoire des Français,* vol. 4 (Brussels, 1836). See his chronology of the years 1160–1256, p. 557ff.

SKEELS, DELL, TRANS. *The Romance of Perceval in Prose* (Seattle and London, 1966).

SKENE, WILLIAM FORBES. *Celtic Scotland,* 3 vols. (Edinburgh, 1956).

———. *Chronicles of the Picts and Scots* (Edinburgh, 1867).

———. *The Coronation Stone* (Edinburgh, 1869).

SKLAR, DUSTY. *Gods and Beasts: The Nazis and the Occult* (1977; New York, 1977, as *The Nazis and the Occult*).

SMITH, ASBURY. *The Twelve Christ Chose* (New York, 1958).

SMITH, GEORGE ADAM. *The Historical Geography of the Holy Land* (New York and London, 1894 or 1896).

SMITH, JOHN HOLLAND. *Constantine the Great* (New York, 1971).

SMYTH, ALFRED P. *Warlocks and Holy Men. Scotland A.D. 80–1000* (London, 1984). See p. 58ff. for a discussion of matriarchy among the Picts.

SÖDERBERT, H. *La Religion des Cathares. Etudes sur le gnosticisme de la basse antiquité et du moyen âge* (Uppsala, 1949).

SOLINUS, CAIUS JULIUS. *Geography. The Excellent and Pleasant Worke, Collectanea Rerum Memorabilium of Caius Julius Solinus,* trans. from the Latin (1587) by Arthur Golding. A facsimile reproduction with an introduction by George Kish (Gainesville, Florida, 1955).

SPENGLER, OSWALD. *Der Untergang des Abendlandes (The Decline of the West)* (Munich, 1918, 1922).

SQUIRE, CHARLES. *The Mythology of the British Islands* (London, 1905; Hollywood, 1975).

STANTON, ELIZABETH CADY. *The Woman's Bible* (New York, 1898).

STEINER, RUDOLF. *Das Christentum als mystische Tatsache and die Mysterien des Altertums* (1961), trans. and rev. as *Christianity as Mystical Fact* by Charles Davy and Adam Bittleston (London, 1914, 1922, 1972).

———. *Le Mystère chrétien et les mystères antiques,* trans. and introduced by Edouard Schuré (Paris, 1947).

STEPHENS, MEIC. *The Oxford Companion to the Literature of Wales* (New York, 1986). For a discussion of *Peredur,* look under *Tair Rhamant, Y,* p. 569ff.

STERZENBACH, THEODOR. *Ursprung und Entwickelung der Sage vom heiligen Gral* (Münster dissertation, 1908). The Grail was a fifth-century portable altar.

STEVENSON, ROBERT LOUIS BALFOUR. *Travels with a Donkey in the Cévennes* (Edinburgh, 1879). The Cevennes Mountains are not exactly in Provence, but they read as if they are.

STRICKLAND, AGNES. *Lives of the Queens of England,* 8 vols. (London, 1852).

STUBBS, WILLIAM. *The Early Plantagenets* (New York, 1902).

SUHTSCHECK, FRIEDRICH VON. *Wolframs von Eschenback Reimbearbeitung des Pârsîwalnâmä* (Leipzig, 1932). A book on the supposed Persian origin of *Parsifal* (Wagner opera).

SUMPTION, JONATHAN. *The Albigensian Crusade* (London and Boston, 1978). See excellent map of southern France, after p. 269.

SWAINSON, C. A. *The Greek Liturgies* (Cambridge, 1884).

TAYLOR, ISAAC. *Words and Places* (or *History, Ethnology, and Geography*) (London, 1885).

TAYLOR, J. W. *The Coming of the Saints* (London, 1969).

TENNYSON, ALFRED. *The Poetical Works of Alfred Tennyson, Poet Laureate* (Boston and New York, n.d.).

TIERNEY, BRIAN. *The Crisis of Church and State, 1050–1300* (Englewood Cliffs, N.J., 1964).

TOLKIEN, JOHN RONALD RENEL, ED. *Sir Gawain and the Green Knight* (Oxford, 1968).

TOYNBEE, ARNOLD, ED. *The Crucible of Christianity,* illus. (London, New York, and Cleveland, 1969).

TREHARNE, R. F. *The Glastonbury Legends* (London, 1967, 1971, 1975).

TRIBBE, FRANK CALVERT. *Portrait of Jesus* (New York, 1983).

TROMBETTI, ALFREDO. *Li Origini della lingua basca* (Bologna, 1966).

TUOHY, WILLIAM. "Vatican Rules Out Allowing Women into Priesthood." *Los Angeles Times* (January 28, 1977), I, pp. 1, 10.

UGARTE, MANUEL. *Visiones de España* (Valencia, n.d.). See "La tierra de Don Quijote," pp. 45–63.

ULRICH VON ZAZIKHOVEN. *Lanzelet,* ed. by Werner Richter (Frankfort, 1934); also ed. by K. A. Hahn (Frankfort, 1845).

VACHER DE LAPOUGE, GEORGES. *Les Sélections sociales* (Paris, 1896).

VELIKOVSKY, EMMANUEL (IMMANUEL). *Ages in Chaos,* 5 vols. (New York, 1950–77).

VENDRYÈS, J. "Les Eléments celtiques de la légende du Graal," *Etudes Celtiques* V (1949): pp. 1–50.

LES VÉRITABLES PROPHÉTIES DE MERLIN, ed. by Le Moyne de la Borderie (Paris, 1883).

VERMEIL, EDMOND. *Germany in the Twentieth Century* (New York, 1956). Published in Great Britain as *The German Scene,* trans. by L. J. Ludovici (1956).

VERSCHAFFELD, DR. WIERSMA. "Les Trois Degrés d'initiation au Graal païen." *Cahiers d'Etudes Cathares* 3, 1949.

VILLEMARQUÉ, HERSART DE LA. *Myrdhinn* (Paris, 1862). Arthurian criticism may be said to have been inaugurated by Count Villemarqué here.

VULGATE CYCLE OF ARTHURIAN ROMANCES, 7 vols., ed. by Oskar H. Sommer (Washington, 1908–16).

WACE AND LAYAMON. *Arthurian Chronicles,* trans. by Eugene Mason. Introduction by Gwyn Jones (London, Toronto, and New York, 1912–77).

WADE-EVANS, ARTHUR W. *Welsh Christian Origins* (Oxford, 1934).

WAGNER, RICHARD (1813–83). *Parsifal,* Royal Opera Guide 34.

Text and trans. by Andrew Porter (London and New York, 1986).

WAINWRIGHT, F. T. *The Problem of the Picts* (Edinburgh, 1965).

WAITE, ARTHUR EDWARD. *The Holy Grail. Its Legends and Symbolism* (London, 1909; New York, 1961).

WAKEFIELD, WALTER L. *Heresy, Crusade, and Inquisition in Southern France, 1100–1250* (London, 1974).

WAKEFIELD, WALTER L., AND AUSTIN EVANS. *Heresies of the High Middle Ages* (New York and London, 1969).

WALKER, BARBARA G. *The Woman's Dictionary of Symbols and Sacred Objects* (New York, 1988).

WALKER, CURTIS HOWE. *Eleanor of Aquitaine* (Richmond, 1950).

WARNER, HENRY JAMES. *The Albigensian Heresy*, 2 vols. (London, 1922–1928, 1967).

WARNER, MARINA. *Alone of All Her Sex. The Myth and the Cult of the Virgin* (London and New York, 1976, 1983).

WARNER, RICHARD. *An History of the Abbey of Glaston and of the Town of Glastonbury* (Bath, 1826).

WATSON, WILLIAM J. *The History of the Celtic Place-Names of Scotland* (Edinburgh, 1926).

WATTS, JOHN. *The Lives of the Holy Apostles* (London, 1716).

WEBBER, FREDERICK ROTH. *Church Symbolism: An Explanation of the More Important Symbols of the Old and New Testament* (Cleveland, 1938).

WECHSSLER, EDUARD. *Die Sage vom heiligen Gral in ihrer Entwicklung bis auf Richard Wagners "Parsifal"* (Halle, 1898).

WEINRAUB, EUGENE J. *Chrétien's Jewish Grail. A New Investigation of the Imagery and Significance of Chrétien de Troyes's Grail Episode Based upon Medieval Hebraic Sources* (Chapel Hill, 1976).

THE WELSH TRIADS. *Trioedd Ynys Prydein*, ed. and trans. with Commentary and Introduction by Rachel Bromwich (Cardiff, 1961, 1979).

WESTON, JESSIE LAIDLAW. *From Ritual to Romance* (Cambridge, 1920).

————. *The Legend of Sir Lancelot du Lac* (London, 1901).

————. *The Legend of Sir Perceval. Studies upon Its Origin, Development, and Position in the Arthurian Cycle*, 2 vols. (London, 1906–09).

————. *The Legends of the Wagner Drama. Studies in Mythology and Romance* (New York, 1964).

————. *The Quest of the Holy Grail* (London, 1913; New York, 1964).

WHITE, T. H. *The Once and Future King* (London, 1958).

WILLIAM OF MALMESBURY. *De antiquitate Glastoniensis ecclesiae, 1129–39*, trans. as *On the Antiquity of the Church of Glastonbury.*

See *De gestis regum anglorum,* ed. by William Stubbs (London, 1887).

WILLIAM OF NEWBURGH. *Historia rerum Anglicarum.* In *Chronicles of the Reigns of Stephen, Henry II, and Richard I* (vol. 1), ed. by R. Howlett (*Rolls Series,* vol. 82) (London, 1884).

WILLIAMS, A. H. *An Introduction to the History of Wales,* 2 vols. (Cardiff, 1941–48).

WILLIAMS, CHARLES, AND C. S. LEWIS. *Arthurian Torso* (Oxford, London, New York, Toronto, 1948).

WILLIAMS, MARY R. *Essai sur la composition du Roman Gallois de Peredur* (Paris, 1909).

WILLIAMSON, HUGH ROSS. *The Arrow and the Sword* (London, 1947).

———. *The Flowering Hawthorn,* illus. by Clare Leighton (New York, 1962).

WILSON, IAN. *The Shroud of Turin* (New York, 1978).

WOLFRAM VON ESCHENBACH. *Parzival,* illus. In Prosa übertragen von Wilhelm Stapel (Munich and Wien, 1980).

———. *Parzival,* ed. by Karl Lachmann (Berlin and Leipzig, 1926).

———. *Parzival,* trans. and Introduction by Helen M. Mustard and Charles E. Passage (New York, 1961); trans. and Foreword by A. T. Hatto (London and New York, 1980).

———. *Parzival,* 2 vols., trans. by E. Tonnelat (Paris, 1934).

———. *Parzival,* trans. by Jessie L. Weston (London, 1894).

———. *Parzival und Titurel,* 3 vols., ed. by Karl Bartsch and rev. by Marta Marti (Leipzig, 1929–35).

———. *Titurel,* trans. and Studies by Charles E. Passage (New York, 1984).

WRIGHT, J. K. *Geographical Lore of the Time of the Crusades* (New York, 1926, 1965).

YATES, FRANCES AMELIA. *The Rosicrucian Enlightenment* (London and Boston, 1972).

YEATS, WILLIAM BUTLER. *A Vision* (London, c. 1910).

ZELLER, B., ED. AND TRANS. *La Gaule et les invasions depuis les origines jusqu'à la mort de Henri IV,* illus. (Paris, 1890–97).

ZIMMER, HEINRICH ROBERT. *Altindisches Leben. Die cultur der vedischen Arier nach den Sambita dargestellt von Heinrich Zimmer* (Berlin, 1879).

———. *The Art of Indian Asia,* 2 vols., ed. by Joseph Campbell (New York, 1955).

———. "Bretonische Elemente in der Arthursage des Gottfried von Monmouth." ZFSL XII (1890): 253–56.

———. *The Irish Element in Medieval Culture,* trans. by Jane Loring Edmonds (New York, 1891, 1969).

———. *Keltische Studien,* 2 vols. (Berlin, 1881–84).

————. *The King and the Corpse,* ed. by Joseph Campbell. Bollingen Series XI (Princeton, 1948, 1956, 1968). See part 1 for four essays on Gawain, Yvain, Lancelot, and Merlin.

————. *Mythes et symboles dans l'art et la civilisation de l'Inde,* ed. by Joseph Campbell (New York, 1946; Paris, 1951).

NOTE TO THE READER

See also "Great Britain" (pp. 390–92) in *Encyclopedia of Early Christianity,* ed. by Everett Ferguson, Michael P. McHugh, and Frederick W. Norris (New York and London, 1990).

About the Author

Norma Lorre Goodrich, Ph.D., K.C., FSA Scot, has been teaching for forty-five years and is a professor emeritus at the Claremont Colleges. She is the author of *King Arthur, Guinevere, Merlin, Heroines, Priestesses, Ancient Myths,* and *Medieval Myths.* She lives in Claremont, California, with her husband.

Index